Entrepreneurial Finance

Entrepreneurial Finance
Finance for Small Business

Second Edition

Philip J. Adelman
DeVry Institute of Technology

Alan M. Marks
DeVry Institute of Technology

Prentice
Hall

Upper Saddle River, NJ 07458

Library of Congress Cataloging-in-Publication Data

Adelman, Philip J.
    Entrepreneurial finance : finance for small business / by Philip
J. Adelman, Alan M. Marks.—2nd ed.
      p.   cm.
    Includes bibliographical references and index.
    ISBN 0-13-085968-0
    1. Small business—Finance. I. Marks, Alan M. II. Title.

HG4027.7 A338 2000
658.315'92—dc21   00-033973

Acquisitions Editor: *Elizabeth Sugg*
Production Editor: *Mary Jo Graham*
Production Liaison: *Eileen M. O'Sullivan*
Managing Editor: *Mary Carnis*
Director of Manufacturing and Production: *Bruce Johnson*
Manufacturing Manager: *Ed O'Dougherty*
Editorial Assistant: *Anita Rhodes*
Cover Design: *Miguel Ortiz*
Formatting/page make-up: *Carlisle Publishers Services*
Printer/Binder: *Banta Harrisonburg*

Prentice-Hall International (UK) Limited, *London*
Prentice-Hall of Australia Pty. Limited, *Sydney*
Prentice-Hall Canada Inc., *Toronto*
Prentice-Hall Hispanoamericana, S.A., *Mexico*
Prentice-Hall of India Private Limited, *New Delhi*
Prentice-Hall of Japan, Inc., *Tokyo*
Simon & Schuster Asia Pte. Ltd., *Singapore*
Editora Prentice-Hall do Brasil, Ltda., *Rio de Janeiro*

10 9 8 7 6 5 4 3 2 1
ISBN 0-13-085968-0

To my wife, Hannah B. Adelman,
for her support and continued belief in my abilities,
and to my children, Eddie, Danny, and Tova, for being my cheerleaders.

Philip J. Adelman

To my loving and supportive family, my wife Cheryl and my children, Jamie and Jared Marks,
who gave me the encouragement to realize that my goal is achievable.

Alan M. Marks

To DeVry Institute of Technology, who gave us the opportunity to use our creative talents to teach.

Contents

Chapter 3

Financial Statements   47

Chapter 4

Analysis of Financial Statements   71

Chapter 5

Profit, Profitability, and Break-Even Analysis   97

Chapter 6

Forecasting and Pro Forma Financial Statements 115

Chapter 7

Working Capital Management 155

Chapter 8
Time Value of Money   189

Chapter 9
Capital Budgeting   219

Chapter 10

Personal Finance 249

Preface

We have written this textbook for the over 90 percent of business owners in the United States who own sole proprietorships, partnerships, or small nonpublic corporations. We are targeting those individuals who wish to learn more about the financial aspects of small business entrepreneurship. We omit complex theory and discuss vital issues with a direct and clear delivery of material. We apply many of the techniques that are found in traditional corporate finance texts to small businesses at an understandable level.

Most people who desire to start a business come from technical and engineering backgrounds. Their formal education is in technology rather than business. This book is written primarily for the community college and junior college market that caters to the concerns of individuals wishing to enhance their abilities in those areas of business that lead to successful entrepreneurship. This text also can be used as a supplementary text by technical colleges and universities offering programs in entrepreneurship. Of the over 20 million businesses in the United States, approximately 74 percent are sole proprietorships, 7 percent are partnerships, and 9 percent are subchapter S-corporations. Fewer than 10 percent are publicly traded; however, typical financial textbooks are written for the corporate finance market. Additionally, over 87 percent of all business establishments have fewer than twenty employees.[1] For these businesses, the owner usually is the chief financial officer, the chief executive officer, *and* the chief operating officer. Such business owners need a working knowledge of finance because they have no staff support on a full-time basis to assist in planning. In addition, the resources used in writing a business plan often omit many of the financial aspects that owners may need to determine the financial health of an existing or future business.

Our textbook differs from the typical financial textbook in the following areas. Most financial texts are written with an emphasis on publicly traded corporations. They are written for college juniors, seniors, or gradu-

---

1. U.S. Bureau of the Census, *Statistical Abstract of the United States: 1995,* 115th ed. (Washington, DC 1995).

ate students, with the assumption that the student has had several courses in accounting. They assume that this student will be working for a major corporation. These may be valid assumptions; however, they do not always apply to a small business and these texts typically do not provide specific examples for the noncorporate market. Our textbook fills this void. Also, because many students who enter into business come from a technical background rather than having a prior formal business education, we begin our text by outlining the basic economic factors affecting finance. We then discuss the advantages and disadvantages of various forms of business ownership. The text provides examples of financial statements for each type of business ownership. We devote more time than most financial texts to discussing working capital and inventory management, because even though the sales of a small business may increase, that business may fail because of poor working capital and inventory management techniques. Most business managers have been trained to judge the profitability of a project in terms of payback and break-even analysis. We have taken corporate capital budgeting techniques and adapted them to small business by showing the weighted average cost of capital as it exists for a small business owner. We also demonstrate the importance of the time value of money as a tool in both business planning and personal financial planning, and we simplify the use of this tool.

Most individuals who work for the traditional publicly traded corporation have access to a 401k or other formal retirement plan. Traditional financial textbooks, for this reason, do not cover personal financial planning. Small business owners are often so involved with current operations that they neglect to plan for their own personal financial future. We believe that it is imperative for small business owners not only to run their business successfully on a day-to-day basis, but also to have those skills that will enable them to plan for their personal future. Therefore, we have included a chapter on personal financial planning. This chapter includes an in-depth discussion of risk management as well as those investment vehicles that enable the entrepreneur to plan for personal financial goals.

Acknowledgments

The authors would like to extend their appreciation to the following professors for their contributions to this second edition. We wish to thank John Cavaliere, Sault College of Applied Arts & Technology, Sault Ste. Marie Ontario and Bill Hefter, San Francisco State University.

The following professors at DeVry Institute of Technology were extremely helpful and highly professional in their review and contributions to this second edition. We wish to thank Joyce Barden, John Draftz, Dr. Evelyn L. Plummer, and Sean T. Wright and acknowledge their individual contributions to this second edition.

Professor Draftz made significant contributions to chapter 8. His eagle eye, attention to detail and contribution of many problems and practice tests are very much appreciated. Professor Wright contributed several problems and provided valuable feedback on the textbook in general. Professors Plummer and Barden made several valuable suggestions on the presentation of both financial statements and financial data. Additionally, we have included several of Professor Draftz' and Professor Wright's problems in the instructor's CD as part of our special instructional package.

Philip J. Adelman
Alan M. Marks

Entrepreneurial Finance

FINANCIAL AND ECONOMIC CONCEPTS

1

Learning Objectives

When you have completed this chapter, you should be able to:

- Understand the basic concept and importance of finance as it relates to individuals and business.
- Understand the basic economic concepts of finance.
- Distinguish between marginal revenue and marginal cost.
- Distinguish between economic capital and financial capital.
- Determine the opportunity cost of making decisions.
- Identify the relationship that exists between savings, income, expenditures, and taxes.
- Identify those factors that affect interest rates.

- Understand the relationships that exist between supply and demand for money and prevailing market interest rates.
- Describe the role of the Federal Reserve and those tools used to achieve the goals of economic growth, price stability, and full employment.
- Understand the relationship that exists between risk and return on investment.
- Compare systematic risk to unsystematic risk and their impact on the small business.

This book is written to provide the individual who has no formal education in finance with a brief overview of finance from both a personal and a business perspective. The book is primarily for people who want to start their own business, or who want to analyze companies and investments, but who do not have the time to pursue a formal course of study in a traditional business college setting. The mathematical concepts in this book are not beyond high-school level, so it can be used as a supplementary text in any college business course. In the United States, approximately

40 percent of all businesses fail in the first five years.[1] This is normally not because the businesses offer poor products or services, but because of poor financial management and/or a lack of adequate financial capital.

 ## BASIC FINANCIAL CONCEPTS

Finance is essentially any transaction in which money or a moneylike instrument is exchanged for other money or another moneylike instrument. An individual who finances a car typically has a specific amount of money set aside for a down payment. That individual needs to obtain the balance of the sale price to purchase the car. He or she can finance the car by signing a promissory note (a loan agreement) for the cash needed to pay the car dealer. The financial part of purchasing the car involves the money used for the down payment and the signing of a promissory note. The actual sale of the car is an exchange process that can be associated with marketing: The seller exchanges the car for the buyer's money; however, the car has been financed by the exchange of a promissory note for money.

For the small business manager who desires to build a new plant, methods of financing may include using cash generated from current sales, borrowing funds from financial institutions such as banks or insurance companies, borrowing funds from select individuals, selling stocks, or using one's own savings. Bonds, which will be discussed in Chapter 10, are not really a viable source of financial capital for the small business. Bonds are normally available only to large corporations. Therefore, small business entrepreneurs will predominantly rely on lending institutions or their own funds to satisfy their needs for additional financial capital.

Businesses acquire capital assets through the use of financial capital. A plant, facility, or factory is a fixed or capital asset. Examples include buildings, machinery, and equipment. Capital assets are used by businesses to increase revenue or sales. Financial assets such as stocks, bonds, or savings may also be used to increase revenue because they can be used to acquire capital assets.

For most individuals and businesses, financial transactions are undertaken for the purpose of exchanging a sum of money today for the expectation of obtaining more money in the future. We buy stock at today's price because we believe that the stock will increase in value or that the corporation will generate a profit and provide us with cash or stock dividends in the future. A dividend is an after-tax payment that may be made by a corporation to a stockholder. We can sell the stock after it appreciates (goes up in value) or not sell and receive dividends. Similarly, we invest money in a business today because we expect greater returns for our money in the future.

---

[1]*Business Failure Record, 1994,* Dun and Bradstreet Corp., Wilton, CN, 1995.

We can stay with the business and pay ourselves from our profits, or wait for the business to appreciate and sell it to another business owner.

IMPORTANCE OF FINANCE

Any individual who starts or manages a business needs a basic understanding of finance. This fact is especially true in today's volatile market where interest rates over the last two decades have been as low as 4 percent and as high as 20 percent. If we expect to obtain greater returns from our investments in the future, we have to understand finance, its relationship to interest rates, and how to obtain proper financing. Without this understanding, our individual and business efforts may fail. However, before we can develop more of an understanding of finance, we must begin by understanding those basic economic concepts that relate to finance.

ECONOMIC CONCEPTS OF FINANCE

The United States operates on the basic principle that all individuals can achieve their own objectives in a free enterprise system, within the confines of the marketplace. Such a system is known as a market economy. A market economy such as ours consists of several markets. A **market** is any organized effort through which buyers and sellers freely exchange goods and services. Some of these markets in our economy include real estate markets, where property is exchanged; retail markets, where final goods and services are exchanged; the internet, where information is exchanged; and the commodity market, where basic commodities (raw materials such as agricultural products, precious metals, and oil) are exchanged. The market that deals with finance is the financial marketplace. The three primary participants in this financial marketplace are individual households, businesses, and government. In our free enterprise financial market system, the primary savers of funds are households. They are the suppliers of funds to other individuals, businesses, and government. The latter participants are the users of funds.

SCARCE RESOURCES

The central theme of economics is one of scarcity. Items are scarce because normal people want more than they currently have. Humans have unlimited desires for goods and services. We live in a world of scarce resources, so we are willing to pay a positive price to obtain goods and services. For the individual, financial means and time are limited resources. Because individuals have limited financial means, they must make choices as to which resources they want to obtain and in what time period they want to obtain those resources. The four types of scarce resources of typical concern in both business and economics are natural resources, human resources, capital resources, and entrepreneurial resources.

Natural Resources

Natural resources consist of natural products such as minerals, land, and wildlife. They exist in nature and have not been modified by human activity. In economic terms, we consider the payment made for natural resources to be rent. Natural resources are referred to in some economic textbooks as **land.**

Human Resources

Human resources are the mental and physical talents of people. Human resources are also referred to by the economist as **labor.** The economic payment for human labor is wages. There are, of course, different levels of wages. Wages are paid by business owners, based on the marginal revenue product of the human resource and the availability of the human resource. We have heard many arguments about the value of professional athletes and their high salaries, but the fact remains that based on marginal revenue product, these people are paid a fair salary.

Before continuing our discussion of this area, we must define some terms. The word **marginal** as we use it here is related to the addition of one more unit of measurement. **Marginal revenue product** is the additional revenue we obtain by hiring one more unit of labor. **Marginal physical product** is the additional product that results from hiring one more unit of labor. **Marginal cost** is the cost of hiring one more unit of labor or the cost of producing one more unit of output.

For example, say that you own a professional basketball team. Your team is average, and for the last two years you have averaged 16,000 ticket sales for an arena that seats 20,000 people. However, you have noticed that when the Los Angeles Lakers come to town, you sell all 20,000 seats. You determine that the additional seats are sold because Los Angeles has a superstar who people are willing to pay to see. Therefore, you seek to hire a superstar. For your own team you want an athlete of the caliber of Kobe Bryant, Shaquille O'Neal, or Jason Kidd. How much would you be willing to pay this basketball player?

You estimate that if you hire a superstar, who is your marginal physical product, you will sell out. The average price of a ticket for your arena is $50. You could sell 4,000 more tickets for each game and then bring in extra revenue of $200,000 ($50 a seat times 4,000 seats) for each home game. Because there are 41 home games, you would make an additional $8.2 million in ticket sales. The $8.2 million in ticket sales is your marginal revenue product. This figure does not include additional television revenue or the sales of food, beverages, or team sports memorabilia. Based on the marginal revenue product of a superstar, you would be willing to pay a marginal cost of up to $8.2 million to hire this basketball player. If you owned this team and could get a player like Jason Kidd for $7 million a year, would you hire him? Of course you would, because you would clear a profit of $1.2 million.

These athletes are obviously a scarce resource. If you advertise in the paper, how many people with the talents of a superstar will apply for the job? Conversely, if you own a pizza parlor and advertise for a delivery driver, how many people with the mental and physical talent to deliver pizza will apply for the job? You will probably have several applicants, because there are hundreds of people in your community who have pizza delivery skills. What is the marginal revenue product of pizza delivery? If your average pizza sells for $10 and the average driver can deliver four pizzas an hour, then the marginal revenue product is $40 per hour. Therefore, the absolute maximum amount you would be willing to pay a driver is $40 per hour; however, considering both marginal revenue product and the availability of pizza delivery people, you may be able to hire a new driver for minimum wage of $5.15 per hour.

Capital Resources

Capital resources are separated into two categories: economic capital and financial capital. **Economic capital** consists of those items that people manufacture by combining natural and human resources. Examples include buildings and equipment of both business and government enterprises, roads, and bridges. The economic payment for capital (which includes both economic and financial capital) is interest. It is absolutely essential that we distinguish between economic capital and financial capital. Economic capital is interchangeable with the terms **physical capital** and **fixed assets,** those capital resources that are used to make more items. **Financial capital** is a dollar value claim on economic capital, and therefore may include several types of assets such as cash, accounts receivable, stocks, and bonds. When a provider of funds holds financial capital, the provider has a dollar value legal claim on economic capital. For example, if you have borrowed money from a bank to finance a new delivery truck for your business, the bank has supplied you with financial capital. The title to your vehicle is actually in the name of the bank. The promissory note that you signed with the bank is the dollar value claim that the bank has on your fixed asset (vehicle).

Entrepreneurial Resources

Entrepreneurial resources are the individuals who assume risk and begin business enterprises. The entrepreneur combines land, labor, and capital

Table 1-1 Expected Financial Returns of Investment Opportunity

Investment Opportunity	Expected Annual Return (%)
Purchase stock	12
Purchase home	10
Purchase bonds	7
Place money in bank savings account	4
Purchase new car	−15

resources to produce a good or service that we value more than the sum of the individual parts. Without the entrepreneur, resources would not normally be combined, except as needed for subsistence, or just enough to sustain life. The economic payment made to the entrepreneur is profit. The entrepreneur seeks to make as much profit as possible. Therefore, when entrepreneurs form businesses, they seek to make a profit that exceeds the wages paid to labor. The owner of a professional sports team, the entrepreneur, will normally make more than any player on that team. The owner of the pizza shop should normally make more in profit than any employee makes in wages.

OPPORTUNITY COSTS

In any market transaction both the buyer and the seller usually believe that they have obtained the best use of their scarce resources. The economic basis for this belief revolves around the concept of opportunity costs. An **opportunity cost** is the highest value surrendered when a decision to invest funds is made. Opportunity cost is a quantifiable term. For example, an individual who has $20,000 may decide to invest in stocks or bonds, place the money in savings, buy a new car, or place a down payment on a house. The individual investor determines what annual return can be expected from these choices and constructs a table that is based on expected financial return. Table 1-1 lists the investment opportunities mentioned here and the expected annual gain or loss from each alternative. The investor will naturally take other factors into consideration such as the risk associated with investing in the stock market or the pleasure received from driving a new car.

In looking at Table 1-1, we see that the car actually depreciates (loses economic value) over time, whereas all other assets increase in value. Nevertheless, the investor decides to buy the car. As mentioned, factors other than pure finance, such as a requirement for transportation or the enjoyment that can be obtained from driving the car, go into the decision. When the decision is made to purchase the car, the opportunity cost is 12 percent. This percentage is the return that the investor can expect to realize from investing in stock, and also the highest value surrendered when the car is purchased. If faced with these alternatives and we had decided to purchase stock, then the opportunity cost would have been the return from the purchase of a home, or 10 percent. The return from the home purchase would have been the highest value surrendered when we chose stock. Once again, choosing the purchase of an asset is the actual decision. The highest value that we would surrender in purchasing the stock is the return from the home, so its return of 10 percent is the opportunity cost of the decision. In other words, we would surrender the opportunity to purchase a home, which appreciates in value at 10 percent, if we chose to invest in stocks at a 12 percent return.

One economic concept of finance central to any market transaction is that every party to the transaction has the expectation of gain from the transaction. In the case of the car purchase, the buyer obviously valued the car more than the $20,000. To the buyer, surrendering the $20,000 to buy the car resulted in a greater benefit than would have been obtained by picking some other item. Otherwise, the car would not have been purchased. The car dealer, on the other hand, valued the $20,000 more than the car. Receiving the $20,000 for the car was of greater benefit to the car dealer than owning the car. Otherwise, the dealer would not have sold the car. This win-win situation is central to all free enterprise market transactions. Both the buyer and the seller believe that they gain from the transaction.

SAVINGS, INCOME, EXPENDITURES, AND TAXES

Let us look at how the $20,000 was made available to purchase the car in the previous example. Most people generate savings to make large market transactions. Savings can only be achieved if all expenditures are less than total income. Therefore it is essential to determine exactly where savings come from. We begin with the concept of gross income.

Gross income for the individual is all the money received from all sources during the year, including wages, tips, interest earned on savings and bonds, income from rental property, and profits to entrepreneurs. Gross income is subject to taxation by our government. One reason for taxation is there are items that we consume or have available that we do not want to pay for directly. Examples include public education, good roads, safe drinking water, and police and fire protection. The money that we use to finance these public goods comes from taxes and government user fees. **Taxes** are payments to government for goods and services provided by government. For most of us, the government collects taxes on our wages prior to our getting paid for our labor. If you have income from sources other than wages, the federal government requires that you pay estimated taxes, normally on a quarterly basis, to lessen what may be a great financial burden when annual income taxes are due.

There are three basic forms of taxes that government can, and does, collect: progressive taxes, regressive taxes, and proportional taxes. **Progressive taxes** take a larger percentage of income as that income increases. With each step up in income, a greater percentage of taxes are due. For example, if Tom Childress makes $20,000 in wages a year and pays $3,000 in taxes, and Jane Smith earns $60,000 and pays $16,800 in taxes, then Tom pays 15 percent of his income in taxes, whereas Jane pays 28 percent. The actual tax rates are established by legislation at the federal, state, and local levels. The percentage is a proportion and is calculated by taking the amount paid, dividing it by the gross income received, and multiplying the answer by 100. The formula for tax percentage is as follows:

$$\text{Tax percentage} = \frac{\text{Tax payment in dollars}}{\text{Income in dollars}} \times 100$$

For Tom Childress,

$$\text{Tax percentage} = \frac{\$3,000}{\$20,000} \times 100 = 15\%$$

For Jane Smith,

$$\text{Tax percentage} = \frac{\$16,800}{\$60,000} \times 100 = 28\%$$

Regressive taxes take a higher percentage of your income as your income decreases. Sales taxes are a typical example of regressive taxes. Lower-income individuals must use a higher percentage of their income to purchase goods and services. For example, a person making $800 per month will probably have to spend all of his income to survive. If we have a 5 percent sales tax, this individual will pay $40 per month in sales taxes on his $800 income. If, on the other hand, another individual makes $5,000 a month, she may spend only $4,000 and save the remaining $1,000 each month. Therefore, she will pay a 5 percent sales tax on $4,000, or $200 per month in sales tax. However, the $200 is only 4 percent of her $5,000 income. Thus, the wealthier individual pays 4 percent of income in sales taxes, whereas the lower-income individual pays 5 percent. Consequently the tax is regressive. Because many politicians realize the hardship that regressive taxes may place on lower-income individuals, we see several cities and states that exempt food and medicine from sales taxes.

Regarding **proportional taxes,** the percentage paid will stay the same regardless of income. For many of us, social security and medicare taxes are proportional. As income increases by one dollar, 7.65 percent of that dollar is paid in social security and medicare taxes. The only true proportional tax

Table 1-2 Flat Tax Proposal

Gross Income ($)	Taxes Paid ($)	Percentage of Income Paid in Taxes (%)
30,000	0	0.00
40,000	1,700	4.25
50,000	3,400	6.80
60,000	5,100	8.50
70,000	6,800	9.71
80,000	8,500	10.63
90,000	10,200	11.33
100,000	11,900	11.90
110,000	13,600	12.36
120,000	15,300	12.75
130,000	17,000	13.08
140,000	18,700	13.36

in the United States currently is the medicare tax which is 1.45 percent of wages with no upper limit. Social security has a tax rate of 6.2 percent, but it is capped at an income level of $72,600 for 1999.[2] Therefore, social security is proportional for wages up to $72,600 but it becomes a regressive tax for people earning more than $72,600.

Flat tax proposals

The proposal goes something like this: There will be no tax paid on the first $30,000 of income for a family of four, and then there will be a 17 percent flat tax on all income that exceeds $30,000. Given the previous descriptions, would implementation of this proposal mean a progressive, regressive, or proportional tax? The answer is not obvious, but the proposal is for a progressive income tax, which is illustrated by Table 1-2.

When evaluating Table 1-2, we notice that there are no taxes paid on our $30,000 income; therefore, the percentage of income paid in taxes is 0 percent. However, we pay an additional $1,700 in taxes on each $10,000 earned above $30,000. Thus, the family earning $70,000 pays $6,800 in taxes, or 17 percent of the $40,000 that was earned above the $30,000 exemption. Notice that this equates to a 9.71 percent income tax on the family income of $70,000. Also, we see that as income increases from $30,000 to $140,000, the tax rate continues to increase as a percentage of income. Therefore, the flat tax proposal is actually a progressive income tax proposal.

The preceding methods may be used by government to collect its income to provide the goods and services previously mentioned. In any event,

---

[2] *Early Release Copies of 1999 Income Tax Withholding and Advance Earned Income Credit Payment Tables.* Internal Revenue Service Notice 1036 (Rev. November 1998).

when we subtract taxes from gross income, we are left with **disposable income,** that which one has after paying federal, state, and perhaps local taxes. **Discretionary income** is disposable income minus fixed expenses such as rent, utilities, and insurance. Discretionary income can be either consumed (spent) or saved. Consumption in economic terms is the same as spending.

Many households generate incomes that exceed their required expenditures. Households can therefore save or invest this excess income as they choose with businesses, financial institutions, or brokerage institutions, and become the suppliers of funds to the financial marketplace. In the financial marketplace the buyers or users of funds are those people and institutions (government and business) requiring money, which they obtain through loans. A loan is a principal amount of money that is exchanged for a promise to repay this principal amount plus interest. The interest charged can be said to be the annual rent for the principal amount of money. The amount of rent paid in dollars and cents is determined by the interest rate in effect at the time of the loan. There are many factors that affect these interest rates, four of which are of primary concern: the supply of money saved, the demand for borrowed funds, the Federal Reserve policy, and risk. These factors are discussed in the following sections.

SUPPLY OF MONEY SAVED

The **supply of money saved** is primarily the total money that is placed in demand deposit (checking) accounts, savings accounts, and money market mutual funds. The **law of supply** states that as the payment for or price of an item increases, the quantity of the item supplied to the market will increase, ceteris paribus. *Ceteris paribus* is a Latin phrase, meaning "all else remains the same." In economic terms the law of supply relates to the price paid and the quantity of the resource that will be provided at that price. In finance the concept of the law of supply can be demonstrated by comparing the amount of money saved with interest rate amounts paid for the money. A simple illustration of this can be given with a supply table that depicts the incomes and expenses of several families. Table 1-3 provides the income and expenses of seven individual households.

The table provides several factors about gross income and discretionary income.

1. We have a progressive tax system. As income increases, the amount of income paid in federal taxes also increases as a percentage of income. The Jones family, earning $30,000, pays 19.43 percent of its annual income in federal taxes; however, the Charles family earns $150,000 and pays 28.72 percent of its annual income in federal taxes.
2. Fixed expenses decrease as a percentage of income, as income increases. For the Jones family, fixed expenses consume 63.58 percent of

Table 1-3 Income and Expenses of Various Households

Household Name	Gross Income ($)	Income, SS, & Medicare Taxes ($)	Federal Taxes Paid as a % of Gross Income	Disposable Income ($)	Fixed Expenses ($)	Discretionary Income ($)
Jones	30,000	5,828	19.43	24,173	19,073	5,100
Roberts	50,000	10,683	21.37	39,318	31,758	7,560
Smith	70,000	17,813	25.45	52,188	38,868	13,320
Brown	90,000	23,864	26.52	66,136	40,936	25,200
Meeks	110,000	30,099	27.36	79,901	41,021	38,880
Adams	130,000	36,589	28.15	93,411	46,611	46,800
Charles	150,000	43,079	28.72	106,921	49,033	57,888

Source: *Early Release Copies of 1999 Income Tax Withholding and Advance Earned Income Credit Payment Tables,* Department of the Treasury, Internal Revenue Service Notice 1036 (Rev. November 1998)

annual income (19,073 ÷ 30,000); but the Charles family spends only 32.69 percent of its income on fixed expenses (49,033 ÷ 150,000).

3. Discretionary income increases as wealth increases. Therefore, the Jones family has 17 percent (5,100 ÷ 30,000) of its income to save or spend as it wishes, but the Charles family has 38.59 percent (57,888 ÷ 150,000) of its annual income to save or spend as it wishes.

Thus, as wealth increases, the amount of discretionary income increases. Because discretionary income can be either consumed or saved, we would expect that the supply of money saved would increase as the price paid for money increases (interest rate).

Supply tables are generated by determining how much of a product or service people or businesses would be willing and able to provide to the market at various prices. Because money is a scarce resource, we can generate a supply table by determining how much money people will place in their savings as interest rates increase. We ask a series of individuals, with different amounts of discretionary income, what percentage of their money they save at different and varying interest rates.

Table 1-4 shows how much money families are willing to save as interest rates increase. Note that some people save money at a 4 percent interest rate, whereas others do not invest in savings until interest rates reach 6 or 8 percent. As interest rates approach 20 percent, virtually every family puts some of its discretionary income into savings. Notice that there is a definite limit to the amount of money that can be supplied regardless of the interest rate. People are limited in their amount of discretionary income. Even though everyone would like to save more money, financial situations dictate that every household has a limit to the amount of money that can be saved, because money is scarce.

Table 1-4 Supply Table: Money Saved for Seven Sample Families

Annual Interest Rate (%)	Annual Savings in Dollars ($)							
	Jones	Roberts	Smith	Brown	Meeks	Adams	Charles	Total
0	$ —	$ —	$ —	$ —	$ —	$ —	$ —	$ —
2	—	—	—	—	—	—	—	—
4	—	—	—	500	780	1,940	5,790	9,010
6	—	—	670	1,250	1,940	2,720	7,530	14,110
8	100	200	930	1,760	2,020	3,890	12,000	20,900
10	200	500	1,500	3,000	3,500	7,000	16,000	31,700
12	250	750	2,500	5,000	6,000	10,000	20,000	44,500
14	300	1,000	3,250	8,500	12,000	15,000	25,000	65,050
16	400	1,200	4,500	12,000	18,000	23,000	31,000	90,100
18	500	1,500	6,000	15,000	25,000	28,000	38,000	114,000
20	500	1,700	8,000	18,000	30,000	32,000	40,000	130,200
22	500	1,700	8,000	18,000	30,000	33,000	41,000	132,200
24	500	1,700	8,000	18,000	30,000	33,000	41,200	132,400

For example, the Jones family has a gross income of $30,000. After paying taxes, rent, utilities, and other contractual obligations, it is left with a discretionary income of only $5,100. This money is all the family has left to pay for items such as food, entertainment, clothing, and savings. For a family in this situation, virtually all the discretionary income will be consumed just to survive. Therefore, regardless of how high interest rates on savings rise, this family can save only $500 a year.

Conversely, the Charles family, with a gross income of $150,000, is left with discretionary income of $57,888. Therefore, this family can afford to save much more as a percentage of its total income. The Charles family can save 71 percent of its discretionary income ($41,200 ÷ $57,888) and still have $16,688 per year ($57,888 − $41,200) for food, clothing, and entertainment. This gives the Charles family almost $1,400 per month for spending, even after it saves 71 percent of its discretionary income.

The total supply of money available in the marketplace can be shown visually with a **supply curve** (Figure 1-1). The curve is generated from the supply table (Table 1-4) by horizontally summing the total money saved by the seven families at varying interest rates. At an interest rate of 10 percent, we can calculate $31,700 in total savings for all these families. At an interest rate of 20 percent, we calculate $130,200 in savings. Of course, if we obtained this figure for all families in the United States, then we would have a supply curve that represented the total supply of money saved.

For the United States, there are four measures of the money supply: M1, M2, M3, and L. Of primary interest to us is M1, which consists mostly of money in circulation and money in checking accounts (demand de-

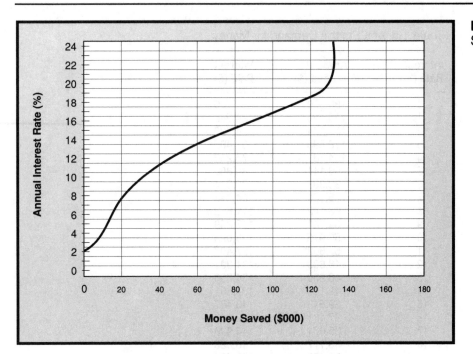

FIGURE 1-1
Supply of Money

posits), and M2, which consists of M1 plus money in passbook savings accounts, retail money market accounts (accounts that use short-term securities), and small time deposits (certificates of deposit, or CDs, in amounts of less than $100,000). For our purposes, when we discuss the money supply and personal savings, we are referring to M2. If we had been able to survey the entire population, and added across the supply table to obtain the total amount of money that would be saved by the population at varying interest rates, we could calculate the amount of money in savings accounts and money market funds for the United States, or M2 minus M1. The problem is that the figures for the United States are difficult to comprehend because the numbers are so large. For example, for January 2000, M1 was $1,122.6 billion, M2 was $4,686.3 billion, and the savings accounts in commercial and thrift institutions totaled $3,563.7 billion,[3] giving the United States over $3.5 trillion in savings. The numbers are so large that the government typically rounds to the closest $100 million. In other words, the figures are fairly accurate, give or take a hundred million.

Because of the size of these numbers, we will stay with our microexamples. When we plot our sample supply curve, we see that the quantity of money supplied for the sample population is upward sloping and is based on horizontally summing the results of the supply table. In the example

---

[3]*Money Stock and Debt Measures,* Federal Reserve Statistical Release H.6, February 3, 2000.

Table 1-5 Ann Smith's Demand for Money

Interest Rate (%)	Amount Financed ($)	Interest Paid ($)
0	180,000	0
1	155,454	24,546
2	135,274	44,726
3	118,595	61,405
4	104,731	75,269
5	93,141	86,859
6	83,396	96,604
7	75,154	104,846
8	68,142	111,858
9	62,141	117,859
10	56,975	123,025
11	52,503	127,497
12	48,609	131,391
13	45,200	134,800
14	42,199	137,801
15	39,543	140,457
16	37,181	142,819
17	35,071	144,929
18	33,177	146,823
19	31,468	148,532
20	29,922	150,078
21	28,516	151,484
22	27,233	152,767
23	26,059	153,941
24	24,980	155,020

given for our sample families (Table 1-4), we find that there is no money in savings at interest rates of 2 percent; approximately $31,700 in savings at interest rates of 10 percent; and $130,200 in savings at rates of 20 percent.

DEMAND FOR BORROWED FUNDS

Another factor that determines interest rates is the demand for money. The **demand for borrowed funds** is all the money that is demanded in our economy at a given price. The **law of demand** states that as the price of an item decreases, people will demand a larger quantity of that item, ceteris paribus. Therefore, as interest rates go down, borrowing increases. It becomes cheaper for us to borrow more money so that we can purchase additional capital assets (see Table 1-5).

In our example, Ann Smith has determined that she wants a new home and can afford monthly payments of $500. If she did not have to pay any interest to finance the home and could obtain a 30-year mortgage (360 monthly payments), she could afford to purchase a $180,000 home. However, if she had to pay 10 percent interest, she could only afford to buy a house worth $56,975, because the interest payments would be $123,025.

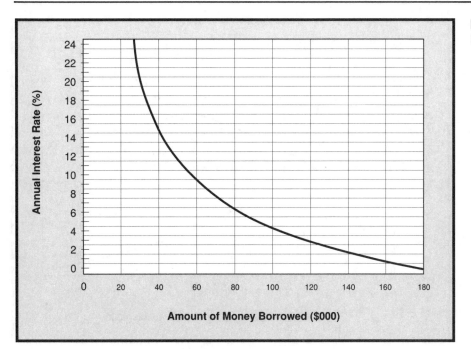

FIGURE 1-2
Demand for Money

What holds true for the individual, in general holds true for the economy. We see that the dollar amount demanded for housing increases as interest rates go down. Additionally, more families in the economy can afford to purchase homes at lower interest rates. This relationship between the cost of financing, or market interest rates, and the demand for items of high dollar value holds true for governments and businesses as well as for individuals.

A **demand table** (Table 1-5) is generated by determining how much individuals are willing to borrow at varying interest rates. We used the home purchase as an example, but in reality, the quantity demanded for big-ticket and literally thousands of other items will increase as the cost of borrowing decreases. The **demand curve** (Figure 1-2) is nothing more than the horizontal summation of a demand table, or in this case, plotting Ann Smith's demand for borrowed funds at varying interest rates.

We cannot look at supply and demand separately. To determine the actual market interest rate, we must integrate both the supply curve and the demand curve. **Supply** and **demand** are obtained by combining the two curves. The interest rate at which the supply curve and the demand curve intersect is known as the equilibrium point, and theoretically, at that interest rate, the financial market will be cleared. In other words, the quantity of money supplied to the market will be exactly equal to the quantity of money demanded in the market. Equilibrium, therefore, is the point at which the quantity supplied and the quantity demanded are equal. If the market is in equilibrium, then the market price is the equilibrium price. If

FIGURE 1-3
Supply and Demand for
Money

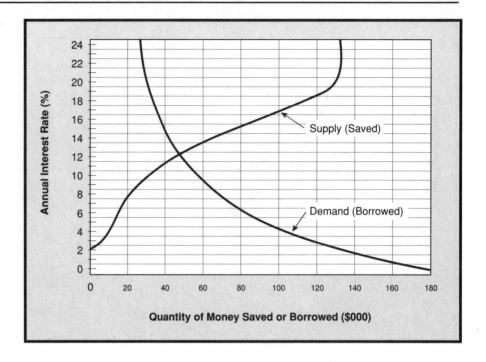

we compare Table 1-4 with Table 1-5, or look at Figure 1-3, we note that Ann Smith can borrow approximately $45,000 at an interest rate between 12 and 13 percent. If she wants to borrow more than this amount, she will have to pay a higher rate, because households are not willing to save more than $45,000 unless interest rates are higher.

Households will borrow funds to invest in businesses, provided that interest rates are within some range that makes the investment seem profitable. If market interest rates are above that range, households will prefer to save their money rather than invest in a business or some other capital asset. At 18 percent, households will save more and borrow less. As this procedure continues, the quantity of money saved increases.

When the supply of money saved exceeds the demand for money, there is a surplus of money in the marketplace. Institutions will pay less for savings, and interest rates will begin to fall. Therefore, as more and more people save, and borrow less, lending institutions will find themselves with money that they cannot loan out. They will not want to attract any more savings, and thus interest rates will begin to fall as lending institutions cut the price they are willing to pay to attract savers.

FEDERAL RESERVE POLICY

Supply of and demand for money are the critical factors affecting interest rates, all other things being equal. In a totally free market system, those factors alone would dominate the interest rates paid for money. We currently do not have a totally free market for money; thus, other factors have to be included such as the Federal Reserve.

The **Federal Reserve** is the central bank of the United States. It is often referred to as the Fed. The Fed is responsible for controlling the monetary policy of the United States. **Monetary policy** is governmental action to change the supply of money to expand or contract economic activity. The U.S. government has some broad general goals, and the Fed is responsible for trying to achieve and maintain these goals. The three basic goals are economic growth, price stability, and full employment. We must have growth in our economy because every year more people enter the nation's workforce and the economy must create jobs for these people. We must have price stability if consumers are to maintain their confidence in the economic system. We must have full employment to ensure that Americans who want to work can find work.

Unfortunately, some of these goals are diametrically opposed to one another and the government must seek to strike a balance between them. For example, we will not have price stability if we have inflation. **Inflation** occurs when the average price of goods increases. The measure of inflation that is most often used is the **consumer price index (CPI).** The CPI represents a market basket of goods that the average American consumer purchases each month. The government prices this basket of goods each month and determines if the basket has increased in price (inflation) or decreased in price (deflation). As individual consumers, we cannot really determine if we have inflation, because we do not purchase the entire basket every month and we normally get mixed signals from our purchases. For example, if gasoline increases in price and food decreases in price, then we do not know if we have inflation. It is only when the average price of the *entire* basket of goods increases that inflation exists for the economy. If the CPI changes and the inflation rate increases by 7 percent between January of one year and January of the next year, then a basket of goods that cost $100 in January of the first year will cost $107 in January of the following year.

Based on our previous discussion of supply and demand, we can see that what is occurring in the marketplace when we have inflation is that the demand for the items in the basket is exceeding the supply of goods in the basket. Therefore, consumers are bidding up the price of the basket of goods and services. The Fed has goals for inflation. If these goals are exceeded, the Fed intervenes by making adjustments in the money supply to dampen demand. If the supply of money available in the marketplace is reduced, then interest rates will go up and consumers will not be able to purchase as many goods and services as before. When this happens, the demand for items in the basket decreases and prices begin to fall. The Federal Reserve has three primary tools that it uses to control the money supply: open market operations, bank reserve requirements, and the discount rate.

Open market operations consist of the Fed's purchasing or selling U.S. securities. Because security obligations (treasury bills, notes, and bonds) of the United States are considered to be the safest possible investment, there is always a demand for these instruments. Open market operations are the most significant tool of the Fed, and this tool is in constant use. The Fed can determine exactly how much the money supply is being expanded or contracted by its open market operations. To increase the money supply, the Fed purchases government securities and pays for them with cash. This provides the economy with more money to lend. Subsequently the money supply is increased. When the Fed wants to decrease the money supply, it sells securities. These securities are paid for with cash by households and institutions. The money supply is decreased because the Fed takes this currency out of circulation.

The Fed also establishes a **reserve requirement** for banks in the United States. These reserves are the percentage of deposits placed in banks that must be maintained to conduct daily operations and cannot be used for lending purposes. These reserves may be kept on deposit with the Fed or can be maintained in each bank's vault. The banking institution must hold the amount of this reserve requirement in reserves. For example, if the reserve requirement is 17 percent and a bank has $100 million on deposit, then the bank can only loan out $83 million because it must keep $17 million in reserves. If the Fed increased the reserve requirement to 25 percent, then the bank could only loan $75 million. Obviously, a small change in reserve requirements drastically affects the money supply. Changes to the reserve requirement ratio are seldom employed.

The **discount rate** is the rate of interest that the Fed charges banks to borrow money from the Fed. Banks can borrow money from the Fed when they want to make loans but find that they do not have sufficient reserves. This makes the Fed the lender of last resort for the banking industry. Although the Fed does not directly control market interest rates, it does have an effect on them. Because banks earn their profits on loans, there must be a difference between what the banks pay for money and what they charge for money that is borrowed by households, governments, and businesses. The discount rate charged by the Fed to its member banks is normally the nation's lowest lending rate, as can be seen in Table 1-6.

If the Fed believes that there is too much borrowing in the marketplace, it may tighten credit by increasing the discount rate. When interest rates increase, it becomes more difficult for us to borrow as the payments on our loans increase. This situation dampens the demand for money and cools off the economy.

RISK

We have discussed three of the four major variables that affect market interest rates. They are supply of money, demand for money, and Federal Reserve monetary policy. The fourth factor is risk.

Table 1-6 Money Rates, as of January 31, 2000

Type of Rate	Definition	Rate (%)
Discount	The charge on loans to depository institutions by the New York Federal Reserve Bank	5.00
Federal funds	The rate banks charge each other for overnight loans in minimum amounts of $1 million	5.87
T-bill, three months	The rate on government treasury bills sold at a discount of face value in units of $10,000	5.56
Prime	The interest rate that banks charge their most creditworthy customers	8.50

Source: Federal Reserve Statistical Release H.15, February 7, 2000.

Risk involves the probability that the actual return on an investment will be different from the desired return. When we talk about risk-taking in business or finance, we are discussing an individual's tolerance for investments. These investments may or may not return what is desired. In general, younger people tend to be risk takers and older people tend to be more risk averse. For example, the purchase of a U.S. bond or treasury bill is considered to be a risk-free investment. The probability that the government will not pay interest and principal on the bond is negligible. Conversely, investing in a new business is more risky. As noted earlier, approximately 40 percent of all new businesses in the United States fail in the first five years. If we were to invest in a new business, we would therefore demand a higher probable return on our investment than if we invested in government securities. It would not be wise to take more risk and not expect a higher return. If we expected the business investment to provide us with the same return as a government bond, we would purchase the bond and eliminate the risk factor.

Risk can be divided into two categories: systematic risk and unsystematic risk. **Systematic risk** is associated with economic, political, and sociological changes that affect all participants on an equal basis. For example, Australia and Brazil had a severe drought in 1995 that affected farm production; as a result, demand for U.S. wheat increased and wheat prices rose in all sectors of the economy. In December 1995, the prime lending rate decreased from 8.75 percent to 8.5 percent. This decrease affected all borrowers who had loans tied to prime lending rates. Both of these examples are factors of systematic risk because the effect was national. **Unsystematic risk** is unique to an individual, firm, or industry. In business, unsystematic risk is often based on management capabilities, competition within the industry, vendor reliability, and variables that relate to microeconomics.

The total risk of a business is based on a series of variables and incorporates both systematic and unsystematic risk. When a person starts a business, lenders consider unsystematic factors such as the type of business and the uncertainty that exists with respect to the firm's earnings and future profitability. Additional items include the experience and financial and capital assets of the owner, business location, and several other factors that relate directly to the business. The lenders will consider all risk factors and determine if they will grant the loan. If unsystematic risk is perceived to be too high, the loan will be denied. If unsystematic risk is within the range specified as acceptable in the lending guidelines of the bank, the loan will be granted. The interest rate charged for this loan will represent a combination of the systematic and unsystematic risk factors. If the prime lending rate is 8 percent and the unsystematic risk factor is considered to be 3 percent, then the financial institution will grant the loan at an interest rate of 11 percent or above, but never less than 11 percent. In effect, the borrower is paying a risk premium of 3 percent to get the loan.

As noted in Table 1-6, the prime lending rate is that rate charged by banks to their best customers. As risk increases, so does the interest rate. Banks may charge less than prime to a customer who they perceive will repay the loan with no problems. Banks may charge prime plus 3 or 4 percent to a company they consider to be risky.

In addition, the amount of the down payment on capital purchases such as land, buildings, and machinery may vary based on the risk assessment of the bank. For example, a veteran may be entitled to a Veterans Administration (VA) loan with no down payment. If the veteran defaults on the loan, the loan is guaranteed by the government of the United States. If another person with the same income tries to obtain a conventional home loan from a bank, the bank may require a down payment of 10 to 20 percent of the home value, due to the fact that the bank perceives unsystematic risk as being higher for the second individual. This loan is guaranteed only by the income of the individual. The base lending rate for business loans is normally the prime rate in existence at the time of the loan request.

Businesses often face the risk of interest rate fluctuations. This risk can impact a business if the business has a variable rate loan. In periods of low interest rates, businesses will tend to borrow more because capital can be obtained at a lower cost. In periods of rising interest rates, capital becomes expensive to obtain and maintain. For example, one of the authors had a $150,000 business loan that was granted by the bank at prime plus 2 percent. When the prime rate rose by 2 percent during one year, the payments on this loan increased by $246 per month. As interest rates move up, businesses are forced to pay a higher price for money they have previously borrowed, which eats away at their profitability.

The management of risk will be dealt with extensively in later chapters. If we are to succeed in business, we must reduce our risk to acceptable limits; otherwise, bankruptcy may be the end result. Therefore, to succeed, the business owner must develop plans to minimize risk and to place the business in a competitive and profitable position.

 # CONCLUSION

In this chapter we introduced basic financial concepts. We discussed the importance of finance and its relationship to those economic concepts involving the scarcity of resources, opportunity costs, savings, income, expenditures, and taxes. Because the small business owner or manager will usually make decisions concerning acquisition of financial capital, interest rates were fully discussed with respect to supply and demand, Federal Reserve policy, and risk.

It is essential that we have a basic knowledge of these factors before we attempt to set goals, establish ownership of a business, and write a business plan prior to starting our own business. These topics will be covered in Chapter 2.

REVIEW AND DISCUSSION QUESTIONS

1. What is finance?
2. What is a market?
    a. Name five types of markets in which you participate.
    b. What markets trade economic resources?
3. Compare marginal revenue, marginal cost, and marginal revenue product.
4. Distinguish between economic and financial capital.
5. Discuss the value of the entrepreneur. What distinguishes the entrepreneur from the labor resource? Why are entrepreneurs unique?
6. What is opportunity cost?
7. What makes up gross income?
8. Compare progressive, regressive, and proportional taxes. Give at least one example of each type of tax.
9. What is the law of supply?
10. What is a supply table? How do you obtain a supply curve from a supply table?
11. What is the law of demand?
12. Explain the concept of a surplus of money versus a shortage of money.
13. What is the Federal Reserve? What are the Fed's three tools for controlling the money supply?
14. What is risk? What is the difference between systematic and unsystematic risk?

EXERCISES AND PROBLEMS

1. Carry Yoki's Lounge consists of the following: Carry, the owner, believed that people would come to hear a band play on Friday, Saturday, and Sunday evenings. During the remainder of the week, she believed her customers would watch sporting events on several television sets located throughout the lounge. Carry employed two bartenders, three servers, two assistant servers, two cooks, one dishwasher, and a cleanup person. She had a bar, 15 bar stools, 4 tables, 40 chairs, 4 television sets, and a satellite dish. She had an oven, stove, grill, refrigerator, sinks, dishes, and glassware. Carry started this business with $50,000 of her own money and borrowed $150,000 from the bank. From the above description, list each of the scarce resources that are used in Carry Yoki's Lounge.

2. Joe Fixit has an appliance repair business. He has more business than he can handle and wants to hire another repair person. Joe estimates that three appliances can be repaired each hour by a qualified person. Joe bills out labor at $45 per hour, but stipulates that the minimum charge for appliance repair estimates is $30 plus parts. What is the marginal revenue product of a qualified repair person? What is the maximum hourly wage that he would pay an employee?

3. Sam Smith is currently employed as a mechanical engineer and is paid $65,000 per year plus benefits that are equal to 30 percent of his salary. Sam wants to begin a consulting firm and decides to leave his current job. After his first year in business, Sam's accountant informs him that he has made $45,000 with his consulting business. Sam also notices that he paid $6,000 for a health insurance policy, which were his total benefits during the year he started his own business. What was Sam's opportunity cost?

4. Sara Lee just graduated from college with a degree in accounting. She had five job offers: Bean Counters CPA, $35,000; Assets R Us, $27,000; The Debit Store, $30,000; J & J's CPAs, $33,000; and The Double Entry Shop, $40,000. What was her opportunity cost if she accepted the job with The Double Entry Shop?

5. Sam Club earned $50,000 and paid taxes of $10,000. Samantha Heart earned $60,000 and paid taxes of $12,000. If these taxes were paid to the same government agency, is the tax on income progressive, regressive, or proportional? Why did you reach this conclusion?

6. You read an article in this morning's paper that stated inflation was accelerating and would reach 6 percent this year. If the Fed believes this statement and it had set a goal of 3 percent inflation, what would it likely do at the next meeting of the Federal Open Market Committee?

7. A friend of yours came into your office and said that his bank was out to kill small businesses. You asked him what he meant by this remark, and he

said that he read an article that said his bank had just loaned $10 million to a major automobile manufacturer at a rate of 8 percent, which is less than prime. But your friend just borrowed $50,000 from the same bank, which charged him prime plus 3 percent, or 11.5 percent. Your friend has been in business for two years, and last year he had a loss of $2,000. How can you explain this difference in interest rates to your friend?

FINANCIAL MANAGEMENT AND PLANNING

2

Learning Objectives

When you have completed this chapter, you should be able to:

- Describe the five basic functions of a manager and how they relate to a small business.

- Distinguish between strategic plans and functional plans.

- Understand the three factors that must be addressed when establishing goals.

- Describe the financial goals of a for-profit organization.

- Trace the three-step process to take when using control.

- Compare and contrast the basic forms of business ownership (sole proprietor, partnership, and corporation).

- Distinguish between limited and unlimited liability.

- Compare and contrast general partnership, limited partnership, and a limited liability company.

- Understand the role that the franchise plays when establishing a small business.

- Understand the basic components of a SWOT analysis.

- Know what basic factors are required to complete a business plan.

To achieve a financial objective, a businessperson must be both a manager and a leader. Although there are no universally accepted definitions of **management,** it can essentially be defined as the process of working with or through others to achieve an individual or business goal by efficiently and effectively using resources.

MANAGEMENT FUNCTIONS

A manager performs five basic functions: planning, organizing, staffing, directing, and controlling operations. These functions are discussed in the following sections.

PLANNING

Planning is a systematic process that takes us from some current state to some future desired state. Planning involves establishing goals and developing processes and methods for achieving these goals. There are several types of planning with which we should be concerned as business owners.

Strategic planning is the development of long-term plans for our business. Strategic planning involves establishing overall company priorities. Additionally, the strategic planner allocates resources and takes the steps necessary to meet the strategic goals. The strategic plan answers the following question: Where do we want our business to be, at some future date? It is important to note that strategic plans have a time horizon that usually exceeds one year. Strategic plans most often have time horizons of five years or more. Some industries require strategic plans that cover fifteen years.

Functional plans for business are driven by the strategic plan. They are related to specific functional areas of business such as accounting, marketing, or human resources. If you currently own a pizza parlor restaurant and would like to open 10 additional restaurants in your community within five years, your goal can be accomplished by using a strategic plan. Each of these restaurants, however, will have to hire personnel. As a result, you need a personnel plan. This functional plan supports the strategic plan. Each restaurant will also require equipment. As a result, you will need a capital budgeting plan. Each restaurant will require a marketing strategy, so you will also have to have a marketing plan. Each restaurant will have to provide products and services to customers in a specific manner to guarantee consistency of quality with respect to the product. As a result, you will need an operational plan. All of the preceding are functional plans that support the strategic plan of your business.

Another functional plan involves financial planning. **Financial planning** consists of the gathering of all of a firm's monetary requirements for the support of each functional plan. The company, therefore, must convert these functional plans into an overall budget for the firm. This budget then drives the financial and financing requirements. The reason so many businesses fail is due to a lack of adequate financial planning. Nobody begins a business with a plan for failure, but too many businesses have been started with a failure to plan.

Goal setting is precursor to establishing a plan. A goal is a measurable objective that can be reached in a specified time frame. All goals must have three characteristics: (1) they must be measurable (10 restaurants); (2) they must be achievable (Is it feasible to open the 10 restaurants?); and (3) they must have a time frame connected to them (e.g., within five years). In many texts, the terms *goals* and *objectives* are interchangeable; however, there is a difference. Goals are normally considered to be long term. Objectives are intermediate goals that measure progress toward the overall long-term goal.

Continuing with the previous example, you might set an objective of having two more restaurants operating next year, and an additional two in the following year. By opening two restaurants each year over the next five years, you will achieve all intermediate goals (objectives) and accomplish the strategic goal of opening ten restaurants in five years.

There are three basic financial goals required by a for-profit organization: to maximize the wealth of the business owners (investors) over the life of the business, to meet interest payments on debt, and to grow.

These goals require that our company have one overall goal: to make money now and to make more money in the future.[1] If a satisfactory return on investment is not reached by the individual owner, that owner will become discouraged and will look to invest elsewhere. A business that is not making a profit may cease to exist. Additionally, if interest payments on debt are not made, banks or other creditors may force the enterprise into bankruptcy. For the individual business owner, bankruptcy can make it difficult, if not impossible, to obtain future credit. Finally, a business enterprise has to grow. If it does not grow, it will probably not be competitive in the marketplace and will cease to exist.

To avoid the preceding problems, the manager must develop business plans based on definite and obtainable goals. Once definite goals have been established, then plans should be written that will allow accomplishment of each goal. The beginning of financial planning requires basic knowledge of financial analysis, financial forecasting, and development of budgets (which are plans converted to financial terms). These items are covered in detail in subsequent chapters.

ORGANIZING

Organizing is the second function of the manager. Once a plan has been written, the owners (managers) must develop an organization that will allow them to carry out the plan. For most start-up companies, structure is fairly simple, with one or two employees, and virtually no departments. As the business grows, however, definite structures and departments must be

---

[1] Eliahu Goldratt, *The Haystack Syndrome: Sifting Information out of the Data Ocean* (Croton-on-Hudson, NY: North River Press, 1990).

established. If you are the single owner of a restaurant, you can probably interview and hire every employee. If you reach your goal of having 10 restaurants, you will need someone to recruit for you. The decision will have to be made as to whether you will give the responsibility for hiring to the managers of each store or to a central personnel office. With small businesses, you are not subject to many government rules and regulations. As the business grows, you need more experts to assist you. Organizing the business is related to planning. A functional plan, previously discussed, should answer the following questions: Who will do it? What skills do they need? What is the time frame that we have set in which to have it accomplished? Where will it be accomplished? How do we get it accomplished? Answers to these questions allow us to define our organization. For example, you may want to interview applicants and hire a manager for each of your 10 stores. You may also permit these managers to hire their own employees. Or, you may want to have your central personnel department screen and test all applicants, and then send only those people who are qualified to your stores to be interviewed by the individual managers whom you have previously selected.

Within the context of financial management, a business's organization involves monitoring financial plans and determining how to obtain the funds required to carry out these plans. In a small business, financial organization may be carried out entirely by the entrepreneur. As the business grows, a definite organizational structure must be developed to obtain and monitor funds.

STAFFING

The **staffing** function requires that the manager obtain the most capable personnel to implement the business plans. Each functional plan involves people. As a result, the overall planning process must also deal with specific jobs. For each specific job, we must determine the job requirements. Job requirements are what the job requires with respect to education, training, and basic skills. Additionally, a job description should be developed for each position. It depicts the duties that must be performed by the employee who will be hired. In the small business, the owner takes care of most of this responsibility.

DIRECTING

The fourth function of a manager is leading or directing. **Directing** is providing proper guidance and direction to others who will accomplish the organization's mission. The entrepreneur is the person who leads and directs the business. Employees try to emulate employers and managers whom they respect. As owners of an organization, we must be honest if we expect our employees to be honest. We must be truthful if we expect them to be truthful. We should guide by the Golden Rule: Treat our employees as we would want to be treated if we were in their situation. Good employers and managers have long-term, loyal employees. Employers and managers who cannot effectively lead will experience high employee turnover.

Directing in the financial arena is carried out through the budgeting process. Through the budgeting process, financial assets are disbursed to specific areas and functions of the business. Managers, to carry out efficient operations, must direct the flow of financial assets properly.

CONTROLLING

Controlling, next to planning, is the most difficult process to undertake. Controlling is essentially a three-step process that involves the following: establishing a standard of measurement, measuring actual performance against the standard, and taking corrective action when actual performance varies from the established standard. Financial control begins with setting standards to follow. It compares actual expenditures and income with projected standards, and determines problem areas. Next, controlling takes corrective action by developing and implementing solutions to problems. Financial control also requires owners to protect the financial assets of the company by developing sound internal auditing (monitoring) and control procedures. This feat cannot be reasonably accomplished without the development of adequate strategic and functional financial plans.

BUSINESS ORGANIZATIONS AND OWNERSHIP

One of the first decisions that must be made when planning a business is what form of ownership it will entail. The four basic forms of business ownership are sole proprietorship, partnership, corporation, and limited liability company. A franchise, although not a specific business form, also will be discussed. Within the context of the partnership form of business, are both general and limited partnerships. There are also several forms of corporate ownership. The two primary types of corporations are public and private. The limited liability company is a hybrid, having some of the characteristics of both the partnership and the corporation. Which form is appropriate depends on the situation of the owner. If you are just starting a business as a single entity, it may be appropriate to begin as a sole proprietor. If you only desire to own a portion of a business, a form of corporate ownership or limited partnership may be in order.

As we continue, it will become apparent that the decision to use a specific form of business ownership will be contingent on several factors. These factors include tax advantages, financial support, the owner's desires, and the

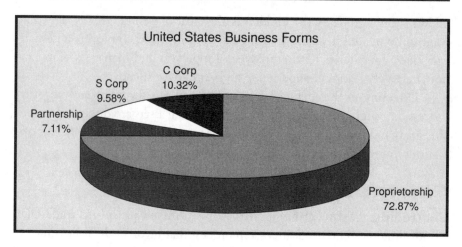

FIGURE 2-1
United States Business Forms
Source: Number of Business Income Tax Returns, by Size of Business for Specified Income
    Years, 1980–1996; IRS, Statistics of Income Bulletin, Winter 1998/99, Publication 1136, Rev.
    2/99. U.S. Securities & Exchange Commission, 1998 Annual Report to Congress.

type and location of the business. It is important to note that tax advantages are subject to change as our government changes tax laws. One should always consult a tax professional to determine the current status of these laws. In 1996 more than 23 million business organizations filed tax returns in the United States.[2] The breakdown of these is shown in Figure 2-1.

SOLE PROPRIETORSHIP

The business form most widely used today is the **sole proprietorship,** which is operated by an individual for profit. Personal incentive and satisfaction contribute to the sole proprietor's ability to make the business work.

Advantages of a Sole Proprietorship

The sole proprietorship has several advantages over the other forms of business ownership. There are no formal federal legal requirements with which to comply to establish the sole proprietorship. Local governments (city, county, or state) may require a license for tax purposes, but the fees are normally quite small and the forms are usually easy to fill out. Title to the property of the business is in the owner's name. The sole proprietor conducts the business alone or within a tight family structure. The business requires no formal organizational structure. For this reason, all that is needed to start a

---

[2]Number of Business Income Tax Returns, by Size of Business for Specified Income Years, 1980–1996; IRS, Statistics of Income Bulletin, Winter 1998/99, Publication 1136, Rev. 2/99.

business (with the exception of local licenses) is an idea and the desire to conduct business in a reputable and legal fashion.

From an accounting standpoint, sole proprietorship business tax procedures can be relatively simple, because all income from the business is reported on the owner's individual tax return. The sole proprietor can determine the type of and contribution to a retirement plan, and can take maximum advantage of tax laws pertaining to sheltering income. The owner is usually the manager of the business and has total control over how managerial authority is exercised on a daily basis. The freedom to take action allows the owner to make decisions and take action without delay. The owner can choose to change products, services, or business locations. The owner can determine goals or sell the business without consulting anyone else. Often this total freedom is the optimum path and provides the most satisfaction to the individual owner.

Disadvantages of a Sole Proprietorship

The sole proprietorship also has several disadvantages. The capital structure (the combination of debt and equity financing) of the business is limited because the owner depends on individual resources to operate the business. Financing the business is totally dependent on the wealth and credit standing of the owner. As a sole proprietor, one may find it difficult to borrow from outside resources. Having a detailed financial plan and the ability to fill out a loan package are necessities if the business owner desires to raise additional capital.

The sole proprietor also has unlimited liability. All property of the business is in the owner's name. The owner is responsible for all debts of the business and is legally liable for any problems that the business may have. For example, if someone is injured in the sole proprietor's store, the owner can be sued, personally. If the owner is found guilty and a large judgment is rendered to the injured party, the proprietor may have to dip into personal assets (e.g., house, car, or furniture) to pay the judgment.

Additionally, the life of the business is limited to the life of the owner. If the business owner dies, the business legally ceases to exist. If the proprietor has left the business to a spouse or child, this person must relicense the business in his or her name. Transfer of ownership will take time, and overall disruptions in business continuity may occur. Thus, the death or poor health of the owner will tend to dissolve the proprietorship.

Two additional disadvantages may plague a sole proprietor. First, a business owner may lack those managerial skills that are necessary to operate a business. Second, the inability of a star employee to obtain ownership (or at least a vested interest) in the business may give the employee the incentive to look elsewhere for employment.

PARTNERSHIP

A **partnership** is an association of two or more persons who carry out a business as co-owners for a profit. There are essentially two types of partnerships, the general partnership and the limited partnership. All partnerships, in the authors' opinion, should be formed with a formal partnership agreement that specifies the legal arrangements and business responsibilities of each partner. Because of the complexities associated with partnerships, it is strongly recommended that any partnership agreement be written in consultation with an attorney.

The **general partnership** has an important advantage over the proprietorship. Because there is more than one owner, there is more expertise; the partners have more expertise than the sole proprietor. Often partnerships are formed because of these differences in expertise. One partner may be an excellent technician, but has no personality. The other may be an excellent salesperson, but has no technical ability. Obviously, if such a situation exists, the firm will be better off using the expertise of both partners. The partners may have an equal voice in management or may be limited by the partnership agreement.

The general partnership also has several disadvantages that are similar to those of the proprietorship. Each partner is personally liable for the acts of the partnership. Financing of the business is limited by the assets and credit ratings of the individual partners. Ownership is difficult to transfer, and profits are taxed to the individual partners on their personal tax returns. The partnership has a limited life and is legally terminated when one partner dies, unless the partnership agreement is very specific with regard to a transfer of ownership. For example, you may have an excellent relationship with your partner, but not get along with your partner's spouse. If your partner dies, you may find yourself with a new partner (partner's spouse) with whom you may disagree or who is totally incompetent, unless there is a specific buy-sell provision in the partnership agreement.

The **limited partnership** involves one or more general partners and normally several limited partners. The most widely used form of limited partnership occurs with real estate development and holdings. In such a partnership the general partner is in charge of day-to-day operations and is personally liable for the partnership. The limited partners are basically investors, and their liability is limited to the amount of their investment in the partnership. They are not involved with the daily operations. For example, John Adams finds a large apartment complex that is for sale for $1 million. John is a real estate management expert who believes that the purchase would provide a good profit if the apartment complex is handled properly. John has $50,000 to invest in this venture. He locates 19 other people who are willing to invest $50,000 each in this apartment complex. John now has the $1 million to purchase the complex. He would become the general partner, and the other 19 investors would be the limited partners.

Now assume that the apartment complex has a major fire in which several tenants are severely injured, and the tenants sue the partnership. The tenants receive a judgment of $3 million. John is personally liable as the general partner. The other 19 partners have a limited liability of $50,000 each. This amount reflects the magnitude of their individual investments. Other than in the general areas of limited and unlimited liability, the limited partnership has the same advantages and disadvantages of the general partnership. To avoid the unlimited liability problem that John faced in the partnership outlined here, he could have formed his organization as a corporation.

CORPORATION

The **corporation** is a legal entity according to U.S. law, so it may accomplish the same tasks as an individual can accomplish. It may buy and sell assets, enter into legal contracts, hire and fire employees, and so forth. Corporations are incorporated in any one of the 50 states or one of the territories of the United States and are chartered by the state or territory for tax purposes. All corporations are C-corporations unless 100 percent of the stockholders vote to select S-corporation status. C-corporations are taxed as corporations; corporate income tax is paid by the corporation on its profit, prior to distributing any profit to the shareholder. S-corporations have special tax status. The corporation does not pay income tax on its profit. The shareholders receive their proportionate share of the S-corporation's profit and report this as income on their individual income tax statements. It is imperative to consult an attorney and a tax professional when forming a corporation because the laws pertaining to forming the corporation, will vary by state and the corporation is subject to state law and federal rules and regulations.

Ownership of a corporation is based on shares of stock or percentage of ownership. The number of shares owned by an individual, divided by the total shares outstanding (sold) determines the percentage of ownership held by an individual. There are essentially two types of corporations: the public corporation and the private or closely held corporation.

A **public corporation** is one whose stock is traded on the open market and represents less than 1 percent of all business organizations in the United States (less than 30,000 of over 23,000,000) (Figure 2-1).[3] These

---

[3]U.S. Securities and Exchange Commission, 1998 Annual Report to Congress at http://www.sec.gov.

corporations are governed by the Securities and Exchange Commission (SEC). They must meet several federal reporting requirements. All public corporations must send an annual report to each stockholder and file an annual form 10K report (basically a set of financial statements) with the SEC. Both of these forms are available to the public. Annual reports can easily be obtained by calling the corporation and requesting a copy. Form 10K reports can also be obtained by calling the corporation, or these may be found at any large public library or university library, or on the internet through the Electronic Data Gathering and Retrieval System (EDGAR), which became effective May 1996. All public corporations must file electronically. Corporate advantages and disadvantages are normally opposite the individual and partnership advantages and disadvantages.

Advantages of a Corporation

Advantages for the corporation are numerous. From a financial standpoint, the corporation has tremendous advantages over the sole proprietorship or partnership. The corporation has almost unlimited access to financial capital because it may raise capital by selling stock (acquiring new owners), by borrowing from banks (as does the sole proprietor), or by borrowing from the public through issuing bonds. A corporate bond, like a government bond, is borrowed money. The corporation must pay interest on the face value of the bond for the duration of the bond's life. On the maturity date of the bond, the corporation must redeem the bond at face value. Stocks and bonds are more thoroughly discussed in Chapter 10. A corporation has unlimited life, as long as it is financially stable and is not forced into a liquidating bankruptcy. Ownership in the corporation is passed from one owner to another either through the sale of the corporation's stock, by gift, or by inheritance.

The owners of the corporation have limited liability insofar as ownership is limited to the number of shares of stock held by an individual. The corporation has unlimited liability because it can be sued for unlimited amounts, until it becomes bankrupt. The individual owner of a corporation, in a court action, is only liable for his or her investment in the corporation. For example, you buy $1,000 in stock in the XYZ Corporation. This corporation is sued for developing and selling a product that results in the death of several customers. In a court action the corporation loses a $100 million lawsuit that forces XYZ Corp. into bankruptcy. Your only liability is the $1,000 investment. Thus, the corporation has unlimited liability, but you, as the individual owner, have limited liability. You can never lose more than your $1,000 investment even if the corporation ceases to exist. When we hear that a corporation has limited liability that means the corporate owner actually has limited liability.

Disadvantages of a Corporation

The corporation also has many disadvantages. There are formal federal and state legal requirements that must be met. These include an annual audit by an independent, impartial, outside auditor, of which the corporation bears the cost. Other requirements include the filing of numerous forms and compliance with several laws that apply only to corporations, including the 10K requirements discussed earlier.

Another disadvantage is that business ownership is widely held. Stockholders elect a board of directors at an annual meeting, and the board selects the key managers of the corporation. Owners are therefore separated from the business and have little or no control over how the business is run on a daily basis. The owner normally has little say in business products, location, or goal setting.

From a financial point of view, the biggest disadvantage of the corporation is double taxation. The corporation pays federal tax on its profits; then the corporation may distribute a share of its profits back to the owner as a dividend. You, as a stockholder, must declare the dividend as ordinary income and pay personal income tax at your current tax rate. For example, in 1999, a corporation was subject to a maximum tax rate of 35 percent of net profit in excess of $10 million. The maximum tax rate for an individual was 39.6 percent.[4] Assume that you owned 1,000 shares in a corporation that was subject to the maximum corporate tax rate of 35 percent. The corporation had to pay 35 percent in federal taxes on each dollar of profit. The corporation then sent you a dividend of $5 per share. You then had an additional $5,000 in income (1,000 shares times $5 dividend per share). If your personal tax rate was 39.6 percent, then you paid 39.6 percent in tax on each dollar of dividend income. What is the total tax paid on each dollar earned by the corporation and paid to you in the form of a dividend? It is *not* 35 + 39.6, or 74.6 percent. The total tax rate on each of these corporate dollars earned was in fact 60.74 percent. For each dollar that the corporation had in operating profit, 35 cents was paid in taxes (35 percent). This left 65 cents for every dollar earned to be paid as a dividend. You then received this 65-cent net profit in the form of dividends. You then paid 39.6 percent of the 65 cents paid to you in dividends, or you paid 25.74 cents in taxes on the dividend distribution. Thus, the total amount of taxes paid on the original dollar of corporate earnings was 35 cents by the corporation and 25.74 cents by you, for a total tax of 60.74 cents, which is also 60.74 percent.

---

[4]IRS Publication 542, Corporations and IRS Notice 1036 (Rev. November 1998), Early Release Copies of 1999 Income Tax Withholding and Advance Earned Income Credit Payment Tables.

Can you be in a corporation and avoid the double taxation rate? You can put your money into a private corporation that has received Subchapter S status from the Internal Revenue Service (IRS). As explained earlier, S-corporation profit is distributed to the stockholder as ordinary income and the stockholder pays income tax on this profit at his or her normal tax rate.

Other Corporations

A **private corporation** is one that has been formed under state law but that does not sell its shares of stock to the public. Federal law allows individuals to form small corporations. An example of a private corporation is the professional corporation, which can have a single owner. We typically find physicians, accountants, and other professionals in this type of corporation. A professional corporation will have the designation "P.C." after the title of the corporation, such as in an individual's name (e.g., Sidney Jones, M.D., P.C.). Like a large corporation, private corporations have the advantages of limited liability. They have the disadvantages of limited management expertise and limited ability to raise cash, like the proprietorship or partnership. They are also subject to double taxation, like the public corporation.

The **Subchapter S-corporation** is privately held and has filed for and been granted Subchapter S status by the Internal Revenue Service. The Subchapter S-corporation must have more than one owner but not more than 75 owners.[5] States authorize these corporations in different forms, and again we advise consulting an attorney and an accountant to determine which form is best for you.

The Subchapter S-corporation is, for the most part, the best of both worlds. It has the advantages of the sole proprietorship or partnership. The form of the business and the business products are determined by a small group of owners. Stock (ownership) can be easily transferred. There is no double taxation as profits flow through to the individual. Federal reporting is minimal, because the corporation simply has to file for a federal tax number and permission to function under one of the IRS codes governing this type of corporation. Once this permission is granted, reporting of corporate profits or losses is included on the owner's personal tax forms.

Liability is limited to the owner's investment in the corporation. Unfortunately, because the stock is not publicly traded, the Subchapter S-corporation is limited in its access to capital. For this reason, some businesses, although they begin as private or Subchapter S-corporations, will change their status to that of a public corporation, by expanding their ownership base and publicly trading stock, as they expand and require more capital.

---

[5] Internal Revenue Service, Instructions for Form 2553 (Revised July 1999), Election by a Small Business Corporation.

Although the owner of a corporation cannot normally be sued as an individual, in several recent cases managers and owners have been sued when they have been shown to have done something blatantly illegal. A famous case involved a president of an Illinois corporation who knowingly failed to provide his worker with proper safety protection, and the worker was killed on the job. The company had been in violation of Occupational Safety and Health Administration (OSHA) guidelines for a long period, and there was substantial evidence that the owner knew what the requirements were, but chose to ignore them. The owner was charged with and convicted of murder.

LIMITED LIABILITY COMPANY

A **limited liability company (LLC)** is a hybrid business entity having features of both partnerships and corporations. If formed properly it will be taxed as a partnership, and its members will enjoy limited liability like corporate shareholders. Like a partnership, an LLC establishes an agreement that defines the functions, responsibilities, and financial and tax provisions of the members. Additionally, the LLC may have either a written or an oral agreement among the members, but we strongly recommend a written agreement. The advantages of an LLC include limited liability of members, income flow and loses to individual member tax returns, and active management by all members of the LLC without the risk of liability associated with a limited partnership. Foreigners may also have ownership in the LLC as well as corporations, trusts, and estates. A disadvantage is that the LLC cannot be used by professionals such as physicians and attorneys. There may be other disadvantages, but it has been authorized for such a short time that there is little legal precedent and it is not available in all states.

When you begin a business, the type of ownership is one of your primary considerations. We advise forming a corporation anytime there may be substantial personal liability for you, the owner. However, one cannot normally begin as a public corporation because there is not demand for the stock of a company unless it develops a revolutionary new product or until it develops a track record of profitability. Therefore, the remainder of this text concentrates on finance for a small business—the financial requirements for a sole proprietorship, partnership, or private corporation. Public corporations will be discussed briefly and only when necessary.

FRANCHISE

Although franchises are not a form of business ownership, we will discuss them at this point. A **franchise** is a business in which the buyer, who is the franchisee, purchases the right to sell the goods or services of the seller, who is the franchiser. Franchisers provide four advantages: name recognition, standardized policies and procedures for product and service delivery, marketing skill in the form of strategy and advertising, and training of employees, managers, and franchisees. The franchisee, in exchange for these services, signs a franchise agreement that obligates the franchisee to conduct business in a manner prescribed by the franchiser. The franchisee normally agrees to provide the franchiser with a percentage of gross sales on a monthly basis. Franchisers essentially own a percentage of your cash flow. One of the disadvantages then of the franchise is that you are not truly your own boss. You must comply with the contractual obligations agreed to in the franchise agreement. However, there are several reasons for entering into a franchise agreement: You have a proven product, a guaranteed sales area, good training, and, in many cases, a guaranteed profit margin. You must understand that some franchises do fail. Some franchisers are better than others. If you are considering this type of business, check out the franchise thoroughly. Talk to franchisees who were not recommended by the franchiser. Find out how many hours are actually involved, what profit margins really exist, and the actual amount of your financial obligation. If you are then satisfied, consider going into the franchise. Whereas over 40 percent of all new businesses fail in the first five years, the franchise failure rate is under 10 percent.

STARTING A BUSINESS

Obviously when we start a new business, one of the first decisions involves legal formation. The business does not exist until the owners establish it. The business cannot exist until the owners choose the legal form under which the business is to operate.

For most new businesses, the owner must determine how much money is required to begin the business. If the owner does not have the financial capital to begin the business with personal equity, then some financing must be obtained from outside parties. The owner would then need a valid loan proposal; but we, the owners, cannot get a loan proposal together unless we have a basic understanding of business forms, forecasting procedures, and business and personal finance, which are covered in subsequent chapters.

The remainder of this chapter pertains to the requirements for starting your own business. Most management texts include a recommendation to perform a SWOT analysis. The acronym **SWOT** stands for **strengths, weaknesses, opportunities,** and **threats.** Strengths and weaknesses pertain to the internal workings of a company. Opportunities and threats pertain to those external factors outside of the company's control, but that the company must take into consideration.

Before you seriously consider venturing into a business, we strongly recommend that you and any of the prospective principals or partners in this business contemplate your individual strengths and weaknesses. Make a list and include under strengths those items that you really enjoy doing. Include your areas of expertise. Under weaknesses, include items that you really dislike and items in which you lack expertise. Include also things that you prefer not to do or things that go against your grain. For example, say that you are a plumber and you take much satisfaction in knowing that when you place fixtures in a new house, the owners will be satisfied. Every fixture will work as advertised. List this quality as a strength. You can make good money doing this job on your own. You would really like to start your own plumbing company, but you do not have any idea of where to begin. List not having a plan for investing your money as a weakness. Wanting to start your own business and not knowing where to begin also is a weakness. We hope that this book will help you in your weak areas and teach you how, as you build your business, to take advantage of your strengths and determine how to overcome those weaknesses.

When you start a business, you plan to be involved for several years. If you detest a certain job function, then you had better include hiring someone to perform this function as part of your business plan. The reason why we recommend listing those things that you really like to do is that you may be doing them for a long time. Most successful businesspeople are those who really enjoy doing whatever it is that makes their business a success.

Understand that when you own a small business, you are "they." For example, say you own a business that is open on a 24-hour basis, and you have just worked the day shift from 7 A.M. to 4 P.M. If you are only an employee, you go home. If it is your business and an employee who is supposed to work from 4 P.M. to midnight calls in sick, you are the one who fills in. It is your baby store, and it just got sick. You are the doctor and the nursemaid. If you want your business to succeed, you must constantly nurture it and pay attention to every important detail. The rewards are astronomically high, and your efforts will pay off in the future.

Opportunities are factors that exist *in* the business environment. If utilized, opportunities will help the business to grow and prosper. For example, you are the plumber previously described, and as you continue your assessment, you realize that your community is growing at a rate of 5 percent a year. A 5 percent growth rate means new construction and more housing. Each new living complex requires plumbing fixtures, which is an opportunity for your new business to grow. Opportunities, then, also are factors that exist *outside* of your business, but that if utilized, also will help your business to grow and prosper.

Threats are factors that exist in the environment which may impede the growth of your business, directly or indirectly. As a plumber, you know there is competition from other plumbers in your area. Each competitor is a potential threat to your ability to land a contract. Additionally, you may have new government regulations that impose different requirements on the attachment of plumbing fixtures—that which was legal last week may not be legal this week. Understand that opportunities and threats are not the same for every business, and when factors in the environment change, the requirements for your business will also change. For example, consider the convenience store industry. Ten years ago, convenience stores were the only places open 24 hours a day. If you needed a container of milk for your child at 2 A.M., the only place to buy this was at a Circle K, a Seven-Eleven, or some other convenience store. With the introduction of bar coding and the expansion of supermarkets, these stores found it profitable to remain open 24 hours a day. If there was a convenience store located on the same block as a supermarket, however, a new threat developed for the convenience store: The milk sold by the supermarket was at a lower price and was just as convenient to buy as that in the convenience store. Several of these stores have disappeared as a result of new competition brought about by changes in technology.

Another threat to the convenience store industry is the gas station. Years ago, gas stations were open only until 6 P.M. Now the oil companies have entered the convenience store market and pose yet another threat to this industry. As a business owner, you must continuously monitor such changes in your environment and adjust your business plans accordingly. If you look at the convenience store industry in large cities, you will see that these stores are now located at major intersections, with gas pumps. The convenience store in the middle of the block has all but disappeared.

If you have finished a SWOT analysis and still want to begin a business, it is time to write a business plan. Your business plan will then result in requirements for financing, as the plan is converted into a budget. Although we do not explain here how to write an actual business plan, we will outline the requirements for a loan proposal, as presented by the Small Business Administration (SBA). The SBA provides a document on the internet that provides all elements of a business plan.[6] In addition, there are several excellent texts on writing a business plan. Our purpose in this text is to illustrate how to develop and interpret the financial data required for the business plan.

ELEMENTS OF A BUSINESS PLAN

The following are the Small Business Administration requirements for a loan proposal. These are normally the minimum requirements for obtaining fi-

---

[6]The SBA home page on the internet is located at http://www.sba.gov.

nancing from any financial institution or venture capitalist. Elements of the business plan should include a cover sheet, statement of purpose, and table of contents. The following are specific elements required by the SBA.

DESCRIPTION OF THE BUSINESS

In addition to legal form and name of the business, date of formation, location, and so forth, the business description should include the following items: a marketing plan for the business, an assessment of the competition, the operating procedures to be used by the business, the personnel required by the business, and the type and limits of insurance.

Legal Form and Name of the Business

Before applying for a loan, you must have already determined the legal form of business organization you will use. For partnerships and corporations, the partnership agreement or articles of incorporation must be included with the loan application. Be aware that you will already have spent some money in forming the business. You should have already selected an attorney and an accountant. The proper agreements must be in place prior to the application, so you must already select the business name and conduct proper research to ensure that the business will not infringe on currently registered trade names or trademarks. You also must apply for business licenses before you can begin the business.

Date of Formation

You must supply the date that the business was formed, which should take into account initial meetings of partners or initial meetings of the corporate board of directors.

Location

Selecting a location is perhaps the most important decision for a small business. If you have no idea of how to select a location, you should consider taking a course in marketing from a local community college. In addition, the SBA has the Service Core of Retired Executives (SCORE), which is a group of retired business owners and managers who have years of experience in various businesses. They can assist you in determining location requirements and in directing you to other help you may need to begin your business.

For a retail enterprise, there are three L's associated with the success of the business: Location, Location, Location! There are several important factors associated with proper location. The federal government and your local governmental agencies can provide you with an abundance of helpful information in this regard.

One valuable resource is *Metropolitan Areas,*[7] which is published by the U.S. Department of Commerce, Bureau of the Census. These publications can be found at any large university or public library. You can select virtually any large intersection within your community and find the population and projected growth rates for that particular area. Information regarding families includes income, age, gender, race, and family size.

Local governmental agencies such as departments of transportation can provide you with information about traffic size during the day, including travel in various directions on major roads. Vehicle movement is extremely important for certain types of retail establishments. For example, a cafe serving breakfast items should be located on the morning commuting side of the road. Locating the business on the opposite side may cut potential sales by as much as 40 percent. People will not normally cross several lanes of traffic to stop for breakfast.

Wholesale establishments must have access to local transportation facilities and be located close to freeways. If the normal method of receiving goods is via railroad, then the facility must be located at a rail siding. Manufacturing facilities also have several factors that influence their location decisions. Some of these include closeness to customers and raw materials, availability of labor force, and local laws with regard to pollution control, taxes, and incentives.

Product or Service

What specific product or service will your business provide? Have you already contacted vendors to ensure that you will have adequate inventories to maintain sales? Are there license agreements that have to be obtained to provide specific services?

Brief History of the Business

If you are purchasing an existing business, gather data to study its profits and profitability. If you are applying for a loan for an existing business, you will have to provide the potential lender with expected growth rates and information on how well the business has functioned up to the time of the loan application. If you are starting a new business, you will have to provide information with regard to your reasons for starting the business.

Proposed Future Operations

How rapidly is the business expected to grow? When will it become profitable? Are there plans for expansion, and if so, during what time frame? Any

---

[7]A complete listing of metropolitan areas and population estimates can be found at the Bureau of the Census home page on the internet at http://www.census.gov/.

information that you can provide the potential lender in this area will enhance your probability of obtaining the loan. This information indicates that you actually have a business plan and are not simply operating on wishful thinking.

Service Area

What is the service area in which you propose to operate this business?

FINANCIAL DATA

The financial data requirements include loan applications (covered in this text under financial statements, chapter 3), capital equipment and supply lists (covered under capital budgeting, chapter 9), balance sheet (covered under financial statements, chapter 3), break-even analysis (methods and analysis covered in this text, chapter 5), pro forma income projections (profit and loss statements covered in detail in this text, chapter 6), and pro forma cash flow (covered in detail, chapter 6). As you can see, this text is written to make it easy for you to comply with government requirements of obtaining a loan.

SUPPORTING DOCUMENTS

Most lenders will also require the following supporting documents: tax returns on principals for the last three years (normally a principal is anyone who will own more than 5 percent of the business); a personal financial statement (see Chapter 3; these forms can be obtained from any bank); and a copy of the franchise contract (if a franchise) and all supporting documents provided by the franchiser. Copies of the following will also have to be provided: a proposed lease or purchase agreement for building space; licenses and other legal documents; resumes of all principals; and letters of intent from suppliers, vendors, and so forth.

 CONCLUSION

In this chapter, we discussed the functions of management and how they relate to small business. Special emphasis was placed on the requirement for the entrepreneur to set specific business goals and its importance to business planning. We distinguished between limited and unlimited liability and compared and contrasted the various legal business forms. The advantages and disadvantages of each business form were discussed. We then provided an outline of the requirements for starting a business and the elements of a business plan.

Notice how many of these elements contain requirements for financial forms that must be submitted to obtain a small business loan. The methods used to generate these forms, and a deeper understanding of the meaning of these forms, will be covered in subsequent chapters. Filling out forms is one thing; making sure that they are correct and will be accepted by a lending institution is another. We hope to facilitate the latter with this textbook.

REVIEW AND DISCUSSION QUESTIONS

1. What is planning? Compare strategic planning with functional planning.
2. What role does goal setting play in the planning process?
3. Develop a list of at least 10 products that exist today that did not exist 10 years ago.
4. What are the five functions of a manager?
5. What are the three steps of controlling?
6. List and briefly explain three forms of business ownership.
7. What is meant by unlimited liability?
8. How does a limited partnership differ from a general partnership?
9. What advantages does a corporation have over the sole proprietorship? What are disadvantages of the corporation?
10. What distinct advantage does a private or Subchapter S-corporation have over the public corporation?
11. What are the pitfalls of franchising?
12. List and describe the components of a SWOT analysis.
13. List the major components of a business plan. What components are of primary concern to you, and why?

EXERCISES AND PROBLEMS

1. Carol Jones wanted her business to increase sales by 50 percent over the next five years. To do this, she would have to hire three more people. She wanted to determine how to evaluate these people, so she began to list their job performances. She also listed where these employees would work and what training they would require. What management functions is Carol performing, and how do they apply to the above scenario?
2. Jerry is a personnel manager for a large retail department store. He just received a memo that stated the company would build three new stores in Phoenix over the next five years, with one store opening in 24 months, one opening in 36 months, and one opening in 60 months. The memo that Jerry received relates to what type of business plan? If Jerry is directed to develop a personnel plan for Phoenix, what type of planning will Jerry be doing?
3. Joe Doe just started a business. He wants the business income to flow directly to his own personal tax return, but he wants to make sure that he has limited liability. What form(s) of business ownership would you recommend for Joe?

4. You buy 1,000 shares of ABC Company at $6 per share. The company is sued for millions of dollars, and ABC Co. is forced into bankruptcy. The newspaper stated that the cost of this suit would amount to $12 per share of stock. What is the maximum amount of money you can lose with this investment? Why?

5. Sam Jones, Mary Adams, and Larry Brown have been talking about starting their own business for several years. Sam is an electronic repairman, Mary is a partner in a large law firm, and Larry is an excellent salesperson. Sam and Larry will work in the business on an equal basis. It will cost $100,000 to start this business. Sam has no money, Mary has $60,000, and Larry has $40,000. If they form a partnership, how would you recommend that they organize?

6. Barry McGuire wants to purchase a dry-cleaning establishment. Barry has heard of the SWOT analysis and wants to use this methodology to determine whether he should purchase the business. He found the following information: The dry cleaner is located in a busy shopping center, and currently does all the cleaning on the premises. It has three commercial accounts that comprise 20 percent of its business. The population in the local area is growing by approximately 6 percent per year. Located across the street is a price-cutting dry cleaner in another shopping center which advertises heavily in the local area. With the exception of this shopping center and the property across the street, all property in this area is zoned residential. Most of the residents in this area are professional people who wear suits to work. The shop has an assumable lease, and the lease has a fixed rental fee for the next five years. Barry has had five years of experience in the dry-cleaning business, and would run the shop full time. Based on the above information, perform a SWOT analysis.

7. You want to open a yogurt shop. Write a brief paragraph describing each of the following elements of a business plan: description of the business, factors affecting location, and product or service to be offered.

FINANCIAL STATEMENTS 3

Learning Objectives

When you have completed this chapter, you should be able to:

- Understand how financial statements are used by businesses.
- Understand the differences and similarities that exist between a personal cash flow statement and a business income statement.
- Distinguish between fixed and variable expenses.
- Understand the changes in income statements that exist with different forms of business.
- Understand the differences and similarities that exist between a personal statement of financial position and a business balance sheet.
- Analyze the components of the basic accounting equation.
- Distinguish between assets and liabilities.
- Understand the relationship between fixed assets and depreciation.
- Given the basic data for a company, construct a financial statement.
- Understand the problems that may exist with financial statements.

Every business, regardless of its legal business form, has the same basic financial statements. These statements are used by the business for the internal control of finance, as well as by external parties who are going to invest in the business or who are going to provide the business with financial capital for start-up or for continuing operations. These external parties are current or potential creditors (banks, vendors, and landlords) and investors (venture capitalists, future partners, stockholders, and owners). Creditors and investors will use these statements to determine the basic health of the business. Data from these statements are used to evaluate a company's track record, present status, and possible future financial direction.

In this chapter we discuss financial statements for individuals, sole proprietorships, partnerships, and corporations. When these forms are identical, we will so note; however, when there is a difference in the forms, we will note each variation with a separate form.

For the public corporation (a corporation whose stock is publicly traded), the SEC requires that financial statements be audited by an independent certified public accountant (CPA) in accordance with accounting principles established by the Financial Accounting Standards Board (FASB). Although audits are not required for small (private) businesses, we recommend that you use an accountant to help you set up the books and provide you with a compilation or review of the business's financial statements. Hiring an accountant is money well spent, because it allows the entrepreneur to concentrate on managing the business, rather than on spending many hours reinventing a wheel that is already round. Additionally, most accountants can save you added expense in the long run by recognizing and solving problems that arise in the normal course of your business.

Most of us as small business owners will not have a full-time accountant—and we do not necessarily need one—but we will definitely need some type of accounting information system that will perform the accounting function. There are several excellent computerized accounting packages on the market for small businesses. Once a system is established, then your accountant may spend very little time evaluating your books, except at year-end when they have to be closed out and taxes have to be paid. The amount of time the accountant will spend on your books depends on the complexity of the business and external user requirements (e.g., lending institution requirements). Lending institutions may require monthly, quarterly, or annual statements.

Most of us are familiar with personal financial statements if we have ever applied for credit, purchased a home, or applied for a bank loan. We begin by looking at a typical bank application form. When any customer applies for a business loan, most banks require a **financial statement (personal form).** This statement is a single form that is actually composed of two segments, the statement of financial position and the personal cash flow statement. This form is shown in Table 3-1. We will cover all the information that is required for this form by looking separately at the component forms; then we will compare what we see with the typical statements required in business.

We begin by looking at the individual's **cash flow statement** and then discussing its business equivalent, the **income statement.** We next evaluate an individual's **statement of financial position** and expand our discussion to show how this form equates, in business, to the **balance sheet,** or a company's statement of financial position.

Table 3-1 Financial Statement, Personal Form

Financial Statement Personal Form

FIRST ANY KIND OF BANK:		OFFICE:	
NAME:		SOCIAL SECURITY NO:	
ADDRESS:		BUSINESS PHONE:	
CITY, STATE, ZIP		HOME PHONE:	
SPOUSE NAME:		SOCIAL SECURITY NO:	
ASSETS:	IN DOLLARS	LIABILITIES:	IN DOLLARS
CASH IN THIS BANK: CHECKING		LOANS PAYABLE THIS BANK:	
SAVINGS:		LOANS PAYABLE OTHER FINANCIAL INSTITUTIONS: (SCHEDULE 6)	
CASH IN OTHER FINANCIAL INSTITUTIONS:		ACCOUNTS PAYABLE OTHER FIRMS & INDIVIDUALS: (SCHEDULE 6)	
		CREDIT CARDS:	
MARKETABLE STOCKS AND BONDS: (SCHEDULE 1)		INCOME & OTHER TAXES PAYABLE:	
ACCOUNTS RECEIVABLE: (SCHEDULE 2)		REAL ESTATE TAXES:	
TOTAL CURRENT ASSETS		TOTAL CURRENT LIABILITIES:	
NOTES OR MORTGAGES RECEIVABLE: (SCHEDULE 3)		OTHER REAL ESTATE INDEBTEDNESS: (SCHEDULE 5)	
CASH SURRENDER VALUE LIFE INSURANCE: (SCHEDULE 4)		LIFE INSURANCE LOANS: (SCHEDULE 4)	
VEHICLES (YEAR & MAKE):		OTHER LONG-TERM DEBTS: (DESCRIBE)	
REAL ESTATE: (SCHEDULE 5)			
OTHER PERSONAL PROPERTY:		TOTAL LIABILITIES:	
TOTAL ASSETS:		TOTAL ASSETS – TOTAL LIABILITIES = NET WORTH	
ANNUAL INCOME:		ANNUAL FIXED EXPENSES:	
GROSS SALARY:		REAL ESTATE PAYMENTS: (SCHEDULE 3)	
SPOUSE'S GROSS SALARY:		RENT:	
BONUSES & COMMISSIONS:		INCOME TAXES:	
INCOME FROM SECURITIES: (SCHEDULE 1)		PROPERTY TAXES:	
RENTAL OR LEASE INCOME: (SCHEDULE 3)		ALIMONY, CHILD SUPPORT:	
MORTGAGES OR CONTRACT INCOME: (SCHEDULE 3)		INSURANCE PREMIUMS:	
OTHER INCOME (DESCRIBE):		OTHER (DESCRIBE):	
TOTAL GROSS INCOME:		TOTAL ANNUAL EXPENSES:	
LESS – TOTAL EXPENSES:			
NET CASH INCOME:			

PERSONAL CASH FLOW STATEMENT

Table 3-2 shows a personal cash flow (income) statement, which evaluates all earnings or inflows and expenses or outflows. Our inflows are basically all annual income before taxes. Included in income are wages and salaries, interest income on investments, dividend income on stock investments, and capital gains on the sale of assets that have appreciated. In addition, outflows also are expenses. We typically have two types of expenses. First are those over which we have some control such as food, clothing, and automobile expenses. These are called **variable expenses,** because the amount that we spend each month or year will typically vary. For example, automobile expenses would include gas, oil, and maintenance. We normally do not spend the same amount per month on automobile expenses. The second type of expenses are those over which we have little or no control such as mortgage payments, automobile loan or lease payments, property taxes, insurance, in-

Table 3-2 Jones Family, Personal Income Statement

The Tom Jones Family
Personal Income Statement
(Cash Flow Statement)
January 1, 2000, to December 31, 2000

INCOME		
Salaries	$ 60,000	
Interest Income	740	
TOTAL INCOME		$ 60,740
FIXED EXPENSES		
Mortgage Payment	$ 9,600	
Automobile Payment	5,040	
Property Taxes	1,235	
Insurance	4,500	
Income Taxes	5,032	
Savings & Investment	1,200	
Personal Loan Payment	900	
TOTAL FIXED EXPENSES		$ 27,507
VARIABLE EXPENSES		
Food	$ 5,485	
Transportation	2,500	
Utilities	1,800	
Clothes & Personal	2,700	
Recreation & Vacation	2,780	
TOTAL VARIABLE EXPENSES		$ 15,265
TOTAL EXPENSES		$ 42,772
(Cash Balance at the end of the year)		$ 17,968

come taxes, and loan payments. These items are called **fixed expenses,** and are often contractual in nature.

After paying all variable and fixed expenses, we arrive at net cash income, which is our personal bottom line. Creditors will look at this figure to determine if we can afford to increase our fixed expenses in the form of a loan, or if we can afford to increase our variable expenses in the form of a credit card. You may therefore consider yourself in financial trouble if you already have a low or negative net cash income.

In looking at Table 3-2, we note that the Tom Jones family has net cash income of $17,968 at the end of 2000. This figure is sufficient for a bank to grant additional credit in the form of a credit card, or for the family to qualify for a fixed loan. For example, if Tom wanted to purchase a new car, with monthly payments of $450, many banks would grant him this loan. If he purchased the new car his annual loan obligation would be $5,400. Table 3-2 shows he has net cash income of $17,968 which is more than enough to cover the new car loan obligation of $5,400. It would not be unusual for the bank to grant additional credit to Tom Jones. Let's be honest; you or I would also grant this loan.

 INCOME STATEMENT

Let us now look at an income statement for a business and see how this equates to the cash flow statement for Tom Jones. The **income statement** is like a motion picture; it shows what has happened to the business during the accounting period with regard to the revenues (income) and expenditures (expenses) of the business. The normal accounting period is one year; however, companies will typically generate an income statement on a monthly basis to determine how the company is doing, and to compare a specific month to the same month in previous years and to past months during the current year.

For external reporting, corporations will typically generate quarterly income statements. They often will issue quarterly reports to stockholders and other creditors and investors. For forecasting and internal auditing, however, they will use monthly income statements. These are used to compare results with those from the same month in previous years. Additionally, if you apply for a business loan through an SBA resource, they will require a monthly pro forma income statement for the first year of a company's operation and quarterly for the next two years. A **pro forma** financial statement is developed to project the future condition of a business based upon a forecast. It projects future income and expenses as determined by a forecast of future operations.

The income statement for a business can be equated to the personal cash flow statement or personal income statement (Table 3-2). When we

Table 3-3 Income Statement for a Sole Proprietorship, Partnership, Limited
Liability Company, or Subchapter S-Corporation

The Tom Jones Company
Income Statement
January 1, 2000, through December 31, 2000

Gross Sales	$ 350,642		
Less: Returns and Allowances	2,366		
Net Sales		$ 348,276	
Cost of Goods Sold		124,276	
Gross Profit			$ 224,000
Operating Expenses:			
Salaries Expense	$ 95,000		
Rent Expense	24,000		
Property Taxes Expense	2,500		
Depreciation Expense	5,000		
Utilities Expense	10,250		
Advertising Expense	9,250		
Insurance Expense	3,000		
Total Operating Expenses		$ 149,000	
Operating Income			$ 75,000
Other Expenses:			
Interest Expense		10,000	
Net Income*			$ 65,000

*This line on an Income Statement for a Corporation appears as Net Income before Income
Taxes (see Table 3-3a)

compare this personal income statement with a company's income statement (Table 3-3), we see several similarities.

A business income statement can be divided into three sections. The
first section shows gross revenues (sales) minus returns and allowances which
equals net sales; net sales minus cost of goods sold equals gross profit. The
second section shows gross profit minus operating expenses which equals
operating income (net income before interest and taxes). The third section
shows operating income minus interest which equals earnings before taxes
minus taxes (if the business is a corporation) which equals net income
(profit).

Let us now define the preceding terms more carefully. **Revenues** are
all sales of products and services for the company. Next we consider **returns
and allowances.** Regardless of how perfect we wish to make our products,
there will always be some customers who are not satisfied, or some products
that were sold and are defective. In such cases we normally provide a refund
of purchase price or grant some allowance (increased warranty, partial credit
on next purchase, etc.) to the customer. Another type of allowance comes
into play when the company is a manufacturer and the customer is a retailer.

The retailer may be given allowances in the form of a trade discount or series of discounts for services that are performed by the retailer for the manufacturer. For example, if you manufacture bicycles, you could give your retailer a trade discount for assembling and displaying your product in a highly marketable fashion. Additionally, you might offer a trade discount for retail promotion or advertising. Some retailers who buy your bicycles for resale might take advantage of one or more of your discounts. Because you do not know in advance how much this amount will be, you keep track of it during the accounting period. **Net sales** are the revenue you have after you have accounted for any sales returns and allowances and any sales discounts.

Cost of goods sold (COGS) is the amount it costs us to obtain the items that we sell. COGS typically includes the costs of materials, direct labor, and overhead allocated specifically to the product. For the retail store, these are the total costs, to the store, of that store's merchandise (including freight and cost of merchandise). For the manufacturing firm, these are manufacturing labor costs, measurable machine costs, and the cost of raw materials, fabricated parts, and the allocation of factory overhead. COGS represents most of the **variable costs** of manufacturing firms. Variable costs are driven directly by the volume of product flow. The **gross profit** of a company is determined by subtracting COGS from net sales. An item is normally variable and is part of COGS if

1. the company allocates a percentage of the sales dollar to the item in question (e.g., factory overhead that is based on a percentage of direct labor or material cost);
2. the company can accurately measure the cost that is used by the item in question (raw material or component parts); or
3. the cost occurs prior to the item being ready for sale.

Operating expenses are normally the **fixed costs** of a business. Salaries for executives and administrative personnel, rental expenses, insurance, and advertising expenses are normally fixed and known in advance. When we say fixed costs, however, we do not necessarily mean that they do not vary; we mean that these are the expenses of a business that are not directly related to revenues or cost of goods sold. For example, the utility bills may vary considerably during the year, but they are still placed under the category of operating expenses. If you live in the northern section of the United States, you know that your heating bill will be much higher for January than it is for July, but this is still considered to be a fixed cost and is placed under operating expenses, because it is not directly related to COGS. If the item cannot be allocated or measured based on sales dollars, it is normally an operating expense.

Operating income appears on the income statement as the result of subtracting the sum of our operating expenses from gross profit. Operating

Table 3-3a Income Statement, Corporation

The Tom Jones Company
Income Statement
January 1, 2000, through December 31, 2000

Net Income before Income Taxes*	$ 65,000
Less: Provision for Income Taxes	15,000
Net Income	$ 50,000
Net earnings per share of common stock:	$ 0.50
(100,000 shares outstanding)	

*Note: This is the Net Income line on Table 3-3 for a sole proprietorship, partnership, Subchapter S-corporation, or limited liability company.

income can also be thought of as earnings from operations before interest and taxes are paid.

Interest expense is the interest accrued during the accounting period on money borrowed by our company. Once this interest expense is subtracted from operating income, we obtain earnings before taxes.

Earnings before taxes (net income before taxes) are the amount of income we have before we pay income taxes to the governments that collect such taxes on the profits of businesses. This amount is the bottom line for the sole proprietorship, partnership, limited liability company (LLC), or Subchapter S-corporation, because the profit of such a company is considered to be personal income and is reported on the individual's income tax statement. As discussed in Chapter 2, however, the corporation is subject to double taxation, and Table 3-3a shows the continuation of the income statement for a corporation.

Provision for income taxes (less income taxes) is based on the fact that corporate incomes are subject to a corporate income tax. This is the corporate tax that is owed to the federal, state, and possibly municipal governments, all of which may charge income taxes on corporate earnings.

Net income is the profit after provision for income taxes and interest expenses for the corporation, and the profit after interest expense for the sole proprietorship, partnership, LLC, or Subchapter S-corporation. (Tables 3-3 and 3-3a show this difference.) For the corporation, this figure is net profit, after paying all expenses including interest and taxes (shown in Table 3-3a as $50,000). For the sole proprietorship, partnership, LLC, or Subchapter S-corporation, this item appears on the income statement immediately after interest expense (shown in Table 3-3 as $65,000), because income taxes for these businesses are paid by the individual owners, rather than by the business.

In this textbook we use C-corporation and corporations as one in the same. Subchapter S-corporations will be referred to as Subchapter S-corps.

Remember that an income statement does not reflect cash flow. Sales for many businesses are recognized when the sale is made. Yet, sales may not all be paid for in cash; some may be on credit. Therefore, the income statement may show a sale as revenue, when in fact we may not collect the money for several months if the customer has charged this sale on a revolving credit line. In addition, expenses are recognized when we incur them, not when we pay them. This is the accrual method of accounting.

Say, for example, that your business pays its employees on the first and the fifteenth of each month. When you close out the books at the end of the month, you will show all wages and salaries that are owed to your employees from the sixteenth to the last day of the month, but the checks will not be written or paid for until the beginning of the next month. In addition, taxes may still be owed, and other expenses may have been incurred, but not yet actually paid for, by your firm.

Earnings per share are how much a corporation has made for each share of common stock outstanding. To obtain this figure, the corporation takes its net income and divides it by the total number of shares of common stock outstanding. For example, as shown in Table 3-3a, the Tom Jones Corporation had net income of $50 thousand and 100 thousand shares of common stock outstanding; its earnings per share were 50 cents. We obtain the number of shares outstanding from the balance sheet, which is discussed shortly.

Corporations are allowed to distribute their profit, in the form of dividends to stockholders, or to retain their earnings for future investment. Retained earnings provide the firm with an internal source of financing that can be used to purchase capital equipment and to acquire or merge with other companies. An advantage of using retained earnings for financing future operations is that the owners provide the capital so the company does not need external financing in the form of debt.

STATEMENT OF FINANCIAL POSITION

The **statement of financial position** (a personal balance sheet) indicates all items that are owned (assets) by the individual (or family) and all items that are owed (liabilities) by the individual (or family) at a specific point in time. Therefore, the statement of financial position is written with an "as of" date (the specific day for which it is valid); see Table 3-4 for the Tom Jones family statement of financial position. This statement is typically part of a bank loan application, and it is also computed by financial planners to assist the individual with planning a financial strategy.

Table 3-4 Statement of Financial Position (Balance Sheet)

The Tom Jones Family
Statement of Financial Position
As of December 31, 2000

Assets
Cash and Cash Equivalents

Cash and Checking Account	$ 1,900		
Savings Account	4,000		
Total Cash and Cash Equivalents		$ 5,900	
Invested Assets			
Stocks and Bonds	19,000		
Life Insurance Cash Value	5,500		
Total Invested Assets		$ 24,500	
Use Assets			
Residence	184,000		
Automobiles	27,000		
Furniture, Clothing, Jewelry, etc.	32,000		
Total Use Assets		$243,000	
Total Assets			$ 273,400

Liabilities and Net Worth
Liabilities

Homeowners Insurance	425		
Credit Card Balance	1,900		
Automobile Note Balance	11,200		
Home Mortgage Balance	138,000		
Total Liabilities			$ 151,525
Net Worth			121,875
Total Liabilities and Net Worth			$ 273,400

As we did for the income statement, we now discuss each item on the statement of financial position to ensure a thorough understanding of this financial statement as business managers or owners. An **asset** is any item that is used or owned by the individual, business, or corporation. Assets are normally listed on these statements in order of **liquidity** (a measure of how fast an asset can be converted into cash). In other words, cash is the most liquid of assets, then savings accounts, certificates of deposit (due to the penalty for turning them into cash before the due date), and then stocks and bonds. The preceding items are **current assets,** because they can normally be converted into cash during the accounting year. Land, buildings, furniture, and clothing are **fixed assets,** because they normally are not used up during the accounting year. They are the least liquid of assets. It may be difficult to dispose of these items and obtain cash.

Looking at Table 3-4, we note that the current assets for Tom Jones and his family consist of cash and cash equivalents in the amount of $5,900 and invested assets of $24,500. The fixed assets, also called *use assets,* on the statement of financial position amount to $243,000. The total assets of the Tom Jones family are worth $273,400, but this does not necessarily reflect the wealth of the family, because many use assets are not normally owned free and clear, and therefore the family may owe something on these items. To determine the family's real worth, we must determine how much is owed (what the family's total liabilities are).

Liabilities are that part of assets that is owed to others. These items are primarily financed by debt. Tom Jones owes $425 on his homeowners insurance, has a credit card balance of $1,900, and owes $11,200 on his automobile, which was listed as a $27,000 asset. He also has a mortgage on his home of $138,000, even though the home is worth $184,000. Therefore, the total liabilities for the Tom Jones family are $151,525. When we subtract total liabilities from total assets, we arrive at the net worth of the family, which is $121,875.

Note that the statement of financial position formula is always

$$\text{Assets} = \text{Liabilities} + \text{Net worth}$$

It can also be written as

$$\text{Assets} - \text{Liabilities} = \text{Net worth}$$

Note that the net worth figure represents how much cash the family could obtain if it disposed of all its assets at the value listed on the statement of financial position. This statement of financial position is equivalent to the balance sheet of a business, as we will now explain.

BALANCE SHEET

The **balance sheet** (or, in accounting texts, the statement of financial position) for the business (Table 3-5) lists all assets and liabilities. It is like a snapshot taken at an instant in time. There are some minor differences in definitions between the individual statement of financial position and the business balance sheet. We will discuss them as we go through Table 3-5.

The balance sheet formula is often referred to as the basic accounting equation and is similar to the equation for the statement of financial position:

$$\text{Total assets} = \text{Total liabilities} + \text{Owner's equity}$$

Assets in the business are like assets for the individual; they are everything that the business has a right to use or own. Current assets normally

Table 3-5 Balance Sheet (Statement of Financial Position), Sole Proprietorship

The Tom Jones Company
Balance Sheet
As of December 31, 2000

Assets			
Current Assets			
Checking Account		$ 2,000	
Certificates of Deposit		50,000	
Accounts Receivable		40,000	
Inventory		35,000	
Total Current Assets			$ 127,000
Fixes Assets			
Land		$ 50,000	
Buildings	$ 250,000		
Less: Accumulated Depreciation	50,000	200,000	
Equipment	$ 50,000		
Less: Accumulated Depreciation	5,000	45,000	
Total Fixed Assets			$ 295,000
Total Assets			$ 422,000
Liabilities and Owner's Equity			
Current Liabilities			
Accounts Payable—Trade		$ 10,000	
Notes Payable—Bank		5,000	
Taxes Payable		3,000	
Total Current Liabilities			$ 18,000
Long-Term Liabilities			
Building Mortgage Payable		$ 180,000	
Equipment Loan Payable		30,000	
Total Long-Term Liabilities			$ 210,000
Total Liabilities			$ 228,000
Owner's Equity			194,000
Total Liabilities and Owner's Equity			$ 422,000

can be converted into cash during the accounting year, and they are not covered by federal depreciation schedules. Like the individual's current assets, those of the business will include cash, savings, and marketable securities. In addition, the business has accounts receivable and inventory listed as current assets. **Accounts receivable** are the credit sales for which money has not been collected. **Inventory** items are those the business has in stock but has not yet sold.

Fixed assets have an expected life in excess of one year and are usually depreciated in accordance with tax laws. All fixed assets for a business are carried on the books at purchase price, less depreciation. These are valued differently than the fixed assets of an individual, because when we generate a statement of financial position (personal balance sheet) we normally use current market value for our fixed assets, but the business balance sheet is prohibited from doing this by generally accepted accounting principles (GAAP).

Depreciation is the wearing out of a business asset during its useful life. The government recognizes that some assets will last for more than one year, and that these items normally wear out as they are used. Therefore, the government establishes depreciation schedules, and for tax purposes, businesses are obligated to depreciate assets according to methods or schedules provided by the government.

The depreciation schedule for an asset is determined primarily by tax law, and the business normally has no choice in determining the life of an asset. The business may have a choice in determining the actual method of depreciation to use for an asset, however. To determine this specific schedule, an owner must contact an accountant, because the laws change on a regular basis. For example, if we constructed a building in 1986 and opened the building in 1986, the building had to be depreciated according to an accelerated cost recovery system (ACRS) schedule over a period of 18 years. If, however, the building was not completed until 1987, then the business had to use a straight-line depreciation schedule, modified accelerated cost recovery system (MACRS), for 31.5 years. The business has no choice in this matter. If the building was opened for use on December 31, 1986, it is depreciated on one schedule, and if it opened on January 1, 1987, it is depreciated on another schedule.

Many businesses, however, will maintain two depreciation schedules, one for tax reporting purposes and one that is realistic for the business in question. Further examples will be provided in Chapter 9 when we discuss capital budgeting.

Several categories of fixed assets will be listed on the balance sheet. **Land** is a fixed asset that does not wear out with normal use, so it is always carried on the books at the price that the company paid for it. Although land may appreciate or depreciate in value, we do not know in advance what will happen, and so no adjustments are made on the balance sheet until the land is actually sold.

Buildings are carried on the books at the price paid, and accumulated depreciation is shown as a deduction on the balance sheet. In other words, every year, the total depreciation shown on the income statement (Table 3-3) is transferred to the balance sheet at the end of the year. For example, the Tom Jones Company has buildings worth $250,000 listed on the balance sheet (Table 3-5), with accumulated depreciation of $50,000. The 1999 balance sheet would have shown the same value for the building ($250,000), but the accumulated depreciation would have been listed as $45,000.

The $5,000 listed on the income statement (Table 3-3) at the end of 2000 would have been transferred to the balance sheet as an addition to the previous year's accumulated depreciation (e.g., $45,000 + $5,000 = $50,000 accumulated depreciation). So depreciated fixed assets are carried on the books at the price paid, but every year accumulated depreciation increases and thus lowers the value of the asset on the balance sheet.

Equipment includes all items such as machinery, fixtures, and automobiles. These assets may have to be broken down by specific type, because of depreciation schedules in use at the time of purchase. When any fixed asset is sold or disposed of, both its cost and accumulated depreciation are removed from the balance sheet.

Total assets are the sum of current and fixed assets. For the Tom Jones Company, total assets are $422,000 ($295,000 in fixed assets and $127,000 in current assets). **Liabilities** for the firm are what is owed by the firm to others (creditors). Liabilities, like assets, are divided into two categories, current and long term. **Current liabilities** are those obligations that the firm expects to pay off during the current accounting year. Those items that are included in current liabilities are accounts payable, notes payable, and taxes payable. **Accounts payable** are the debts that are owed to vendors. Any present goods or services that were delivered to the firm but that were not paid for as of the date of the balance sheet are listed as accounts payable. **Notes payable** are promises to pay a creditor or lender the amount owed plus interest for a specified period of time, normally one year or less. They can be owed to a bank, an individual, or a group of persons. **Taxes payable** are the accrued taxes that are owed but not actually paid as of the date of the balance sheet. Examples include city and state sales taxes which were collected during December, but that are not actually paid to the state until January of the following year. This also would include taxes taken out of employee pay, but not yet actually paid to the government, such as income taxes and taxes for the Federal Insurance Contribution Act (FICA) which includes social security and medicare. Most of us combine FICA and medicare and call it social security, but for the business owner these are calculated separately (6.20 percent social security + 1.45 percent medicare = 7.65 percent).

Total current liabilities are nothing more than the sum of all current liabilities for a company, as depicted on the balance sheet. For the Tom Jones Company, total current liabilities as of midnight, December 31, 2000, were $18,000.

Long-term debt is the amount the company owes but does not expect to pay during the current accounting year. Examples include mortgages on buildings, loans on equipment, and possibly bonds. (Bonds were discussed briefly in Chapter 2 under corporate financing, and will be discussed more fully in Chapter 10 on personal finance). Note that the portion of long-term debt that we expect to pay during the current accounting period would be shown under current liabilities. For example, if our company had $1,000,000 in bonds and was expecting to retire $100,000 this year, then we would show current maturities of long-term debt under current liabilities of $100,000 and bonds under long-term debt of $900,000.

Total liabilities are the sum of current liabilities and long-term debt. The Tom Jones Company has total liabilities of $228,000.

Owner's equity is the net worth of a company. It is the same as the net worth of the individual Tom Jones as shown on the statement of financial position (personal balance sheet). Using our balance sheet formula, the owner's equity must be $194,000, because the total assets must always equal the sum of total liabilities plus owner's equity. In other words, the balance sheet must always balance. We will show cases of negative owner's equity in Chapter 5, when we discuss bankruptcy.

How the owner's equity is shown on the balance sheet is determined by the form of business ownership. We show three different owner's equity tables to illustrate the differences in the bottom portion of the balance sheet. For all business, regardless of type of ownership, assets and liabilities would be treated the same; however, the owner's equity portion of the balance sheet is depicted differently for each type of ownership.

SOLE PROPRIETORSHIP

For the sole proprietor, the owner's equity is simply the business assets minus the business liabilities. This remainder is the amount that the owner could obtain for the business if it were sold at its current book value, as shown in Table 3-5. **Book value** is the value of an asset on the company's books after depreciation has been determined. It is probably an unrealistic figure in regard to the actual value of the business, because it is based on historical value rather than fair market value. Land and buildings normally appreciate in value over time, whereas equipment and machinery depreciate in value.

PARTNERSHIP

For the partnership, the owner's equity is shown according to the partnership agreement, as shown in Table 3-6. The actual money invested in the firm has nothing to do with this figure, because it represents what the business could be sold for (at book value) and how much would remain after paying off all liabilities.

The method of dividing owner's equity and profits is always determined by the partnership agreement. For example, say that Tom Jones had a great idea for a business, but had little money. He contacted two friends, Larry Smith and Kathy Moore, and convinced them to invest in his business. Tom had to raise

Table 3-6 Balance Sheet, Partnership

Tom Jones and Partners

Partners' Equity		
Tom Jones	$ 19,400	
Larry Smith	87,300	
Kathy Moore	87,300	
Total Partner's Equity		$ 194,000
Total Liabilities and Partners' Equity		$ 422,000

$100,000 to start the business and obtain the bank loans to finance the purchase of the land, the building, and equipment. He had $10,000, and Larry and Kathy each agreed to put up $45,000. Now he had the $100,000. The partnership agreement that was drawn up stated that each partner would receive profits in accordance with his or her original investment, and that Tom would be the working partner and would receive a salary of $20,000 per year. Tom's salary is listed as part of the $95,000 salaries expense on the income statement (Table 3-3). The $65,000 net income, or profit, that was made in year 2000 would be split, with 10 percent going to Tom, 45 percent to Larry, and 45 percent to Kathy. So Tom would receive $6,500 (10 percent of the $65,000 net income) from the profit plus his $20,000 salary, or a total of $26,500. Larry would get $29,250 (45 percent of the $65,000 net income) and Kathy would get $29,250. Because this business is a partnership, these incomes would be reported on each partner's income tax forms, with each partner paying taxes based on his or her individual income.

The partner's equity portion of the business would be the same as the corporation's equity; thus, $194,000 (Table 3-6) would be divided in accordance with the partnership agreement (10 percent for Tom and 45 percent each for Larry and Kathy). As Table 3-6 indicates, Tom has $19,400 in equity ($194,000 × 10 percent), and Larry and Kathy each have $87,300 ($194,000 × 45 percent). The total equity for the partners is $194,000 ($19,400 + $87,300 + $87,300).

PUBLIC CORPORATIONS

Table 3-7 shows the owner's equity portion of the balance sheet for a corporation. As explained in Chapter 2, corporations can raise funds by selling bonds (long-term debt) or by selling stock. The Tom Jones Corporation sold 10,000 shares of preferred stock (Table 3-7) at $5 per share which equals $50,000. It also sold 100,000 shares of common stock at 60 cents a share. Of the 60 cents per share (Table 3-7), 10 cents is the par value and 50 cents is the paid-in capital in excess of par. This is the 100,000 shares that was used to determine earnings per share of common stock on the income statement (Table 3-3a). The

Table 3-7 Balance Sheet (Statement of Financial Position), Corporation

The Tom Jones Corporation
Balance Sheet
As of December 31, 2000

Assets			
Current Assets			
Checking Account		$ 2,000	
Certificates of Deposit		50,000	
Accounts Receivable		40,000	
Inventory		35,000	
Total Current Assets			$ 127,000
Fixed Assets			
Land		$ 50,000	
Buildings	$ 250,000		
Less: Accumulated Depreciation	50,000	200,000	
Equipment	$ 50,000		
Less: Accumulated Depreciation	5,000	45,000	
Total Fixed Assets			$ 295,000
Total Assets			$ 422,000
Liabilities and Stockholder's Equity			
Current Liabilities			
Accounts Payable—Trade		$ 10,000	
Notes Payable—Bank		5,000	
Taxes Payable		3,000	
Total Current Liabilities			$ 18,000
Long-Term Liabilities			
Building Mortgage		$ 180,000	
Equipment Loan		30,000	
Total Long-Term Liabilities			$ 210,000
Total Liabilities			$ 228,000
Stockholders' Equity			
Preferred Stock, $5 par (10,000 Shares)		$ 50,000	
Common Stock, $0.10 par (100,000 Shares)		10,000	
Paid-in Capital in Excess of Par—Common		50,000	
Total Paid-in Capital		$ 110,000	
Retained Earnings		84,000	
Total Stockholders' Equity			$ 194,000
Total Liabilities and Stockholder's Equity			$ 422,000

figure for paid-in capital in excess of par is what the Tom Jones Corporation actually obtained, above par value, for its stock offer. In other words, the corporation sold 100,000 shares of common stock and raised capital of $60,000. Because the par value is 10 cents, the 100,000 shares show up on the balance sheet as common stock at par $10,000; and the capital in excess of par ($50,000) indicates that the corporation raised $60,000 with its common stock offer. Accumulated retained earnings is money that is not distributed to stockholders, but is retained by the corporation for future investment.

OWNER'S EQUITY

How owner's equity is depicted on the balance sheet depends on the form of company ownership. In all cases, however, the balance sheet formula must be maintained. For a sole proprietorship,

$$\text{Assets} = \text{Liabilities} + \text{Owner's equity}$$

For a partnership,

$$\text{Assets} = \text{Liabilities} + \text{Partner's equity}$$

For a corporation,

$$\text{Assets} = \text{Liabilities} + \text{Stockholder's equity}$$

STATEMENT OF CASH FLOWS

The income statement and balance sheet do not actually show cash flow during the accounting period if the business is using an accrual system of accounting, because revenue is recognized when *earned* and not paid, whereas expenses are recognized when *incurred* and not paid. To determine what has happened to our working capital account (the amount of cash available) between the beginning and the end of the current year, we must show how the company's cash has flowed into and out of the business during the year. Table 3-8 shows the statement of cash flows for the Tom Jones Corporation.

The first section of the cash flow statement identifies all operating sources and uses of cash and is referred to as **cash flows from operating activities.** On the receipt side of this section, we see that the corporation collected $308,276 from sales. We note that, on the income statement (Table 3-3), sales were listed as $350,642, but the Tom Jones Company had returns and allowances of $2,366, which left the company with net sales of $348,276. In addition, the balance sheet (Table 3-5) shows accounts receivable of $40,000. Because the returns and allowances and the amount still owed to the company did not result in cash, the Tom Jones Company had cash flows of only $308,276 on sales of $350,642.

On the payment side of this section are all payments actually made in conducting operating activities. Again, we must look at both the income statement and the balance sheet. Note that the company had a cost of goods

Table 3-8 Statement of Cash Flows

The Tom Jones Corporation
Statement of Cash Flows
For the Year Ended December 31, 2000
Increase (Decrease) in Cash and Cash Equivalents
(Amounts in thousands)

Cash Flows from Operating Activities Receipts:		
Collections from Customers		$ 308,276
Interest Received on Certificates of Deposit	$ 4,000	
Total Cash Receipts		$ 312,276
Payments:		
To Suppliers	(114,276)	
To Employees	(95,000)	
For Rent	(24,000)	
For Utilities	(10,000)	
For Advertising	(10,000)	
For Insurance	(3,000)	
For Property Tax	(2,000)	
For Income Tax	(12,000)	
Total Cash Payments		$ (270,276)
Net Cash Flow from Operating Activities		$ 42,000
Cash Flows from Investing Activities:		
Acquisition of Plant Assets	(50,000)	
Net Cash Outflow from Investing Activities		(50,000)
Cash Flows from Financing Activities:		
Proceeds from Issuance of Preferred Stock	50,000	
Proceeds from Issuance of Common Stock	60,000	
Payment of Long-Term Debt	(24,000)	
Net Cash Inflow from Financing Activities		$ 86,000
Net Increase in Cash		$ 78,000
Cash Balance, December 31, 1999		30,000
Cash Balance, December 31, 2000		$ 108,000

sold of $124,276 (income statement), but still owed $10,000 to suppliers on the last day of the accounting year (balance sheet). Therefore actual cash payments to suppliers were $124,276 minus $10,000 which equals $114,276.

The method that we use in calculating cash flows is as follows: We use the income statement to determine the total accumulated expense for an item, and we then subtract from this expense any item remaining on the balance sheet as a current liability. In other words, we can take the figures off of the income statement's operating expense column, provided that there is not a balance remaining in the current liabilities section of the balance sheet. For example, if we had $3,000 listed under current liabilities on the balance sheet as salaries payable, then the statement of cash flows would show payments to employees as $92,000 rather than the $95,000 that is currently on the income statement. The cash flows from the operating activities section of the statement of cash flows include all activities conducted in the normal operation of the business during the accounting period.

The remaining sections of the statement of cash flows show how the firm managed its cash with relationship to long-term debt and owner's equity. The **cash flows from investing activities** section reflects any long-term investments made by the firm. It includes cash paid in the acquisition of land, buildings, or equipment; loans to other companies; and the proceeds from the sale of any land, buildings, or equipment. For our purposes, we assume that the company paid $50,000 for a plant addition. The actual value of the plant addition could have been considerably more than this; but it is only the actual cash paid by the firm that is reflected here. The total value of the purchase would be reflected on the balance sheet under fixed assets, and the portion financed would be shown on the balance sheet as long-term debt. For example, in 1999 the Tom Jones Company had land valued at $50,000 and buildings valued at $100,000 on its balance sheet with an $104,000 mortgage. In 2000, the company built a $150,000 addition, paying $50,000 down (shown on Table 3-8 as acquisition of plant assets) and financing the remainder with a $100,000 mortgage giving the company a total mortgage of $204,000. During the year 2000, the company issued all of its stock and paid $24,000 to the bank to reduce its mortgage to $180,000. This $180,000 mortgage is now reflected on the year 2000 balance sheet (Table 3-5). Then the 1999 balance sheet would show buildings of $100,000, and the 2000 balance sheet would show buildings of $250,000. This latter figure would include the total cost to the company of both buildings, the $100,000 for the original building plus the $150,000 for the addition.

The section **cash flows from financing activities** includes actual cash received from the sale of stocks or bonds, and the actual cash paid to others in the form of dividends to owners and the repayment of long-term debt. For our purposes, we are assuming that the Tom Jones Corporation actually issued all of its stock in the year 2000, receiving proceeds of $50,000 from preferred stock and $60,000 from common stock. It used these proceeds to reduce its mortgage by $24,000.

As shown, the income statement and balance sheet do not accurately reflect the actual cash flow during the accounting year. If owners and other interested parties are to determine the company's effectiveness, we must also have a statement of cash flows.

PROBLEMS WITH FINANCIAL STATEMENTS

We must remember that financial statements are written by people, and that they are governed by tax and other laws. Therefore, when evaluating financial statements, we must be cautious. It is important to note that in some cases fixed assets are carried on the balance sheet in an amount that does not necessarily reflect their true value, because even though depreciation is shown, the item is always placed there at the value paid (book value).

For example, in 1996 an office building was purchased for $33 million (book value to the buyer) in Phoenix, Arizona, and then sold for $44 million (market value) in 1999. How? In 1996 the rental value of commercial real estate was much lower than it was in 1999, therefore the building increased in value by 33 percent in only three years. Another example of the difference between book and market value is the Scottsdale Galleria which was valued at $125 million (initial book value) and sold at auction for $6 million (market value) in 1993 and has remained vacant for the last seven years.[1] What are these assets really worth?

Book value may not show the actual value of a business; and different people use different methods of accounting. Some businesses use the accrual method, in which sales are recognized as completed when the transaction is made, even though the customer may still owe a considerable amount which is carried on the seller's books as accounts receivable. Can the accounts receivable actually be collected at their face value in the future? Yes if the customer is a good credit risk. Sometimes accounts receivable may have to be sold to a factor for a fraction of their worth. At times, balance sheets also show large inventories that are obsolete; in this case the inventories would have to be sold at a considerable loss. For example, consider a computer supply house that purchased several hundred 386 computers just before Pentiums became popular. The company may show $50,000 worth of computers on its books, but these items could not be given away, because they no longer serve a practical purpose and have no demand.

 ## CONCLUSION

In this chapter, we introduced personal and business financial statements and discussed their similarities and differences. We compared financial statements for different forms of business ownership. Additionally, we showed the relationship between income statement, balance sheet, and cash flow statement. We also pointed out some of the problems that may exist with financial statements. We discussed the relationship between fixed assets and depreciation and its impact on both book value and fair market value.

When reading any financial statement, be cautious, find out some background on the company, and determine for yourself how accurate the statement is.

---

[1] *The Arizona Republic,* Section D, "Business & Money," Page 1, March 9, 2000.

REVIEW AND DISCUSSION QUESTIONS

1. How are financial statements used by business?
2. Compare variable and fixed expenses.
3. Describe the basic format of an income statement, listing all its sections.
4. What is the primary difference between the income statement of a sole proprietorship or partnership and the income statement of a corporation?
5. What is a personal statement of financial position?
6. What is the difference between the time periods listed on an income statement and on a balance sheet?
7. What is the importance of liquidity?
8. List the categories that are on the balance sheet for a business.
9. What is the accounting equation for the balance sheet?
10. What is the difference between a current asset and a fixed asset?
11. Compare owner's equity in a sole proprietorship, partners' equity in a partnership, and stockholders' equity in a corporation.
12. What is the purpose of the statement of cash flows?
13. List the components of the statement of cash flows.
14. Why are fixed assets carried on the balance sheet at a price that may not reflect the true value of the assets?

EXERCISES AND PROBLEMS

1. Given the personal cash flow statement in Table 3-2, use your own data to determine your disposable income at the end of the current year. Please include income from all sources, fixed expenses, and variable expenses.
2. Given the statement of financial position in Table 3-4, use your own data to determine your net worth. Make sure that student loans are included in liabilities, if applicable.
3. The Happy Auto Shop has the following annual information: gross sales, $700,000; net sales, $696,000; and gross profit, $448,000. What are Happy's returns and allowances and cost of goods sold?
4. Construct a personal income statement for the Davey Jones family, using the following information: salaries $42,000; mortgage payment $7,980; food, $2,400; interest income, $150; transportation $1,200; dividend income, $190; automobile payment, $3,060; clothes and personal, $2,000; student loan payment, $1,700; property taxes, $1,100; Utilities, $3,000; Insurance, $2,100; income taxes, $9,700; recreation and vacation, $2,000. What is the families disposable income?
5. Construct a statement of financial position (balance sheet) for the Davey Jones family, using the following information: cash $50; checking account $2,500; student loan balance, $6,000; Stocks and Bonds, $2,600; savings account $5,850; Residence $110,000; automobile, $12,000; savings account,

$5,800; automobile loan balance, $12,000; 401K retirement account, $15,000; furniture, clothing, jewelry, $8,000; credit card balance, $4,000; mortgage loan balance, $99,000.

6. Construct an income statement using the following information: net sales, $500,000; salaries, $100,000; rent, $24,000; COGS, $250,000; utilities, $25,000; payroll taxes, $25,000; insurance, $12,000; and interest expense, $5,450. Make sure that you include gross profit, operating expenses, and net profit.

7. George's Pizzeria has the following information as of December 31, 2000: cash, $2,000; pizza ovens, $25,000; furniture, $12,500; accounts payable, $3,500; notes payable, $12,500; accumulated depreciation, $10,000; wages payable, $1,500; taxes payable, $2,500; and equipment loan, $18,000. Construct a balance sheet for George. Do you think he has a problem with his current balance sheet? If so, what is it?

8. State the stockholder's equity of the Alphabet Corporation if it has a current net profit of $1,500,000; beginning of the period retained earnings of $3,675,000; 1 million shares of common stock issued at a par value of $1 per share; and paid-in capital in excess of par $12.50 per share.

9. State your current cash balance if you have the following information: total cash receipts of $624,000; a cash balance at the end of last year of $60,000; total cash payments of $540,000; cash outflow from investing activities of $100,000; and cash inflows from financial activities of $172,000.

ANALYSIS OF FINANCIAL STATEMENTS

4

Learning Objectives

When you have completed this chapter, you should be able to:

- Understand the purpose of financial statement analysis.
- Perform a vertical analysis of a company's financial statements by:
  Comparing those accounts on the income statement as a percentage of net sales and comparing those accounts on the balance sheet as a percentage of total assets for a period of two or more accounting cycles.
  Determining those areas within the company that require additional monitoring and control.
- Perform a horizontal analysis of a company's financial statements by:
  Comparing the percentage change of components on a company's income state-

ment and balance sheet for a period of two or more years.
  Determining those areas within the company that require additional monitoring and control.

- Perform ratio analysis of a company and compare those ratios with other companies within the same industry using industry averages.
- Analyze the relationships that exist between the several categories of ratios in determining the health of a business.
- Distinguish between liquidity, activity, leverage, profitability, and market ratios.
- Know how to obtain financial statements and financial information from various sources.

Understanding financial statements provides little knowledge unless you can use the financial statements to determine potential profitability—either for your own firm or for a potential investment. As an entrepreneur, you will find that there is often no difference, in the eyes of a potential lender, between the financial statements of your firm and your own financial statements. As explained in the previous chapter, the personal statement of financial position is in most cases an offshoot of the business's balance sheet. For example, most of the sole proprietor's assets are invested in the business. If the proprietor wishes to obtain a loan, then it is imperative that his or her financial statements provide the lender with a picture of profitability, or potential profitability, that is at least as good as that of other firms in the same type of industry.

For example, if Linda Brown wants to open and operate a soft-serve yogurt shop, she will be required to furnish her lender with a statement of financial position, which in essence can be equated to a company's balance sheet. Linda must demonstrate sufficient net worth to secure a loan from her creditors. Often a lending institution will use measurable criteria, established for businesses of a similar nature, to determine if Linda will qualify for the loan. Lenders are primarily concerned with the financial health of potential borrowers. Financial statement analysis is predominately used by lenders to determine how healthy an existing or potential business is.

So, potential creditors use this analysis to determine if they will lend money to our firm (through loans, mortgages, bonds, the issuance of credit cards, or the extension of lines of credit). Financial statement analysis is also used externally by potential investors to determine if they will invest in our firm (through the purchase of stock or entry into partnerships).

The purpose of financial statement analysis also is to generate information that can be used internally by the business itself. Internally, as managers of a company, we use financial statement analysis to monitor and control specific items on the financial statements, and to compare our business with those of our competitors in the same industry. If operating expenses are increasing and revenue is decreasing, for example, monitoring the data will allow us to take corrective action. We know that we have to develop a course of action that will either decrease our expenses, increase our revenue, or produce a combination effect of both cutting expenses and increasing revenue. If action is not taken, the net profit of the company will decline. For Linda, if the cost of goods sold for soft-serve yogurt in 1999 was 30 percent of sales, and in 2000 the cost of goods is 35 percent of sales, then she will probably find that she is losing money, or that at least her shop is not as profitable in 2000 as it was in 1999 unless she can determine some method of cutting operating expenses.

Several methods are available for us to use in comparing our business with those of our competitors. If other firms are publicly owned, we can obtain their financial reports by contacting the firm and asking for an annual report. We also can go to the library and look at their annual reports or SEC form 10K. We also may make use of published financial data in sources such as *The Value Line Investment Survey,* or obtain the same or additional information from sources on the internet. One such resource is the SEC's Electronic Data Gathering and Retrieval System (EDGAR), mentioned in Chapter 2. The internet address for this source is http://www.freeedgar. com/. Additional information is available in industry reports and data published by trade journals on specific industries.

There are essentially three methods of analyzing financial statements: vertical analysis, horizontal analysis, and ratio analysis. All **calculations** in this chapter shall be **rounded to two decimal places,** because most items are reported as either a fraction or a percentage of dollar items. The authors believe that decimal places beyond two when using dollars do not significantly add to the results.

VERTICAL ANALYSIS

Vertical analysis is the process of using a single variable on a financial statement as a constant and of determining how all other variables relate as a percentage of the single variable. The vertical analysis of the income statement is used to determine, specifically, how much of a company's net sales is being consumed by each individual entry on the income statement. For example, if our sales were $100,000 and the cost of goods sold was $70,000, then 70 percent of net sales was consumed by the cost of goods sold. On the income statement, when conducting a vertical analysis, we always use net sales as 100 percent; therefore, each item on the income statement is divided by net sales to determine what percentage of net sales is being consumed by the item. The following formula is used in vertical analysis of an income statement:

$$\text{Percentage of net sales} = \frac{\text{Income statement item in \$}}{\text{Net sales in \$}} \times 100$$

Table 4-1 contains a vertical analysis of a hypothetical firm, Markadel Retail Store. Note that cost of goods sold for 1999 was 34.27 percent of net sales. If the industry average for this type of firm was 28 percent, then we could conclude that costs were excessive and this might be a reason for lower profits.

Additionally, vertical analysis can help in pricing products, because a pattern of relationships exists between net sales, overhead, and profitability. Businesses generally, by way of a vertical analysis over time, can determine the relationships between percentage of overhead, profitability, and net sales. For example, the Markadel Retail Store has computed total operating expenses of 46.48 percent of net sales (25.38 + 11.92 + 9.18) and operating income of 19.25 percent of net sales; therefore Markadel, having used

Table 4-1 Sample Income Statement Data

Markadel Retail Store
Income Statement Data
From January 1 through December 31, 1999 and 2000

Account	Year 1999	Year 2000	Vertical Analysis 1999 (%)	Horizontal Analysis 1999– 2000 (%)
Gross sales	$300,580	$315,487	101.73	4.96
Less returns	5,124	9,253	1.73	80.58
Net sales	295,456	306,234	100.00	3.65
Cost of goods sold	101,250	120,002	34.27	18.52
Gross profit	194,206	186,232	65.73	(4.11)
Operating expenses				
Administration	74,983	76,450	25.38	1.96
Advertising	35,214	37,250	11.92	5.78
Overhead	27,120	28,300	9.18	4.35
Operating income	56,889	44,232	19.25	(22.25)
Interest	7,000	6,250	2.37	(10.71)
Earnings before taxes	49,889	37,982	16.89	(23.87)
Taxes	7,483	5,697	2.53	(23.87)
Net profit	$ 42,406	$ 32,285	14.35	(23.87)

vertical analysis, can determine its average markup requirements as a percentage of sales.

Vertical analysis of the balance sheet is always carried out by using total assets as a constant, or 100 percent, and dividing every figure on the balance sheet by total assets. This tells us how much of our total assets is claimed by owners and how much is obligated to creditors. The following formula is used in vertical analysis of a balance sheet:

$$\text{Percentage of total assets} = \frac{\text{Balance sheet item}}{\text{Total assets}} \times 100$$

Looking at Table 4-2, we see that Markadel has current assets of $65,830, which is 30.77 percent of total assets. On initial analysis, this would appear to be an extremely liquid firm; however, a further look indicates that only 7.24 percent of current assets are liquid enough (cash is 4.77 percent and notes receivable are 2.47 percent) to meet a creditor's claim. Accounts receivable (7.16 percent) and inventory (16.37 percent) amount to 23.53 percent of total assets. Thus, vertical analysis would indicate that the firm may have to take drastic steps to either expedite accounts receivable or decrease inventory (possibly with a sale) in order to meet its obligations. Looking at current liabilities, we note that they are only 27.70 percent of total assets, but because cash and notes receivable are only 7.24 percent of total assets, this firm has a serious problem in its ability to meet short-term debt.

Table 4-2 Sample Balance Sheet Data

Markadel Retail Store
Balance Sheet Data
As of December 31, 1999 and 2000

Category	Year 1999	Year 2000	Vertical Analysis 1999 (%)	Horizontal Analysis 1999–2000 (%)
Current assets				
Cash	$ 10,210	$ 8,175	4.77	(19.93)
Notes receivable	5,280	8,102	2.47	53.45
Accounts receivable	15,320	18,025	7.16	17.66
Inventory	35,020	50,515	16.37	44.25
Total current assets	65,830	84,817	30.77	28.84
Fixed assets				
Land	25,000	25,000	11.69	0.00
Buildings	135,000	135,000	63.10	0.00
Accumulated depreciation	(47,000)	(50,000)	21.97	6.38
Equipment	58,250	58,250	27.23	0.00
Accumulated depreciation	(23,150)	(28,150)	10.82	21.60
Total fixed assets	148,100	140,100	69.23	(5.40)
Total assets	$213,930	$224,917	100.00	5.14
Current liabilities				
Accounts payable	$ 34,250	$ 40,003	16.01	16.80
Notes payable	25,000	33,035	11.69	32.14
Total current liabilities	59,250	73,038	27.70	23.27
Long-term debt				
Mortgage payable	65,000	63,000	30.38	(3.08)
Bank loan payable	10,000	15,000	4.67	50.00
Total long-term debt	75,000	78,000	35.06	4.00
Total liabilities	$134,250	$151,038	62.75	12.51
Owner's equity	79,680	73,879	37.25	(7.28)
Total liabilities and owner's equity	$213,930	$224,917	100.00	5.14

HORIZONTAL ANALYSIS

Horizontal analysis is a determination of the percentage increase or decrease in an account from a base time period to successive time periods. The basic formula for horizontal analysis of any statement is

$$\text{Percentage change} = \frac{\text{New time period amount} - \text{Old time period amount}}{\text{Old time period amount}} \times 100$$

The formula will show us whether the change is positive or negative.

If we use the income statement data (Table 4–1) and choose net profit for our horizontal analysis, we get the following:

$$\text{Percentage change} = \frac{\$32,285 - \$42,406}{\$42,406} \times 100 = -23.87\%$$

Note that net profit declined by 23.87 percent between 1999 and 2000, even though gross sales increased by 4.96 percent. This would indicate that we must attempt to determine which areas of the business contributed to the declining profit. We note that returns increased by 80.58 percent and COGS increased by 18.52 percent, thereby contributing to a decline in gross profit of 4.11 percent. This would indicate that the firm requires either a change in pricing policy, so that sales prices reflect increases in COGS, or a thorough evaluation of COGS to determine if the firm can do something to reduce costs. The firm must also look at returns to determine if quality of merchandise is deteriorating.

Note: There is no relationship between percentages and actual dollar figures with horizontal analysis. The horizontal analysis percentage merely shows how rapidly a given line item on the income statement or balance sheet has changed during the period of analysis.

For example, the increase in returns and allowances of 80.58 percent represents only $4,129, whereas the increase in gross sales of 4.96 percent represents $14,907. Horizontal analysis is most useful for determining those areas that must be closely monitored.

A horizontal analysis of the balance sheet data (Table 4-2) indicates that the cash position is deteriorating, whereas accounts receivable and inventory are increasing by 17.66 and 44.25 percent, respectively. We would expect to find that total liabilities are increasing, because of the firm's inability to generate cash, and that the equity position is deteriorating. This is in fact true; total liabilities increased by 12.51 percent and owner's equity declined by 7.28 percent. The balance sheet itself does not provide us directly with owner's equity. To obtain this, we must always apply the accounting equation:

$$\text{Assets} = \text{Liabilities} + \text{Owners equity}$$

In 1999, owner's equity was $79,680, and in 2000 it was $73,879. Using the percentage change formula, we find that owner's equity declined by 7.28 percent, or, after rounding, 7 percent. If the firm attempted to attract new investors or obtain additional borrowing, it might find it difficult with the deteriorating profit and equity position noted on both the income statement and the balance sheet. As managers, we would use the analysis internally to determine a course of action for our firm. As creditors or investors, we would use the analysis to determine if we want to either loan to or invest in this firm.

 **RATIO ANALYSIS**

Vertical and horizontal analyses are primarily methods of analyzing a single firm. Although we could use vertical and horizontal analyses to compare two firms in the same industry, it is easier to use ratio analysis for this comparison. Normally, when we want to determine how our firm is doing with relationship to other firms in our own industry, we use ratio analysis.

Ratio analysis is used to determine the health of a business, especially as that business compares with other firms in the same industry or similar industries. A ratio is nothing more than a relationship between two variables, expressed as a fraction. Therefore, a single ratio, by and of itself, is meaningless. It is only through comparison, using industry averages as a barometer, that we can determine the well-being of our business. This comparison allows us to succeed in determining whether our company is healthy or in need of repair.

There are several categories of ratios, each of which is used to measure the health of an organization in specific areas. If we use the human body as an example, we can say that one would not go to a gynecologist with a heart problem. In a business context, one does not go to a banker with an inventory problem. Each ratio discussed in the following sections is of particular interest to specialists within the business community. Note, however, that if the total body is not in balance, then several apparently nonrelated health problems may occur. Likewise, although a business in disarray may look healthy in some areas, the overall picture is one that lacks stability. There are several categories of ratios that are important. Like the human body, if the business is to survive and prosper, then all those categories of ratios must operate in a healthy fashion.

TYPES OF BUSINESS RATIOS

There are several categories of business ratios, including liquidity, activity, leverage (debt), profitability, and market ratios. Each category addresses a particular area of financial health within a company. A company that is profitable usually has all areas working in harmony. We begin by discussing these various categories of ratios.

LIQUIDITY RATIOS

Liquidity ratios determine how much of a firm's current assets are available to meet short-term creditors' claims. Liquidity ratios are of primary interest to potential investors and creditors, banks, and other lending institutions. The specific ratios that fall into this category are the current ratio and the quick, or acid test, ratio.

Current Ratio

The **current ratio** is calculated by dividing total current assets by total current liabilities. For example, using Table 4-2, we find that current assets for 2000 were $84,817 and current liabilities were $73,038.

$$\text{Current ratio} = \frac{\text{Current assets}}{\text{Current liabilities}} = \frac{\$84,817}{\$73,038} = 1.16$$

This indicates that for every dollar of short-term creditors' claims, the company had $1.16 to pay for these current obligations. If we divide 1 by 1.16, we see that the company would have had to dispose of approximately 86 percent of its current assets to meet its current obligations. The general rule for most industries is that the current ratio should be 2 or higher. However, one must also look at the industry average, because some industries are very capital intensive and have tremendous capital tied up in plant and equipment (e.g., utility firms, heavy-manufacturing firms), whereas others are highly labor intensive and have little tied up in plant and equipment (e.g., law firms, computer software development firms).

Quick (Acid Test) Ratio

The **(acid test) ratio** is given by the following:

$$\text{Quick ratio} = \frac{\text{Current assets} - \text{Inventory}}{\text{Current liabilities}}$$

Taking 2000 data for our example firm from Table 4-2, we get

$$\text{Quick ratio} = \frac{\$84,817 - \$50,515}{\$73,038} = 0.47$$

Therefore, for every dollar in creditors' claims, the company had only 47 cents to satisfy them using cash on hand. This ratio does not include the sale of the company's inventory. It measures the ability of the firm to meet its short-term obligations without liquidating its inventory, which is extremely important in certain industries, especially for those firms that have high seasonal sales (e.g., toy stores, garden equipment companies, and pool supply firms) or are in industries that have rapid changes in product lines (e.g., personal computer dealers). If inventory should have to be eliminated during low-demand periods, the loss to the firm could be excessive. For example, if a pool supply store has to generate cash during the off-season (January), then the sales prices for its products may have to be so low that the company would be forced to sell at below its own cost of goods. Notice that in such a case the firm will actually lose money on every sale. Therefore, companies having a high current ratio may have so much inventory that they are giving an unclear picture of their ability to meet creditors' claims. Such a company may have so much tied up in inventory that it is actually overinvesting its own excess funds in inventory. An acid test will reveal this problem.

ACTIVITY RATIOS

Activity ratios indicate how efficiently a business is using its assets. Assets are meaningless if they cannot be turned into cash in a timely manner to generate the revenue that the firm requires to meet its obligations. The following ratios are included in this category.

Inventory Turnover Ratio

The **inventory turnover ratio** (or, simply, inventory turnover) indicates how efficiently a firm is moving its inventory. It basically states how many times per year the firm moves its average inventory. There are two formulas that may be used to calculate inventory turnover: One is net sales divided by average inventory at retail, and the other is COGS divided by average inventory at cost. Because both COGS and average inventory at cost can be obtained from figures readily available on the income statement and balance sheet of the company, we normally use the second formula, as shown here for our sample firm:

$$\text{Inventory turnover} = \frac{\text{COGS}}{\text{Average inventory at cost}}$$

The average inventory at cost is obtained by adding beginning and ending inventory for the year in question and dividing by two.

$$\text{Average inventory} = \frac{\text{Beginning inventory} + \text{Ending inventory}}{2}$$

Beginning inventory for one year is typically the ending inventory for the previous year. It stands to reason that if we close our books on December 31, 1999, the beginning inventory for 2000 would be the same value as that listed for inventory on the balance sheet for 1999. Therefore, for the Markadel Retail Store, average inventory is ($35,020 + $50,515) ÷ 2 = $42,767.50. Cost of goods sold for 2000 was $120,002. The inventory turnover for Markadel was $120,002 ÷ $42,767.50 = 2.81. This means that Markadel turned its inventory over approximately 2.81 times in 2000.

To determine how long the average item is in stock, we would divide 366 (number of days in the year 2000) by inventory turnover. Thus, Markadel carries its average inventory for 366 ÷ 2.81, or approximately 130 days. Depending on cash flow, the company may need financing to carry its inventory for this period of time.

Accounts Receivable Turnover Ratio

The **accounts receivable turnover ratio** allows us to determine how fast our company is turning its credit sales into cash. The formula for this ratio is

$$\text{Accounts receivable turnover} = \frac{\text{Credit sales}}{\text{Accounts receivable}}$$

For Markadel in 2000, if we assume that all sales were credit sales, then we use $306,234 for net sales, and accounts receivable were $18,025. So accounts receivable turnover would be $306,234 ÷ $18,025 = 16.99.

Accounts receivable turnover is most often used to determine the average collection period for a company. This formula is as follows:

$$\text{Average collection period} = \frac{\text{Days per year}}{\text{Accounts receivable turnover}}$$

This means that Markadel turned its credit sales into cash approximately 17 times a year in 2000, or waited an average of 21.54 days (366 ÷ 16.99 = 21.54) to collect a credit sale. The year 2000 is a leap year and has 366 days. In 1999 the accounts receivable turnover ratio was $295,456 ÷ $15,320 = 19.29 and the average collection period was 18.92 days (365 ÷ 19.29). Therefore, it took an average of 2.62 days longer to collect money in 2000 than it did in 1999. Nothing is inherently good or bad about the outcome of this ratio. It does reflect on how well the company's actual collections compare with its credit policy. If Markadel has terms of 30 days, then its credit policy is probably too tight, because it is collecting much faster than its terms indicate. We will discuss this in more detail in Chapter 7 when we determine credit policies.

Fixed Asset Turnover Ratio

The **fixed asset turnover ratio** indicates how efficiently fixed assets are being used to generate revenue for a firm. The formula is

$$\text{Fixed asset turnover} = \frac{\text{Net sales}}{\text{Fixed assets}}$$

To obtain the figures for fixed asset turnover, we refer to both the income statement (Table 4-1) and the balance sheet (Table 4-2) for the company. For Markadel in 2000, fixed asset turnover was ($306,234 ÷ $140,100) = 2.19. In 1999, fixed asset turnover was ($295,456 ÷ $148,100) = 2.00. Markadel improved its use of fixed assets between 1999 and 2000, because in 1999 it generated $2.00 in sales for every dollar of fixed assets committed, and in 2000 it generated $2.19. If we are running our business properly, and have not invested in new equipment, we will normally have a goal of improving this ratio on an annual basis, as the ratio should normally increase because of the depreciation aspect of fixed assets. Because we subtract depreciation on an annual basis, the book value of fixed assets will decline each year. Even if sales remain constant, we should see a larger ratio, which may be deceiving. When we purchase large quantities of fixed assets, however, we will expect this ratio to decline, because our fixed asset book value will increase by the purchase price of the fixed assets.

Total Asset Turnover Ratio

The **total asset turnover ratio** indicates how efficiently our firm uses its total assets to generate revenue for the firm. The formula used to calculate total asset turnover is

$$\text{Total asset turnover} = \frac{\text{Net sales}}{\text{Total assets}}$$

This ratio, like the preceding one, requires that we use both the income statement and the balance sheet to obtain the proper numbers. For Markadel in 2000, total asset turnover was ($306,234 ÷ $224,917) = 1.36, whereas in 1999, total asset turnover was ($295,456 ÷ $213,930) = 1.38. When total assets are considered, Markadel generated 2 cents less revenue on each dollar's worth of total assets in 2000 than it did in 1999. We saw from the fixed asset turnover ratio that Markadel generated an additional 19 cents on each dollar of fixed assets in 2000 as compared with 1999. Because fixed assets and current assets make up total assets, we know that Markadel actually used fixed assets much more efficiently than current assets. Because of this, Markadel must spend more time managing current assets, or it could find itself with a very serious liquidity problem.

LEVERAGE RATIOS

Leverage (debt) ratios indicate what percentage of the business assets is financed with creditors' dollars. In other words, it indicates what percentage of the business's assets actually belongs to the owners and what percentage is subject to creditors' claims.

Debt-to-Equity Ratio

The **debt-to-equity ratio** indicates what percentage of the owner's equity is debt, or for every dollar of equity, how many dollars of debt the firm owes. The formula for the debt-to-equity ratio is

$$\text{Debt-to-equity ratio} = \frac{\text{Total liabilities}}{\text{Owner's equity}}$$

or

$$\text{Debt-to-equity ratio} = \frac{\text{Total liabilities}}{\text{Total assets} - \text{Total liabilities}}$$

All information for the debt-to-equity ratio is obtained from the balance sheet (Table 4-2). For Markadel in 2000, the debt-to-equity ratio was ($151,038 ÷ $73,879) = 2.04. Therefore, debt was slightly more than two times the value of the ownership of the firm. This indicates that the company is highly debt capitalized, which might be a result of the company's being new (when a lender may loan up to 80 percent of the total assets of the firm) or its being highly capital intensive. This situation is similar to that of the purchase of a new home in which the owner pays $20,000 down on a $100,000 home; if the home is the individual's only asset, he or she will have a debt-to-equity ratio of [($80,000 ÷ ($100,000 − $80,000)] = 4. This indicates that for every dollar in assets that the individual actually owns, he or she has $4 in debt. The ratio is neither good nor bad in itself, but should be compared with that of other individuals, comparable firms within the industry, or industry averages. The reason for this comparison is that debt must be paid for by you and/or your firm. Debt payments include both principal and interest. If you have a considerably higher ratio than your competitors, then you will have much lower profit margins in a competitive industry. In a highly competitive industry, we are not free to set prices to cover debt. For example, McDonald's, Wendy's, and Burger King all have 99-cent specials. One of these firms could not decide to increase its price to $2 just because it had more debt.

Returning to our debt-to-equity calculation for Markadel, we notice that the debt-to-equity ratio for 1999 was [$134,250 ÷ ($213,930 − $134,250)] = ($134,250 ÷ $79,680) = 1.68. Once again, this indicates that $1.00 of owner's equity is supporting approximately $1.68 of creditors' claims. Therefore, Markadel increased its debt-to-equity ratio between 1999 and 2000. Because assets increased between 1999 and 2000, we can conclude that the purchase of these assets was financed with more debt than equity.

Debt-to-Total-Assets Ratio

The **debt-to-total-assets ratio** indicates what percentage of a business's assets is owned by creditors. The formula for the debt-to-total-assets ratio is

$$\text{Debt-to-total-assets ratio} = \frac{\text{Total liabilities}}{\text{Total assets}}$$

The information for the debt-to-total-assets ratio is obtained from the balance sheet (Table 4-2). For Markadel in 2000, this ratio was ($151,038 ÷ $224,917) = 0.67. Therefore, approximately 67 cents of every dollar in assets used by the business was subject to creditors' claims. In 1999, the debt-to-total-assets ratio was ($134,250 ÷ $213,930) = 0.63. The ratio increased by 4 percent between 1999 and 2000, so in 2000, this company owed approximately 4 cents more to creditors on every dollar of assets owned.

Times-Interest-Earned Ratio

The times-interest-earned ratio shows the relationship between operating income and the amount of interest in dollars the company has to pay to its creditors on an annual basis. The formula for this ratio is

$$\text{Times-interest-earned ratio} = \frac{\text{Operating income}}{\text{Interest}}$$

The figures for calculating this ratio are obtained from the income statement (Table 4-1). For Markadel in 2000, this ratio was ($44,232 ÷ $6,250) = 7.08. So Markadel's operating profit could decline by seven times and the firm would still be able to meet its annual interest obligation. If operating income declined from $44,232 to $37,982, then the ratio would decrease by one, to 6.08. If it declined by another $6,250, the ratio would again decline by one, to 5.08. As mentioned, operating income could decline by seven times this $6,250 figure and Markadel would still be able to pay interest on its debt. Again, this ratio by itself does not convey much information. What we should do is compare Markadel's ratio with the industry average to determine if the firm is better off than the average firm in the industry. We also can use a comparison of annual figures to determine if Markadel's ability to pay interest on debt is increasing or decreasing.

PROFITABILITY RATIOS

Profitability ratios are used by potential investors and creditors to determine how much of an investment will be returned from either earnings on revenues or appreciation of assets. They are also used internally by managers to gauge how well their firms are performing in fiscal and calendar years. If a firm experiences sound current asset management as reflected in liquidity ratios, favorable leverage as determined by leverage ratios, and a substantial degree of turnover as reflected in activity ratios, then the profitability ratios should also be positive and improving. Both internal managers and outside investors will compare the ratios of our company with those of our competitors or with industry averages.

Gross Profit Margin Ratio

The **gross profit margin ratio** is used to determine how much gross profit is generated by each dollar in net sales. To calculate gross profit margin, we use the following formula:

$$\text{Gross profit margin ratio} = \frac{\text{Gross profit}}{\text{Net sales}}$$

The data for this ratio are obtained from the income statement (Table 4-1). For Markadel in 1999, this ratio was ($194,206 ÷ $295,456) = 0.66, and in 2000 it was ($186,232 ÷ $306,234) = 0.61. Therefore, Markadel was less profitable in 2000 than it was in 1999. An analysis indicates that although sales increased, the percentage increase in COGS exceeded the percentage increase in sales, resulting in a lower gross profit margin. Looking at the horizontal analysis of sales and COGS for 1999 and 2000, we see that net sales increased by 3.65 percent, whereas COGS increased by 18.52 percent. This situation could very well lead Markadel into bankruptcy if its managers cannot determine how to control COGS in the future. In some situations the firm may have little or no control due to a natural disaster. For example, in 1999, the northeastern section of the United States experienced the worse drought in 105 years of record keeping.[1] Many farmers reported crop yields 30 to 40 percent below previous year yields. Consider what would happen to the operating profit margin of our sample firm if sales decreased by 40 percent and cost of goods sold remained the same. This is the situation of the farmer in a severe drought.

Operating Profit Margin Ratio

The **operating profit margin ratio** is used to determine how much each dollar of sales generates in operating income. The following formula uses operating income, which is actually a company's earnings before interest and taxes (EBIT):

---

[1] National Oceanic and Atmospheric Administration, press release, August 6, 1999.

$$\text{Operating profit margin ratio} = \frac{\text{Operating income}}{\text{Net sales}}$$

We continue to use Table 4-1 to obtain our data. For Markadel in 1999, the operating profit margin was ($56,889 ÷ $295,456) = 0.19, and in 2000 it was ($44,232 ÷ $306,234) = 0.14. Therefore, we see that Markadel earned about 19 percent, or 19 cents, on each dollar of sales in 1999, but only 14 percent or 14 cents in 2000. This decrease was not the result of a decrease in sales, but the result of increases in both COGS and some operating expenses. The overall operating earnings figures may actually have exceeded the figures for other firms in the industry and may not necessarily have been bad.

Net Profit Margin Ratio

The **net profit margin ratio** tells us how much a firm earned on each dollar in sales after paying all obligations including interest and taxes. The formula is

$$\text{Net profit margin ratio} = \frac{\text{Net profit}}{\text{Net sales}}$$

Looking at our income statement data in Table 4-1, we see that Markadel's net profit margin in 1999 was 14.35 percent ($42,406 ÷ $295,456), and in 2000 was 10.54 percent ($32,285 ÷ $306,234). Overall, there was a decline in net profit of over 23 percent between 1999 and 2000, even though net sales actually increased by 3.65 percent. This situation indicates that Markadel's managers have not been attentive to those details that contribute to a satisfactory bottom line.

Note: All of the preceding profitability ratios for 1999 were already calculated, because of our vertical analysis of Markadel's income statement.

Operating Return on Assets Ratio

The **operating return on assets ratio,** or operating return on investment, allows us to determine how much we are actually earning on each dollar in assets prior to paying interest and taxes. The formula for operating return on assets is

$$\text{Operating return on assets} = \frac{\text{Operating income}}{\text{Total assets}}$$

The calculation of this ratio requires us to use both the income statement and the balance sheet. For Markadel in 1999, operating return on assets was ($56,889 ÷ $213,930) = 0.27, and in 2000 it was ($44,232 ÷ $224,917) = 0.20. Thus, for every dollar in assets committed in 1999, 27 cents was generated in operating income, but in 2000, only 20 cents was generated.

Net Return on Assets Ratio

The **net return on assets (ROA) ratio** is also referred to as net return on investment and tells us how much a firm earns on each dollar in assets after paying both interest and taxes. This ratio is useful when deciding if the firm is a good investment compared with other alternatives. The formula for net return on assets is

$$\text{Net return on assets ratio} = \frac{\text{Net profit}}{\text{Total assets}}$$

We must again use both the income statement and the balance sheet. For Markadel in 1999, this ratio was ($42,406 ÷ $213,930) = 0.20, and in 2000 it was ($32,285 ÷ $224,917) = 0.14. Note that Markadel returned almost 14 percent (rounded up to 14 percent from 0.1435) on its assets in 2000, which was considerably more than one could have earned by investing in government bonds or by placing the money in a savings account, because government bonds were paying between 4 and 7 percent annual interest, depending on the length of maturity, and bank savings accounts were typically paying less than 4 percent. Because the net return on assets ratio allows us to compare possible investment alternatives, we may see this ratio listed as simply return on investment, or ROI.

Return on Equity Ratio

The **return on equity (ROE) ratio** tells the stockholder, or individual owner, what each dollar of his or her investment is generating in net income. The formula for return on equity is

$$\text{Return on equity ratio} = \frac{\text{Net profit}}{\text{Owner's equity}}$$

or

$$\text{Return on equity ratio} = \frac{\text{Net Profit}}{\text{Total assets} - \text{Total liabilities}}$$

When we look at the income statement and balance sheet for Markadel, we find that in 1999 the return on equity ratio was ($42,406 ÷

$79,680) = 0.53 and in 2000 it was ($32,285 ÷ $73,879) = 0.44. When discussing ROE we must note that there is constant pressure on corporate CEOs to increase annual earnings, because the denominator of the equation normally increases due to the increase in retained earnings. If earnings remain stagnant, then ROE decreases, because a portion of earnings are normally added to owner's equity in the form of retained earnings. Therefore, with stagnant earnings the numerator remains constant and the denominator increases in value, so ROE declines. Debt can also distort a company's ROE. The more debt a company has, the higher will be the calculation of ROE, because the accounting equation will show decreased owner's equity when debt is increased. Another method that companies employ to reduce equity and increase ROE is the buyback or retirement of shares of stock.

MARKET RATIOS

Market ratios are used to compare firms within the same industry. They are primarily used by investors to determine if they should invest capital in the company in exchange for ownership.

Earnings per Share Ratio

The **earnings per share ratio** is nothing more than the net profit or net income of the firm, less preferred dividends (if the company has preferred stock), divided by the number of shares of common stock outstanding (issued). The formula for calculating earnings per share ratio is

$$\text{Earnings per share ratio} = \frac{\text{Net income} - \text{Preferred dividends}}{\text{Number of common shares}}$$

If the firm is publicly held and has issued preferred stock, then preferred stock dividends are subtracted from net earnings prior to calculating earnings per share. The preferred stockholders are quasi owners of a corporation (they do not normally have a vote), but they receive a specific dividend income. Therefore, the earnings per share ratio is typically more meaningful to the common, rather than the preferred, stockholder.

Let us say that a corporation had net income after taxes in 2000 of $1,500,000. It also had 10,000 shares of preferred $100 stock that paid 7 percent, so the preferred stock dividend was $70,000 (10,000 shares times $100 value per share times 0.07). The balance sheet shows 100,000 shares of common stock outstanding; therefore, the earnings per share were

$$\text{Earnings per share} = \frac{\$1,500,000 - \$70,000}{100,000} = \frac{\$1,430,000}{100,000} = \$14.30$$

This indicates that common stockholders were earning $14.30 for each share of stock they owned.

Price Earnings Ratio

The **price earnings ratio** is a magnification of earnings per share in terms of market price of stock. The price earnings ratio formula is

$$\text{Price earnings ratio} = \frac{\text{Market price of stock}}{\text{Earnings per share}}$$

For example, if the earnings per share are $14.30 and today's business section of the newspaper lists the corporate stock as selling for $143, then the price earnings ratio is ($143 ÷ $14.30) = 10. In other words, the stock is selling approximately at 10 times its earnings. If investors believe that the earnings per share will increase in the future, then the market price will eventually increase. If, on the other hand, the company receives adverse publicity (e.g., the ValueJet crash in Florida in 1996, litigation against the tobacco companies by the state attorney general), then the public may perceive that the price earnings ratio will decrease in the future, and the price of the stock will drop.

A company will have a price earnings ratio only if it earned a profit (has a positive net income on its income statement) during the previous reporting quarter. If the company had a loss, then there can be no price earnings ratio. Note that a decrease in earnings will give you a price earnings ratio, but it will be higher than in the previous quarter. Often we hear that a company had a loss during the current quarter, when in fact the reporter means that earnings per share decreased. This loss is not a true loss, because the income statement will still show a positive net income.

SOURCES OF COMPARATIVE RATIOS

Several public sources of comparative ratios are readily available to the investor or business owner. It is essential that these ratios be obtained to determine how well the individual firm is doing as compared with other firms in the same or similar industries. Most of these source publications are available at local public libraries, or at college or university libraries, and also on the internet. Some of the sources are as follows:

♦ *Industry Norms and Key Business Ratios.* New York: Dun & Bradstreet Credit Services.

- *Dun's Review.* New York: Dun & Bradstreet.
- *Quarterly Financial Report for Manufacturing, Mining, and Trade Corporations.* Washington, D.C.: Federal Trade Commission.
- *Statement Studies.* Philadelphia: Robert Morris Associates.
- *The Value Line Investment Survey.* New York: Value Line Publications, Inc.

Other sources include the financial statements of other companies (if firms are publicly held, then the annual reports and form 10K reports are available from the corporation), trade journals, and business and industry publications. Because both the sources and firm sizes vary, the entrepreneur may have to use a combination of vertical, horizontal, and ratio analyses to obtain a complete and clear picture of an industry.

 CONCLUSION

No single method of analysis will give us a complete picture of our firm. Therefore, we presented the three most widely used, and easily understood, methods in this chapter.

1. Vertical analysis is extremely useful to the business owner as a monitoring tool because most businesses complete monthly financial statements to be used internally. Software programs can be set up to automatically calculate a vertical analysis for the owners or managers of the business. Vertical analysis is a rapid method of catching fluctuations in income statement or balance sheet items. It uses pivotal accounts as a measure of how good the financial health of the company is with regard to these accounts.

2. Horizontal analysis is useful as a control tool to compare actual annual fluctuations with established company goals. Horizontal analysis can also be performed on a monthly or quarterly basis, if the owner believes that circumstances call for tighter control. This type of analysis is also used to determine if short-term objectives are being accomplished from period to period.

3. Ratio analysis is a means of identifying trends in a firm's liquidity, leverage, activity, profitability, and marketability. It is also used to determine if your firm compares favorably with other firms in the same industry. Ratio analysis makes you, as an owner or manager, more aware of the sore spots in your firm that may be in need of repair.

As an entrepreneur, you will use financial analysis as a means of monitoring both your own and your competitors' performance. Additionally, it will allow you to establish standards and goals for your own firm for control purposes. If financial analysis is used properly, it allows the owner to identify variances in performance and to determine a course of corrective action in a timely manner.

REVIEW AND DISCUSSION QUESTIONS

1. What is the purpose of financial statement analysis?
2. Give an example of how financial statements can be used internally by the managers of a company.
3. List and briefly describe the three types of financial statement analysis.
4. If a company had sales of $2,587,643 in 1994 and sales of $3,213,456 in 1999, by what percentage did sales change during this time period? If the company had a goal of increasing sales by 5 percent during 1999, did it meet its objectives?
5. If the company in question 4 had set a goal of increasing sales by 8 percent in 1999, what should the sales goal have been for 1999?
6. List and briefly describe the five categories of business ratios.
7. If a company computes its current ratio to be 3.56, what does this mean in terms of the company's current assets and current liabilities?
8. Why might a company have a high current ratio, but a low quick ratio (acid test ratio)?
9. If a company has a beginning inventory of $30,000 and ending inventory of $55,000, compute its average inventory. If the COGS is $140,000, compute its inventory turnover and determine how many days the average item is in stock.
10. A company computes its accounts receivable turnover to be 20. Based on this information, find the average collection period. If the company has a credit collection period of 30 days, explain the relationship between the credit collection period and the average collection period.
11. If a company finds that its fixed asset turnover (net sales/fixed assets) has fallen below 1, what does this indicate?
12. If a company has $181,000 in total liabilities and $225,000 in total assets, what percentage of total assets is being financed with the use of other people's money?
13. Distinguish between gross profit margin, operating profit margin, and net profit margin and provide the formula for each ratio.
14. Why is the operating return on assets ratio also referred to as the operating return on investment?
15. If a company's stock is currently selling for $12 per share and its price earnings ratio is 6, what are its earnings per share? What does this figure mean?

EXERCISES AND PROBLEMS

1. Samantha Knight is applying for a small business loan. She provides the bank with the following information: cash in checking accounts, $5,000; cash in savings, $10,350; home market value, $145,500; first mortgage on house, $25,000; home equity loan limit, $70,000; home equity loan, $10,000; automobile market value, $19,000; automobile loan outstanding, $15,000; credit card debt, $1,500.
   a. Calculate the debt-to-asset ratio.
   b. Calculate the debt-to-equity ratio.
   c. What percentage of Samantha's assets are owned by others?

2. You receive the following partial balance sheet (Table 4–3) for 2000 and 1999 for a company that you are considering making an investment in. Perform a vertical analysis for each year on these accounts. Compare the two years, and in a sentence describe those changes that were beneficial or detrimental to this company.

Table 4-3 Balance Sheet, Sample Company

Category	1999	Vertical Analysis 1999	2000	Vertical Analysis 2000
Current assets	$ 7,000,000	_____	$ 9,000,000	_____
Total fixed assets	8,000,000	_____	6,000,000	_____
Total assets	15,000,000	_____	15,000,000	_____
Current liabilities	$ 3,000,000	_____	$ 1,000,000	_____
Long-term debt	4,000,000	_____	4,000,000	_____
Owner's equity	8,000,000	_____	10,000,000	_____
Total liabilities & owner's equity	$15,000,000	_____	$15,000,000	_____

3. You were not totally satisfied with the vertical analysis, so you now want to run a horizontal analysis of this company. Complete Table 4-4. Perform a horizontal analysis on these accounts. Compare the changes in accounts, and in a sentence describe those changes that were beneficial or detrimental to this company.

Table 4-4 Sample Balance Sheet

Category	1999	2000	Horizontal Analysis
Current assets	$ 7,000,000	$ 9,000,000	_____
Total fixed assets	8,000,000	6,000,000	_____
Total assets	15,000,000	15,000,000	_____
Current liabilities	$ 3,000,000	$ 1,000,000	_____
Long term debt	4,000,000	4,000,000	_____
Owner's equity	8,000,000	10,000,000	_____
Total liabilities & owner's equity	$15,000,000	$15,000,000	_____

4. Last month you were vacationing in Phoenix and noticed that there were several Starbucks Coffee locations. You do not have any coffee locations in your city, except for a few local cafes. You also have a large college in your town and believe that if Starbucks Coffee opened a location they would be very successful. If you went to your public library, what sources would you use to find out more information about this company? If you are on the internet, how can you obtain additional information on this company?

5. Given the balance sheet for Starbucks Corporation (Table 4-5), answer the following:
   a. For each year calculate the following ratios: current, quick, debt-to-asset, and debt-to-equity.
   b. In a written explanation, state what each of these ratios means.
   c. Compare the ratios for the two-year period and determine if Starbucks is sufficiently liquid.
   d. How well is Starbucks managing its debt?

Table 4-5 Starbucks Corporation Consolidated Balance Sheets*

(in thousands, except share data)

	Sept 27, 1998	Sept 28, 1997
Assets		
Current Assets:		
Cash and cash equivalents	$101,663	$ 70,126
Short-term investments	21,874	83,504
Accounts receivable	50,972	31,231
Inventories	143,118	119,767
Prepaid expenses and other current assets	11,205	8,763
Deferred income taxes, net	8,448	4,164
Total current assets	337,280	317,555
Joint ventures and other investments	38,917	34,464
Property, plant, and equipment, net	600,794	488,791
Deposits and other assets	15,764	16,342
Total Assets	$992,755	$857,192
Liabilities and Shareholders' Equity		
Current Liabilities:		
Accounts payable	$ 54,446	$ 47,987
Checks drawn in excess of bank balances	33,634	28,582
Accrued compensation and related costs	35,941	25,894
Accrued occupancy costs	17,526	12,184
Other accrued expenses	37,928	30,829
Total current liabilities	179,475	145,476
Deferred income taxes, net	18,983	12,946
Convertible subordinated debentures	—	165,020
Commitments and contingencies (notes 5, 9, and 13)		
Shareholders' Equity:		
Common stock—Authorized, 150,000,000 shares; issued and outstanding, 89,633,478 (includes 424,275 common stock units) and 80,559,023 shares, respectively	589,214	391,284
Retained earnings, including cumulative translation adjustment of $(6,631) and $(1,511) respectively, and net unrealized holding (loss)/gain on investments of $(532) and $63, respectively	205,083	142,426
Total shareholders' equity	794,297	533,710
Total	$992,755	$857,152

6. Perform a horizontal analysis of the Starbucks balance sheet (Table 4-5).
   a. Compare assets, liabilities, and owner's equity from one year to the next.
   b. Is the corporation better off in 1998 or in 1997?
7. Perform a vertical analysis of the Starbucks balance sheet (Table 4-5) for September 27, 1998.
8. Given the income statement for Starbucks Corporation (Table 4-6), and balance sheet (Table 4-5), answer the following:
   a. Calculate the following ratios for each year: operating profit margin, net profit margin, operating return on assets, net return on assets, and return on equity.

Table 4-6 Starbucks Corporation Consolidated Statement of Earnings
(Income Statement)*

(in thousands, except earnings per share)			
Fiscal year ended:	Sept 27, 1998	Sept 28, 1997	Sept 29, 1996
Net revenues	$ 1,308,702	$ 975,389	$ 697,872
Cost of sales and related occupancy costs	578,483	436,942	336,658
Store operating expenses	418,476	314,064	211,575
Other operating expenses	43,479	28,239	19,787
Depreciation and amortization	72,543	52,801	36,019
General and administrative expenses	77,575	57,144	37,258
Merger expenses	8,930	—	—
Operating income	109,216	86,199	56,575
Interest and other income	8,515	12,393	11,029
Interest and other expense	(1,381)	(7,282)	(8,739)
Gain on sale of investment	—	—	9,218
Earnings before income taxes	116,350	91,310	68,083
Income taxes	47,978	36,099	26,373
Net earnings	$ 68,372	$ 55,211	$ 41,710
Net earnings per common share - basic	$ 0.78	$ 0.69	$ 0.56
Net earnings per common share - diluted	$ 0.75	$ 0.66	$ 0.53
Weighted average shares outstanding:			
Basic	88,055	79,645	74,667
Diluted	91,885	90,159	80,916

*Securities and Exchange Commission, Washington DC 20549, Form 10-K, Annual Report.

    b. In a written explanation, describe what each of these ratios means.

    c. In a brief paragraph, describe the overall profitability of Starbucks.

9. Perform a horizontal analysis for the Starbucks Corporation income statement (Table 4-6). Write an explanation of this analysis.

10. Using both the balance sheet (Table 4-5) and the income statement (Table 4-6) for Starbucks Corporation, answer the following:

    a. Calculate the following ratios for each year: inventory turnover, times interest earned, fixed asset turnover, and total asset turnover.

    b. In a written explanation, describe what each of these ratios means.

    c. In a brief paragraph, describe how well you believe Starbucks is managing its assets and its ability to meet interest payments on debt.

11. Given the profit loss (income statement) and balance sheet for Sam's Sandwich Delivery (Table 4-7), answer the following:

    a. Calculate the following ratios: current, quick, accounts receivable turnover, fixed asset turnover.

    b. Using the inventory figure on the balance sheet as average inventory, calculate the inventory turnover ratio.

    c. Calculate the debt-to-equity ratio, debt-to-total asset ratio, and operating profit margin ratio.

    d. Perform a vertical analysis of the income statement.

Table 4-7 Financial Statements for Sam's Sandwich Delivery

Profit Loss (Income Statement) for Six Months Ending 06-30-2000

Revenues			
Retail Sales	$ 68,283		
Wholesale Sales	104,417		
Total Revenues		$172,700	
Cost of Sales	52,067		
Gross Profit		$120,633	
Total Operating Expenses	111,117		
Operating Profit		$ 9,516	
Other Income/Expenses			
Interest Income	41		
Interest Expense	(651)		
Depreciation-Store Equipment	(292)		
Total Other Income/Expenses		(902)	
Net Profit			$8,614

Balance Sheet as of 06-30-2000			
Assets			
Current Assets			
Change Fund		$ 569	
Cash in Bank-Checking		8,612	
Cash in Bank-Savings		9,622	
Accounts Receivable		6,843	
Inventories		2,607	
Total Current Assets			$ 28,253
Fixed Assets			
Furniture and Fixtures	4,296		
Less: Accum Depreciation	4,110	186	
Equipment	68,293		
Less: Accum Depreciation	67,725	568	
Transportation Equipment	31,168		
Less: Accum Depreciation	11,571	19,597	
Total Fixed Assets			$20,351
Total Assets			$48,604
Current Liabilities			
Accounts Payable Trade		6,208	
Accrued Payroll Taxes		3,464	
Accrued Sales Taxes		987	
Total Current Liabilities			$10,659
Long-Term Liabilities			
Auto Loans Payable		18,626	
Total Long-Term Liabilities			$18,626
Total Liabilities			$29,285
Stockholder's Equity			
Common Stock	83,081		
Retained Earnings	(72,376)		
Net Profit/Loss	8,614		
Total Equity			19,319
Total Liabilities and Equity			$48,604

e. Perform a vertical analysis of the balance sheet.

f. Based on your analysis, would you consider investing in Sam's Sandwich delivery business?

12. Go to your local library or on the internet and look up the industry averages for the following groups of ratios: liquidity, activity, debt utilization, and profitability.

a. Compare these ratios to the Starbucks ratios.

b. After your analysis of Starbucks in the previous exercise, would you still recommend that Starbucks establish a location in your town?

13. The Handy Dandy Corporation has an income statement which indicates that operating income is $2,375,486 and net profit is $1,375,486. The corporation currently has 2 million shares of common stock outstanding and 1 million shares of preferred stock which pays a dividend of $1.00 per share. What is this corporation's approximate earnings per share?

14. The Handy Dandy Corporation has an income statement which indicates that operating income is $2,375,486 and net profit is $1,375,486. The corporation currently has 3 million shares of common stock outstanding and 1 million shares of preferred stock which pays a dividend of $1.00 per share. What is this corporation's approximate earnings per share?

PROFIT, PROFITABILITY, AND BREAK-EVEN ANALYSIS

5

Learning Objectives

When you have completed this chapter, you should be able to:

- Understand the difference between efficiency and effectiveness.

- Distinguish between profit and profitability.

- Compare accounting and entrepreneurial profit.

- Understand the relationship of profit margin and asset turnover on the earning power of a company.

- Understand the use of leverage and its relationship to profitability and loss.

- Distinguish between chapter 11 and chapter 7 bankruptcy.

- Given the variable costs, revenue, and fixed costs of a business, determine the break-even point and contribution margin.

- Construct and analyze a break-even chart when given variable costs, revenue, and fixed costs of a business.

In Chapter 4 we gained an understanding of financial statements and their analysis. In this chapter we begin exploring those methods that are necessary for planning our financial strategy. Prior to developing this strategy, it is necessary to define some key financial concepts that the entrepreneur will often be asked about by a potential lender (bank) or investor. Typical questions include the following:

1. What profit do you expect to obtain?
2. How profitable will your firm be in the future?
3. How profitable is your firm now?
4. What is your break-even point?

Before these questions can be adequately answered, we must understand the basic concepts behind them. Although a question pertaining to efficiency and effectiveness may not be asked directly, having a clear understanding of these terms will help when talking with a lender/investor. In the chapter we will review the concepts of efficiency and effectiveness, and then relate them to profit and profitability.

EFFICIENCY AND EFFECTIVENESS

Efficiency is obtaining the highest possible return with the minimum use of resources. **Effectiveness** is accomplishing a specific task or reaching a goal. For example, assume you are in the automobile repair business and employ two mechanics. Both mechanics are asked to complete a specific job (e.g., changing an alternator in a 1996 Chevrolet). One mechanic completes the job in 1.5 hours, and the other mechanic completes the job in 2.3 hours. Both mechanics were effective, because they both completed the job, accomplished the task, and reached the goal. The first mechanic was more efficient, however, because that mechanic completed the job using less of the time resource. In this example, mechanic-hours-worked (the resource used) is the measure of efficiency for automobile repairs.

In financial planning the same principle applies. Assume that two people, James and Joan, want to make an investment and eventually earn $1,000 during one year. They both would be effective if they accomplished this task. If James decided to earn the $1,000 by keeping money in a savings account that returned 5 percent per year, then he would have to invest $20,000 ($20,000 $\times$ 0.05 = $1,000) to earn his $1,000. If Joan purchased a one-year certificate of deposit (CD) that returned 10 percent, then she only would have to purchase a $10,000 CD ($10,000 $\times$ 0.10 = $1,000) to earn her $1,000. James and Joan were both effective, because they both attained their goal, which was the target return of $1,000; however, Joan was more efficient, because she used less money to achieve the same goal. We find that both effectiveness and efficiency are normally related to manufacturing and personal accomplishments (e.g., constructing a building, making a product, or writing a book). Businesses must consistently strive to achieve both efficiency and effectiveness. Today, however, the greatest emphasis in the business community appears to be on a constant quest to improve both profit and profitability.

Businesses use both profit and profitability in the financial marketplace as measures of efficiency and effectiveness. The terms profit and profitability, like efficiency and effectiveness, are regarded as two separate concepts.

PROFIT

Profit is an absolute number earned on an investment. Other terms that indicate a profit include earnings per share for stockholders, interest for savers, and coupons for bondholders. There are two basic types of profit, accounting profit and entrepreneurial profit. For a business's financial statements, we use **accounting profit,** which is typically shown at the bottom of an income statement. This profit is basically what a business has left from its revenues after paying all expenses, including cost of goods, administrative expenses, overhead, interest, and taxes.

Entrepreneurial profit differs from accounting profit, as it is based on the economic concept of opportunity costs (defined in Chapter 1). An entrepreneurial profit is the amount earned above and beyond what the entrepreneur would have earned if that person had chosen to invest time and money in some other enterprise. For example, assume that Sam Jones, an electrical engineer, quit his job with a major firm to open a business that manufactures a small electrical component. The job that Sam quit paid $50,000 per year. After his first year in business, Sam's income statement indicated that his firm had made a profit of $30,000. Thus, Sam had an accounting profit of $30,000, but an entrepreneurial loss of $20,000.

The opportunity cost surrendered to go into business on his own was $50,000, because Sam gave up a $50,000 job to go into a business that earned $30,000. His earnings of $30,000 resulted in an entrepreneurial loss of $20,000. At the end of the second year, Sam's business showed a profit of $90,000. Because Sam could have earned $50,000 in his old job (opportunity cost surrendered), he then had an entrepreneurial profit of $40,000. It is important for us to understand this concept, because the small business owner hopes to make an entrepreneurial profit in addition to an accounting profit. Profit is directly related to the concepts of efficiency and effectiveness. The owner establishes a profit goal (measure of effectiveness) and attempts to reach this goal in the most efficient manner (the manner making the best use of resources).

PROFITABILITY

Profitability can be measured in a business by using a ratio that is obtained by dividing net profit by total assets. Profitability, therefore, is our return on investment and is related more to the concept of efficiency than that of effectiveness. For the business owner, profitability is how efficiently the business assets are being used in generating profit. To illustrate, assume that Mary Jones owns two businesses, a computer software sales company and a computer consulting firm. She invested $100,000 in the sales company and received a profit of $2,000; she invested $10,000 in the consulting firm and received a profit of $1,500. Therefore, Mary made a higher profit or dollar amount off of the sales company. On the other hand, the consulting firm had greater profitability. With $10,000 in assets committed, the consulting firm generated a profit of $1,500, as opposed to $2,000 of profit generated on $100,000 in assets committed by the sales company.

We determine profitability by using the net return on assets ratio. As mentioned in Chapter 4, this ratio is sometimes referred to as simply return on investment, or ROI.

$$\text{ROI} = \frac{\text{Net profit (income)}}{\text{Total assets}}$$

For the sales company,

$$\text{ROI} = \frac{\$2,000}{\$100,000} = 0.02 = 2\%$$

For the consulting firm,

$$\text{ROI} = \frac{\$1,500}{\$10,000} = 0.15 = 15\%$$

Hence, Mary's investment in the consulting firm was much more profitable than her investment in the sales company. Profitability is one method of determining the efficiency of an owner's investment, as compared with another investment. Another method of determining if a business is using its assets efficiently is to compute its earning power.

EARNING POWER

The **earning power** of a company can be defined as the product of two factors: (1) the company's ability to generate income on the amount of revenue it receives, which is also known as net profit margin; and (2) its ability to maximize sales revenue from proper asset employment, also known as total asset turnover. Therefore, earning power is equal to net profit margin times total asset turnover. To calculate the earning power of a company, the following formulas are used.

$$\text{Net profit margin} = \frac{\text{Net profit (income)}}{\text{Net sales}}$$

and

$$\text{Total asset turnover} = \frac{\text{Net sales}}{\text{Total assets}}$$

Therefore,

$$\text{Earning power} = \text{Net profit margin} \times \text{Total asset turnover}$$

$$= \frac{\text{Net profit (income)}}{\text{Net sales}} \times \frac{\text{Net sales}}{\text{Total assets}}$$

Because sales cancel in the preceding formula,

$$\text{Earning power} = \frac{\text{Net profit (income)}}{\text{Total assets}}$$

Companies that have a low inventory turnover (as discussed in Chapter 4) have to compensate for low asset use by maintaining a high net profit margin. A high margin is achieved by having a selling price that far exceeds the cost of the good. The markup must be greater in those companies that are not able to efficiently turn over their assets as readily as other companies. An example would be a company that sells specialized heavy machinery. These companies do not do a high-volume business and so must compensate for decreased turnover by having higher margins. Supermarkets, on the other hand, have very high inventory turnover ratios, and can therefore operate on low profit margins and still generate earning power.

When discussing the assets of a company, we have to consider the debt and equity supporting them. For most businesses the ownership of assets is divided into two portions. Recall that the basic accounting formula is Total assets = Total liabilities + Owner's equity, or Total assets − Total liabilities = Owner's equity. Hence the higher the liabilities, the lower the owner's equity. The liability portion of this formula indicates how much of a company is being financed by other people's money.

FINANCIAL LEVERAGE

Financing a company with other people's money is known as using **financial leverage.** The higher the amount of liabilities, the greater your financial leverage and the lower the amount of equity you have invested in the company. Any net income generated by the company ultimately will give you a greater return on equity if you use very little of your own money and more of other people's money.

For the small business owner, financial leverage is the proportion of the company that is financed by debt. Leverage is a universal tool. It is a small force that can move a much larger force. In business terms, a small amount of owner's equity is supporting a large amount of assets. Any change in income will magnify the return on equity either positively or negatively. Most of us are familiar with a school seesaw, on which a small child's force can move a much larger child. As the small child moves farther from the center of the seesaw, the fulcrum of the seesaw acts like a lever, and the larger child is supported by the smaller child. The larger child is said to be leveraged. The fulcrum, or pivot point, of the seesaw can be compared with the fixed costs of financing. The fixed costs of financing are the interest expenses paid on the amount of debt incurred. A small amount of equity uses this fulcrum to support the assets of a company (the larger child). A firm is said to be in heavy financial leverage if its fixed costs of financing are high.

You use financial leverage when, rather than using your own capital or equity, you use debt to finance your business. In highly leveraged businesses, owners use very little of their own resources (money) and instead use someone else's capital. This is referred to as debt financing, as opposed to equity financing.

The resulting profits will give the business owner a greater return on equity, because one's own financial capital is not tied to the business and can therefore be used in some other capacity. As the business owner pays off the debt and continues to earn a profit, the returns can be extremely high.

Servicing the debt (paying interest on the loan) does not always have a positive ending. In a recession or economic downturn, leverage can work the other way. As you service the debt, and profits decrease, you may have to raise your prices to make a profit. If you are in a highly competitive business, an increase in price may result in decreased sales. Additionally, if you are in a highly leveraged company and are competing with another firm that uses equity financing, you will find that the other company can charge a lower price and be more profitable because your margin has to include the cost of servicing the debt. If you cannot raise prices, you will have to cut expenses, which also may negatively affect sales, service, and quality. Another thing to consider when using leverage is that business loans are often tied to prime lending rates; thus, interest payments on debt will vary based on fluctuations in the prime rate of interest.

Financial leverage must be carefully managed, because too much leverage may place you in a noncompetitive position. Financial leverage is like a balloon that is being blown up. The air is the buildup of debt within the balloon. Because only a certain amount of surface area can withstand the increased air pressure, sooner or later the balloon will burst from too much air. A business also can burst when the debt burden (the fixed costs of financing) becomes too much for the supporting structure of the business to handle. When the bubble bursts for a business, the business may be heading for bankruptcy.

 **BANKRUPTCY**

Bankruptcy for a business occurs when the liabilities of the firm exceed the assets and the business lacks sufficient cash flow to make payments to

Table 5-1 Balance Sheet, The Tom Jones Company

The Tom Jones Company
Balance Sheet
As of December 31, 2000

Assets

Current Assets			
Checking Account		$ 2,000	
Accounts Receivable		10,000	
Inventory		35,000	
Total Current Assets			$ 47,000
Fixed Assets			
Land		$ 50,000	
Buildings	$250,000		
Less: Accumulated Depreciation	100,000	$150,000	
Equipment	50,000		
Less: Accumulated Depreciation	30,000	$ 20,000	
Total Fixed Assets			220,000
Total Assets			$267,000
Liabilities and Owner's Equity			
Current Liabilities			
Accounts Payable Trade		$ 20,000	
Notes Payable Bank		20,000	
Taxes Payable		3,000	
Total Current Liabilities			$ 43,000
Long-term Liabilities			
Building Mortgage		$200,000	
Equipment Loan		30,000	
Total Long-Term Debt			$230,000
Total Liabilities			$273,000
Owner's Equity			(6,000)
Total Liabilities and Owner's Equity			$267,000

creditors. This situation places the business in a negative equity situation, as shown in Table 5-1.

The sequence of events typically runs along this path: If this business has only $2,000 in cash, it cannot pay the taxes that are due, the vendors, or the bank. The owner then starts missing payments to the vendors and the bank. The vendors then stop issuing credit to this company and begin to deliver on a cash on delivery (COD) basis. In order to have the cash to pay the vendor, the business misses another bank payment. The bank then calls the note and demands full payment. The owner does not have the cash to pay the bank, and the bank seeks to foreclose on the buildings and equipment.

The owner applies for protection under chapter 11 of the bankruptcy code. There are essentially two types of bankruptcy for a business, chapter 11 and chapter 7.

Chapter 11 bankruptcy occurs when a business seeks court protection while it develops a plan to pay off its creditors. While the business is in chapter 11, it can continue operating and its creditors are effectively held at bay by the courts. Once the plan is submitted, the majority of the creditors must approve the effectiveness of the plan. The plan often includes such provisions as paying creditors a portion of the money owed, reorganizing loans, and possibly refinancing mortgages. If the majority of the creditors reject the reorganization plan, then the company may be forced into chapter 7 bankruptcy.

Chapter 7 bankruptcy requires liquidation of all assets of the business, and payment to the creditors. As we see from the balance sheet in Table 5-1, even if all assets are sold for book value of $267,000, the debt holders will not receive all of the $273,000 that is owed to them by the Tom Jones Company. The stockholders have a negative equity position of $–6,000. Common stockholders, or owners, are always last in line to be paid. In the present example, they will receive nothing for their investment. In most cases the assets of the company, especially the inventory and equipment, are sold for considerably less than book value. If this is the case, the debt holders will receive pennies on each dollar that is owed to them.

Before we take on debt, it is essential to determine if our business will be able to support the debt, and provide us with a profit. One method of determining profit in advance of making an investment is through break-even analysis.

 # BREAK-EVEN ANALYSIS

Break-even analysis is a process of determining how many units of production must be sold, or how much revenue must be obtained, before we begin to earn a profit. The decision of whether to use units sold or revenues obtained in calculating break-even is based on several factors. One factor involves the firm's ability to determine its sales units. For a retail firm that deals in hundreds and perhaps thousands of individual items, break-even in terms of sales dollars is easier to compute than break-even in sales units. For the manufacturing firm that produces discrete units, however, break-even in units of production may be more appropriate.

In any event, we must identify several variables prior to determining break-even. These variables are fixed costs, variable costs, and sales, either in total dollar amount or in price per unit.

BREAK-EVEN QUANTITY

Determining the break-even point using the **break-even quantity (BEQ)** method is achieved with the following formula:

$$BEQ = \frac{FC}{P - VC}$$

where

FC = fixed costs

P = price charged per unit

VC = variable cost per unit

Fixed costs (as discussed) are the costs of running a business that are not tied to the amount of production or sales, and are normally found on the income statement of a business as operating expenses. In other words, fixed costs will be incurred even if there are no sales or revenues. For example, when you sign a lease, payments are due to the property owner every month and typically will not change even though sales may increase or decrease. Normally, fixed costs include but are not limited to rent, utilities, insurance, executive salaries, clerical salaries, and servicing of debt.

Price is what the company charges for the product or service. In manufacturing, wholesale, or retail industries, it is the actual price received for the product. In service industries (for legal, accounting, consulting, plumbing, and electrical services), we often measure price in terms of hourly charges.

Variable costs are all costs associated with producing or procuring a product or service that is sold by a firm. They are costs that are directly related to sales. For a manufacturing firm, variable costs would include costs of raw materials, possibly production labor, and often costs of running production machinery (utility costs), because these items are not used unless a product is being manufactured. For a wholesale or retail firm, variable costs (cost of goods sold on the income statement) are those paid by the firm for the items that are sold, including freight, insurance of items in transit, and the price of merchandise.

Consider the following example: Carl Einfeld manufactures toy trucks. He wants to know how many trucks he must sell to make a profit. He has used his cost data to generate Table 5-2. For break-even analysis, Carl will have to go through the following process:

1. Carl must first determine the values of the variables in our break-even formula (i.e., fixed costs, variable costs, and price).
2. Next, Carl must determine the time period that will be used for break-even analysis. Let us assume that Carl wants to determine

Table 5-2   Cost Data for Carl's Toy Trucks

Cost Category	Payment Basis	Cost ($)
Rent	Monthly	2,000.00
Salaries	Monthly	5,000.00
Employee Benefits	Annually	7,000.00
Insurance	Quarterly	1,500.00
Property Taxes	Annually	3,000.00
Wood	Per truck	1.25
Paint and Finishing	Per truck	0.25
Labor	Per truck	2.50
Packing and Shipping	Per truck	2.00

break-even on an annual basis. When examining Table 5-2, we note that fixed cost items are paid in different time frames (rent and salaries are paid monthly, employee benefits and property taxes are paid annually, and insurance is paid quarterly).

3. Carl now must convert all fixed costs to the break-even time period. In our example, Carl is using annual break-even quantity. He could just as easily have determined break-even on a quarterly, monthly, or even daily basis. Note that to convert items that are paid weekly to a monthly basis, the following procedure should be used: Multiply the weekly figure by 52 (weeks per year) and divide the answer by 12 (months per year). This will give an accurate monthly charge.

4. Carl must use the break-even formula to determine the quantity of units that must be produced during the time period. This will provide Carl with the number of trucks that he must produce each year in order to break even.

The fixed costs from Table 5-2 are rent, salaries, employee benefits, insurance, and property taxes. To determine total fixed costs, we annualize all figures as follows:

$FC = $ (Rent $\times$ 12) + (Salaries $\times$ 12) + Employee benefits + (Insurance $\times$ 4) + Property taxes

$= (\$2,000 \times 12) + (\$5,000 \times 12) + \$7,000 + (\$1,500 \times 4) + \$3,000$

$= \$24,000 + \$60,000 + \$7,000 + \$6,000 + \$3,000$

$= \$100,000/\text{year}$

Carl sells each toy truck for $10:

$$P = \$10/\text{truck}$$

The variable costs are added, as follows:

VC = Wood + Paint and finishing + Labor + Packing and shipping

= \$1.25 + \$0.25 + \$2.50 + \$2.00

= \$6.00/truck

Substituting these values into the BEQ formula, we have

$$BEQ = \frac{FC}{P - VC}$$

$$= \frac{\$100,000/\text{year}}{\$10/\text{truck} - \$6/\text{truck}} = \frac{\$100,000/\text{year}}{\$4/\text{truck}}$$

$$= 25,000 \text{ trucks/year}$$

Notice that we kept all units constant throughout our calculations, and therefore we finished with a break-even quantity of 25,000 trucks per year. If we had not converted fixed costs to annual costs, our calculations would have been incorrect. This point cannot be overemphasized: If units are not constant and used consistently in calculations, then your answers will be vague and confusing. If we had not converted all fixed costs to annual costs, then we would have

FC = \$2,000 + \$5,000 + \$7,000 + \$1,500 + \$3,000 = \$18,500

Placing this into our formula, we would have calculated our break-even quantity as follows:

$$BEQ = \frac{FC}{P - VC}$$

$$= \frac{\$18,500}{\$10/\text{truck} - \$6/\text{truck}} = 4,625 \text{ trucks}$$

If Carl had set up his assembly line to manufacture 4,625 trucks per year, rather than 25,000, he would have lost several thousand dollars.

Several other items can be obtained from the basic break-even formula, including contribution margin and revenue. In the BEQ equation, $P - VC$ is the **contribution margin,** or the amount of profit that will be made by a company on each unit that is sold above and beyond the break-even quantity. It is also the amount the company will lose for each unit of production by which it falls short of the break-even point. The contribution margin formula provides us with the profit that is made on each unit of production once break-even has been passed. In the case of Carl's toy trucks, Carl will lose \$4 on every truck that is sold below the break-even quantity, and make a profit of \$4 on every truck that is sold above it.

Revenue for any business is simply the sales price times the quantity sold ($R = P \times Q$). Therefore, Carl's revenue at break-even will be $250,000 ($10/truck $\times$ 25,000 trucks/year).

With a slight modification, the BEQ formula can be used to determine the sales needed (in units) to make a specific profit. This is calculated as follows:

$$\text{Total quantity} = \frac{FC + \text{Desired net profit}}{P - VC}$$

Let us assume that Carl would like to make a profit of $30,000 on his toy truck line. He would use the BEQ formula, but add the profit of $30,000 to the fixed costs. He would then have the following:

$$\text{Total quantity} = \frac{\$100,000/\text{year} + \$30,000/\text{year}}{\$10/\text{truck} - \$6/\text{truck}}$$

$$= 32,500 \text{ trucks/year}$$

Therefore, Carl must manufacture 32,500 trucks per year in order to realize a $30,000 net profit.

If the total quantity figure does not come out to an even number, we normally round up, because we cannot produce or sell less than one complete unit. If, in the previous example, we had a sales price of $9 per truck and a variable cost of $6, we would then have a quantity of $130,000/($9 − $6) = 43,333.33 trucks, and so we would round up to 43,334 trucks because we cannot sell 33 percent of a truck. Additionally, note that our profit would be less than $30,000 if we sold 43,333 trucks.

Consider the fact that most manufacturing firms such as Toyota or General Motors spend several hundred million dollars to build a manufacturing plant that produces a particular line of automobiles. They have to know how many units they will produce each day. They must order all parts for assembly so that they arrive at the assembly lines within a specified time frame. If Toyota makes 60 Camrys per hour at their Tennessee plant and has two eight-hour shifts, they make 960 Camrys per day. They need 5 tires for each car or 4,800 tires per day. Quantity break-even points are extremely important, because there are thousands of parts that must be ordered for an assembly line each day. On the other hand, if we have a store such as Safeway, then total volume of sales in dollars is of utmost importance. We do not need to know how many cases of soda pop will be sold at a particular store each day, but we must know what total dollar sales will be required in order to break even, pay all bills, and make a profit on our investment in the store. For this type of firm, we will compute break-even in dollars rather than in units.

BREAK-EVEN DOLLARS

The variables and formula used to compute **break–even dollars (BE$),** or revenue required for break–even, are basically the same as those used for BEQ, except that we express the contribution margin as a percentage of sales rather than as a dollar amount. Using Carl's toy truck company, the price is $10 for each truck and the variable costs of producing a truck are $6. Therefore, *VC* as a percentage of sales is *VC/P,* or $6/$10, which yields 0.60 (60 percent of each sales dollar is consumed by variable costs of production). Thus, the contribution margin is 40 percent of each sales dollar. Our contribution margin formula for this calculation is Contribution margin $= 1 - VC$ (expressed as a percentage of the sales dollar). (As previously explained, a retail sales company may list COGS as a dollar figure without being able to determine the cost of each unit with regard to COGS. Such a company would use vertical analysis on its income statement data to determine COGS as a percentage of sales dollars.) We can now compute BE$ for Carl's toy truck company as follows:

$$BE\$ = \frac{FC}{1 - VC} = \frac{\$100,000/\text{year}}{1 - 0.60}$$

$$= \frac{\$100,000/\text{year}}{0.40} = \$250,000$$

Note that as the variable costs as a percentage of sales increase, the contribution margin decreases and the break–even amount in dollars or units sold will increase. This means that if sales remain stable as variable costs increase, the break–even amount will change. For example, if lumber costs increase so that Carl has to pay $1.75 for wood per truck, then *VC* increases by 50 cents per unit to $6.50. The contribution margin now decreases to 0.35 from 0.40. To break even, the company would now have to generate revenues of $285,714 rather than the $250,000 that we previously calculated.

As noted, with a slight modification, the break–even formulas can be modified to determine the sales required in order to make a specific profit. Assume that Carl wants to make a profit of $50,000 next year. Variable costs remain at 60 percent of sales, and fixed costs are $100,000 per year. The formula for break–even dollars with profit is

$$BE\$ = \frac{FC + \begin{matrix} \text{Desired} \\ \text{net profit} \end{matrix}}{1 - VC} = \frac{\$100,000 + \$50,000}{1 - 0.60} = \frac{\$150,000}{0.40} = \$375,000$$

Therefore, if Carl wants to make a profit of $50,000, then he has to generate total toy truck revenue of $375,000.

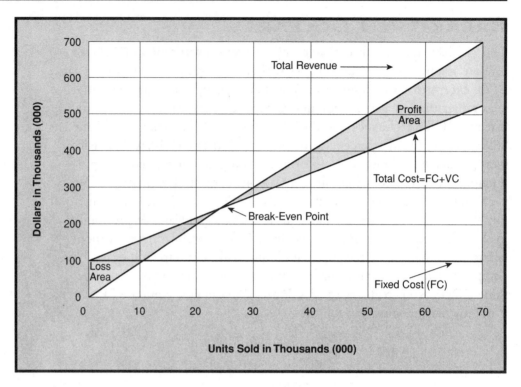

FIGURE 5-1
Break-Even Chart for Carl's Toy Trucks

BREAK-EVEN CHARTS

Plotting a **break-even chart,** or graph, can be done quite easily. Using Carl's toy truck company, we set up the vertical axis as dollar units and the horizontal axis as sales in units. We then plot a horizontal line indicating fixed costs $100,000 (see Figure 5-1). Next we plot the total revenue line from the intersection of the horizontal and vertical axes. This is rather easily accomplished, because if there are no sales then revenue is zero. We choose a couple of points for the revenue line based on sales of even units (for example, 50,000 units and $500,000 in sales, since the price is $10 per unit and revenue equals sales times units sold). Then we plot our total cost line by plotting variable costs beginning from the intersection of the vertical axis and the fixed cost line. Break-even charts are easy to analyze, allowing the businessperson to see how much profit or loss the company will have, based on various sales volumes.

In analyzing a break-even chart, note that all points to the right of the break-even point indicate the profit of the firm. The profit for any number of units or amount of revenue is obtained by taking the difference between the total revenue line and the total cost line. We can choose any quantity to the right of the break-even point, move vertically, and determine the profit. For example, we can determine that if Carl sells 50,000 units, he should earn a profit of $100,000. Additionally, note that any sales quantity to the left of the break-even point will result in a loss, because for these quantities the total cost line lies above the total revenue line.

 CONCLUSION

Now that we have some understanding of profitability, profit, and break-even analysis, we must determine if our business will be profitable. Is it worth the entrepreneurial effort? Will we make a profit in our business, and can we obtain financing? To answer these questions, we must be able to predict the sales and expenses of our firm, and this is accomplished with financial planning, forecasting, and budgeting, which are the subjects of our next chapter.

REVIEW AND DISCUSSION QUESTIONS

1. Compare efficiency and effectiveness.
2. What is the difference between accounting profit and entrepreneurial profit?
3. What financial ratio is predominantly used to determine profitability?
4. Describe the earning power of a company.
5. How is financial leverage related to bankruptcy?
6. Compare chapter 11 bankruptcy with chapter 7 bankruptcy.
7. What is the relationship between fixed costs, contribution margin, and the break-even point?
8. What are some factors that affect variable costs?
9. What are the basic steps that you must take to determine if you will be able to make a profit?
10. The Handy Doll Manufacturing Company has the following information: The average doll selling price is $12, raw materials for a doll are $4, and it takes 15 minutes to assemble a doll. Production labor is paid $8 per hour. Operating expenses are as follows: salaries, $2,500 per week; insurance, $1,200 per quarter; rent, $1,500 per month; and utilities, $800 per month. How many dolls must be sold per month to break even? How many dollars in sales does this represent? What is the contribution margin for each doll sold?
11. For the company in question 10, if the goal is to make a profit of $5,000 per month, how many dolls will have to be sold?
12. What is the effect of an increase in variable costs as a percentage of sales on the contribution margin and on the break-even dollar amount?

EXERCISES AND PROBLEMS

1. John and Mary work for a direct marketing firm. They make calls to customers for a local carpet cleaning service. In a typical hour John completes 50 calls and gets two sales; Mary completes 50 calls and gets one sale. Compare these two people from the viewpoint of effectiveness and efficiency.

2. Joan purchases a government bond for $10,000 that pays 7% annual interest. Jim purchases $20,000 worth of corporate bonds that pay 10% annual interest. Joan's goal is to earn $700 per year on her investment, and Jim's goal is to earn $2,000 per year on his investment.
   a. Is Joan or Jim more efficient and why?
   b. Is Joan or Jim more effective and why?

3. Sam quit a $30,000-a-year job with a local heating and air conditioning firm to go into business for himself. After his first year in business his accountant showed him an income statement, which indicated Sam's firm had a profit of $40,000. During this year Sam had drawn a salary of $20,000.
   a. What was Sam's accounting profit and entrepreneurial profit?
   b. Explain the difference between accounting and entrepreneurial profit.

4. Maury quit his job as an accountant with We Keep Books Accurately to open his own accounting firm. He earned $40,000 with the accounting firm We Keep Books Accurately. During the current year Maury had revenues of $150,000 and total expenses of $110,000.
   a. What was Maury's accounting profit?
   b. What was Maury's entrepreneurial profit?

5. James builds brick walls for custom homes. His annual sales are approximately $300,000, and his net income is $18,000. He has assets of $100,000 invested in this business. Tom sells window shades. His annual sales are approximately $900,000, and his net income is $27,000. He has assets of $150,000 invested in his business.
   a. Compute the net profit margin for both James and Tom.
   b. Compute the asset turnover for both James and Tom.
   c. Compare the profitability of these two firms, and discuss the similarities and differences.

6. The Faster Modem Corporation was founded by two engineers who managed to capitalize their firm with $150,000. They were able to raise this money because their test model performed much faster than current modems on the market and they received an initial commitment from a national firm to market their modem. However, a national modem manufacturer beat them to the market, and they found that they had invested $140,000 in obsolete technology. They now find that they have no sales, $500 in cash, and a $2,000 payment due to their creditor on the first of next month. What are the owners options?

7. You are going to open a business making custom cabinets. You can sell each cabinet for $80. It takes a cabinetmaker approximately 45 minutes

to make one cabinet. Each cabinetmaker works an eight-hour day, earning $18 per hour. Each cabinet will use $25 in raw materials. You normally produce cabinets 20 days a month, and can employ two cabinetmakers. You estimate that your fixed costs will be $5,000 per month.

   a. What is your contribution margin?

   b. How many cabinets must you make each month to break even?

   c. What dollar sales volume will you have to make to earn a monthly profit of $2,000?

   d. What is your total monthly revenue if you want to make a $2,000 profit?

   e. Construct a break-even chart for the custom cabinet firm.

8. Wanda wants to open a health food store. She will pay rent of $1,500 per month, utilities of $500, insurance of $100 per month, and payroll of $1,250. She estimates that her cost of goods will be approximately 65 percent of sales. Wanda would like to make $2,000 a month for herself.

   a. What is her contribution margin?

   b. How much does she need in monthly sales to break even?

   c. How much does she need in monthly sales to make a profit of $2,000?

   d. Construct a break-even chart for Wanda's health food store.

9. Woody's Widget Shop has the following information: The average widget has a selling price of $18; raw materials for the widget are $4 and it takes 30 minutes to assemble one widget. Production labor is paid $8 per hour. Operating expenses are as follows: salaries $2,500 per week; insurance $1,200 per quarter; rent $3,000 per month and utilities $1,000 per month.

   a. How many widgets must be sold each month in order to break even?

   b. How many dollars in sales does this represent?

   c. What is the contribution margin for each widget sold?

   d. If the goal is to make $100,000 profit per month, how many widgets will have to be sold?

10. You want to open up a custom skate board shop. You can sell each skate board for $160. It takes 3 hours to make each skate board. Each skate board maker earns $25 per hour. Each skate board costs $15 in raw materials. You estimate that your fixed costs are $20,000 per month.

   a. What is the contribution margin?

   b. How many skate boards must be sold each month in order to break even?

   c. What is the breakeven dollar amount?

   d. How many skate boards will have to be sold in order to earn a $10,000 profit each month?

   e. What is your total monthly revenue if you want to earn a profit of $8,000?

FORECASTING AND PRO FORMA FINANCIAL STATEMENTS

6

Learning Objectives

When you have completed this chapter, you should be able to:

- Understand the importance of a sales forecast to a business.
- Understand the basic steps used in selecting a forecasting model.
- Know how to evaluate a forecasting model.
- Given a business situation, choose the proper forecasting model.
- Calculate a forecast using time series data.
- Explain the role that the mean absolute deviation (MAD)

plays in selecting a forecasting model.

- Understand the relationship between a business's revenue base, sales forecast, assets, and need for financing.
- Construct pro forma financial statements from available data on a proposed or existing business.
- Apply the percentage of sales method in determining any required new financing needed for a business.

We now understand how to read and analyze financial statements. We also know that lending institutions, to comply with SBA guidelines, will require pro forma (projected) financial statements for at least three years into the future. Because the first line on the income statement is total sales or total revenue, we cannot begin a financial statement without an estimate of sales. Our main objective in this chapter is to learn the procedure for obtaining an estimated sales figure. This procedure for estimating a future sales figure is called *forecasting*.

The sales forecast is what drives all other factors in our pro forma (projected) financial statements. These financial statements will be used both by our firm and by any external users whom we want to have a stake in our firm. We need pro forma statements to develop internal budgets for the functional departments of our business. If we seek to convince investors to provide equity capital for our business, then we also will have to provide them with pro forma financial statements. The reason that lenders want these financial statements is they need to ensure that our business will generate enough profit to pay back both the principal and the interest on the loan; potential investors also will want to ensure that the business is profitable enough to provide them with the desired return on their invested capital.

Because of the need for these pro forma financial statements, forecasts of future sales and revenues are required. The time horizon for these forecasts must meet or exceed that required by the lender or investor. Forecasting is a necessary beginning point for actually developing plans. The forecast of the demand for our products and services will in most cases determine the size of our physical plant. The forecasted demand for our products and services also will help us plan for the purchase of equipment (capital expenditures) and the hiring of personnel (wages, salaries, and benefits). Finally, the financial plan must be developed to ensure that all of the money required for the physical plant, purchase of equipment, and hiring of personnel will be available. In addition, the financial plan must ensure that sufficient profit will be available to meet the requirements of lenders and investors.

 ## FORECASTING

A **forecast** is a quantifiable estimate of future demand. **Forecasting** in business is the process of estimating the future demand for our products and services. Forecasting for the financial manager also requires estimates of future interest rates. Because we are using an estimate, we know in advance that our forecast will not be completely accurate; however, firms that use forecasts have a much higher success rate than firms that do not. The process used involves several basic steps: (1) Determine the type of forecasting model to be used; (2) determine the forecast horizon; (3) select one or more forecasting models; (4) evaluate the models; (5) apply the chosen model; and (6) monitor the model to ensure that it is still appropriate. If the model is not appropriate, go back to step 1 and begin again.

1. **Determine the type of forecasting model to be used.** The criteria for selecting a forecasting model will require us to ask six basic questions: (1) Who will be using the forecast and what information do they require? (2) How relevant and available are historical data? (3) How accurate does the forecast have to be? (4) What is the time period of the forecast? (5) How much time do we have to develop the forecast? (6) What is the cost or benefit (value) of this forecast to our company? Questions 3, 4, and 5 are tied together. The more ac-

curacy you want, the higher the cost of gathering data. Long-term forecasts normally include more variables. Gathering information for more variables is more costly and time consuming. The more time spent in gathering the information, the higher the cost.

2. **Determine the forecast horizon.** Several factors influence the length of the forecast horizon. The basic premise to remember is that there is an inverse relationship between forecast accuracy and time horizon. The longer the time horizon, the more inaccurate the forecast will be. The forecast horizon should be at least as long as the time period of your strategic plan. Utility companies may have to use forecast horizons of 10 to 15 years, because of the time that it takes to construct new plants. Product life cycles also influence the length of forecasts. Some products such as milk are very stable, and forecasts concerning these products can be made for years into the future. Other products such as videocassettes normally have very short life cycles, and forecasts of their sales and rentals are normally for less than one year.

3. **Select one or more forecasting models.** When selecting a forecasting model, it is important to consider the previous criteria (the six basic questions). In some instances you may want to use a combination of forecasting models.

4. **Evaluate the models.** We can compare several similar forecasting models with evaluation criteria such as mean absolute deviation (MAD). MAD is a measure of how closely a forecasting model compares with actual sales data. We will demonstrate the use of MAD after we develop our first time series model. We also can evaluate models based on our basic information requirements. A forecasting model is meant to assist us in managing our business—it is not supposed to make decisions for us. With modern computers, it is often too easy to allow the computer to generate a forecast and then to blindly follow that forecast. The environment of business is constantly changing. Changing tastes of our customers, new competitors entering our area, and general economic changes that affect our business are not normally built into our forecasting models. As business owners and managers, we must be aware that changing market and economic conditions require us to constantly evaluate our forecasting models, and change them when they no longer perform as desired.

5. **Apply the chosen model.** We apply the forecasting model in our business and use it to determine future requirements. Application of the model and the specific units of measurement used therein depend on the area of our business for which we are using the model. Long-range general business plans are typically expressed in terms of dollars. Production planning requires that these plans be expressed in

units of production to determine future requirements for plant, equipment, and personnel. Personnel and production planners also require that forecasts be broken down into human resource requirements. The financial planner must determine the cost of obtaining the required financing to support all of the various plans. Many small businesses have owners who perform all of the preceding functions. Using a forecasting model will often require us to develop several functional business plans to support the forecast.

6. **Monitor and control the model.** Forecasts should be adjusted by us as managers anytime they do not reflect reality; however, we must always keep in mind that the forecast will not be completely accurate. If it is good enough to allow us to write business plans that accurately reflect our needs as managers, then the forecast is adequate. When a forecasting model no longer allows us to do this, then the model must be adjusted or a new model must be developed.

TYPES OF FORECASTING MODELS

There are several forecasting models from which to choose. The three types of methods used in these models are qualitative, quantitative, and cause and effect. Qualitative methods use expert opinions to predict sales. Quantitative methods use mathematical formulas and statistics to predict sales. Cause-and-effect methods use statistical formulas based on models to predict sales. An example of cause and effect would be an increase in the sale of soda pop when the temperature increases. High temperatures are the cause of increased sales, which are the effect.

There are three basic categories of forecasting models, each of which is associated with a particular type of method: (1) **judgmental models,** which use qualitative methods, (2) **time series models,** which use quantitative methods, and (3) **causal models,** which use cause-and-effect methods. We begin by discussing the methodology used by each of these categories of models. We then discuss specific models that are associated with each category. Prior to the discussion about time series models, we provide a brief section on determining mean absolute deviation (MAD).

Judgmental Models

Judgmental models are qualitative and essentially use estimates based on expert opinion. People who are experienced in these specific areas develop both an intuitive feel and a scientific method for determining what will sell and what the customers want. Judgmental models forecast future sales for both existing and new products. Judgmental models for determining the forecast for future sales of existing products and services use surveys of both sales forces and customers, and various other types of market research. Judgmental models for forecasting sales for a new business or new product use historical analogies, market research, and the Delphi method.

Surveys of sales forces are conducted by managers to determine future sales within the company's sales territories. Managers combine individual sales estimates collected into a total company sales forecast. This method is the proper way to determine sales if your company already has a sales force in place, if the sales force is stable and reliable, and if sales are made directly to major customers. Models based on these surveys are most appropriate for manufacturing and wholesale firms.

Surveys of customers are effective for virtually all firms, but particularly for the company that has a few large customers. Examples include firms that manufacture parts for a few large national chains, original equipment manufacturers, and unique specialty shops. Because the customers normally have sales forecasts of their own or know what their requirements will be, they can provide fairly accurate requirements for future time periods. Surveys of customers also are appropriate for firms that want to know customer demographics. For a small firm with a limited advertising budget, a survey of customers will allow the firm to target its advertising based on factors such as zip codes.

Historical analogy is useful in several areas. It can be used when a new product is introduced that has characteristics similar to those of previous products. For example, a bakery plans to introduce an oat bran bread because of customer's concerns regarding fiber in their diets. If the bakery has previously introduced a seven-grain bread or other bread because of customer dietary concerns, then they can use this historical analogy (how did the previous product sell?) to determine demand for the new bread product. Historical analogy also can be used when a company is going to expand by opening a new store or sales outlet. Firms that have several outlets use historical analogy to determine where to place new outlets. If you shop in malls, you have probably noticed that jewelry stores normally locate at mall entrances where they are visible to all shoppers. These stores are visible to shoppers entering the mall and to shoppers who are walking through the mall from one large department store to another.

Historical analogy also can be used in planning for a new business, or for business expansion. It is rare to find a new business that is not similar to some other business in some given location. Many franchises and chain stores use historical analogy to determine what level of sales can be expected when a new facility is built. They use sales from previous locations with similar characteristics, such as population density, local population income, and traffic patterns, to determine the expected level of sales in the new location. For example, new convenience stores and gas stations are normally located at major intersections with high traffic flows.

Market research can include surveys, tests, and observation. Surveys can be conducted via telephone interviews, mail questionnaires, field interviews, and even interest groups on the internet. Tests often involve marketing products in certain test areas. Results of surveys and tests are statistically extrapolated, and a forecast is developed based on those results. Market research is useful for introducing new products or for introducing existing products into new areas. It also can be used to start new businesses in specific areas where the products and services being offered are in short supply. Many firms use market research to build a customer profile in order to determine specific demographic characteristics about their customers. For example, if you have purchased a new appliance recently, you probably filled out a customer survey that you mailed in as part of the warranty card. Another example is being asked to give your zip code to the checkout clerk at your local appliance store. This information helps the store determine exactly where its customers live.

The **Delphi method** uses a panel of experts to obtain a consensus of opinion. Normally the Delphi method is used for unique new products or processes for which no previous data exist. It also has been used in areas where market research might provide competitors with too much information about a new product or service; this holds true for high-tech products that easily can be copied by competitors. A committee of experts is selected by the Delphi model developer. Members of the committee are widely dispersed and typically do not even know the other committee members. A monitor is selected, and a questionnaire is developed describing the proposed project. Committee members are asked for their best estimates of sales and other information that the monitor believes will be significant. The monitor gathers and evaluates the information. A revised questionnaire is developed that includes relevant data from the first round. The revised questionnaire with new data is then sent out to the committee. The process is continued until committee members reach a consensus.

As discussed, judgmental models are considered to be qualitative because they use opinions and previous experience to determine the forecast. The forecast itself is quantitative, however. It provides us with the number of units or dollar volume of expected sales during a specific time period. A new business entrepreneur should be somewhat of an expert or have a specific area of expertise in the type of business. Entrepreneurs normally know several other people who can provide them with expert opinions. They also subscribe to trade journals and professional magazines that provide them with essential data.

Time Series Models

Time series forecasting models normally use historical records that are readily available within the firm or industry to predict future sales. For this reason they are often referred to as internal or intrinsic models. In marketing they may be referred to as primary data models. Marketing texts normally refer to internal data as primary data, and to information that is gathered from external sources as secondary data. The specific time series model that will be chosen by a firm depends on the historical sales patterns of the firm and the use of evaluation criteria. The assumption in time series forecasting is that past sales are a fairly accurate predictor of future sales. We will discuss four time series models in order of their simplicity, moving from the easiest models to the most complex. They are (1) the moving average model, (2) the weighted moving average model, (3) the exponential smoothing model, and (4) the linear regression model.

The following references will be used in this chapter when discussing the variables associated with mathematics used is forecasting:

A = actual observation of the variable to be forecast

F = forecast of the variable

t = current time period. Time periods can be a measure of any time period (e.g., hour, day, month, year, decade). If time periods are being measured in months and the current month is April, then t = April.

$t - 1$ = one time period in the past. If time is being measured in months and t is April, then one time period in the past is March.

$t - 2$ = two time periods in the past. If time is being measured in months and t is April, then two time periods in the past is February.

$t + 1$ = one time period in the future. If time is being measured in months and t is April, then one time period in the future is May.

$t + 2$ = two time periods in the future. If time is being measured in months and t is April, then two time periods in the future is June.

Δ = the difference between two numbers. For example ΔAF would be actual observation of variable minus forecast.

Σ = sum of several numbers, normally in a column

n = the number of observations used in a calculation. The n for months in a year equal 12 and n for years in a decade are 10.

Moving Average Model.   The **moving average model** assumes that actual sales for some recent previous time periods are the best predictor of future sales. It also assumes that each time period taken in succession has an equal influence on the prediction of future sales. The procedure is to obtain the arithmetic average of actual sales for several past time periods. This average is then used as the forecast for the next time period. To obtain an arithmetic average, we sum actual sales for several time periods and divide this total by the number of time periods. Mathematically we use the following formula.

$$F_{t+1} = \frac{A_{[t-(n-1)]} + \ldots + A_{t-1} + A_t}{n}$$

For our example, we will use a three-month moving average. Actual sales for two years (1999 and 2000) are shown in Table 6-1. In our example we assume that actual sales during the previous three months will be a reasonable estimate of future sales in the following month. The procedure, therefore, is to add the previous three months' actual sales and divide by three to obtain the arithmetic average. To obtain a forecast for month 4 (Apr-99), we would add known sales for months 1 (Jan-99), 2 (Feb-99), and 3 (Mar-99) and divide the total by three, as shown here:

$$F_{t+1} = \frac{A_{t-2} + A_{t-1} + A_t}{3}$$

$$F_{April} \frac{(245 + 244 + 250)}{3} = 246.33$$

We then use this figure, 246.33, as our forecast for month 4 (Apr-99). When actual sales for month 4 (Apr-99) are received, we drop month 1 (Jan-99) and use months 2, 3, and 4 to predict sales for month 5 (May-99).

$$F_{t+1} = \frac{A_{t-2} + A_{t-1} + A_t}{3}$$

$$F_{May} = \frac{(244 + 250 + 260)}{3} = 251.33$$

Our forecast for month 5 (May-99) is therefore 251.33. This procedure is repeated for every month, as shown in Table 6-1. We can use any number of previous time periods we believe to be relevant; however, most models use three months due to quarterly sales patterns and quarterly reporting requirements. Table 6-1 illustrates moving average forecasts using three and four months.

Mean Absolute Deviation

Three of the times series models discussed in this chapter—moving average, weighted moving average, and exponential smoothing—are for short-range forecasts. They are useful for determining the forecast for the next time period. As business owners and managers, when we need to use a short-term forecast, we want to determine which of the three models to use for our particular situation. In addition we also want to know what weights to use for the weighted moving average model, and what value of alpha is most ap-

Table 6-1   Moving Average Model

$$\text{Formula for Moving Average: } F_{t+1} = \frac{A_{[t-(n-1)]} + \ldots + A_{t-1} + A_t}{n}$$

Moving Average = Forecast

Month and Year	Time Period	Actual Sales	3-Month Moving Average	Deviation = Actual − Forecast	Absolute Deviation $\Delta|A-F|$	4-Month Moving Average	Absolute Deviation $\Delta|A-F|$
	0						
Jan-99	1	245					
Feb-99	2	244					
Mar-99	3	250					
Apr-99	4	260	246.33	13.67	13.67		
May-99	5	265	251.33	13.67	13.67	249.75	15.25
Jun-99	6	260	258.33	1.67	1.67	254.75	5.25
Jul-99	7	255	261.67	−6.67	6.67	258.75	3.75
Aug-99	8	245	260.00	−15.00	15.00	260.00	15.00
Sep-99	9	240	253.33	−13.33	13.33	256.25	16.25
Oct-99	10	255	246.67	8.33	8.33	250.00	5.00
Nov-99	11	265	246.67	18.33	18.33	248.75	16.25
Dec-99	12	270	253.33	16.67	16.67	251.25	18.75
Jan-00	13	250	263.33	−13.33	13.33	257.50	7.50
Feb-00	14	250	261.67	−11.67	11.67	260.00	10.00
Mar-00	15	258	256.67	1.33	1.33	258.75	0.75
Apr-00	16	267	252.67	14.33	14.33	257.00	10.00
May-00	17	273	258.33	14.67	14.67	256.25	16.75
Jun-00	18	278	266.00	12.00	12.00	262.00	16.00
Jul-00	19	260	272.67	−12.67	12.67	269.00	9.00
Aug-00	20	256	270.33	−14.33	14.33	269.50	13.50
Sep-00	21	255	264.67	−9.67	9.67	266.75	11.75
Oct-00	22	270	257.00	13.00	13.00	262.25	7.75
Nov-00	23	275	260.33	14.67	14.67	260.25	14.75
Dec-00	24	283	266.67	16.33	16.33	264.00	19.00
Jan-01	25		276.00			270.75	
$\Sigma\Delta|A-F|$ =				62.00	255.33		232.25
n =				21	21		20
MAD =				2.95	12.16		11.61

propriate for the exponential smoothing model. We obviously want to select the model that comes closest to predicting our actual sales for our particular business. One method of determining the error of a forecasting model is mean absolute deviation.

Mean absolute deviation (MAD) is a tool used to measure the forecasting error of a model. MAD is simple to calculate and provides us with a method of determining which weights or alpha to choose for our model, and which model is most appropriate for predicting sales. For each time period for which we have calculated a forecast, we subtract the absolute value of forecast sales from actual sales. The absolute value of any number is positive and is represented mathematically by vertical lines drawn on either side

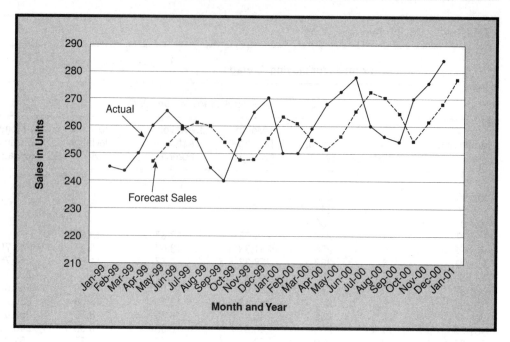

FIGURE 6-1
Plot of Actual Sales and Forecast Sales

of the number or formula. The formula for absolute deviation in our forecasting models is

$$\text{Absolute deviation} = |A - F|$$

Referring back to Table 6-1, we notice that the sixth column is absolute deviation $\Delta|A-F|$, where A equals actual sales and F equals forecast sales. If we go down the column to Aug-99, we notice that the difference (deviation) between our actual sales of 245 and our forecast sales of 260 is a negative 15; however, the absolute difference is 15 because the absolute value of any number is positive.

Mean absolute deviation (MAD) is the measure of the overall forecast error. It represents the average difference between our forecast and actual sales data. Figure 6-1 shows a plot of our actual sales and forecast sales using the data for a three-month moving average taken from Table 6-1.

Notice that our forecast is below actual sales for Apr-99 by 13.67 units, but above actual sales in Sep-99 by 13.33 units. If we try only to obtain the arithmetic average of this difference, then we would add the two numbers and divide by two to obtain 0.17 units as the average error of the forecast.

$$\text{Average arithmetic deviation} = \frac{13.67 + (-13.33)}{2} = \frac{0.34}{2} = 0.17$$

If, on the other hand, we use the average absolute deviation, then we would have

$$\text{Average absolute deviation} = \frac{|13.67 + 13.33|}{2} = \frac{27}{2} = 13.5$$

Therefore, just taking the average difference does not give us an accurate overall forecast error, for this we must use the absolute difference.

To obtain the mean absolute deviation, we sum the absolute difference and then obtain the average difference as shown in column six of Table 6-1. The mean absolute deviation is calculated by the formula:

$$\text{MAD} = \frac{\Sigma|\text{Actual sales} - \text{Forecast sales}|}{n}$$

$$\text{MAD} = \frac{\Sigma|A - F|}{n}$$

Using the formula for MAD in column 6 of Table 6-1, we have a sum of the absolute differences of 255.33; we then divide by the total number of differences which is 21 and obtain a mean absolute deviation of 12.16 units. Table 6-1 also shows the calculation of MAD for our four-month moving average forecast of 11.61 units. The inaccuracy of the arithmetic average is shown in a separate column, 2.95 versus 12.16 for MAD.

Weighted Moving Average Model. What if we believe that previous-period actual sales are not equal in their influence on the next periods' sales? We can then choose a weighted moving average model. The **weighted moving average model** assumes that the closest time period is a more accurate predictor of future sales than previous time periods, although previous time periods have some influence on future sales. The forecaster using this model will assign weights to the time periods based on personal judgment. The sum of the weights normally equals one. When using one as the sum of the weights, we have a simple formula because the denominator in the following equation equals one. If the forecaster does not want to use a sum of one, then we sum the weights and use this sum as the denominator in our equation. The value of each weight is based on how much of an influence the forecaster believes the corresponding time period has on overall sales. The formula for this method, using three months, is as follows:

$$F_{t+1} = \frac{(W_1)(A_{t-2}) + (W_2)(A_{t-1}) + (W_3)(A_t)}{\Sigma W}$$

Forecast for the next time period = Weight assigned to time period 1 × Actual sales for month 1 + Weight assigned to time period 2 × Actual sales for time period 2 + Weight assigned to time period 3 × Actual sales for time period 3 ÷ Sum of the weights. If the sum of the weights equals one, then there is no need to divide because any number divided by one is the number (e.g., 25 ÷ 1 = 25). For our example we use the sales data in Table 6-2 and first assign weights of 0.1, 0.3, and 0.6. Because the sum of the weights equals one (.01 + 0.3 + 0.6 = 1), we do not have to divide. We then plug values into our formula as follows: Forecast for Apr-99 = (0.1)(245) + (0.3)(244) + (0.6)(250) = 247.70.

$$F_{t+1} = (W_1)(A_{t-2}) + (W_2)(A_{t-1}) + (W_3)(A_t)$$
$$F_{Apr-99} = (0.1)(245) + (0.3)(244) + (0.6)(250)$$
$$F_{Apr-99} = 247.70$$

When actual sales are received for April (260), we drop the January sales figure and use actual sales for February, March, and April to obtain our forecast for May. Hence, the forecast for May-99 = (0.1)(244) + (0.3)(250) + (0.6)(260) = 255.40.

We can assign weights of any values provided that we use the sum of the weights in the denominator. In Table 6-2 we also illustrate use of the weighted moving average model using weights of 0.25, 0.35, and 0.40 and weights of 4, 5, and 8. Also, as with the moving average model, we can use any number of time periods. Let us work one more example and obtain the forecast for May 2000 using weights of 4, 5, and 8 and actual sales for February of 250, March of 258, and April of 267. Plugging these values into the following formula, we obtain a forecast of 260.35.

$$F_{t+1} = \frac{(W_1)(A_{t-2}) + (W_2)(A_{t-1}) + (W_3)(A_t)}{\Sigma W}$$
$$F_{May-00} = \frac{(4)(250) + (5)(258) + (8)(267)}{4 + 5 + 8}$$
$$F_{May-00} = \frac{(1,000) + (1,290) + (2,136)}{17} = \frac{4,426}{17}$$
$$F_{May-00} = 260.35$$

After calculating our forecasts as shown in Table 6-2, we would also calculate MAD to determine which series of weights would be most appropriate for our company. If we chose a weighted average model for our forecast, we would use weights of 0.1, 0.3, and 0.6 to do our forecasting as MAD of 10.42 is the lowest. These weights 0.1, 0.3, and 0.6 provide us with the smallest overall forecasting error.

Exponential Smoothing Model.   The **exponential smoothing model** uses a smoothing constant, alpha (α), as an adjustment in deter-

Table 6-2   Weighted Moving Average Model

Formula for weighted moving average: $F_{t+1} = \dfrac{(W_1)(A_{t-2}) + (W_2)(A_{t-1}) + (W_3)(A_t)}{\Sigma W}$

Month	Time Period	Actual Sales	$W_1=0.1$ $W_2=0.3$ $W_3=0.6$	Δ|A−F|	$W_1=0.25$ $W_2=0.35$ $W_3=0.40$	Δ|A−F|	$W_1=4$ $W_2=5$ $W_3=8$	Δ|A−F|
	0							
Jan-99	1	245						
Feb-99	2	244						
Mar-99	3	250						
Apr-99	4	260	247.70	12.30	246.65	13.35	247.06	12.94
May-99	5	265	255.40	9.60	252.50	12.50	253.29	11.71
Jun-99	6	260	262.00	2.00	259.50	0.50	260.00	0.00
Jul-99	7	255	261.50	6.50	261.75	6.75	261.47	6.47
Aug-99	8	245	257.50	12.50	259.25	14.25	258.82	13.82
Sep-99	9	240	249.50	9.50	252.25	12.25	251.47	11.47
Oct-99	10	255	243.00	12.00	245.50	9.50	245.00	10.00
Nov-99	11	265	249.50	15.50	247.25	17.75	248.24	16.76
Dec-99	12	270	259.50	10.50	255.25	14.75	256.18	13.82
Jan-00	13	250	267.00	17.00	264.50	14.50	265.00	15.00
Feb-00	14	250	257.50	7.50	260.75	10.75	259.41	9.41
Mar-00	15	258	252.00	6.00	255.00	3.00	254.71	3.29
Apr-00	16	267	254.80	12.20	253.20	13.80	253.76	13.24
May-00	17	273	262.60	10.40	259.60	13.40	260.35	12.65
Jun-00	18	278	269.70	8.30	267.15	10.85	267.71	10.29
Jul-00	19	260	275.40	15.40	273.50	13.50	273.94	13.94
Aug-00	20	256	266.70	10.70	269.55	13.55	268.35	12.35
Sep-00	21	255	259.40	4.40	262.90	7.90	262.35	7.35
Oct-00	22	270	255.80	14.20	256.60	13.40	256.47	13.53
Nov-00	23	275	264.10	10.90	261.25	13.75	262.29	12.71
Dec-00	24	283	271.50	11.50	268.25	14.75	268.82	14.18
Jan-01	25		279.30		276.95		277.59	
$\Sigma\Delta$|A−F| =				218.90		244.75		234.94
n =				21.00		21.00		21.00
MAD =				10.42		11.65		11.19

mining the forecast. A **smoothing constant** is a value assigned by the forecaster to adjust the forecast based on the forecaster's assumption of the relationship between sales in one time period and sales in the next time period. Alpha can have any value between 0 and 1; however, alpha is normally 0.1, 0.2, or 0.3. The higher the value of alpha, the greater the emphasis given to sales for the current time period. The lower the value of alpha, the greater the emphasis given to the smoothed forecast for the current time period. A higher value of alpha is assigned when the forecaster believes that current sales are more predictive of future sales. Conversely, a lower alpha will be chosen when the forecaster believes that the smoothed forecast is more predictive of future sales. With exponential smoothing we must begin with an assumed rather than an actual forecast. (Most models use actual sales in the first period of observation as the assumed forecast.)

Table 6-3　Exponential Smoothing Model

			With $\alpha = 0.1$		With $\alpha = 0.2$		With $\alpha = 0.25$	
Month and Year	Time Period	Actual Sales	Forecast	$\Delta\lvert A-F\rvert$	Forecast	$\Delta\lvert A-F\rvert$	Forecast	$\Delta\lvert A-F\rvert$
	0							
Jan-99	1	245						
Feb-99	2	244	245.00		245.00		245.00	
Mar-99	3	250	244.90	5.10	244.80	5.20	244.75	5.25
Apr-99	4	260	245.41	14.59	245.84	14.16	246.06	13.94
May-99	5	265	246.87	18.13	248.67	16.33	249.55	15.45
Jun-99	6	260	248.68	11.32	251.94	8.06	253.41	6.59
Jul-99	7	255	249.81	5.19	253.55	1.45	255.06	0.06
Aug-99	8	245	250.33	5.33	253.84	8.84	255.04	10.04
Sep-99	9	240	249.80	9.80	252.07	12.07	252.53	12.53
Oct-99	10	255	248.82	6.18	249.66	5.34	249.40	5.60
Nov-99	11	265	249.44	15.56	250.73	14.27	250.80	14.20
Dec-99	12	270	250.99	19.01	253.58	16.42	254.35	15.65
Jan-00	13	250	252.89	2.89	256.86	6.86	258.26	8.26
Feb-00	14	250	252.60	2.60	255.49	5.49	256.20	6.20
Mar-00	15	258	252.34	5.66	254.39	3.61	254.65	3.35
Apr-00	16	267	252.91	14.09	255.11	11.89	255.49	11.51
May-00	17	273	254.32	18.68	257.49	15.51	258.36	14.64
Jun-00	18	278	256.19	21.81	260.59	17.41	262.02	15.98
Jul-00	19	260	258.37	1.63	264.07	4.07	266.02	6.02
Aug-00	20	256	258.53	2.53	263.26	7.26	264.51	8.51
Sep-00	21	255	258.28	3.28	261.81	6.81	262.38	7.38
Oct-00	22	270	257.95	12.05	260.45	9.55	260.54	9.46
Nov-00	23	275	259.16	15.84	262.36	12.64	262.90	12.10
Dec-00	24	283	260.74	22.26	264.89	18.11	265.93	17.07
Jan-01	25		262.97		268.51		270.20	
$\Sigma\Delta\lvert A-F\rvert =$				233.54		221.36		219.80
$n =$				22.00		22.00		22.00
MAD $=$				10.62		10.06		9.99

Formulas for exponential smoothing model:
$$F_{t+1} = \alpha(A_t) + (1 - \alpha)(F_t)$$
$$F_{t+1} = (F_t) + \alpha(A_t - F_t)$$

Table 6-3 gives an example of the exponential smoothing model, applied to our two years' worth of sales data. The formula used in Table 6-3 is either

$$F_{t+1} = \alpha(A_t) + (1 - \alpha)(F_t)$$

or, simplified

$$F_{t+1} = (F_t) + \alpha(A_t - F_t)$$

The authors have seen this formula presented both ways in various texts. The formula that you use is one of preference.

The following symbols are used in the exponential smoothing formula:

F_{t+1} = the smoothed forecast for the next time period
Alpha (α) = the smoothing constant
A_t = actual sales for the current time period
F_t = the smoothed forecast for the current time period

We will use actual sales for January 1999 as the assumed smoothed forecast for February 1999 to begin our calculations. Using an alpha of 0.1 (less weight given to actual sales, more weight given to smoothed forecast), we plug the data into our formula to obtain the forecast for period 3, or Mar-99, as follows:

$$F_{t+1} = \alpha(A_t) + (1 - \alpha)(F_t)$$
$$F_{\text{Mar-99}} = (0.1)(244) + (1 - 0.1)(245) = 24.4 + (0.9)(245)$$
$$= 24.4 + 220.5$$
$$F_{\text{Mar-99}} = 244.90$$

Let us do one more example using the other formula. We want to obtain a forecast for January 2001. Using Table 6-3 and an alpha of 0.25, we obtain the actual sales for Dec-00 of 283 and the forecast for Dec-00 of 265.93. Substituting in our formula, we obtain a forecast of 270.20 for Jan-01. The procedure is as follows:

$$F_{t+1} = (F_t) + \alpha(A_t - F_t)$$
$$F_{\text{Jan-01}} = (265.93) + (0.25)(283 - 265.93)$$
$$= (265.93) + (0.25)(17.07)$$
$$F_{\text{Jan-01}} = 270.20$$

We show the results of the exponential smoothing forecast for months 3 through 25 in Table 6-3 for alphas of 0.1, 0.2, and 0.25.

After calculating our exponential smoothing forecasts as shown in Table 6-3, we also would calculate MAD to determine which value of alpha would be most appropriate for our company. If we chose an exponential smoothing model for our forecast, we would use an alpha of 0.25 as it produces a MAD of 9.99 units, which is the lowest.

Selecting the Model.   If we are going to use one of the three models (moving average, weighted moving average, or exponential smoothing) for the business demonstrated in this chapter, we would compare MAD in Tables 6-1, 6-2, and 6-3. We would use an exponential smoothing model with an alpha of 0.25 for this business, because a MAD of 9.99 is the smallest.

Linear Regression Model.   MAD can be used for short-term forecasts such as those obtained with moving average, weighted moving average, and exponential smoothing models. In business, however, we must also forecast for the intermediate and long term. For intermediate and long-term forecasts, the model most often used is simple linear regression. **Linear regression** does not use MAD, but rather a statistical method known as least squared regression. The statistical formulas are beyond the scope of this text.

To develop a regression model, we analyze the actual sales data that we have used for Tables 6-1, 6-2, and 6-3. The sales data show certain variations. The four areas of variation present in data that are gathered over time are as follows:

1. **Seasonal variation is caused by the predictable shopping habits of our customers, or by annual climatic conditions.** Seasonal variation for retail establishments may be expressed on a weekly basis. For a restaurant, Monday is normally the slowest day of the week. Sales on Friday and Saturday are normally the best. For general retail sales, the fourth quarter of each calendar year shows the strongest sales, because of the Christmas shopping season.

2. **Trend variation is caused by growth or decline in demand for our product or service over time.** The change in sales over time is represented by a trend line. This straight line is the regression line. It is calculated by using linear regression. For industries that have relatively new products, this trend line may show annual growth of 20 to 50 percent. For mature products, the trend line may increase with population growth. For some products that are being replaced by newer ones, the trend line might be negative or downward sloping.

3. **Cyclical variation is caused by general economic factors that affect our industry.** For most products and services, when the economy expands, sales also grow. When we enter a recession, sales normally decline.

4. **Noise is random variation in our data that is not explained by the preceding factors.** The value of noise is calculated in statistical models that are beyond the scope of this text. As an example of noise, let us say that a business experienced weekly sales of $50,000, $52,000, $54,000, $25,000, and $56,000 during a five-week period. The economy has been good and sales, in general, have shown consistent growth. However, in week 4 of our example, sales were only $25,000. We check historical records, question others in the same business, and do everything else in our power to try to determine why sales were only $25,000 in this particular week. We conclude that there is no logical explanation. This variation, then, would be labeled as noise or random variation. It is unexplained.

Linear regression is used to determine two factors: the slope of the regression line and the intercept of the regression line. As noted, the regression line is our trend line. The basic formula for the regression line as displayed in statistical texts is $y = a + bx$. This formula is similar to that for a straight line used in many math text books, $y = mx + b$. Following are definitions of the variables used in the regression formula:

- y is the dependent variable. A **dependent variable** is one that relies on other variables for its value. The value of y is normally observed, but the value observed depends on the other variables in our equation.
- x is the independent variable. An **independent variable** is one that does not depend on other variables for its value. In forecasting models, x is often a time period.
- b is the slope of the regression line. **Slope** is defined as rise over run. This is the change in y divided by the change in x, or the change in the dependent variable divided by the change in the independent variable. For our example problem it is the change in sales over the change in time. Algebraically it is expressed as

$$\text{slope} = \frac{\Delta y}{\Delta x} = \frac{y_2 - y_1}{x_2 - x_1}$$

When slope is positive, the resulting regression line moves up and to the right. When slope is negative, the resulting regression line moves down and to the right.

- a is the y-intercept. The y-intercept is the value of y when x equals zero.

The easiest method of introducing the regression function is to show a scatter diagram of basic sales data (see Figure 6-2). On a graph, the vertical y-axis represents sales, and the horizontal x-axis represents time. A point has been plotted showing the sales value for each time period. In analyzing the diagram, we can see that sales appear to be seasonal. Sales in the first quarter of each year are low, and then increase in the second quarter, decline in the third quarter, and show a substantial increase in the fourth quarter. We also see that there is an increase in sales from one year to the next. If we could draw a straight line through the points in this diagram, we would have the trend line. Because we must produce a forecast covering several years into the future, we must determine the value of the trend line, which is accomplished with the regression formula.

The mathematical steps for calculating regression are time consuming, but the actual calculations are relatively easy. If you have a computer with a spreadsheet program such as Lotus 123 or Microsoft Excel, it will take you very little time to calculate the values of the intercept and slope. We will discuss the mathematical calculation of the regression line as shown in Table 6-4.

FIGURE 6-2
Scatter Diagram

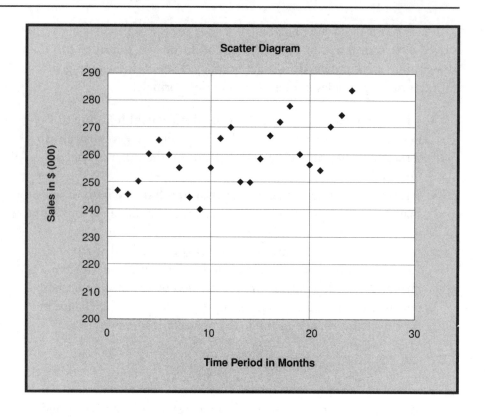

The formulas for the intercept (*a*) and slope (*b*) are given in Table 6-4. You must first construct columns representing the variables in the formulas. We already have the time periods (*x*) and sales (*y*), from our basic data in Table 6-1. We therefore need two additional columns to calculate the intercept and slope. We construct one column for x^2 and another column for the product of *x* and *y*. We then perform the required calculations. After accomplishing this, we sum (Σ) each column to arrive at the total. We then plug the required numbers back into our formula, as shown in Table 6-4. The value of the y–intercept (*a*) is calculated as 246.8841, which is the value of *y* when *x* equals zero. The slope is calculated as 1.0126, which means that for every increase of one in the value of *x*, *y* will increase in value by 1.0126. However, because *y* is sales in thousands of dollars, sales will increase by $1,012.60 each month.

If you have access to a computer with Microsoft Excel, you can simply use a function wizard to place the values of *x* and *y* into the function for slope. When you hit the return key, the value of the slope will be returned as 1.0126. Do the same thing for intercept, and the value of 246.8841 will

Table 6-4 Calculation of the Regression Line

Month	Time Period (x)	Actual Sales (y)	x^2	xy
JAN YR 1	1	245	1	245
FEB	2	244	4	488
MAR	3	250	9	750
APR	4	260	16	1040
MAY	5	265	25	1325
JUN	6	260	36	1560
JUL	7	255	49	1785
AUG	8	245	64	1960
SEP	9	240	81	2160
OCT	10	255	100	2550
NOV	11	265	121	2915
DEC	12	270	144	3240
JAN YR 2	13	250	169	3250
FEB	14	250	196	3500
MAR	15	258	225	3870
APR	16	267	256	4272
MAY	17	273	289	4641
JUN	18	278	324	5004
JUL	19	260	361	4940
AUG	20	256	400	5120
SEP	21	255	441	5355
OCT	22	270	484	5940
NOV	23	275	529	6325
DEC	24	283	576	6792
SUMS (Σ)	300	6,229	4,900	79,027

Using the formulas below, we substitute from Table 6-3 above and obtain an intercept (a) of 246.8841 and a slope (b) of 1.0126

$$y = a + bx$$

$$a = \frac{\Sigma x^2 \Sigma y - \Sigma x \Sigma xy}{n \Sigma x^2 - (\Sigma x)^2} = \frac{(4,900)(6,229) - (300)(79,027)}{(24)(4,900) - (300)^2} = \frac{(30,522,100) - (23,708,100)}{(117,600) - (90,000)} = \frac{6,814,000}{27,600} = 246.8841$$

$$b = \frac{n \Sigma xy - \Sigma x \Sigma y}{n \Sigma x^2 - (\Sigma x)^2} = \frac{(24)(79,027) - (300)(6,229)}{(24)(4,900) - (300)^2} = \frac{1,896,648 - 1,868,700}{117,600 - 90,000} = \frac{27,948}{27,600} = 1.0126$$

be returned. This process takes approximately 30 seconds with a spreadsheet program. Once the slope and intercept are derived, we can plot the regression line for any future time periods. The regression line eliminates the seasonal and noise variation in our data. It assumes a linear relationship between the value of y and x as shown in Figure 6-3.

Using the data in Table 6-5, we have determined the value of the regression line for 36 time periods and plotted this data in Figure 6-3. Table 6-5 demonstrates how we take the data for slope and intercept and calculate the regression (trend) line for future time periods.

The regression forecast column in Table 6-5 provides the value of the regression line for time periods 1 through 36. This represents a regression

FIGURE 6-3
Sales Chart with
Regression Line

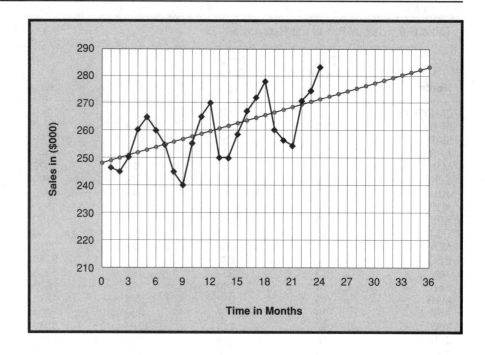

forecast for y for these time periods. The actual calculation is performed mathematically by plugging the values of the slope and intercept into our regression formula as follows:

$$y = a + bx = 246.8841 + (1.0126)(x)$$

For $x = 0$,

$$y = 246.8841 + (1.0126)(0) = 246.8841$$

For $x = 1$,

$$y = 246.8841 + (1.0126)(1) = 247.8967$$

For $x = 36$,

$$y = 246.8841 + (1.0126)(36) = 283.3377$$

Here we have substituted values of 0, 1, and 36 for x. We can, in the same way, obtain a value of y for any time frame we choose.

We also can use the regression line and our current data to obtain a forecast of future sales that includes seasonal data. To obtain the seasonal ratio, we divide actual sales by the regression forecast for the time period. Column 5 in Table 6-5 was calculated using this seasonal ratio formula. The seasonal ratio for Jan-99, equals 245/247.8967, which equals 0.9883, which we rounded to 0.988. We calculated the seasonal ratio for each period for which we have actual sales data.

Table 6-5 Forecast of Sales, Including Seasonal Adjustment

$y = a + bx$
$a = 246.8841$
$b = 1.0126$

Month	Time x	Actual Sales (A) Jan-99 - Dec-00	Regression Forecast (F) y = a + bx	Seasonal Ratio (A)/(F)	Seasonal Forecast of Sales
	0		246.88		
Jan-99	1	245	247.90	0.988	245
Feb-99	2	244	248.91	0.980	244
Mar-99	3	250	249.92	1.000	250
Apr-99	4	260	250.93	1.036	260
May-99	5	265	251.95	1.052	265
Jun-99	6	260	252.96	1.028	260
Jul-99	7	255	253.97	1.004	255
Aug-99	8	245	254.98	0.961	245
Sep-99	9	240	256.00	0.938	240
Oct-99	10	255	257.01	0.992	255
Nov-99	11	265	258.02	1.027	265
Dec-99	12	270	259.04	1.042	270
Jan-00	13	250	260.05	0.961	250
Feb-00	14	250	261.06	0.958	250
Mar-00	15	258	262.07	0.984	258
Apr-00	16	267	263.09	1.015	267
May-00	17	273	264.10	1.034	273
Jun-00	18	278	265.11	1.049	278
Jul-00	19	260	266.12	0.977	260
Aug-00	20	256	267.14	0.958	256
Sep-00	21	255	268.15	0.951	255
Oct-00	22	270	269.16	1.003	270
Nov-00	23	275	270.17	1.018	275
Dec-00	24	283	271.19	1.044	283
Jan-01	25		272.20	0.975	265
Feb-01	26		273.21	0.969	265
Mar-01	27		274.22	0.992	272
Apr-01	28		275.24	1.026	282
May-01	29		276.25	1.043	288
Jun-01	30		277.26	1.038	288
Jul-01	31		278.27	0.991	276
Aug-01	32		279.29	0.960	268
Sep-01	33		280.30	0.944	265
Oct-01	34		281.31	0.998	281
Nov-01	35		282.33	1.022	289
Dec-01	36		283.34	1.043	296

To obtain average seasonal ratios, we calculate the average seasonal ratio for each similar time period. For example, we add the seasonal ratio for Jan-99, year 1, and Jan-00, year 2, and divide by two [(0.988 + 0.961)/2]. We can then obtain an average seasonal ratio for Jan-01, year 3 of 0.975. We multiply our average seasonal ratio for Jan-01 of 0.975 by the regression forecast for Jan-01, year 3, of 272.20 and obtain a seasonal sales forecast for

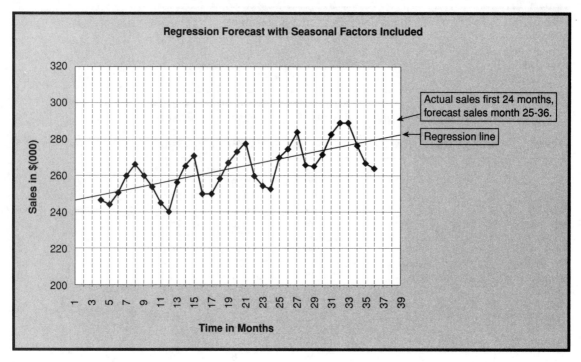

FIGURE 6-4
Three-Year Regression and Seasonal Forecast

Jan-01, year 3 of 265. The results of these calculations are shown in the seasonal forecast of sales column 6 of Table 6-5, and graphically in Figure 6-4.

Often a trend can be computed using simple sales data and basic mathematics. The trend in business is normally expressed as a percentage increase or decrease in sales during a time period, normally one year. Once we determine this trend, we can apply it to a sales forecast to determine future sales. For example, if, for a given business, total sales in year 1 were $320,000 and sales in year 2 were $352,000, then the sales growth was 10 percent. To determine this, we would use the same formula as in analyzing financial statements using horizontal analysis [i.e., (New − Old) ÷ Old]. For this example, it would be $352,000 minus $320,000, divided by $320,000, or $32,000/$320,000, which is 0.1, or 10 percent. If our assumption is that the business will continue to grow at a rate of 10 percent per year, then our forecast of sales for year 3 would be $387,200. This would be computed by taking 10 percent of year 2 sales and adding it to year 2 sales. We also could compute this by multiplying current-year sales by 1.10. The formula is

$$F_{t+1} = F_t(1 + g)$$

where F_{t+1} is the sales forecast for time period t plus one unit of time, F_t is actual sales during time period t, and g is the growth rate expressed as a percentage.

Causal Models

Causal models also are known as external or exogenous models. Causal models take into account variables in the general economy that affect the revenue obtained by a company. Causal models can be simple or quite complex. Most require multiple regression analysis, which is normally beyond the scope of a small business manager, yet the manager should be aware of the effect these variables have on business. We can often include causal modeling as part of our forecasting technique. For example, if we sell home appliances to building contractors, then building permits allow us to predict sales growth or decline several months into the future. Also, consider that most businesses have their short- and long-term loans tied to the prime lending rate; therefore, a change in this interest rate will directly impact how much interest we will pay on future and current loans.

The forecast drives our business planning. Good plans will answer the questions of what, who, where, when, and how: What is to be done (mission and goals)? Who will do it? Where will they do it? When will they do it (specific goal)? How will it be done (resource allocation and use of resources)? The basic sales forecast also provides us with one very important number: projected sales in dollars. This dollar figure is the necessary beginning point for developing pro forma financial statements.

PRO FORMA FINANCIAL STATEMENTS

A **pro forma financial statement** is a projected statement based on the forecast.

As our business increases its revenue base, increased sales create the need for additional assets. For example (see Hannah's Donut Shop case study, Appendix D), when Hannah's Donut Shop increased its number of wholesale customers, it had to purchase an additional delivery truck. Accounts receivable also increased because new wholesale customers were in fact credit customers. Although Hannah extended credit to these customers, she experienced a direct buildup in fixed assets (delivery truck) and an indirect buildup in current assets in two areas: the increase in accounts receivable because of the increase in credit customers, and an increase in raw materials inventory because Hannah had to purchase additional donut mixes to make more donuts. Therefore, Hannah recognized the need for financial planning in her business.

To best address such concerns, a business should begin with a preparation of estimated financial statements for the future. This process is call **pro forma financial analysis.** Its goal is to predict individual financial variables and integrate each into the preparation of several pro forma financial

Table 6-6   Pro Forma Income Statement

Income Statements for Time Periods Indicated

	Actual Sales for 1999	Pro Forma Sales for 2000
Sales	$100,000	$150,000
COG	60,000	90,000
Gross Profit	$ 40,000	$ 60,000
Operating Expenses		
Rent	12,000	12,000
Utilities	2,000	2,500
Insurance	1,500	2,000
Equipment	4,500	8,500
Total Operating Expenses	$ 20,000	$ 25,000
Operating Profit	$ 20,000	$ 35,000
Interest Expense	5,000	5,000
Net Profit	$ 15,000	$ 30,000

statements. We of course realize that pro forma analysis is based on the sales forecast. Because total sales are the top line on an income statement, we begin our pro forma analysis by developing the pro forma income statement. This is used to determine the expected future profit of our firm.

PRO FORMA INCOME STATEMENT

Most businesses develop a pro forma income statement by using information from a current statement. For example, if we project an increase in sales, then cost of goods sold also will increase. Table 6-6 shows a pro forma income statement for a hypothetical company whose forecast indicated that sales would increase by 50 percent from 1999 to 2000. Cost of goods sold can be expected to be the same percentage of sales year after year. Because COGS was 60 percent of sales in 1999, COGS for 2000 is expected to be 60 percent of $150,000, or $90,000. Therefore, gross profit will increase by 50 percent, to $60,000. One factor to remember is that operating expenses reflect some fixed costs that will not increase with increased sales; however, other operating expenses will increase with increased sales. Mortgage and lease payments will not normally increase with sales. In our case study, Hannah had to purchase a new truck to support the increase in sales; hence, her fixed bank payments increased. Operating expenses must be separated into two categories: those that we know will not increase with sales, and those that will increase by some amount as sales increase. Since many operating expenses have a specific supplier or vendor, we can often check with them to forecast changes in these fixed expenses. For example, we can call our insurance agent and check rate changes for utility companies.

When sales increase, we often have to increase our fixed assets by the purchase of additional equipment and machinery. This purchase of assets is frequently financed by long-term debt. Although the increase in monthly bank payments will increase our operating expenses, the percentage increase in these expenses will normally not be as great as percentage increases in sales. The result is that our operating income will often increase by a margin that is greater than our increase in sales. In our pro forma income statement example (Table 6-6), sales increase by 50 percent, but operating profit increases from $20,000 to $35,000, which reflects a 75 percent increase. The interest payments on our loans may increase, depending on what additional assets are acquired during the year and how we choose to finance them. In any event, if we plan properly, our future net profit also should increase. In most cases, net profit should increase at a rate that exceeds the rate of increase in sales, because many of our operating expenses do not increase.

The pro forma income statement shown in Table 6-6 is for a business that has an historical record. For a start-up business, the pro forma income statement is more difficult to generate. (Start-up business costs will be discussed in more detail at the end of this chapter.) For the start-up business, the owner must estimate sales using one or more of the qualitative methods discussed at the beginning of this chapter. Once the owner has an estimate of sales, then COGS should be a percentage based on industry standards. If the owner cannot obtain goods at or below this industry standard, chances are that he or she will not be able to generate a profit. All operating expense figures must be inserted based on the owner's obtaining the necessary data. Once a location is determined, the owner will have actual lease or mortgage payment amounts. The owner must then obtain an estimate of utility costs from the utility companies for the location selected. Insurance premiums also will, in most cases, be based on the facility selected. Marketing expenses will have to be estimated. Each area of the income statement will have to be completed based on estimates of operating expenses, because historical records do not exist. Once the pro forma income statement is developed, the owner should determine if the operating expenses are in line with industry averages. It is only then that the owner can determine if the new venture will be profitable.

PRO FORMA CASH BUDGET

Now that we have a pro forma income statement, we must look at how the categories on the income statement affect our pro forma balance sheet. When we initially discussed financial statements, we indicated that an income statement is not a cash flow statement. The next step, then, is to determine cash flow requirements by developing a pro forma cash budget. Once this budget is developed, we can construct a pro forma balance sheet.

A **pro forma cash budget** projects future receipts and expenditures and determines how much financing is needed on a monthly basis to correct any shortfalls in cash flow. It is important to note that a positive change (increase) in sales may have a negative impact on the business if financial planning does not occur. For example, when Hannah experienced increased donut sales, she was faced with a complicated chain of results. The increased sales of wholesale donuts required the purchase of an additional delivery truck. Where does one get the money to support such additional assets? The delivery truck could be paid for in cash or financed through a financial institution. In addition, we must note that an increase in sales often results in the granting of additional credit; and credit sales are not collected immediately. Hannah had to make monthly payments to the bank for the delivery truck, and to her vendors for the donut mixes. Many of the accounts receivable customers paid monthly; however, the donut vendor delivered weekly and wanted to be paid within two weeks of delivery (net 15 days). Such a situation initially results in a negative cash flow, but the monthly income statement indicates a profit. This creates a discrepancy between the amount of sales stated on the income statement and the actual amount of cash available to pay bills. If a business has $100,000 in sales, and they are all on credit, then the business may have a serious cash flow problem. It is for this reason that we must generate a pro forma cash budget on a monthly basis.

The method used is to go back to our seasonal forecast for the individual months to get the monthly sales figure for our cash budget. We next turn to our historical records. For our sample company, an analysis of the historical records indicates that 30 percent of current-month sales are collected in cash. The remaining 70 percent are accounts receivable. We also find that 60 percent of the accounts receivable will be collected in the month following the sale. The remaining 40 percent will be collected in the second month following the sale. We show this information in Table 6-7. We then use this information to determine the total receipts for each month of our projected year.

Additionally, cash payments are arrived at for each month by taking into account inventory purchases, labor costs, operating expenses, and interest payments. Finally, a net cash flow figure for each month is derived, and subsequently a cash budget is constructed. We look at each month's net cash flow and determine those months for which we have a shortfall. We should set up a line of credit with a bank or lender so that we have access to required capital for those months. This access to capital also may include the entrepreneur's savings.

Under December on our pro forma cash budget are two figures that will be transferred to our pro forma balance sheet: accounts receivable and cash. Accounts receivable are $14,000; cash on hand is $3,339. Accounts payable are 60 percent of December's sales forecast, or ($20,000 × 0.60) =

Table 6-7 Pro Forma Cash Budget

Monthly Cash Receipts					
	August	*September*	*October*	*November*	*December*
Sales	$ 10,000	$ 15,000	$ 18,000	$ 22,000	$ 20,000
Current Month Collection at 30% of Sales	3,000	4,500	5,400	6,600	6,000
Outstanding Current Month Accounts Receivable (AR)	7,000	10,500	12,600	15,400	14,000
60% of AR Collected Month Following Sale		4,200	6,300	7,560	9,240
40% of AR Collected in 2nd Month Following Sale			2,800	4,200	5,040
Total Receipts			$ 14,500	$ 18,360	$ 20,280

Monthly Cash Payments					
Accounts Payable (AP), Previous Month			$ 9,000	$ 10,800	$ 13,200
Labor Costs			3,600	4,400	4,000
Operating Expenses			1,667	1,667	1,667
Interest Payments			600	600	600
Total Payments			$ 14,867	$ 17,467	$ 19,467

Monthly Cash Budget					
Total Receipts			$ 14,500	$ 18,360	$ 20,280
Total Payments			14,867	17,467	19,467
Net Cash Flow			$ (367)	$ 893	$ 813

Cash Budget With Borrowing and Repayment					
Net Cash Flow			$ (367)	$ 893	$ 813
Beginning Cash Balance			2,000	2,000	2,526
Total Cash Balance			1,633	2,893	3,339
Monthly Loan or Repayment			367	(367)	0
Cumulative Loan Balance			367	0	0
Ending Cash Balance			$ 2,000	$ 2,526	$ 3,339

Note: Shaded rows, Sales and Outstanding Current Month Accounts Receivable, do not represent cash flow.

$12,000. We confirm this with December's accounts payable, which is November's forecast times 60 percent or ($22,000 × 0.60) = $13,200. We are now ready to generate our pro forma balance sheet.

PRO FORMA BALANCE SHEET

The **pro forma balance sheet** is a projected balance sheet for a future time period. The increase in sales will cause a buildup in assets and will be reflected in the pro forma balance sheet. Looking at Table 6-8, we see that cash is projected to increase from $2,000 to $3,339. At the same time, we expect to experience an accounts receivable and inventory buildup as a result of increased sales. As of December 2000, accounts receivable and inventory are expected to be $14,000 and $27,500, respectively.

Table 6-8   Pro Forma Balance Sheet

Balance Sheets for Year Ending December 31

	Actual for 1999	**Pro Forma for 2000**
Current Assets		
Cash	$ 2,000	$ 3,339
Accounts Receivable	10,000	14,000
Inventory	15,000	27,500
Total Current Assets	$27,000	$44,839
Fixed Assets		
Net Machinery & Equipment	30,000	40,000
Total Assets	$57,000	$84,839
Liabilities and Owner's Equity		
Current Liabilities		
Accounts Payable	$10,000	$12,000
Notes Payable	9,000	—
Total Current Liabilities	$19,000	$12,000
Long-Term Liabilities		
Long-Term Loan	$30,000	$55,000
Total Liabilities	$49,000	$67,000
Owner's Equity	8,000	17,839
Total Liabilities & Owner's Equity	$57,000	$84,839

Equipment is expected to increase to $40,000. When sales increase substantially, we have to determine if additional machinery and equipment are required to support this increase in sales. The purchase of this additional equipment is shown on our pro forma balance sheet as an increase in fixed assets. As we can see in Table 6-8, total assets increase from $57,000 in 1999 to a projected $84,839 for 2000. This additional $27,839 in assets must be financed by increasing liabilities, equity, or both.

With the increased sales, our company is expected to generate enough cash to completely pay off $9,000 of notes payable. Accounts payable, on the other hand, increase from $10,000 to $12,000. This is a result of the additional inventory that we expect to purchase each month to support the additional sales. Overall, total assets increase by $27,839 ($84,839 pro forma for 2000 minus $57,000 actual for 1999). This buildup in assets is to be financed by an additional $18,000 in total liabilities ($67,000 pro forma for 2000 minus $49,000 actual for 1999) and $9,839 ($17,839 pro forma for 2000 minus $8,000 actual for 1999) in additional owner's equity. Going back to the pro forma income statement (Table 6-6), we see that net profit increases to $30,000. The difference between the $30,000 and the $9,839 increase in owner's equity is what the owner expects to take out of the business as profit.

A business owner has several choices in combinations of debt and equity financing. In this example, if net profit decreased, then the owner would be forced to seek more debt financing. Depending on the economic situation, the owner would have to choose between short-term and long-term financing, or a combination of both. Long-term financing is less risky, but costs more; short-term financing is more aggressive, but costs less. Be aware that most lending institutions will only finance commercial buildings and equipment at 70 percent of market value. Inventory and accounts receivable also can be used as collateral for financing; however, the lending institution will base its loan on the type of inventory that your firm carries. If you are in a business with perishable inventory such as fresh vegetables, you cannot expect to be able to use inventory to obtain a loan. If your inventory is not perishable such as automobiles, you can expect to receive higher value. You must check with your lending institution to determine the percentage of inventory value that can be financed. For the firm in our current example, we would not expect assets to be sufficient to support the increase in long-term debt from $30,000 to $55,000. The owner would have to decrease long-term debt and increase internal financing from profit for this company to be viable.

The balance sheet in Table 6-8 was generated by using the pro forma income statement, capital budget, and cash budget to determine the pro forma balance sheet figures. Another manner of generating a pro forma balance sheet is by using a percentage of sales method.

Pro Forma Balance Sheet Using Percentage of Sales

The **percentage of sales method** is based on the fact that assets and liabilities historically vary with sales; thus, any increase in sales will cause a subsequent buildup in both assets and liabilities. Both profit margins and dividend (owner) payout ratios determine the amount of internal financing that can be applied to support increased asset buildup. To use the percentage of sales method, take the previous years balance sheet as shown in Table 6-9. Using the column, actual for 1999, we divide each entry by the actual net sales for 1999 ($100,000 taken from Table 6-6) and display the result in a separate column, percentage of sales.

$$\text{Percentage of sales} = \frac{\text{balance sheet entry in \$}}{\text{Actual net sales in \$}}$$

$$= \frac{\$2,000}{\$100,000} = 0.02, \text{ or } 2\%$$

For example, cash of $2,000 divided by $100,000 equals 0.02, which is 2 percent of sales. We then take our pro forma sales of $150,000 from

Table 6-9　Pro Forma Balance Sheet Using Percentage of Sales Method

Balance Sheets for Year Ending December 31

	$ 100,000 Actual for 1999	Percentage of Sales (%)	$150,000 Pro Forma for 2000
Current Assets			
Cash	$ 2,000	2	$ 3,000
Accounts Receivable	10,000	10	15,000
Inventory	15,000	15	22,500
Total Current Assets	$27,000	27	$ 40,500
Fixed Assets			
Net Machinery & Equipment	30,000	30	45,000
Total Assets	$57,000	57	$ 85,500
Liabilities and Owner's Equity			
Current Liabilities			
Accounts Payable	$10,000	10	$ 15,000
Notes Payable	9,000	9	13,500
Total Current Liabilities	$19,000	19	$ 28,500
Long-Term Liabilities			
Long-Term Loan	$30,000	30	$ 45,000
Total Liabilities	$49,000	49	$ 73,500
Owner's Equity	8,000	8	12,000
Total Liabilities & Owner's Equity	$57,000	57	$ 85,500

Table 6-6 and multiply this figure by the percentage of sales to obtain our pro forma balance sheet for 2000 as shown in Table 6-9.

$$\frac{\text{Pro forma}}{\text{balance sheet entry}} = (\text{Pro forma sales})(\text{Percentage of actual sales})$$

$$= (\$150,000)(0.02) = \$3,000$$

Our pro forma balance sheet entry for cash is $3,000. Pro forma accounts receivable would be calculated as 10 percent of $150,000 or $15,000.

Using Percentage of Sales to Determine New Financing

When using the **percentage of sales method for determining new financing,** use the following formula:

$$\text{Required financing} = \Delta \text{Sales}\left(\frac{\text{Assets}}{\text{Sales}}\right) - \Delta \text{Sales}\left(\frac{\text{Liabilities}}{\text{Sales}}\right) - (S_2)(P)(1 - \text{Owner payout})$$

$$= (\$150,000 - \$100,000)\left(\frac{\$57,000}{\$100,000}\right) - \left(\$150,000 - \$100,000\frac{\$49,000}{\$100,000}\right) - (\$150,000)(0.15)(1 - 0.66)$$

$$= (\$50,000)(0.57) - (\$50,000)(0.49) - (\$150,000)\,(0.15)(0.34)$$

$$= \$28,500 - \$24,500 - \$7,650$$

$$= -\$3,650$$

In our formula, ΔSales is the sales forecast minus current sales. Assets divided by sales is derived from our historical percentages. Liabilities divided by sales is derived from our historical percentages. S_2 is the sales forecast, and P is historical profit margin, which is net profit divided by sales. In the previous example, we assume the owner takes 66 percent of the firm's profit as income.

We take the dollar amount of change in our sales as determined by our forecast and multiply it by the percentage that assets occupy with respect to sales. We subtract the dollar amount of change in our sales multiplied by the percentage that liabilities occupy with respect to sales. We then subtract the sales forecast times the profit margin times one minus the percentage of profit that the owner takes out of the business. If the number obtained is positive, we require new financing. If the number obtained is negative, owner's equity is sufficient, with the buildup in liabilities, to carry the increase in assets; therefore, additional financing is not required.

MONITORING AND CONTROLLING THE BUSINESS

We now have pro forma income statements, cash budgets, and balance sheets. These are required internally not only to project future needs, but also to monitor the actual performance of our company. The use of capital budgets as a monitoring and control tool is discussed in Chapter 9. We must realize, however, that all pro forma statements should be used as monitoring tools. When we monitor an activity, we essentially ask ourselves several questions: Are the actual sales meeting projections? Are the actual costs meeting projections? Are the profit margins meeting projections?

Most small businesses require only two budgets for monitoring and controlling purposes, the capital budget and the cash budget. Several other budgets also can be developed for a business. Most of these budgets, however, are developed as the business grows. Small businesses are not normally divided into departments; once they are, then separate budgets should be developed for each department. Once department budgets are developed, then the owner must determine if the department is one that generates revenue or one that only spends money. Departments that generate revenue, such as production or marketing departments, are normally designated as profit centers for budgeting purposes. Departments that only spend money are designated as cost centers. These would include personnel and research and development.

The controlling process, as previously discussed, requires three steps: (1) establishing a standard, (2) comparing actual performance to the standard, and (3) taking corrective action if necessary. For our company, the standards are the budgets and pro forma financial statements that have been developed. The monitoring process, as we have discussed, compares actual performance (revenues and expenses) with the budget and pro forma statement. Ultimately, controlling consists of the corrective action that we take when actual performance deviates sufficiently to pose a problem.

Because these budgets are estimates of the future, we must realize that the actual numbers will vary from our forecast. The difference between our actual figure and the budgeted figure is known as a variance. As managers, we must establish an acceptable range of parameters for the variance. Corrective action is taken only when the variance exceeds the parameters that we have established. Careful monitoring and taking necessary corrective action will maximize the usefulness of the budget as a tool in accomplishing the goals of financial management.

START-UP BUSINESS COSTS

You must understand that when you begin a business, generating financial statements is difficult. The tendency is to underestimate both the costs and time that it takes to begin a business. How many times have you seen a storefront sign that stated, "Coming soon, Joe's Deli"? When you passed the same location three months later the sign and Joe's Deli were gone.

Start-up costs are associated with getting the enterprise up and running prior to generating any sales, which is a major project for any business owner. For example, when Hannah began her donut business, the utility companies required deposits equal to two months of total utility bills, based on the utility's estimates of the highest monthly payments for similar businesses. The electric company required a $1,400 deposit (estimates of bills for July and August), and the gas company required a $500 deposit (estimates of bills for December and January). Because of the high failure rates for small business, these utilities required that bills be paid on time for two years before the money was refunded. In the case of the gas company, Hannah was late by 10 days on one payment. The gas company began recounting the two-year period after the late payment. As a result, it was three years before she received her deposit from the gas company. Additionally her equipment costs were $65,000, but the bank would only finance 75 percent ($48,750), so she had to come up with $16,250 in cash. It took three months to install the equipment, hire and train all employees, and actually open the business. Total start-up costs, including her $25,000 franchise fee, exceeded $75,000. These start-up costs were incurred before the first donut was sold.

GANTT CHART

Because of time and cost factors, we strongly recommend that the entrepreneur use a Gantt chart to assist in writing a business plan when expanding or starting a business.

A **Gantt chart,** (Figure 6-5), shows all tasks that have to be performed and the time that it takes to accomplish these tasks. The method suggested for using a Gantt chart is to develop a list of each task that must be performed to complete a project. A project is a unique one-time activity with a definite goal and desired completion date. To perform this activity, several tasks must be accomplished. If you are going to open a new business by a specific date, then you need a name, location, lease, utilities, licenses, and so forth. Each of these items is a task, which may have several subtasks associated with it. Many of these tasks also have a cost. Some tasks can be accomplished in conjunction with others (such as making utility down payments and selecting equipment). Some will have to be done in sequence; you need a location before you can negotiate a lease.

After listing all tasks, review them and place them in sequential order. Then fill in your Gantt chart, listing the start and finish time for each task. Using a highlighter, draw a line from the beginning to the end of each task. When you begin a task, use a different color highlighter to show progress. Obtain the estimated cost of each task so you can accurately estimate the cash required for starting up your business and avoid the pitfall of underestimating both the time and money it takes for start-up.

Estimate critical tasks that must be accomplished in a specified time period. For example, if you plan to open your business in April, find out when the phone company requires a listing for the Yellow Pages. If the listing must be in by December, obtain a phone number and get your listing in on time. If you open in April and have not done this, you may go an entire year without a phone number listing. This can kill a small business. For some businesses, especially service businesses such as plumbing and refrigeration repair, if you are not in the phone book, you do not exist. When the hot water heater starts leaking, how do you select a plumber? Make sure that critical tasks are accomplished on time.

 ## CONCLUSION

We now know how to obtain a forecast and to generate those pro forma financial statements required for our internal use and by external parties interested in our business. We also understand the importance of analyzing cash flow to determine our financing requirements. The basic unique requirements of the start-up business also were discussed. Our next task is to manage our current assets and liabilities to ensure that the business survives

Project:		Manager:		Phone:		Page: ___
Plan Area:		Manager:		Phone:		of ___ Pages

Tsk No.	Task Description:	Task Time	Resource	Phone	Time Periods													

FIGURE 6-5
Gantt Chart, Basic Entry Form

and that sufficient cash is generated to pay our bills and to provide us with a steady source of income as business owners and managers. Current assets and liabilities make up the working capital of any business. The management of working capital is the subject of our next chapter.

REVIEW AND DISCUSSION QUESTIONS

1. What is the purpose of pro forma financial statements (Tables 6-6 through 6-9)?
2. What are the basic criteria for selecting a forecasting model?
3. What role does MAD play in evaluating a forecasting model?
4. Compare judgmental, time series, and causal forecasting models.
5. List and describe at least three time series models.
6. In linear regression, compare independent and dependent variables.
7. Describe how to develop a pro forma income statement (Table 6-6).
8. What role does the pro forma cash budget play in financial forecasting (Table 6-7)?
9. What role does the pro forma balance sheet play in financial forecasting (Table 6-8)?
10. In generating a pro forma balance sheet, on what is the percentage of sales method based?
11. How are budgets used as a monitoring and control tool?

EXERCISES AND PROBLEMS

1. Jane White has recorded the following sales figures for last year for her business: January, $35,645; February, $35,456; March, $31,270; April, $32,129; May, $34,456; June, $35,256; July, $36,218; August, $35,456; September, $34,250; October, $32,156; November, $30,125; and December, $32,275. She wants to select from one of three models: a three-month moving average, a weighted moving average (she believes that the weights should be 0.2, 0.3, and 0.5), and an exponential smoothing average in which she uses an alpha of 0.2, and an assumed forecast for January of year 1 of $35,000.
   a. Construct a table that shows each of these forecasts for the current year, and provide the forecast for January of year 2.
   b. Using the available data and your forecasts, which model would you suggest that Jane use for her business?
2. Gary Fisher owns five successful health clubs. He believes that he can put a health club in a new community that currently has no such facility. His research indicates that communities such as this can support two health clubs.
   a. What type of information should Gary gather when selecting a specific site for his health club?

   b. What type of forecasting model will he use to determine the new location for a health club?

3. PERIOD   1   2   3   4
   DATA   32   14   41   10

   a. Make an exponential smoothing forecast for periods 3-5 with 2 values of alpha, 0.05 and 0.60 and an assumed forecast for period 1 of 30.
   b. Compute the MAD for each of the above forecasts.
   c. Which value of alpha will you choose?

4. Develop a linear regression equation to predict demand in the future from the following data:

Demand	23	24	31	28	29
Year	1993	1994	1995	1996	1997

   a. Write the regression equation
   b. Predict demand for the year 2,000
   c. Name the independent variable
   d. Name the dependent variable

Table 6-10   Actual Sales Data

Time Period	Actual Sales $(000)
1	445
2	478
3	525
4	660
5	570
6	600
7	632
8	648
9	690
10	725
11	750
12	

5. Using the data in Table 6-10, calculate a three month moving average forecast for month 12.

6. Using the data in Table 6-10, calculate the following:
   a. A weighted moving average forecast for months 1 through 12, using weights of 3, 5, and 9.
   b. What is MAD for this forecast?

7. Using the data in Table 6-10, calculate the following:
   a. What is the slope?
   b. What is the intercept?
   c. Write the regression equation?
   d. Calculate a regression forecast for month 25.

8. You have just completed the first year of operation for your business and have the following information: sales, $200,000; cost of goods, $140,000; rent, $18,000; utilities, $8,400; insurance, $2,000; equipment, $3,500; and

interest, $10,000. Your forecast indicates that your sales will increase by 20 percent. Your rental agreement provides for a 3 percent increase per year. You read an article indicating that utility costs in your area will increase by 10 percent next year. You just received a notice from your insurance company stating your quarterly premium is increased to $600 beginning the first quarter of next year. Your equipment expense will not change, but the amortization schedule on your current loan indicates that interest expense for next year should be $9,000.

a. Using this data, construct an actual income statement for this year and a pro forma income statement for next year.

b. By what percentage did your net income change?

c. What is your current profit margin and your pro forma profit margin?

d. In your business, assets and liabilities have historically varied with sales. Assets are normally 80 percent of sales, and liabilities are normally 55 percent of sales. You anticipate that you will have no owner payout of net profit. Using the percent of sales method, determine if any additional financing is needed for your business next year.

9. Sam Jones has two years of historical sales data for his company. He is applying for a business loan and must supply his projections of sales by month for the next two years to the bank.

a. Using the data from Table 6-11, provide a regression forecast for time periods 24 through 48.

b. Do Sam's sales data show a seasonal pattern?

Table 6-11   Twenty-four Months of Actual Data

Month	Actual Sales ($000)
1	345
2	350
3	355
4	360
5	365
6	360
7	358
8	352
9	348
10	353
11	362
12	370
13	375
14	382
15	390
16	380
17	375
18	368
19	363
20	373
21	380
22	391
23	397
24	408

10. Your projected sales for next year are as follows: January, $15,000; February, $20,000; and March, $25,000. Based on last year's data, cash sales are 20 percent of total sales for each month. Of the accounts receivable, 60 percent is collected in the month after the sale, and 40 percent is collected in the second month following the sale. Sales for November and December of the current year are $15,000 and $17,000, respectively. You have the following estimated payments: January, $4,500; February, $5,500; and March, $5,200.

  a. Using the data in Table 6-7, what is your monthly cash budget for January, February, and March?

  b. What will your accounts receivable be for the beginning of April?

  c. Will your company have any borrowing requirements for any month during this three-month period?

11. Using Table 6-12: Create a pro forma balance sheet using the percentage of sales method. If net income next year is $50,000, answer the following:

  a. How much did the owners take out of the business?

  b. What is the profit margin for next year?

12. Using Table 6-12: What is required new financing if next years sales forecast increases to $400,000, profit margin is 10 percent, and the payout ratio is 90%?

Table 6-12   Sample Balance Sheet

	Total Sales Current Year $275,000	Percentage of Sales (%)	Forecast Sales Next Year $350,000
Assets			
Current Assets			
Cash	$ 5,694		
Accounts Receivable	19,662		
Inventory	3,381		
Total Current Assets	$ 28,737		_____
Fixed Assets			
Furniture & Fixtures	5,595		
Transportation Equipment	25,456		
Total Fixed Assets	$ 31,051		_____
Total Assets	$ 59,788		══════
Liabilities and Owner's Equity			
Current Liabilities			
Notes Payable	$ 15,456		
Accrued Taxes Payable	3,598		
Total Current Liabilities	$ 19,054		_____
Long Term Debt	18,654		
Total Liabilities	$ 37,708		_____
Owner's Equity	22,080		
Total Liabilities and Owner's Equity	$ 59,788		══════

REFERENCES

Brase, Charles Henry, and Corrinne Pellillo Brase. *Understandable Statistics,* 3rd ed. Lexington, Mass.: D. C. Heath and Company, 1987.

Gaither, Norman. *Production and Operations Management,* 6th ed. New York: Dryden Press, 1994.

Heizer, Jay, and Barry Render. *Principles of Operations Management,* 3rd ed. Upper Saddle River, N.J.: Prentice-Hall, 1999.

Neter, John, and William Wasserman. *Applied Linear Statistical Models, Regression, Analysis of Variance, and Experimental Designs.* Homewood, Ill.: Richard D. Irwin, 1974.

Ruch, William A., Harold E. Fearon, and David C. Wieters. *Fundamentals of Production: Operations Management,* 5th ed. New York: West Publishing Company, 1992.

WORKING CAPITAL MANAGEMENT 7

Learning Objectives

When you have completed this chapter, you should be able to:

- Understand the general concept of working capital management.
- Describe the asset categories that are included in working capital management.
- Determine the methods of managing disbursement and collection of cash to increase business profitability.
- Understand how a business balances extending credit and its ability to manage increased accounts receivable.
- Explain how accounts receivable are analyzed.

- Understand the role that proper inventory management plays in the profitability of a business enterprise.
- Understand how a business's current liabilities are managed.
- Understand the relationship of accrued liabilities management and obligations to federal and local government agencies.
- Understand the relationship of trade and cash discounts to the minimization of accounts payable.

Probably one of the most difficult tasks faced by the small business owner is the proper management of working capital. In the normal course of conducting business, we accumulate current liabilities that often must be paid in lump sums: Rent, insurance, payroll taxes, sales taxes, and accounts payable are a few examples. Revenues, on the other hand, often flow in a sporadic but somewhat steady stream, and it can be difficult to equate the steady income stream to a lumpy payment schedule. The purpose of this chapter is to assist us in grappling with this problem.

WORKING CAPITAL

Working capital consists of the current assets and the current liabilities of a business. Current assets, as covered in Chapter 3, consist of those items that our business normally converts into cash within one year. Current assets also are referred to as **gross working capital,** and consist of cash, marketable securities, accounts receivable, and inventory. Current liabilities are those debts of our company that we normally expect to pay within one year. These are typically accounts payable, fixed payments (rent, utilities, insurance, and the current portion of our long-term debt), and accrued liabilities (payroll and taxes). **Net working capital** is the difference between a business's total current assets and its total current liabilities. If assets are what our business has a right to own, and liabilities are what our company owes, then what is left (the difference between them) is net working capital. It is a measure of our company in terms of liquidity, which is the ability of our firm to turn its assets into cash. The formula for working capital is

Net working capital =
Gross working capital (current assets) − Current liabilities

For example, if our company has $5,000 in current assets, we have $5,000 in gross working capital. If our company has $3,000 in current liabilities, then we have $2,000 in net working capital. This $2,000 is a margin of safety for our business in its ability to pay short-term debt.

WORKING CAPITAL MANAGEMENT

Working capital management is our ability to effectively and efficiently control current assets and current liabilities in a manner that will provide our firm with maximum return on its assets and will minimize payments for its liabilities. Proper working capital management promotes operational efficiency, but not necessarily long-term effectiveness. Creditors look at excess liquidity as a safety margin for paying short-term debt. As owners, however, we should look at excess liquidity as an opportunity to invest in items that will increase future productivity and profitability.

We will discuss working capital management in general terms to see the relationship between these items. Once we have covered the general relationships, we then will recommend specific methods of dealing with current asset management and current liabilities management.

Current assets must be managed properly. In a retail business, cash is used to buy inventory, which we plan on selling at a markup to generate a return on our cash investment. Sales are typically made for cash or on credit. Credit sales become our accounts receivable, which are converted into cash that may be used to pay off liabilities and to purchase more inventory for sale. We can enhance productivity by investing cash in fixed assets. For the retail establishment this may involve new display cases or computerized cash registers that assist us in controlling inventory. For a manufacturer, this investment may be in new machinery that will increase quality or speed of production. Regardless of the type of business, we always should try to manage working capital so that there is an excess of current assets over current liabilities. One reason is the possibility that some liabilities will have to be paid at the beginning of the next accounting period which are not currently listed as liabilities.

For example, let us assume that our company pays its employees twice monthly, on the fifth and the twentieth of each month. When we close our books on the last day of the month, the employees' time cards are still in the work area; therefore, the wages due from the twenty-first of the month until the end of the month will not appear on the books. Conversely, in managing working capital we do not want an excess of cash. We can find some method of investing cash to increase the profitability of our firm. Increased profitability is obtained by increased productivity, which is obtained by investing in fixed (long range) rather than current assets. Making long-range decisions involves capital budgeting, which will be the topic of Chapter 9.

Note that an excess of working capital must be studied closely to determine how the excess cash aspect of the net working capital is being managed. Excess cash should not be left idle: We must determine if it should be invested in marketable securities (certificates of deposit or treasury bills) or inventory. To accomplish this, we must determine inventory needs in terms of quantity and timing, so that future cash requirements can be matched to inventory demand.

Additionally, if we have credit accounts, then our business must be able to convert these accounts receivable into cash. If we cannot collect on accounts receivable in a timely manner, then we may not have enough cash to ensure timely payment to our own creditors. Therefore, if we are going to have credit accounts, we also must establish a plan for managing credit. Too strict a credit policy could very well turn away potential customers, who will then purchase from other firms. Too loose a credit policy may cause cash flow problems, because we will be granting credit to people who do not pay their bills on time. In fact, we may be granting credit to people who will never pay their bills.

A loose credit policy may cause two significant problems for our company: one, a cash flow problem, because much of our cash is tied up in accounts receivable; and two, we may be overstating the value of our current assets if we have accounts receivable on the books that are not collectable.

This second situation tends to make our business look much healthier on the books than it actually is. For example, let us say that we have a business with $100,000 in current assets, which are broken down as follows: cash, $10,000; accounts receivable, $75,000; and inventory, $15,000. Our current liabilities total $38,460.

We normally determine the health of businesses in the same industry with ratio analysis. Recall from Chapter 4 that the current ratio provides us with a relative measure of liquidity.

$$\text{Current ratio} = \frac{\text{Current assets}}{\text{Current liabilities}}$$

In our example, the current ratio is determined by dividing $100,000 by $38,460, which is 2.60. This current ratio of 2.60 means that our firm has $2.60 in current assets for every dollar of current liabilities.

Let us now assume that of our $75,000 in accounts receivable, $25,000 is not collectable. Therefore, our real current assets are only $75,000 (cash, $10,000; accounts receivable, $50,000; and inventory, $15,000). Consequently, our actual current ratio is $75,000/$38,460, or 1.95. As discussed in Chapter 4, a healthy firm normally has a current ratio in excess of 2. We looked quite healthy with a current ratio of 2.60, but the actual current ratio, because of our noncollectable accounts, is 1.95.

The previous discussion and examples explain why it is important to understand the relationships that exist between different items of working capital management. Now we will discuss specific strategy for managing each area of working capital.

CURRENT ASSET MANAGEMENT

Current asset management consists of managing cash, marketable securities, accounts receivable, and inventories.

CASH MANAGEMENT

The goal of cash management is to obtain the highest return possible on cash. This requires the firm to deposit cash and process checks as soon as possible and to disburse cash, by paying bills, as late as possible. At the same time, effective cash management involves investing idle cash in those short-term marketable securities that offer not only safety of principal but also a positive rate of return. Cash management is a part of effective working capital management that involves a trade-off between risk and return. On one hand, enough cash prevents the risk of insolvency caused by cash flowing in and out of our business at different rates, but on the other hand, too much cash will result in less of a return. If we keep excess cash, we can pay our bills but we lose interest on this money by not investing it for the short term.

For most businesses, cash consists of the following items:

1. **Petty cash.** A petty cash fund normally is used to pay for small daily items such as postage or minor supplies. We determine how much petty cash is required and store it in a cash box or drawer that is reserved for this purpose only. Petty cash is exchanged for receipts, and every expenditure must have a matching receipt. When the petty cash fund has to be replaced, we draw a check for petty cash and record all receipts in the books for our business.

2. **Cash on hand.** Cash on hand normally consists of daily sales and a change fund. The change fund is established when we determine how much cash is required for each cash register or cashier's station and stock a change depository with rolls of coins and small bills (typically $1 and $5 bills) required for daily transactions. Depending on the size of our business, the change fund may involve as little as $200 (for a small lunch counter with only one cash register and a check cashing policy that limits checks to the exact amount of purchase), or as much as several thousand dollars (for a supermarket with several cash registers and a check cashing policy that accepts checks in excess of the amount of purchase). For a retail establishment, the change fund will vary with the size of the business, the day of the week, and the season of the year. Wholesale businesses often can run with a small amount of cash on hand, because the vast majority of sales are on credit and transactions are frequently by check. Because cash on hand does not provide us with interest, and excess cash on hand increases business risk (possible robbery or theft), we should make daily deposits to minimize the amount. If our business deals with large cash deposits, we will normally contract with a security firm to pick up deposits for us; but if our business is small, our bank will provide us with drop bags and keys so that deposits can be made when the bank is closed.

3. **Cash in bank, checking.** Business checking accounts may draw interest, but normally are charged for each check that is written against the accounts. To minimize these charges, we should try to write the minimum number of checks. For example, we can normally arrange to pay vendors weekly or monthly, rather than with each delivery (trade credit is a current liability, and management of this item will be discussed later in this chapter).

4. **Cash in bank, savings.** Most businesses will want to maintain a savings account in addition to a checking account for several reasons:

(1) Savings accounts normally earn higher interest rates than checking accounts; (2) the small business must set aside employee taxes, sales taxes, and other payments due to governmental agencies; and (3) some funds should be reserved for emergency repairs and services (e.g., a broken window).

Thus, it makes sense for us to keep most of our business cash in the bank, so that we can earn interest and keep proper records. In addition, there are several advantages to maintaining as many records as possible via a checking account. The most obvious one is that the business has a record of all expenses, and if there is ever an audit by a government agency or other interested parties, canceled checks are considered to be absolute proof of payment. Another advantage of paying by check is that we can utilize the "float."

The two types of float are disbursement float and collections float. The **disbursement float** is the time that elapses between payment by check and the check's actually clearing the bank, at which point funds are removed from our checking account. Most businesses write checks totaling several hundred thousands of dollars per year, and of course large businesses write checks totaling millions of dollars. Most government agencies, and many vendors, will accept a U.S. post office postmark date as date of payment. We are all familiar with this concept because of our annual income tax payments, which are due on April 15 of each year. Obviously the Internal Revenue Service does not actually receive payment on the fifteenth, but it will accept the postmark as proof of payment on that date. It takes time for a check to clear, especially if the creditor's bank is several thousand miles from the debtor. The longer the check takes to clear, the longer we collect interest on the funds that have not been removed from our account.

For example, let us say that our checking account earns interest of 5 percent per year. Then, interest earned on each $100,000 that we can keep for a five-day period, due to the float, will amount to approximately $68.50. This was computed as follows: Annual interest of 5 percent means daily interest of 0.000137, which is derived by dividing the annual interest (0.05) by 365, the number of days in the year.

$$\text{Daily interest} = \frac{\text{Annual interest}}{\text{Days in year}} = \frac{0.05}{365} = 0.000137$$

Next we multiply the amount by the interest rate, and then by the time period during which that interest is earned. Five days' worth of interest equals $100,000 × 0.000137 (daily interest) × 5 (number of days).

If you are the creditor rather than the debtor, then you will try to counteract the use of float as much as possible by speeding collections time.

Collections float is the amount of time that elapses between your depositing a debtor's check in your account and the check's clearing at which point the funds are actually placed in your account. Obviously the same principle applies here as applied in the preceding example: Cash in the bank will earn interest; therefore, we want to speed collections time.

There are several methods of handling this collection with today's interstate banking. One method is to establish a lockbox system in conjunction with the bank. A **lockbox** is a post office box that is opened by an agent of the bank, and checks received there are immediately deposited in our account. Several collection points can be established throughout our marketing area, so that debtors will send payments to lockboxes at these collection points. Daily, a bank designated by us will open each payment and process it. At the end of the business day, the bank wires the funds that have cleared to our bank. For the lockbox system to be profitable, your firm must be involved in high-volume transactions and realize a greater return on short-term investments than the cost incurred in bank charges for the lockbox system. An excellent method for making this determination is to calculate total cost. We would calculate the total cost of the lockbox and total interest earned on invested short-term funds that have cleared the bank. If total interest earned is greater than the cost of the lockbox, we would use a lockbox.

Another method used to speed cash receipt time is electronic funds transfer. **Electronic funds transfer** is accomplished when funds are immediately transferred from one bank account to another via computer. Electronic funds transfer currently makes use of high technology and can immediately provide our customer with a receipt and our account with cash. The most familiar example of use of this method is at pay points that exist in many service stations and grocery and convenience stores. At these pay points, you use your check guarantee card as a debit card. You insert the card in the machine, punch in your personal identification number (PIN), and enter the amount of the purchase or cash desired. The funds are immediately taken from your checking account and deposited in the business's account. For a business, using this system is much better than accepting a check, because the funds, if the transaction goes through, are immediately in the bank, so the business does not have to worry about returned checks due to insufficient funds.

Using yet another method for speeding collections time, many large firms make arrangements for banks to accept payments to the firm when banking customers make deposits in the bank. Most utility companies make these arrangements. It is convenient for us to pay utility bills when making a deposit at the bank, because it saves the cost of postage and lessens the possibility of lost payments. For the utility, it speeds collection of checks and increases the earnings on interest-bearing accounts.

MARKETABLE SECURITIES MANAGEMENT

Marketable securities normally are those investment vehicles that include U.S. treasury bills, government and corporate bonds, and stocks. If our business has cash in excess of our requirements for paying monthly bills, then it makes sense to take the money out of our checking or savings account and invest it in some profit-making or interest-bearing instrument that normally pays more than we can obtain by keeping the funds in checking or savings accounts. We will develop investment strategy for marketable securities in the chapter on individual investment, because we are not dealing with public corporations in this text; however, a corporation can use the same strategy as the individual in handling excess cash.

ACCOUNTS RECEIVABLE MANAGEMENT

Obviously not all business transactions are handled in cash. Many of us, to stay competitive, must establish a credit accounting system. Accounts that are not paid in cash are referred to as receivables (debts owed to our firm). As with cash, our business must manage its accounts receivable properly to maximize profit.

The goal of accounts receivable management is to increase sales by offering credit to customers. However, we must weigh the costs incurred in having increased sales tied up in accounts receivable against the possible loss of business due to factors beyond the utility of a product or service. Many customers will choose to deal with those businesses that offer instant credit rather than those that demand cash. As a business, we can use certain methods to provide credit to our customers, without having to establish a credit department. The most common method is to use a credit factor.

Factoring is the process of selling our accounts receivable to another firm at a discount off of the original sales price. Factoring allows us to have credit sales and still obtain immediate cash for all sales. If you have ever bought a set of tires and charged them at the tire store, and then found that your payments were to be made to some financial management firm, then you have had an account factored. The tire store sold your bill to a third party at a discount.

Although banks do not like to consider themselves as factors, they in fact perform the functions of a factor for many businesses. The factoring system most often used by a small business involves making arrangements with a bank or financial institution to accept their credit card. For most businesses it is cheaper to allow customers to make use of credit cards such as MasterCard or VISA than to establish a credit system. The cost of billing, processing, and record keeping, in addition to the problem associated with having to wait 30 to 60 days for cash that has already been earned through a sale, can become a business nightmare.

The fact remains that the business owner, in making use of MasterCard, VISA, or some other card for credit sales, merely takes the day's credit transactions to the bank and receives a discounted amount of cash immediately. Although this discounted amount will reduce the proceeds of the sale, we now have cash for working capital without the expense of determining if the customer is a good credit risk. The factor will give us immediate cash for sales receipts, provided that we abide by the rules of the factor. For example, say that we own a restaurant, and a customer charges a $32 restaurant bill on a credit card. We are thus assured that we will be paid $32 minus a nominal discount of 4 to 5 percent of the bill. If the discount is 4 percent, then we receive $30.72 for the $32 charge and the bank charges us $1.28 for their processing. We receive $30.72 in cash immediately, rather than having to process a check, which could be uncollectable. Authorization by the credit card company is required and accomplished electronically. From a businessperson's point of view, the reduced proceeds of the sale may be made up by charging a higher price, or just from the savings on the processing costs of credit.

If we choose not to use a factor, and still must establish a credit policy, then we will have to determine (1) to whom we will grant credit, (2) the terms of the credit granted, and (3) how we will monitor credit and deal with delinquent accounts. Often, the industry in which we establish our business will dictate if we use a factor or establish our own credit department. For example, most retail firms accept bank cards, but wholesale and manufacturing firms establish their own credit departments.

Credit Evaluation

In determining which customers are allowed to use credit, we should adhere to established credit standards. These will serve as a yardstick in determining if a potential credit customer will successfully pay a bill or default. Among the primary considerations used in deciding to grant credit to a customer are the three C's of credit—character, capacity, and collateral. A customer's **character** is favorable if that customer has paid bills on time in the past and has good credit references from other creditors. This information is normally obtained from the customer application form which lists other creditors and contains a signed statement that allows us to check these references. **Capacity** to pay refers to whether the customer has enough cash flow or disposable income to pay back a loan or pay off a bill. This information also is normally obtained from the credit application, which lists assets and bank references. Having a high capacity does not necessarily mean that applicants will pay their bills, because they may be saddled with other bills or debt to pay off. A business that grosses $100,000 may be paying off $90,000 in debt. **Collateral** is the ability to satisfy a debt or pay a creditor by selling assets for cash. When evaluating collateral, however, we also must determine if a market exists for the asset. The credit decision involves making sure that the customer is a good credit risk. If the applicant is a business, we often look for a specific rating from a credit rating service, such as Dun and Bradstreet. If the applicant is an individual, we often check credit references and obtain a credit rating from a commercial credit agency. The credit decision is based on all the facts that convey to the lender whether a customer is a good credit risk. Because the credit decision involves allowing a customer (individual or business) to borrow money from our firm, we normally set a limit on that amount when we make the credit decision.

Credit terms are the requirements that our business establishes for payment of a loan (the use of credit by a customer). The terms that are most familiar to us are those associated with bank cards such as VISA or MasterCard. If the account is paid in full within some specified period, normally 30 days or less, then there is no interest charged on the outstanding balance. If the account is not paid in full, then a monthly interest charge is made on the unpaid balance. In addition, a portion of the debt must be paid each month to guarantee the continuation of credit. The terms also will establish a maximum amount of credit allowed the creditor. If we are in a business that requires the issuance of credit in order to stay competitive, then the terms we use are most often dictated by the standards of the industry. It is impossible to list all of the variances in this text; you must determine what the industry standards are and how you will apply them in your firm. We do provide, in later sections of this chapter, illustrations of cash and trade discounts that are normally used by business.

Analyzing Accounts Receivable

Analyzing accounts receivable is an important factor in determining how well our granting of credit matches our collection procedures. It is through this process that we are able to control credit. As stated previously, the control procedure involves establishing a standard, measuring actual performance against the standard, and taking corrective action if required. Let us say that we have established a credit policy of 60 days. In other words, people who have credit with our firm are supposed to pay their balances in full within 60 days of making a credit purchase. Recall from Chapter 4 that accounts receivable turnover is computed by taking credit sales and dividing them by accounts receivable.

$$\text{Accounts receivable turnover} = \frac{\text{Credit sales}}{\text{Accounts receivable}}$$

If our firm has $300,000 in credit sales and $50,000 in accounts receivable, then our accounts receivable turnover ratio is

$$\text{Accounts receivable turnover} = \frac{\$300,000}{\$50,000} = 6$$

Again from Chapter 4, the number of days in a year, divided by our turnover ratio, gives us the number of collection days.

$$\text{Collection days} = \frac{365}{6} = 60.833 \text{ days} \approx 61 \text{ days}$$

Therefore, we have 60.833 (or 61) days outstanding for our credit accounts. If this were our actual situation, then our credit terms and our granting of credit would be in line with our goals. Our customers would be paying their bills within the allocated time period. What if we find that we have $300,000 in credit sales, but our accounts receivable are $100,000? Then, using the same mathematics, we find that our turnover ratio is three ($300,000 ÷ $100,000) and that our average collection days are 121.666 (365 days ÷ 3), or 122 days. This would indicate that corrective action must be taken with regard to our credit policy. We must reevaluate our three C's of credit and tighten our procedures.

Aging of Accounts Receivable

Aging of accounts receivable is accomplished by determining the amounts of accounts receivable, the various lengths of time for which these accounts have been due, and the percentage of accounts that falls within each time frame. If a situation existed as in our second example, then aging of accounts receivable would be necessary. The procedure can be described by following Table 7-1.

Table 7-1 consists of a listing of our customers, the outstanding balance of their accounts, and the number of days since the credit purchase was made. As discussed, the outstanding balance for all accounts is $100,000. We take this information and create an aging schedule. If all of our accounts were in fact collected within the 60-day period established with our credit policy, then this procedure would not be necessary. However, because our accounts receivable turnover ratio is three, rather than six, it is necessary to analyze our outstanding credit accounts.

To construct the aging schedule, we take customer, balance, and number of days outstanding and arrange the information as shown in the bottom half of Table 7-1. We then obtain a total dollar figure for each time period and determine what percentage of our accounts receivable falls within each period. This amount is computed by dividing the total for each time

Table 7-1   Aging of Accounts Receivable

Customer	Outstanding Balance	Days Outstanding
1	$ 5,000	25
2	7,000	45
3	15,000	30
4	12,000	70
5	8,000	90
6	15,000	60
7	6,000	120
8	10,000	100
9	13,000	45
10	9,000	85
Total	$100,000	

Aging Schedule

| Customer | Days Outstanding | | | |
	0–30	31–60	61–90	91+
1	$ 5,000			
2		$ 7,000		
3	15,000			
4			$12,000	
5			8,000	
6		15,000		
7				$ 6,000
8				10,000
9		13,000		
10			9,000	
Totals	$20,000	$35,000	$29,000	$16,000
Percentage Outstanding	20.00%	35.00%	29.00%	16.00%

period by the total credit accounts that are outstanding. For example, we have $20,000 in accounts that have been outstanding from 0 to 30 days. We divide this $20,000 by the $100,000 total outstanding balance from the top portion of the table and determine that 20 percent of our credit accounts fall within the 30-day time period. Thirty-five percent fall within 31 to 60 days, 29 percent fall within 61 to 90 days, and 16 percent have been outstanding for over 90 days. Therefore, 45 percent of our accounts fall outside of the period that we established for our credit policy (60 days). Clearly we have a problem that calls for corrective action.

Our action involves several alternatives. The first is to notify these customers and try to obtain payment. Second, we can deny further credit to these customers if they do not bring their accounts to within our criteria. Third, we can turn delinquent accounts over to a collection agency. Our last resort, if we determine that the account is not collectable, is to write off the account as a bad debt. The customer in this last situation may have filed for bankruptcy, gone out of business, or left the state without leaving a forwarding address.

Our decision will depend on several factors. We should consider the following questions: How good a customer has this person been in the past? Can we afford to carry the customer during this temporary setback? Can we work with the customer on a cash-only basis until some payment is made on the outstanding debt? We cannot tell you how to handle each situation, because it will depend on the specific relationship between your firm and the creditor. However, it should be clear that in addition to working with current accounts that are in arrears, we must reevaluate our credit terms. It would appear that we have a policy that is too loose, as discussed in the first section of this chapter. We must, then, tighten our collection procedures to bring our creditors back in line.

INVENTORY MANAGEMENT

The final part of our current asset management involves managing inventory. For many businesses, in inventory is where most of the current assets are located. Proper management of inventory is critical to operating efficiency. The goals of inventory management appear to be contradictory. We must have enough inventory on hand to satisfy customer demand, but we also must keep inventory at a minimum value to free up cash. If we maintain an inventory that is too large, we may be stuck with obsolete items or items that have short shelf lives (items that spoil or lose their effectiveness, such as milk products or vitamins) and have to be disposed of with no sale. If our inventory is too small, we may lose sales and possibly customers to our competitors. The overall goal of inventory management is therefore to minimize total inventory costs while maximizing customer satisfaction. To accomplish this, there are two primary decisions that must be made: how to establish both the reorder quantity (the number of items to order) and the reorder point (that level of inventory at which a new order will be placed).

Economic Order Quantity Formula

To minimize inventory costs, we must have some idea of the value of our inventory. This can be obtained by determining the total cost of inventory, which includes ordering costs, carrying costs, the price of the good to be ordered, and the losses incurred by lost sales (opportunity costs). The most widely used formula for determining the reorder quantity is the economic order quantity (EOQ) formula. This formula takes into consideration all of the factors mentioned, with the exception of the lost opportunity costs. The EOQ formula attempts to balance ordering costs against storage costs and provides us with the most economic quantity to order to minimize overall inventory costs.

The EOQ formula is

$$EOQ = \sqrt{\frac{2DS}{IP}}$$

where

D = total annual demand for the item
S = total ordering cost for the item
I = carrying cost for the item, normally expressed as a percentage
P = unit cost of the item

The total ordering cost (S) is an administrative expense and is normally determined by taking the cost of the purchasing department or activity and dividing it by the number of orders placed per year. Let us say that Markadel has two purchasing agents whose combined salaries are $80,000 and who have administrative expenses allocated of $20,000 per year. They process 10,000 orders per year. In this case, we would compute S by dividing $100,000 (the total cost of purchasing) by 10,000 (the number of orders placed per year); so we would use $10 in our EOQ formula for the value of S.

We determine inventory carrying costs (I) in a similar manner. The carrying cost would be the cost of storing all inventory for a year, as a percentage of the average inventory value. For example, Markadel has a separate warehouse for inventory. The warehouse, on average, holds $3,000,000 in inventory. We total all costs of running the warehouse for a year, which would include salaries of warehouse workers, insurance, rent, and utilities, and arrive at a figure of $300,000. Therefore, for Markadel, the value of I would be 10 percent of the average inventory value (300,000 ÷ 3,000,000).

Total annual demand (D) is simply the number of units ordered per year, and price (P) is the cost per unit.

Let us say that Markadel orders 16,000 units of a particular item each year, and the unit cost is $20. Using the values for S and I we just computed, we would arrive at an EOQ of 400 units.

$$EOQ = \sqrt{\frac{2DS}{IP}} = \sqrt{\frac{(2)(16,000)(\$10)}{(0.10)(\$20)}} = \sqrt{160,000} = 400$$

Although the preceding formula is the one most often used, there are several other factors that the small business owner must take into consideration. Most vendors require a minimum order for delivery. If the business is small or storage space is at a premium, then orders that are smaller than the EOQ may have to be placed. If the business is large or uses items in quantity, then quantity discounts may override the EOQ formula.

Determining EOQ with quantity discounts requires the following procedures:

1. Compute EOQ for each discounted price.
2. If the computed EOQ falls within the discounted quantity area, then order the EOQ.
3. If the EOQ does not fall within the discounted quantity area, then compute total inventory costs.
4. Order the minimum quantity that provides the lowest overall inventory costs.

When quantity discounts are offered, and the EOQ given by the formula does not fall within the quantity discount range, then you should compute total inventory costs at each of the discount points and determine if the benefits of ordering the larger quantity override the costs of storage. This will require us to compute total costs unless the EOQ formula provides us with results that fall within the quantity discount area.

In determining total costs, the following assumptions are used:

1. Inventory is used at a constant rate during the time period. Therefore, the average inventory in stock at any given time is half the order quantity, or $Q \div 2$, where Q is the order quantity.
2. The number of orders placed per year will be equal to annual demand divided by the order quantity, or $D \div Q$.
   Therefore, our total cost (TC) formula would be

$$TC = DP + \frac{QIP}{2} + \frac{DS}{Q}$$

where

$D \times P =$ total cost of units
$Q \times I \times P \div 2 =$ annual cost of carrying the inventory
$D \times S \div Q =$ annual ordering cost

Table 7-2 presents the following problem with relationship to quantity discounts and shows the solution to this type of problem. We have a warehouse for which annual storage costs are 40 percent of inventory costs. It costs us $10 to place an order, and annual demand for the item is 16,000 units. The vendor provides us with a price list that indicates a price of $20 per unit for orders of 1 to 500 units, $19 per unit for orders of 501 to 1,000 units, and $18.90 per unit for orders in excess of 1,000 units. We first compute EOQ for each price, using the previous formula. The calculation of EOQ for a price of $20 is

$$EOQ = \sqrt{\frac{2DS}{IP}} = \sqrt{\frac{(2)(16,000)(\$10)}{(0.40)(\$20)}} = \sqrt{40,000} = 200$$

Table 7-2   EOQ with Quantity Discounts

Warehouse storage cost (I) = 0.40
Ordering cost (S) = $10.00
Annual demand (D) = 16,000

| | | | Total costs for each quantity | |
Price	Discount Quantity	EOQ	Quantity to Order	Total Cost
$20.00	0–500	200.00	200	$321,600.00
$19.00	501–1,000	205.20	501	$306,223.16
$18.90	Over 1,000	205.74	1,001	$306,343.62

Calculation of EOQ for the $19 price yields an EOQ of 205.2, and for the price of $18.90 we obtain an EOQ of 205.74. Note that we cannot get the quantity discount price of $19 unless we order 501 units; therefore, we must calculate total cost at each discount quantity to determine which quantity provides us with the lowest total cost. Calculation for total cost with a price of $19 is

$$TC = DP + \frac{QIP}{2} + \frac{DS}{Q}$$

$$= (16,000)(\$19) + \frac{(501)(0.4)(\$19)}{2} + \frac{(16,000)(\$10)}{501}$$

$$= \$306,223.16$$

Notice that when we calculate total cost with a discount, P equals the discount price, and Q is the minimum discount quantity that can be ordered to obtain the price. When we solve the equation for each price and quantity, note that our lowest total cost is with a price of $19. Therefore, we would order quantities of 501 if we had adequate storage space. Solving the above equations will give us an idea with regard to how much to order. Unfortunately one of the assumptions made in the EOQ model is that the order is received instantaneously. Since we know this is not true, we also have to determine when to place the order (our reorder point).

Reorder Point Calculations

The **reorder point (ROP)** has three factors that are used in determining the quantity of an item that exists when we actually place an order; lead time and safety stock (ss). **Lead-time** (L) is the time that lapses from order placement to order receipt. Daily demand (d) is the quantity of a product that is used per day. **Safety Stock** (ss) is the quantity of stock held for variations in demand. The formula for calculating the reorder point is:

$$ROP = Ld + ss$$

In our previous example, if we use 16,000 units of an item per year, and are open 250 days per year, then daily demand is 64 units (16,000 units/year ÷ 250 days/year = 64 units/day).

$$\text{Daily demand}\,(d) = \frac{\text{Annual demand}\,(D)}{\text{Number of days open per year}}$$
$$= \frac{16{,}000\ \text{units/year}}{250\ \text{days/year}}$$
$$= 64\ \text{units/day}$$

If it now takes three days from the time that we place an order until we receive the order, then our reorder point for lead time would be 3 days × 64 units = 192 units. Our safety stock is the number of units that we want on the shelf when the new order arrives. Safety stock accounts for daily variation in sales. The actual calculation of safety stock is based on statistical probability factors that are beyond the mathematics of this textbook. The following example can be used. Let's say that the item we are discussing is one that you definitely want to have in stock. In looking at your store records, the best day's sales of this item were 95 units. Therefore, you would have safety stock of 95, the best day's sales in addition to the safety lead-time quantity of 192. We would then calculate our reorder point as:

$$ROP = Ld + ss = (3)(64) + 95 = 287$$

When in-store inventory reached 287 units, if we were not taking advantage of the quantity we would reorder our EOQ of 200 units; if we were taking advantage of the quantity discount we would order 501 units.

Just-in-time (JIT)

Although EOQ, quantity discount, and reorder point calculations are the traditional method of calculating how much to order and when to order, many firms are moving to a JIT model. If daily demand can be accurately predicted, vendor delivery reliability is outstanding, and vendors will deliver on an hourly or daily basis, then JIT inventory can be used. The automobile industry is one example of JIT. Many automobile factories operate two or more shifts with an automobile coming off of the assembly line every minute. This means in 16 hours the plant will produce 960 automobiles (16 hours × 60 minutes × 1 car per minute). Each car requires 4 regular tires and one spare. The plant can schedule the delivery of 3,840 regular tires (960 automobiles × 4 regular tires) and 960 spare tires every day the plant produces. Because of the large quantity of tires, the plant may actually schedule several tire deliveries per day, and totally eliminate the warehouse. Items are delivered directly to the assembly line.

If a company can operate on JIT, it does not have to calculate EOQ, quantity discounts or reorder points. The requirement is to know how many of each part is required for each unit being assembled and to arrange with the vendor to deliver the exact quantity every day.

Many businesses will operate with some combination of the above. For example, Hannah's Donut Shop (Appendix D) received vendor delivery every Wednesday. She ordered from the vendor Monday afternoon, after the day's baking had been completed. Hannah knew her weekly and daily demand for each item. For example, she used 950 cubes of shortening per year (Table 7–4) and was open 365 days a year. Daily demand was therefore 2.6 cubes of shortening (950 cubes ÷ 365 operating day per year). She used a safety stock of one cube, and ordered two days before delivery. When she took inventory on Monday, she would normally order 18 cubes of shortening (7 days × 2.6 cubes) if she had between 6 and 7 cubes in stock (2.6 cubes per day × 2 days lead time + 1 cube of safety stock). If she had less than 6 cubes, she would increase the order by one for each cube she was short. This is a simple application of our ROP formula.

Types of Inventories

Inventory falls into four basic classifications, or types:

1. **Raw materials** are the items that a company uses in producing its final product. These can be basic raw materials (iron ore, coal) for an industrial manufacturing firm, assembly parts (microchips, disk drives, power supplies) for a computer manufacturing firm, or ingredients (flour, yeast) for a bakery. Raw materials are transformed in some manner between their receipt by a business and their being offered for sale by that business as part of the final product.

2. **Work-in-process** inventories consist of those items that are in the midst of the transformation process just mentioned. For example, the computer manufacturer would take microchips, disk drives, and other raw materials out of storage and put them into the assembly process. These items would then be considered as work in process until the finished computer was ready for shipment.

3. **Finished goods** inventories consist of those items that are actually sold by the business—sheet steel for the steel company, computers for the computer manufacturer, or bread for the bakery. Finished goods also include spare parts and repair parts for the end item. For example, a computer manufacturing firm would also have disk drives, mother boards, and other items that might fail in use, which it would sell to authorized computer repair facilities.

4. **Maintenance, repair, and operating (MRO)** inventories consist of those items that are used by the firm in normal operations, but are not manufactured or sold by the firm. These can range from lubricating oil and spare parts for machinery to business forms and paper clips.

ABC Inventory Analysis

In evaluating inventory for financial purposes, the cost of inventory items is an important consideration. It is difficult to determine which inventory items to emphasize unless we have some idea of the importance of these items with relationship to the overall operation of the business. One useful method of inventory analysis is **ABC analysis.** In most business operations, 5 to 10 percent of the inventory items (i.e., individual stock numbers or stock-keeping units) comprise approximately 75 percent of total costs (A items); 10 to 15 percent of the inventory stock numbers comprise 10 to 15 percent of the total costs (B items); and the remaining 75 to 80 percent of the stock numbers account for only 10 to 15 percent of total costs (C items). For manufacturing firms, A items are normally raw materials; for retail stores, the A items are the best-selling items and are finished goods. The B items are intermediate raw materials and next-best-selling items, whereas C items are normally MRO types of items. Table 7-3 gives a partial inventory for Hannah's Donut Shop, the company used in our case study in Appendix D. Table 7-4 shows the ABC analysis for that partial inventory.

The method of determining A, B, and C items is to take the total quantity purchased and multiply it by the unit cost to determine total cost for the item, as shown in Table 7-3. Notice that the total cost is a function of both quantity and price. For example, Hannah uses 104 bottles of bleach per year, but bleach only costs 60 cents a gallon, so the total cost is only $62.40 a year. On the other hand, she uses only 45 cases of urn coffee a year, but each case costs $46.50; therefore the annual cost of coffee is $2,092.50. Once we have determined the total cost of each inventory item, we are ready to perform an ABC analysis, as shown in Table 7-4. We take the inventory items and list them in descending order, based on total cost. We sum the total cost of our inventory and then compute the percentage of total cost that each inventory item consumes by dividing each individual item's total cost by the total cost of the inventory. For example, to determine the percentage of total cost consumed by shortening, we take the annual cost of shortening, divide it by the total cost of inventory, and multiply the result by 100:

$$\text{Shortening percentage} = \frac{(\$21{,}660.00)(100)}{\$83{,}194.75} = 26.04\%$$

We continue this procedure with each inventory item, listing the percentage consumed in a separate column. We then determine ABC by summing

Table 7-3   Hannah's Donut Shop Inventory List

Item Number	Item Description	Annual Demand	Unit Cost	Total Cost
1	Bavarian cream filling	100.0	$15.00	$1,500.00
2	Bleach	104.0	0.60	62.40
3	Blueberry filling	15.6	20.10	313.56
4	Bread flour for raised donuts	990.0	6.10	6,039.00
5	White frosting base	15.6	29.90	466.44
6	Buttermilk mix	35.0	23.30	815.50
7	Cake donut mix	625.0	30.50	19,062.50
8	Raised mix	990.0	21.50	21,285.00
9	Cherry fruit bits	26.0	13.80	358.80
10	Chocolate fudge base	26.0	37.60	977.60
11	Chocolate donut mix	52.0	25.10	1,305.20
12	Chunky apple	20.8	16.95	352.56
13	Comet	26.0	0.40	10.40
14	Degreaser	10.4	6.40	66.56
15	Dishwashing lotion	52.0	3.99	207.48
16	H&R all-purpose flour	52.0	6.99	363.48
17	Lemon mist filling	10.4	13.20	137.28
18	Oat bran	26.0	25.95	674.70
19	Old-fashioned donuts	26.0	22.55	586.30
20	Raspberry filling	50.0	14.44	722.00
21	SAF instant yeast	45.0	33.15	1,491.75
22	Shortening	950.0	22.80	21,660.00
23	Stirrers, coffee	10.4	2.49	25.90
24	Straws, wrapped	5.2	4.00	20.80
25	Sugar packets	5.2	8.99	46.75
26	Sweet N Low	2.6	8.39	21.81
27	Trash bags	10.4	8.70	90.48
28	Urn coffee	45.0	46.50	2,092.50
29	#1 Donut trays	60.0	22.00	1,320.00
30	#2 Donut trays	52.0	21.50	1,118.00
	Total inventory cost			$83,194.75

the percentages in the next column. Shortening is 26.04 percent, plus raised mix of 25.58 percent equals 51.62 percent of total inventory cost. When we reach approximately 75 percent of total cost, we have identified the A items. For Hannah's Donut Shop, the A items are shortening, raised mix, and cake donut mix. Notice that there are three A items out of the inventory list of 30 items. This represents 10 percent of the total inventory items by stock-keeping unit. We continue adding until we reach approximately 90 percent of total cost. The items between 75 percent and 90 percent would be classified as B items. For the donut shop, items 4 through 8 are B items. Notice that out of total items, five are B items, representing approximately 17 percent of the stock-keeping units. The remaining items are C items and comprise over 73 percent of total stock-keeping units.

Why would a business owner go through this procedure? The ABC analysis is based on the 20-80 rule, which is a phenomenon observed in many aspects of business. Twenty percent of your customers will normally

Table 7-4 Hannah's Donut Shop, ABC Analysis

Item Number	Item Description	Annual Demand	Unit Cost	Total Cost	Percentage	Cumulative Percentage
1	Shortening	950.0	$22.80	$ 21,660.00	26.04%	26.04%
2	Raised mix	990.0	21.50	21,285.00	25.58%	51.62%
3	Cake donut mix	625.0	30.50	19,062.50	22.91%	74.53%
4	Bread flour for raised donuts	990.0	6.10	6,039.00	7.26%	81.79%
5	Urn coffee	45.0	46.50	2,092.50	2.52%	84.31%
6	Bavarian cream filling	100.0	15.00	1,500.00	1.80%	86.11%
7	SAF instant yeast	45.0	33.15	1,491.75	1.79%	87.90%
8	#1 Donut trays	60.0	22.00	1,320.00	1.59%	89.49%
9	Chocolate donut mix	52.0	25.10	1,305.20	1.57%	91.06%
10	#2 Donut trays	52.0	21.50	1,118.00	1.34%	92.40%
11	Chocolate fudge base	26.0	37.60	977.60	1.18%	93.58%
12	Buttermilk mix	35.0	23.30	815.50	0.98%	94.56%
13	Raspberry filling	50.0	14.44	722.00	0.87%	95.43%
14	Oat bran	26.0	25.95	674.70	0.81%	96.24%
15	Old-fashioned donuts	26.0	22.55	586.30	0.70%	96.94%
16	White frosting base	15.6	29.90	466.44	0.56%	97.50%
17	H&R all-purpose flour	52.0	6.99	363.48	0.44%	97.94%
18	Cherry fruit bits	26.0	13.80	358.80	0.43%	98.37%
19	Chunky apple	20.8	16.95	352.56	0.42%	98.79%
20	Blueberry filling	15.6	20.10	313.56	0.38%	99.17%
21	Dishwashing lotion	52.0	3.99	207.48	0.25%	99.42%
22	Lemon mist filling	10.4	13.20	137.28	0.17%	99.59%
23	Trash bags	10.4	8.70	90.48	0.11%	99.69%
24	Degreaser	10.4	6.40	66.56	0.08%	99.77%
25	Bleach	104.0	0.60	62.40	0.08%	99.85%
26	Sugar packets	5.2	8.99	46.75	0.06%	99.91%
27	Stirrers, coffee	10.4	2.49	25.90	0.03%	99.94%
28	Sweet N Low	2.6	8.39	21.81	0.03%	99.96%
29	Straws, wrapped	5.2	4.00	20.80	0.03%	99.99%
30	Comet	26.0	0.40	10.40	0.01%	100.00%
	Total inventory cost			$ 83,194.75	100.00%	

account for 80 percent of your sales. Twenty percent of your customers will file 80 percent of your complaints. Twenty percent of your employees will pose 80 percent of your employee problems. Likewise, 20 percent of your inventory items will consume approximately 80 percent of your inventory investment. In managing inventory, however, this rule provides us with a tremendous management advantage.

The 20–80 rule is also known as the Pareto rule. When A items are identified, because they consume approximately 75 percent of your costs, they should be managed carefully. Your concentration should be on these items. You want to have time to negotiate contracts, obtain competitive bids, and establish control procedures in regard to these items. A small savings on the purchase of A items can increase profits and reduce inventory costs tremendously, whereas a large savings on a C item will do little to boost your profit or reduce inventory cost. For example, in the case of Hannah's Donut Shop, Hannah managed to obtain bids from several vendors and reduce the cost of shortening from $22.80 a cube to $19.25. This is a savings of $3.55 a cube, or 15.57 percent. Because she uses 950 cubes of shortening a year, this is an annual savings of $3,372.50. Not only is it an annual savings, but it actually increases profit by the same amount. She has spent $3,372.50 less on cost of goods, but generated the same amount in sales. If you refer back to an income statement, notice that a reduction in cost of goods, with no decrease in sales, results in an increase in profit of the amount saved in inventory expense.

For C items, on the other hand, you merely want a reliable vendor who will deliver on time. We do not shop for C items, but spend our time on A and B items. C items should normally be purchased with open purchase orders, from dependable vendors. Referring again to Table 7-3, notice that Hannah uses 52 bottles of dishwashing detergent a year. Detergent costs $3.99 per bottle. Let us assume that she finds detergent for $1.98 a bottle and can therefore save over 50 percent. Her annual cost for detergent is $207.48. If she buys all 52 bottles on sale, she saves $104.52 a year. But can she store 52 bottles of detergent? If not, then she probably will buy a single case of only 6 bottles, which will save only $12.06. How much time will she spend in buying the detergent? In other words, is it worth shopping for C items? The answer is obviously no.

For C items, we normally do not go through the calculations of EOQ, or establish elaborate control procedures. We establish some minimum quantity, and once that minimum is reached, we place an order to our vendor. We do not shop or negotiate for these items, because we should spend most of our time on A items, an amount of time proportionate to their importance on B items, and as little time as possible on C items. You may find that many business owners who do not spend the time to develop an ABC analysis place their emphasis on the wrong items, because the C items comprise 75 percent of inventory items by stock number or item description. How many times have you seen people in your office shop for business cards, pencils, or paper clips? These are, for most businesses, C items. Could this time be better spent on A items?

CURRENT LIABILITIES MANAGEMENT

Current liabilities management consists of minimizing our obligations and payments for short-term debt, accrued liabilities, and accounts payable.

SHORT-TERM DEBT MANAGEMENT

Short-term debt consists of business obligations that will be paid within the current accounting period. These are normally (a) current payments on long-term debt (e.g., if we have a mortgage with a monthly payment of $2,000, then our current obligation would be $24,000 per year) or (b) payments on short-term loans such as bank lines of credit, or loans that will be paid during the current accounting year that appear on the balance sheet as notes payable. Long-term debt consists of obligations that normally are incurred as a result of capital budgeting, and is covered more fully in Chapter 9. Our primary concern in current liabilities management is merely to pay these obligations when they are due. Because notes payable normally are used to defer the payment of cash and may indicate an inadequate cash flow, we should discuss this area in some detail.

The primary method of incurring notes payable for our business is through extending lines of credit or using promissory notes. A **line of credit** is similar to a credit card. With it, we obtain a credit limit, but we are not obligated to make payments unless we actually borrow the money. A line of credit is normally obtained from our primary bank. We determine the dollar requirement for this line based on our maximum estimated cash requirement that exceeds cash income. We apply for a line of credit for this amount through our bank. The bank will grant this line of credit if we meet their standards, which are often based on the three C's of credit discussed in the previous section.

The requirement for a line of credit is based on the fact that our cash flow may be insufficient to meet current monthly obligations, as a result of seasonal sales and general economic factors. Recall from Chapter 3, when we discussed the statement of cash flow, that in some months cash flow exceeded our requirements, and at other times was insufficient to meet our obligations. If we want to maintain a good credit rating, then we must make payments on time even when our business does not generate sufficient cash. One way of making sure that we can make timely payments is to establish a line of credit that exceeds our estimate of any shortfall. Then when we run short of cash, we borrow against the line of credit and pay it off as rapidly as possible.

Assume that in our business we believe that our maximum shortfall during any single month will be $8,000, and that total borrowing will never exceed $10,000. If we establish a line of credit of $10,000, we will be covered. The advantage of the line of credit is that no payments are required and no interest is accrued until the line is actually used. For example, say that we have a $10,000 line of credit at 12 percent annual interest. In February, we run short of cash by $2,000 and borrow the money. Because we established the line of credit, we now have the use of this $2,000 to pay our creditors on time. If the cash flow in March is sufficient, we can then pay back the $2,000 plus interest for one month. We would pay the bank $2,000 plus 1 percent interest on the money, or $2,020, because we actually borrowed the money for one month, and a 12 percent annual interest rate is computed at 1 percent per month. This procedure saves us considerable interest because we pay interest only when we have a loan outstanding.

In some circumstances, however, we either cannot obtain a line of credit that is sufficient to meet our obligations or we want to borrow a large sum of money for less than one year. Such circumstances would call for obtaining a short-term loan. A short-term loan is taken for one year or less. The procedures are the same as those listed for the line of credit. We determine the amount and apply to the bank for the loan. The primary difference between the line of credit and the loan is, with the loan, we borrow the entire sum at one time and are obligated to make monthly payments. Because we borrow for a longer period of time, we will pay more interest and incur a fixed monthly payment that will increase our current liabilities. In some cases, we can arrange for the loan to be paid in one lump sum, which will involve a single payment plus accrued interest.

A short-term loan is typical if our business has a very short season that generates the majority of our sales. A toy business would be a good example, in which 75 percent of annual sales are made during the three months from October through December. Say that we are in the toy business, and we must contract for a large increase in inventory during the summer months to ensure sufficient stock during our peak selling season. We might obtain a six-month loan on the first of July, with a single balloon payment that is due on the first of January. If we borrowed $100,000 in July at 12 percent interest, we would owe the bank $106,230 in January, because the bank normally computes interest owed on outstanding loans on a daily basis. Therefore, at the end of July we would owe $100,000 plus 31 days of interest, or a total of $101,024. The bank would then compute the next month's interest on the $101,024. This process is known as compounding interest, which will be discussed fully in Chapter 8.

ACCRUED LIABILITIES MANAGEMENT

In addition to paying short-term debt, we also are obligated to pay accrued liabilities. **Accrued liabilities** are those obligations of the firm that are accumulated during the normal course of business and are primarily payroll taxes and benefits, property taxes, and sales taxes. It is with accrued liabilities that the small business owner can get into the most trouble, because of the severe penalties that government agencies can impose on a business. The IRS charges a 10 percent penalty on tax deposits made 16 or more days late, and a 2 percent penalty on deposits made a day late.[1] Government agencies treat businesses as collection agencies for taxes. When you take payroll taxes out of an employee's pay, this money, which the employee earned, is not yours to keep. Therefore, you must pay this obligation to the IRS on the day that it is due or incur a severe penalty. Sales taxes are treated exactly the same

---

[1] Employers Tax Guide Publications, Circular E (rev. January 1999), Department of the Treasury, Internal Revenue Service.

by state and local municipalities. If you use a cash register to ring up sales, then sales taxes are normally added to the sale, and collected by the business. Your closing daily report, normally a Z (a zero balance report), will list the total sales tax collected that day.

It is our contention that the best way to avoid a problem with the government is to make sure that this money for these liabilities is set aside as they are accrued. The easiest method is to establish a separate savings account. Every time a payroll is met, determine how much has been withheld from your employees' paychecks, add the appropriate employer federal, state, and municipal taxes, and deposit this sum into the savings account. Then the money will be in the bank on the day that it must be paid. **Federal employment taxes** consist of income, social security, medicare, and unemployment taxes. In addition, the employer is obligated to match the social security and medicare tax that has been paid by the employee. **State employment taxes** normally consist of income, unemployment, and workmen's compensation taxes. Municipal employment taxes normally are only income tax.

On a daily or weekly basis, determine how much sales tax has been collected and deposit this amount in the savings account. This will provide you with the funds to pay state and local agencies. In addition, if you own property or operate with a triple-net lease (lessee pays rent plus share of property and rental taxes), then you will receive an annual property tax bill which is normally paid in two installments (every six months). Determine the monthly obligation of this tax and set it aside in your savings account, otherwise you may use the money to pay other obligations and not have the cash to pay these taxes when they are due. Government agencies can impound your bank accounts and lock the doors of your business if these taxes are not paid in a timely manner. Therefore, accrued liabilities management must be of primary concern.

Accounts Payable Management

The last item to be discussed in this section on current liabilities is accounts payable. The largest portion of accounts payable normally consists of the obligations of our firm that were obtained by purchasing inventory on credit. Of course, other items such as travel expenses, maintenance services, and entertainment expenses also may be charged. Our purpose in managing accounts payable is to minimize the cash paid for inventories and these other obligations. Because inventories comprise the largest portion of accounts payable, we can normally minimize these cash payments by taking advantage of the discounts that are offered by vendors. The three primary types of discounts that vendors typically use are trade discounts, cash discounts, and quantity discounts.

Trade Discounts

Trade discounts are amounts deducted from list prices of items when specific services are performed by the trade customer. Trade discounts may be expressed as a single amount, such as 30 percent, or in a series, such as 30/20/10. If the discounts are expressed as a series or chain, the customer must accomplish specific tasks of the agreement to qualify for the entire chain discount. This may involve purchasing large quantities of an item or performing specific intermediary functions such as providing point-of-sale displays or local advertising. When taking advantage of trade discounts, it is important to calculate them properly.

Calculation of trade discounts is accomplished by moving backward from the list price. In the previous example, the discount chain of 30/20/10 does not mean that the item may be purchased with a 60 percent discount (30 + 20 + 10 = 60). Rather, we calculate the total discount, in three steps or in one step, by using the net cost rate factor. The following example will be used to illustrate both methods.

Tom's Appliance Store receives a washing machine that has a list price of $300 and for which the manufacturer shows discounts of 30/20/10. The manufacturer's wholesale catalog provides an explanation of each discount. For example, the manufacturer may specify that 30 percent is the normal markup from wholesale to retail, 20 percent is the allowance for free delivery and installation service, and 10 percent is an allowance for point-of-sale display and local advertising. Then Tom may take all three discounts if he is going to comply with all contractual obligations.

There are two methods of calculating discounts. One method is to work the long way, working backward from list with each discount. We determine what would be paid if we took each discount individually, as follows: List price minus the first discount would be

$$\text{List price} - \text{Trade discount} = \text{Discounted price}$$
$$\$300 - (\$300 \times 0.3) = \$210$$

The discounted price minus the second discount would be

$$\$210 - (\$210 \times 0.2) = \$210 - \$42 = \$168$$

The second discounted price minus the third discount would be

$$\$168 - (\$168 \times 0.1) = \$168 - \$16.80 = \$151.20$$

The total invoice price paid, divided by the list price, provides us with the net cost rate factor. The **net cost rate factor** is the actual percentage of the list price paid after taking all successive trade discounts—50.4 percent in this case. One minus the net cost rate factor is the **single equivalent discount.**

Therefore, trade discounts of 30/20/10 amount to a single equivalent discount of 49.6 percent, not 60 percent.

A second, simpler way of determining the net cost rate factor is to multiply the complements of the trade discounts. For example, in the preceding problem the trade discounts were 30/20/10. The complement of a number is found by subtracting the number from 1. So for 30/20/10, the complements are 0.7 (1 − 0.3), 0.8 (1 − 0.2), and 0.9 (1 − 0.1), respectively. Then, multiplying these complements together results in a net cost rate factor of 0.504, or 50.4 percent. Again, the mathematical calculations are as follows:

$$\text{First complement} = 1 - 0.3 = 0.7$$
$$\text{Second complement} = 1 - 0.2 = 0.8$$
$$\text{Third complement} = 1 - 0.1 = 0.9$$
$$\text{Net cost rate factor} = (0.7)(0.8)(0.9) = 0.504$$

The invoice price (the price that you actually pay the vendor) can be calculated simply by the following formula:

$$\text{Invoice price} = \text{List price} \times \text{Net cost rate factor}$$
$$= (\$300)(0.504) = \$151.20$$

The invoice price of $151.20 is the amount that we will pay the washing machine manufacturer if we take all discounts. A trade discount is very much involved in establishing the invoice price. Note, however, that the invoice price can be paid either in cash or on credit. If Tom does not pay for the merchandise when he receives it, then he is a credit customer.

Cash Discounts

Cash discounts are offered to credit customers to entice them to pay promptly. The seller views a cash discount as a sales discount; the customer views it as a purchase discount. The terms of a cash discount play an important role in determining how the invoice will be paid. Cash discounts normally appear on an invoice in terms such as 2/10, n/30, which means that customers may deduct 2 percent off of the invoice price if they pay within 10 days. If customers pay within 30 days, the net (n), or total amount of the invoice is due. If they pay after 30 days, the credit agreement with the sellers normally stipulates that a monthly interest charge be added to the unpaid balance.

Suppose that Markadel sells goods to Tom's Appliance Store for $10,000 (the invoice price), terms 2/10, n/30, with an invoice date of November 1. Terms of 2/10, n/30 mean that Tom's Appliance Store can deduct 2 percent from the invoice price if payment is made within 10 days of the invoice date (up to November 11). If Tom's does not take advantage of the cash discount, then Tom must pay the entire invoice amount within 30 days of the invoice date. If payment is not made by day 30 (December 1), then interest charges of 1.5 percent monthly (18 percent annually) will be added to the unpaid balance. (The interest charged on the unpaid balance will vary, and it is normally listed on the credit application that is signed by the business owner or agent of the business.)

In our example, Tom has several options. (a) He can pay off the $10,000 with a payment of $9,800 within 10 days of the invoice date. This amount is computed by multiplying the invoice price by 1, minus the discount $(1 - 0.02 = 0.98$, and $\$10,000 \times 0.98 = \$9,800)$, or by taking the invoice price times the discount and subtracting it from the invoice price $(\$10,000 \times 0.02 = \$200$, and $\$10,000 - \$200 = \$9,800)$. (b) He can choose to pay the invoice price of $10,000 if payment is made anytime between the eleventh and thirtieth day after the invoice date. If this option is chosen, he will pay the equivalent of 36.7 percent annual interest because of his delaying payment.

How do we determine that his effective rate of interest resulting from his not taking the discount is 36.7 percent? The following procedures and assumptions are used to calculate the effective rate of interest. If Tom does not take the discount, then this is the same as borrowing $9,800 for 20 days and paying $200 in interest on the loan, because after the eleventh day, he still has to pay the $9,800 by the thirtieth day, plus the additional $200. Annual interest is computed by going on the assumption that Tom chose to borrow $9,800 for 20 days and made an interest payment of $200 on this loan. In other words, he chose to forfeit or pay $200 that could have been kept in order to keep the $9,800 debt for an additional 20 days (30 days − 10 days). Thus, Tom pays $200 on $9,800 for 20 days, or an interest rate of 2.04 percent [($200 ÷ $9,800) × 100]. The result is an effective annual interest rate of 36.7 percent [2.04 × (360÷20)]. The effective annual interest rate is obtained by multiplying the time period interest rate by the number of time periods. Most of us are familiar with this computation because of our use of credit cards, which may state, for example, that the unpaid balance will be charged at an interest rate of 1.5 percent per month or 18 percent per annum (1.5 × 12 months). In our cash discount example, we pay interest of 2.04 percent for 20 days and assume twelve 30-day business months per year, or 360 days per year (360 ÷ 20 = 18 payment periods per year).

Many times it may be more profitable for our business to borrow money to take advantage of a cash discount. This holds true if borrowing rates are lower than the rate or cost of money forfeited if the discount is not taken. Consider, for example, that the $9,800 can be borrowed by Tom's Appliance Store on the tenth day from a bank, to take advantage of the cash discount. Assume that a bank is charging a 12 percent annual interest rate. We use 20 days as the time period, because $9,800 plus interest in both cases would have to be paid back after 20 days. Tom's, at the end of 20 days, would have to pay back the following amount:

$$S = \frac{P}{1 - dt}$$

where

S = amount to be paid back, or maturity value
P = proceeds borrowed from bank at a discount
d = discount rate
t = time period

When we substitute into the preceding formula, we obtain

$$S = \frac{P}{1 - dt} = \frac{\$9,800}{\left[1 - (0.12)\left(\frac{20}{365}\right)\right]} = \$9,864.86$$

So $9,864.86 is the amount due to the bank at the end of 20 days if Tom signs a bank note or uses his line of credit (10 days of discount period plus 20 days remaining until the entire amount is due). If he does not borrow the money, then he will have to pay the vendor $10,000 at the end of 30 days. Thus, he saves $135.14 by discounting a note and taking advantage of the cash discount, which adds to working capital. In other words, it costs the firm $64.86 to borrow $9,800 and take advantage of the cash discount. Tom also saves the cost of $200 by paying his creditor $9,800 instead of $10,000. If economic conditions were such that bank lending rates were very high, then the amount saved would decrease because more money would have to be paid to the bank to use the $9,800 for 20 days.

Quantity Discounts

Quantity discounts are offered by vendors to increase their own cash flow when they offer discounts to customers who purchase items in large quantities. Quantity discounts may be one-time discounts or cumulative discounts. A single quantity discount is offered on a single large purchase order. For example, a manufacturing catalog may offer an item with the listing seen in Table 7-5.

Table 7-5   Quantity Discounts

Item Number	Quantity	Unit Cost
10010	1–99	$15.00
	100–499	14.50
	500–999	14.00

If we choose to purchase any quantity up to 99 units, then we would be billed $15 for each unit. An order of 100 to 499 units would be billed at $14.50 per unit, and an order of 500 to 999 units would be billed at $14 per unit. Often these discounts are not advantageous for our business, because if the overall cost of inventory is not reduced by ordering in quantity, then we are just acting as a storage agency for our vendor, and are decreasing our cash. Additionally, inventory items are subject to becoming obsolete or spoiling if we hold them for too long. If we sell high quantities of the item in a short period of time, however, then single quantity discounts provide us with several advantages. These include reducing our total inventory cost and providing us with more throughput and cash flow.

Cumulative Discounts

Cumulative discounts normally are offered on total purchases of an item during the vendor's fiscal year. When cumulative discounts are used, the vendor will keep track of the total quantity purchased during the year and provide the customer with a refund check based on this quantity at the year's end. These discounts are similar to frequent flyer club discounts offered by airline companies. If we assume that our company purchases 10 units of item 10010 each month, then each monthly invoice will be for $150 (10 × $15). At the end of the year we will have purchased 120 units of item 10010. Therefore, if the vending company is offering cumulative discounts, it will give us the cumulative discount price of $14.50 and provide us with a refund check for $60 (120 × $0.50). Cumulative discounts are primarily given to improve customer loyalty, especially if the majority of a firm's customers are small businesses that cannot take advantage of single quantity discounts.

CONCLUSION

Proper management of working capital can improve the overall health of our business by increasing current assets and minimizing current liabilities. Several issues are important here. The only item that is definitely a current asset is cash. Accounts receivable can only be turned into cash if the customer pays the bill. Long-term accounts receivable, although carried as current assets, do nothing to increase our cash position and therefore should be carefully analyzed. Inventory is the single category of item contained within current assets that is subject to the most criticism by both business owners and the academic profession.

The basic problem is that an accountant and a business owner may look at inventories differently. Inventories are only an asset if they can be turned into cash. If not, they are actually a liability, even though Generally Accepted Accounting Principles (GAAP) require that they be listed as a current asset on the balance sheet. For the retail firm, if an item loses popularity, has a short shelf life, or becomes obsolete, then the cost of goods often cannot be recovered, even with a sale. We would have to conclude, then, that such an item is actually a liability. It often must be disposed of, rather than sold.

For the manufacturing firm, the situation can be worse. Raw materials and work-in-process inventories cannot be sold until they are turned into finished goods. Finished goods have no value unless they can be sold. Ideally, the manufacturing firm should not even acquire the raw materials until there is a firm order for the finished goods. Then the raw materials should be turned into finished goods as rapidly as possible for cash. One primary goal of a for-profit firm is to make money now and to make more money in the future. This can only be accomplished when inventory is turned into cash.[2]

Current liabilities management is much more straightforward, because items that are listed as current liabilities are all liabilities. The primary problem for the small business owner is in managing accrued liabilities. These items often do not appear on the books as they are accrued, but only afterward. The business owner must therefore establish some meaningful method for determining their value and ensuring that the cash is available when a payment is required.

Fixed assets and long-term liabilities are normally accumulated through the process of investing excess cash in items that will provide us with more money in the future. The method of determining where to invest this money, and how to evaluate the investment prior to making the commitment, is the subject of Chapter 9.

REVIEW AND DISCUSSION QUESTIONS

1. Compare gross working capital and net working capital.
2. For most businesses, what does cash consist of?
3. In current asset management, what is the float? How would paying by check allow a business to take advantage of the float?
4. List and describe at least three methods a business can use to speed cash receipt time from its debtors.
5. What role do marketable securities play in current asset management?
6. What methods can be used by small businesses to speed the collection of money that is owed to them?
7. What are the three C's of credit? How do these serve as a yardstick for credit evaluation?
8. What corrective action can be taken for customers whose outstanding balances exceed our credit terms?

---

[2]Eliyahu M. Goldratt and Jeff I. Cox, *The Goal: A Process of Ongoing Improvement,* rev. ed (Croton-on-Hudson, N.Y.: North River Press, 1986).

9. What is an ABC analysis with regard to inventory?
10. List and describe three types of inventory.
11. How is a line of credit issued by a bank similar to a credit card?
12. What is the difference between a line of credit and a short-term loan?
13. If a firm does not provide for accrued liabilities, what problems may the firm face?
14. Compare standard quantity discounts to cumulative quantity discounts.

EXERCISES AND PROBLEMS

1. Joe Fellows is attempting to categorize several items from his company's financial statements so that he can determine his working capital. Joe notices the following categories of accounts and amounts: cash, $3,500; accounts payable, $10,200; accounts receivable, $15,000; sales taxes due the city of Phoenix, $750; sales taxes due the Arizona Department of Revenue, $3,450; inventory, $17,500; wages payable, $5,350; taxes payable (federal), $2,570; money market fund, $12,300; and computer, $3,400.
   a. List those accounts that would be classified as current assets and as current liabilities.
   b. Determine the amount of gross working capital.
   c. Determine the amount of net working capital.
   d. What is Joe's current ratio?
2. If you have $50,000 in an interest-bearing savings account that pays 5 percent annual interest, how much interest will you earn during a 30-day month?
3. Jane James owns an appliance store. She normally receives $50,000 worth of appliances per month. She does not like to owe people money and always pays her bills on the day she receives the invoice. Someone told her that if she delayed payment, she could actually increase her profit, because the money would be earning interest in her account. She went through her bills and found that she actually had an additional 10 days, on average, to pay her invoices. She also found that she was earning 5 percent interest on the money she had in her money market savings account.
   a. If she delayed payment by the 10 days, how much additional interest would she earn for the year?
   b. Explain how this problem represents a disbursement float.
4. Jane Marks has a restaurant where she accepts credit cards and checks. Several of the places that Jane shops now accept debit cards and do not accept checks. Jane's banker explained that a debit card would immediately transfer money into her account, but would cost $50 per month for the equipment and bank charges. Although she requires proper identification, Jane loses approximately $590 a year due to bad checks. She also determined that on average she loses three days' interest on all checks because the banks are closed on holidays and weekends. Jane currently

earns 3 percent interest on her bank accounts and accepts an average of $400 a day in checks.

  a. What is the total annual cost to Jane for the debit card service?

  b. What is the benefit?

  c. Should Jane implement the system?

5. Larry's Lawn Equipment Company gives terms of 2/10, n/30. Larry has annual credit sales of $500,000, and average accounts receivable of $60,000.

  a. What is Larry's accounts receivable turnover?

  b. What is Larry's average daily collection?

  c. What is the relationship between the terms that Larry is giving and his average daily collection?

6. A firm has $400,000 in credit sales and $100,000 in accounts receivable. Compute accounts receivable turnover and average number of collection days. How do these numbers relate to the terms of 2/10, n/30?

7. If Larry had accounts receivable of $100,000 rather than $60,000:

  a. What is Larry's accounts receivable turnover?

  b. What is Larry's average collection period?

  c. What should Larry do, if anything?

8. You are managing a company that stocks and distributes hardware. The company employs two purchasing agents who receive a combined salary of $90,000. They process 6,000 purchase requests per year. Average inventory in storage is $600,000, and the total cost of running the warehouse is $200,000. You are told that the company purchases 5,000 hammers per year at a cost of $5.34 per hammer.

  a. Using the EOQ formula, how many hammers should be ordered at one time?

  b. If the hammer vendor stated that it would charge $5.00 per hammer if you ordered 200 or more at a time, what would you do?

9. Calculate the economic order quantity, or EOQ, if annual demand is 10,000 units, inventory storage costs average 20 percent, unit price is $50, and ordering costs are $30.

10. Harriet has been told about an ABC inventory analysis. She has accumulated the following annual figures for her flower shop: roses, $10,000; ribbon, $100; bud vases, $1,000; pins, $15; glass bowls, $500; ceramic pots, $3,000; wrapping paper, $250; and carnations, $5,500.

  a. Using the percent of total inventory cost, if these were her total inventory costs, what items would be classified as A items?

  b. What items are C items?

11. Your firm sells home appliances at retail. When ordering washing machines from the manufacturer, you notice the following terms listed in the catalog:

  ◆ List price, $400

  ◆ Trade discounts of 25/15/5

If you take advantage of all trade discounts, find the net price you will pay for the washing machine.

12. Explain the following terms:
    a. 2/10, n/30
    b. 3/15, n/60
    c. n/40
    d. What is the effective rate of interest you will pay if you do not take advantage of the cash discounts described?

13. Bernie's Bike Shop receives the following trade discounts: 35/25/15. The vendor's price list indicates that 35 percent off list price is for purchasing bikes in quantities of 100 or more, 25 percent off list price for assembling the bikes for customers, and 15 percent for sales promotion and local advertising.
    a. If the manufacturer's list price is $470, what should Bernie pay for each bike if he orders 110 bikes at a time, assembles the bikes, and displays and advertises them?
    b. What is Bernie's single equivalent discount rate?
    c. How much will Bernie pay the manufacturer for each bike if he orders 10 bikes at a time and takes advantage of the other discounts?

14. In the above problem, Bernie is given terms of 4/15, n/30, and he pays by day 15.
    a. How much will he pay the manufacturer for the order of 110 bikes?
    b. For how much will the manufacturer credit Bernie's account?
    c. If Bernie has a cash flow problem and waits until day 30 to pay the manufacturer, what is his effective cost of financing for the year?

TIME VALUE OF MONEY 8

Learning Objectives

When you have completed this chapter, you should be able to:

- Explain the relationship between the time value of money and inflation.
- Distinguish between simple interest and compound interest.
- Distinguish between effective rate and stated rate.
- Explain the differences between an ordinary annuity and an annuity due.
- Calculate the future value and present value factors that are used to solve time value of money problems.

- Integrate several of the methods provided in time value of money to solve real-life financial problems.
- Use a financial calculator to solve time value of money problems.
- Present spreadsheet applications of the mathematics of finance.
- Use financial tables to solve time value of money problems.

All businesses have to invest in plant and equipment to continue growing and to generate additional revenue now and in the future. The decision to invest is referred to as the capital budgeting decision. Chapter 9 is a detailed chapter on the various techniques that we can use in making capital budgeting decisions. Before going into detail concerning the steps and various techniques involved in making the capital budgeting decision, it is important to understand some basic terms or tools that will further aid us in our evaluation of a capital budgeting proposal. We begin in this chapter by discussing the time value of money. Mathematically, the **time value of money** is the loss of purchasing power that occurs over time as a result of inflation. **Inflation** is an increase in average prices over time. It will take more future dollars than current dollars to buy the same items, because the future dollar is inflated. In other words, a dollar received now can purchase more than a dollar received five years from now; and the dollar received five years from now is more valuable than the dollar received forty years from now, ceteris paribus.

If you were a child in 1957, the cost of going to a movie was 25 cents; two hot dogs, French fries, and a beverage at a delicatessen cost 55 cents; and popcorn and a candy bar cost 20 cents. This appears to be a dollar well spent. In 1999 the movie alone cost $5.75. In 1999 we spent $13.50 to purchase the identical items we bought for $1.00 in 1957 (movie, $5.75; two hot dogs, $3.50; fries, $0.75; beverage, $0.75; popcorn, $1.75; and candy bar, $1.00). If the inflation rate averages 6 percent over the 40 years, the purchasing power of a dollar 40 years from now will be 9.72 cents. Therefore, the dollar loses over 90 percent of its purchasing power over 40 years. The method used to calculate this scenario will now be discussed so that we can fully understand the time value of money. Once this concept of time value of money is understood fully, we can apply this tool in evaluating the capital budgeting decision.

We first discuss the concepts of simple interest, bank discount, and compound interest and then distinguish between the two types of interest. However, prior to illustrating the mathematics of the time value of money, note that not all items can be measured by using these formulas. Some items, especially those that are produced by means of high technology, actually decrease in price over time. Examples are color television sets, computers, digital watches, and VCRs. Other factors that are not considered are opportunity costs, as discussed in Chapter 1. There are several alternatives that we can spend a dollar on today that we may not be able to accomplish in the future. This does not negate the fact that mathematical calculations are absolutely necessary when we are making business and personal plans. Therefore, we should use time value of money calculations when making many business decisions.

SIMPLE INTEREST

Simple interest is the amount of interest earned on the principal amount stated. The **principal amount stated** is the base amount that we borrow or save. If $1,000 is borrowed at 8 percent for one year, then simple interest is $80. This is computed as follows:

$$I = Prt$$

where

I = interest
P = principal
r = rate
t = time

$$I = (\$1{,}000)(0.08)(1) = \$80$$

If \$1,000 is borrowed for one-half year at 8 percent, then simple interest (I) equals \$40. This is computed as follows:

$$I = (\$1{,}000)(0.08)(0.5) = \$40$$

Simple interest is used in many short-term (less than one year) transactions and is computed initially based on original principal amount, interest rate, and time span. It is added onto the principal to determine the total amount owed or due.

Simple interest added onto \$1,000 borrowed for three years at 8 percent is exemplified in the following manner:

$$I = Prt$$
$$= (\$1{,}000)(0.08)(3) = \$240$$
$$S = P + I$$
$$= \$1{,}000 + \$240 = \$1{,}240$$

where S is the total amount due (maturity amount). Thus, \$1,240 would have to be paid back at the end of three years. Or, if we placed \$1,000 in an account earning 8 percent, then we would expect to have \$1,240 in our account at the end of three years.

Notice that the formula for simple interest is a basic formula which can be manipulated to find any of the components. If we know any three of the four values in the formula, we should be able to calculate the missing factor. For example, consider the previous data. If we know that the interest amount is \$240, and the rate and time are 8 percent and three years, respectively, then we can find the amount of the principal by the following method:

$$I = Prt$$
$$\$240 = P(0.08)(3)$$
$$P = \frac{\$240}{(0.08)(3)} = \frac{\$240}{0.24} = \$1{,}000$$

Another example occurs when your vendor is owed \$1,000 and is scheduled to receive \$1,300 on a promissory note that you signed at a simple interest rate of 8 percent. You wish to determine how long it will take to pay off your vendor. First you must calculate the interest of $300 by subtracting $1,000 from the $1,300 you promised to pay the vendor. Thus, the following can be applied:

$$I = Prt$$
$$\$300 = (\$1000)(0.08)(t)$$
$$t = \frac{\$300}{(\$1,000)(0.08)} = \frac{\$300}{\$80} = 3.75 \text{ years}$$

Note that simple interest is calculated up front and is immediately added onto the principal to determine the amount owed.

BANK DISCOUNT

The bank discount is an amount of interest deducted from the amount you wish to borrow. It is calculated by multiplying the amount you wish to borrow times the bank discount rate and the amount of time the loan is in effect. This is computed as follows:

$$D = Sdt$$

where

D = bank discount
S = maturity value of loan
d = discount rate
t = time

If we borrow $1,000 for one year at 8 percent, then bank discount (D) is equal to $80. This amount is deducted from the $1,000 that you wish to borrow. You will receive proceeds of $920.

$$D = Sdt$$
$$= (\$1,000)(0.08)(1) = \$80$$
$$\text{Proceeds} = S - D$$
$$= \$1,000 - \$80 = \$920$$

The amount that is paid back to the bank one year later is $1,000 ($S$). This amount is the maturity value of the loan. The problem is that proceeds of $1,000—not $920—are what we need. Thus, we employ the following formula which allows us to calculate the amount that we have to borrow:

$$\text{Amount borrowed} = \frac{\text{Proceeds}}{1 - dt} = \frac{\$1,000}{1 - (0.08)(1)} =$$

$$\frac{\$1,000}{0.92} = \$1,086.96$$

Notice that the stated rate of interest by the bank is 8 percent. However, if we have to borrow $1,086.96 to have the use of $1,000 proceeds, then interest of $86.96 is calculated on the $1,086.96 that we borrow which is the cost of the $1,000 proceeds. The result is an effective annual interest rate of not 8 percent as stated by the bank, but 8.696, or rounded to 8.7, percent. The effective annual interest rate is the actual interest rate paid, taking into account the cost of the money borrowed and the actual amount of the money used. The effective rate is:

$$\text{Effective annual interest rate} =$$

$$\frac{\text{Interest paid}}{(\text{Proceeds})(t)} = \frac{\$86.96}{(\$1,000)(1)} = 0.08696$$

It is important to note that 8.696 is 8 percent plus 69 or (70 because of rounding) hundredths of a percent. Each hundredth of a percent is a basis point; 8.70 is 8 percent plus 70 basis points. Thus, for every dollar that we borrow using bank discount, we are not actually paying 8 percent or $8 interest on every $100 used, but $8.70.

Entrepreneurs often need money for short periods of time, typically less than one year. Several bills must be paid on a quarterly or semiannual basis (e.g., taxes, insurance, or vendor deliveries). When revenues are significantly less than expenditures, borrowing money for a short time may be required. For example, you need $2,000 of proceeds for a period of 90 days, and the going bank discount rate is 8 percent. The amount to be borrowed can be calculated as follows:

$$\text{Amount borrowed} = \frac{\text{Proceeds}}{1 - dt} = \frac{\$2,000}{1 - (0.08)\left(\dfrac{90}{365}\right)} =$$

$$\frac{\$2,000}{1 - 0.0198} = \frac{\$2,000}{0.9803} = \$2,040.25$$

Using our formula for effective annual interest rate we see that the $40.25 paid on borrowed funds of $2,040.25 for the use of $2,000 for 90 days is an effective annual rate of 8.16 percent.

$$\text{Effective annual interest rate} =$$

$$\frac{\text{Interest paid}}{(\text{Proceeds})(t)} = \frac{\$40.25}{(\$2,000)\left(\dfrac{90}{365}\right)} = 0.0816$$

Notice that you can cross multiply to check the math, as the interest paid ($40.25) is the product of the amount of money you are using ($2,000), multiplied by the effective rate (8.16 percent), multiplied by the time (90 ÷ 365).

Federal Treasury Bills

In certain situations, the entrepreneur can actually perform the function of a bank. Businesses oftentimes have excess cash that they want to invest and collect interest on for a short period of time. The businesses need both safety of principal and ease of liquidity. What better source of investing than to lend the U.S. government money for a short time? The government is the borrower and the business is the lender. The government issues treasury bills in denominations of $10,000 for three months, six months, and one year. Consider a three-month treasury bill. As a business owner, you can send a check for $10,000 directly to the Federal Reserve Bank. The Federal Reserve calculates the bank discount to be paid on borrowing $10,000 for three months or 91 days. They will then send you a check for this amount of bank discount and borrow the remaining proceeds. For example, if the discount rate on three-month T-bills is 4.73 percent, then a check for $117.93 of bank discount will be sent to you. The government will use the remaining proceeds of $9,882.07. At the end of three months they will return your entire $10,000. The Treasury auction of 91-day treasury bills as of October 7, 1999, used an interest rate of 4.73 percent. This can be exemplified by the following:

$$D = Sdt$$

$$= (\$10,000)(0.0473)\left(\frac{91}{365}\right) = \$117.93$$

$$\text{Proceeds} = S - D$$

$$= \$10,000 - \$117.93 = \$9,882.07$$

Thus, the government has the use of $9,882.07 (proceeds) for 91 days and pays interest of $117.93. This results in an effective rate of

$$\text{Effective annual interest rate} =$$

$$\frac{\text{Interest paid}}{(\text{Proceeds})(t)} = \frac{\$117.93}{(\$9,882.07)\left(\dfrac{91}{365}\right)} = 0.0479, \text{ or } 4.79\%$$

Uses of Simple Interest and Bank Discount

As we have seen, entrepreneurs borrow and lend capital to others. For example, your friend needs $10,000 immediately as a down payment on a house. You decide to become a lender. Both of you agree that 8 percent would be a fair interest rate for 180 days. His current house is on the real estate market and he is sure it will sell within the 180 days, after which he will repay you. Your friend signs a note that is based on simple interest.

$$I = Prt$$
$$= (\$10{,}000)(0.08)\left(\frac{180}{365}\right) = \$394.52$$
$$S = P + I = \$10{,}000 + \$394.52 = \$10{,}394.52$$

Your friend agrees to repay you $10,394.52 in 180 days for use of $10,000 now. He is the payer and you are the payee. In 60 days, you find that you need cash to take advantage of a cash discount on equipment that you are buying for your business. You go to a bank and ask if it will buy the note from you. The bank says it will be happy to discount the note at 12 percent (prime plus 3.5 percent). The bank multiplies the maturity value of the note ($10,394.52) by 12 percent interest for 120 days remaining (120 days remaining ÷ 365 days per year) and calculates the bank discount in dollars ($410.09). The bank subtracts the $410.09 from the maturity value ($10,394.52) of the note and gives you proceeds of $9,984.43 as shown:

$$D = Sdt$$
$$= (\$10{,}394.52)(0.12)\left(\frac{120}{365}\right) = \$410.0852$$
$$\text{Proceeds} = S - D$$
$$= \$10{,}394.52 - \$410.09 = \$9{,}984.43$$

Notice that the payee actually lost money in discounting the note; however, he needed money very fast. If he did not need the money after 60 days and could wait until day 150, then the note would only have 30 days left until maturity. He would then receive $10,292.00 of proceeds and would have made $292 in interest while relinquishing $102.52 to the bank for discounting the note 30 days before the maturity date.

$$D = Sdt$$
$$= (\$10{,}394.52)(0.12)\left(\frac{30}{365}\right) = \$102.52$$
$$\text{Proceeds} = S - D$$
$$= \$10{,}394.52 - \$102.52 = \$10{,}292.00$$

Of course we realize that many loans are for long periods of time and many of us have savings accounts, retirement accounts, and investments on which we expect to earn interest for several years. For these areas we typically will use compound interest.

 # COMPOUND INTEREST

Compound interest is the interest earned or charged on both the principal amount and on the accrued interest that has been previously earned or charged. With compound interest, we earn interest both on the principal amount and on the interest that has already accrued.

If $1,000 is saved for three years and is compounded yearly, or annually, at 8 percent, then the following interest amounts are computed for each of the individual years, using the formula $I = Prt$.

$$\text{Interest for year 1} = (\$1,000)(0.08)(1) = \$80$$

Because our bank balance after the first year is equal to the principal of $1,000 plus the interest earned of $80, when computing our interest for the next year, we begin with a new principal amount of $1,080.

$$\text{Interest for year 2} = (\$1,080)(0.08)(1) = \$86.40$$

Our bank balance at the end of year 2 will be $1,080 plus the interest of $86.40 earned in year 2. We begin computing interest for year 3 with a new principal amount of $1,166.40.

Over the course of three years, $259.71 of interest has been earned through compounding. This is a higher amount than the $240 earned through simple interest; or, stated another way, $19.71 more will be earned if interest is earned on both principal and interest, as a result of compounding, rather than on principal alone.

Although the simple interest formula can be used to determine compound interest, as we have shown, imagine the complexity of computing interest on a long-term investment in this way. For example, if you won a lottery worth $1 million and chose to take the cash and invest it in a money market account earning 8 percent interest compounded annually for twenty years, what would the value of your account be in twenty years? As you can see, it would be quite tedious to run the simple interest formula twenty times.

We can bypass the multiple individual steps in computing compound interest by using the following compound interest formula to determine future value:

where

FV = Future value
PV = Present value, or current principal amount
$\quad i$ = Interest rate earned per period of compounding
$\quad n$ = Number of compounding periods that the money will be
invested

Once the future value factor is found, all that has to be done is to multiply the principal amount (PV) by the future value factor (FVF) to obtain the future value amount (FV). Thus, using the previous example of saving $1,000 for three years at 8 percent compounded yearly, we observe the following:

$$FV = PV(1 + i)^n = \$1,000(1 + 0.08)^3 =$$
$$\$1,000(1.2597) = \$1,259.71$$

Note that this answer is exactly the same as that obtained using the simple interest formula. By using one simple formula, we have eliminated the previous tedious steps of calculating interest for each year's principal amount and adding all resulting interest amounts. This formula allows us (especially now that many of us own home computers or calculators that include power functions) to easily calculate future values of virtually any investment.

Many of us buy lottery tickets. If you were to win a $1 million lottery, several states would allow you to choose from two options: (1) take the cash at a discounted rate of 50 percent and immediately pay taxes on this amount, or (2) take an annuity payable at $50,000 per year for 20 years. If you take the cash, you will receive a check for $300,000 ($500,000 minus taxes of about 40 percent, counting federal and local taxes). If you invest this money in a stock mutual fund that historically has averaged 10 percent return, how much money will you have in your account at the end of 20 years? Using our formula, we find that you will have $2,018,250 in your account at the end of 20 years.

$$FV = PV(1 + i)^n = \$300,000(1 + 0.10)^{20} =$$
$$\$300,000(6.7275) = \$2,018,250$$

We can obtain the same information by using the tables in Appendix B. To use Appendix Table B-1, we need to know two items: the interest rate per period of the investment, and the number of periods. Going to Appendix Table B-1, Future Value of a Lump Sum, we look for the FVF by going across to the 10 percent column and surfing down to the 20-period row. We find that the FVF is 6.7275. We then multiply the FVF by our present value of $300,000 to find that we will have $2,018,250 in the bank. Notice that we obtain the same answer by either method.

EFFECTIVE RATE

Interest rates take on two dimensions: (1) the rate that is stated or quoted by the lending institution, and (2) the actual, or effective, rate that is earned or charged. The **stated** or **quoted rate** is the rate of interest that is listed, normally on an annual basis, and it disregards compounding. The **effective annual rate** is the actual rate paid by the borrower or earned by the investor when compounding is taken into consideration. For example, if you borrow money for a new car and the bank quotes a rate of 8 percent, then you may be under the impression that you will be paying back $8 a year in interest for every $100 you borrow. However, if the bank compounds the loan quarterly, it will actually cost you more than 8 percent. Because the rate per period is 2 percent and there are four periods in a year, the effective rate can be calculated by using the following formula:

$$\text{Effective annual rate} = (1 + i)^n - 1$$

where

$i =$ interest rate per period (found by dividing the quoted rate by the number of compounding periods)

$n =$ number of compounding periods per year

Using our formula, 8 percent compounded quarterly for one year gives an effective annual rate of $(1.02)^4 - 1$. The solution gives us $1.0824 - 1 = 0.0824$, or 8.24 percent. Therefore, if you borrow $10,000 to purchase a new car, and the stated rate is 8 percent, you might think that the annual interest would be $800, but because the effective rate is 8.24 percent, you would actually pay $824 in annual interest. In reality, though, banks now charge daily interest on the outstanding balance; therefore, the effective rate of interest is actually much higher. Because banks now use a 365-day year, the effective annual rate of interest on an 8 percent loan is 8.33 percent $[(1.0002)^{365} - 1]$.

$$\text{Effective annual rate} = (1 + i)^n - 1 =$$
$$\left(1 + \frac{0.08}{365}\right)^{365} - 1 = (1.0002)^{365} - 1 = 1.0833 - 1 = 0.0833$$

Therefore, the interest rate is normally the stated or quoted rate. The effective rate is the interest rate adjusted for compounding and is what should be used to determine the worth of funds that are to be received in the future or the actual payment that will be made.

TIME VALUE OF MONEY METHODS

Now that we have a general understanding of the concept of the time value of money, we want to expand our knowledge to include the basic tools used by businesses in capital budgeting and financial planning. There are six different time value of money formulas that can be used in making capital budgeting decisions. They can be used separately or in conjunction with one another. The actual formulas will be discussed in this chapter, and tables that can be used in lieu of the formulas are included in Appendix B at the end of the book. Each method will be described here, with the basic question that it can answer. All formulas have a basis of total *amount* equals *investment* (made or received) times the *factor*. To use any of the formulas, we must know two of these three items.

FUTURE VALUE OF A LUMP SUM

What is the future value of a lump sum amount for n periods and at i rate of return? A company sells a piece of equipment for $10,000. It deposits the amount received for five years at 8 percent compounded quarterly. What dollar amount (future value) will the company have if it does not use the money for five years? The company will have approximately $14,859 in the bank at the end of five years. This is calculated as follows:

$$FV = PV(1 + i)^n$$

where

FV = future value
PV = present value
i = interest rate
n = number of periods
$(1 + i)^n$ = FVF (future value factor)

Using our calculator, we take 1.02 and raise it to the twentieth power and obtain a multiplier of 1.485947. We then multiply our present value of $10,000 by this factor to obtain $14,859.47. We also could utilize Appendix Table B-1. Going to the 2 percent column and down to 20 periods, we find a multiplier of 1.4859. Then, when we multiply this factor, we get a dollar value of $14,859. Although the table is not as accurate as the calculator, it is easier for many people to use and provides approximately the same results.

PRESENT VALUE OF A FUTURE LUMP SUM

What is the present value of a future lump-sum amount for n periods and at i rate of return? A company plans to sell a piece of equipment in five years at a salvage value of $10,000, and current interest rates are 8 percent, compounded quarterly. The present value of this future sale of assets is $6,729.71. This is calculated as follows:

$$PV = FV\left[\frac{1}{(1 + i)^n}\right] = \$10,000\left[\frac{1}{\left[\left(1 + \frac{0.08}{4}\right)^{20}\right]}\right]$$

$$= \$10,000\left(\frac{1}{1.485947}\right) = \$10,000(0.672971) = \$6,729.71$$

where the term in the square brackets is known as the present value factor (PVF).

Using our calculator, we find the future value factor of 1.485947 and divide 1 by this factor to obtain the present value factor shown in the formula. We obtain a present value factor of 0.672971. Multiplying this factor by our lump-sum amount of $10,000, we get a present value of $6,729.71. If we go to Appendix Table B-2, Present Value of a Future Lump Sum, go across to the 2 percent column, and surf down to the 20-payment row to obtain a value of 0.6730. This gives us a present value of $6,730. Again the slight error is due to rounding in the table.

FUTURE VALUE OF AN ORDINARY ANNUITY

What is the future value of a stream of payments for n periods and at i rate of return when the money is invested at the end of each compounding period? We find that we can save $100 per month, to be compounded monthly for three years at an annual interest rate of 12 percent. Let us assume that we invest the money at the end of each monthly period. This type of annuity is referred to as an **ordinary annuity** and is calculated as follows:

$$FV = A\left[\frac{(1 + i)^n - 1}{i}\right]$$

The annuity (A) is the payment made during each period of compounding. Note that the mode of paying the annuity (paying monthly) must match the period of compounding for the formula (compounding monthly) to be used correctly. The number of periods n is the number of periods that the annuity will be compounded (invested); FV is the value of the annuity at the end of the compounding periods; and i is the interest rate per period of compounding, which is the stated rate (annual rate) divided by the number of compounding periods during the year. For example, if 12 percent is compounded monthly, then we would divide 0.12 by 12 to obtain a per-period rate of 0.01.

$$FV = A\left[\frac{(1 + i)^n - 1}{i}\right] = \$100\left[\frac{\left(1 + \frac{0.12}{12}\right)^{(12 \times 3)} - 1}{\frac{0.12}{12}}\right]$$

$$= \$100\left[\frac{(1 + 0.01)^{36} - 1}{0.01}\right]$$

$$= \$100(43.0769) = \$4,307.69$$

For this problem, using the annuity formula as shown, we obtain a future value factor of 43.076878. We then multiply our annuity of $100 by this factor to obtain a future value of $4,307.69. We also can use Appendix Table B-3, Future Value of an Ordinary Annuity. Using the 1 percent column and going to a value for n of 36, we obtain a future value factor of 43.0769. Multiplying this factor by our annuity of $100, we obtain $4,307.69. In this case, it is identical to the answer obtained with our calculator.

FUTURE VALUE OF AN ANNUITY DUE

What is the future value of a stream of payments for n periods and at i rate of return when the money is invested at the beginning of each compounding period? When we invest the money at the beginning of each monthly period, this is referred to as an annuity due. The value of our account in three years is calculated as follows:

$$FV = A\left\{\left[\frac{(1 + i)^{(n+1)} - 1}{i}\right] - 1\right\} = \$100\left\{\left[\frac{(1 + 0.01)^{(37)} - 1}{0.01}\right] - 1\right\}$$

$$= \$100(43.5076) = \$4,350.76$$

If we invest the money at the beginning of the month, rather than at the end, we find that our $100 grows to $4,350.76, rather than the $4,307.69 obtained by our previous investment. If we go to Appendix Table B-4, Future Value of an Annuity Due, and look up the future value factor, we obtain 43.5076, which is the same factor that we obtained with the calculator. The difference between the future value of this annuity and the future value we obtained for the ordinary annuity is a result of the fact that our investment has one extra period of time to compound, because the payment is made at the beginning of the period. That is why we use 37 as the exponent

Table 8-1 Payment Schedule for Future Value of an Ordinary Annuity and Annuity Due

Ordinary Annuity									
Payment made	100	100	100	100	100	100	100	100	100
Time	1	2	3	4	5	6	7	8	9

Annuity Due									
Payment made	100	100	100	100	100	100	100	100	100
Time	1	2	3	4	5	6	7	8	9

(i.e., $n + 1$) rather than 36. Additionally, we would actually make one less payment during the three years. Table 8-1 demonstrates the difference between the payment schedule of an ordinary annuity and that of an annuity due. Table 8-1 shows our investment during the first nine months of our three-year term. In the case of the ordinary annuity, we make nine payments during the nine periods numbered from 1 to 9. Because the payments are made at the end of the period (month), the ninth payment does not compound (receive any interest). Therefore, the ordinary annuity uses an exponential factor of n. For the annuity due, we make the same number of payments, but each payment receives interest for the entire compounding period (month). Therefore, the first payment, because it is put in at the beginning of the period, receives interest, resulting in one more period of interest than in the ordinary annuity. Hence, our exponent in the formula for an annuity due is $n + 1$, rather than n.

PRESENT VALUE OF AN ORDINARY ANNUITY

What is the present value of a stream of payments for n periods at i rate of return? How much do we have to place in an account today to receive a stream of $100 payments each month for 36 months, or three years? In other words, what is the present value of such a stream of payments? We know that we will receive a total of $3,600 during the three-year period. Let us say that we are retiring, and will receive a retirement payment of $100 per month for three years; we assume the same interest rate of 12 percent as was used for calculating future values of annuities. Again, let us first assume that the money is received at the end of each month (an ordinary annuity). The present value in this case is

$$PV = A\left[\frac{(1 + i)^n - 1}{i(1 + i)^n}\right] = \$100\left[\frac{(1 + 0.01)^{36} - 1}{0.01(1 + 0.01)^{36}}\right]$$
$$= \$100(30.1075) = \$3,010.75$$

Table 8-2   Payment Schedule for Present Value of an Ordinary Annuity and Annuity Due

				Ordinary Annuity					
Payment received	100	100	100	100	100	100	100	100	100
Time	1	2	3	4	5	6	7	8	9

				Annuity Due					
Payment received	100	100	100	100	100	100	100	100	100
Time		1	2	3	4	5	6	7	8	9

Using the preceding formula, we obtain a present value factor of 30.1075. In this example, the present value of the retirement payments, which we receive at the end of the month, is $3,010.75. If we use Appendix Table B-5, Present Value of an Ordinary Annuity, we obtain a present value factor of 30.1075, which is identical to our calculator result. Multiplying the annuity of $100 by the present value factor, we get an identical answer of $3,010.75. Therefore, if we place $3,010.75 in an account today, we can receive monthly payments of $100 for the next three years.

PRESENT VALUE OF AN ANNUITY DUE

Now let us consider the same situation as in the previous section, except that the money is received at the beginning of each month. The present value of this annuity due is:

$$PV = A\left\{\left[\frac{(1 + i)^{(n-1)} - 1}{i(1 + i)^{(n-1)}}\right] + 1\right\} = \$100\left\{\left[\frac{(1 + 0.01)^{35} - 1}{0.01(1 + 0.01)^{35}}\right] + 1\right\}$$
$$= \$100(30.4086) = \$3,040.86$$

Using the formula, we obtain a present value factor of 30.4086. In this example, the present value of the retirement payments, if we receive them at the beginning of the month, is $3,040.86. If we use Appendix Table B-6, Present Value of an Annuity Due, we find a present value factor of 30.4086. Notice the significant difference in the present value of these two annuities. If we receive the payment at the beginning of the month, we will have to place $3,040.86 in our account. The reasons for this difference are shown in Table 8-2. The table shows the payments received during the first nine months of our three-year term. In the case of an ordinary annuity, we receive nine payments during the nine periods numbered from 1 to 9. Because the payments are received at the end of the period (month), the last payment we receive will have nine periods to compound (receive interest). Therefore, the ordinary annuity uses an exponential factor of n.

In the case of an annuity due, however, we receive the same number of payments, but the ninth payment does not receive interest for the ninth period (month). The present value of the last payment compounds for one less period, because the last payment is received immediately upon the last time period's beginning; hence, our exponent in the formula is $n - 1$, rather than n. Additionally, the formula for the present value of an annuity due has a "plus 1" at the end, because you receive your first payment immediately upon beginning the annuity.

This is the reason why we have to start with more money in the case of an annuity due to receive the same payment as we would with an ordinary annuity. So our example showed that we have to invest $3,010.75 to receive $100 a month with an ordinary annuity, but $3,040.86 with an annuity due, to receive the same payment. In addition, because we begin withdrawal of money immediately with an annuity due, the money received in the first period has not accumulated any interest.

Present Value and Amortization

You are probably thinking at this point that all of this is nice to know, but what value does it have for me in real life? Most likely you have a mortgage or know someone who has a mortgage. All of us, at one time or another, finance items such as automobiles, furniture, and houses. As business owners, we finance equipment, facilities, and inventory. So let us look at a real-life example.

The present value of a stream of monthly payments (an ordinary annuity) is actually the mortgage amount that you agree upon when you financed your home. It is the amount that is agreed upon by the borrower and the lender. For example, if you borrow $100,000 for 30 years at 8 percent interest, then the $100,000 is the present value of the stream of payments (monthly mortgage payments) paid at the beginning of each month, but calculated as an ordinary annuity, which would make payment due at the end of the month. Why? The bank wants to collect your mortgage payment one month in advance, because they will not let you live in the house free. For example, the bank requires you to make the mortgage payment for the month of January on January 1, but the payment is calculated as if you made the payment on January 31. You always pay the bank one month is advance for the privilege of living in your house for the month. Thus, if you borrow $100,000, the mortgage payment for the agreed-upon fixed interest rate of 8 percent compounded monthly for 30 years is $733.76. Because you are obligated to make monthly payments for 30 years, you will be making 360 payments (30 years $\times$ 12 months). We will plug this into our equation for an ordinary annuity, which is

$$PV = A\left[\frac{(1 + i)^{(n)} - 1}{i(1 + i)^{(n)}}\right]$$

$$\$100,000 = A\left[\frac{\left(1 + \dfrac{0.08}{12}\right)^{360} - 1}{\dfrac{0.08}{12}\left(1 + \dfrac{0.08}{12}\right)^{360}}\right]$$

$$= A(136.2835)$$

$$A = \frac{\$100,000}{136.2835} = \$733.76$$

Therefore, $733.76 is the monthly mortgage payment or ordinary annuity. This payment will be made for 30 years, or 360 months times $733.76, for a total of $264,153.60. Note that your mortgage is only $100,000; therefore, you will pay $164,153.60 in interest over the life of the loan. Total interest on a loan equals total payments minus loan amount.

Now if you borrow the same $100,000, but decide to pay it off in 15 years, what is the difference in mortgage payments and total amount of interest paid? You now borrow $100,000 for 15 years at 8 percent interest. The $100,000 is the present value of the stream of payments (monthly mortgage payments) paid one month in advance at the beginning of each month at the agreed-upon fixed interest rate of 8 percent compounded monthly but calculated by the bank as an ordinary annuity. We now plug the new values into the same formula:

$$PV = A\left[\frac{(1 + i)^{(n)} - 1}{i(1 + i)^{(n)}}\right]$$

$$\$100,000 = A\left[\frac{\left(1 + \dfrac{0.08}{12}\right)^{180} - 1}{\dfrac{0.08}{12}\left(1 + \dfrac{0.08}{12}\right)^{180}}\right]$$

$$= A(104.6406)$$

$$A = \frac{\$100,000}{104.6406} = \$955.65$$

With a 15-year mortgage at the same 8 percent interest rate, $955.65 is the monthly mortgage payment or ordinary annuity. This payment will be made for 15 years, or 180 months times $955.65, for a total of $172,017. Note that your mortgage is still $100,000; therefore, you now pay $72,017 in interest over the life of the loan. As we can see from comparing the two mortgages, ($164,153.60 of interest on the 30 year mortgage − $72,017 of interest on the 15 year mortgage)= $92,136.60 will be saved in interest if you finance for 15 versus 30 years. The key question is whether you can afford the additional $221.89-a-month payment for the 15-year mortgage. If you are not sure, you can take the 30-year mortgage and make additional principal payments when possible. You can be sure that additional payments made toward reducing the outstanding principal amount will result in your paying off the mortgage sooner, and subsequently you will pay less in interest over the life of the loan.

Banks are in business to make as much profit as possible. Therefore, they normally use the ordinary annuity rather than the annuity due method of calculating payments for all loans. The reason for using the ordinary annuity is that it is easy to understand. If we take the same $100,000 mortgage over a 15-year payment schedule but calculate the payment using the annuity due, then you will have a smaller monthly payment and, over the 180 months, you will pay the bank less interest. These calculations are as shown:

$$PV = A\left\{\left[\frac{(1 + i)^{(n-1)} - 1}{i(1 + i)^{(n-1)}}\right] + 1\right\}$$

$$\$100,000 = A\left\{\left[\frac{\left(1 + \dfrac{0.08}{12}\right)^{179} - 1}{\dfrac{0.08}{12}\left(1 + \dfrac{0.08}{12}\right)^{179}}\right] + 1\right\}$$

$$= A(105.3382)$$

$$A = \frac{\$100,000}{105.3382} = \$949.32$$

We see that with a 15-year mortgage at the same 8 percent interest rate, $949.32 is the monthly mortgage payment or annuity due. This payment will be made for 15 years, or 180 months times $949.32 (versus the $955.65 ordinary annuity payment), for a total of $170,877.60 rather than the $172,017. Note that the bank collects an additional $1,139.40 in interest over the life of the loan by calculating the mortgage using the ordinary annuity formula. Considering the thousands of loans that banks finance each year, this difference in profit is huge.

Amortization

At this point it is important for us to understand that the monthly payment made to the lender consists of an interest amount calculated on the previous loan balance and a principal amount which will serve to reduce that loan balance. The reduction of the loan balance by applying each month's principal payment is known as **amortization.** To further clarify amortization, Table 8-3 addresses several components that include payment number, date

Table 8-3 Loan Amortization for Mortgage

	Loan Date of Origin	Loan Amount	Annual Interest Rate	# of Payments	Monthly Payment
	1/1/99	$100,000.00	8.00%	360	$733.76

Payment Number	Date of Payment	Monthly Payment	Monthly Interest	Principal Payment	Remaining Loan Balance
					$100,000.00
1	1/1/99	$ 733.76	$ 666.67	$ 67.10	99,932.90
2	2/1/99	733.76	666.22	67.55	99,865.36
3	3/1/99	733.76	665.77	68.00	99,797.36
4	4/1/99	733.76	665.32	68.45	99,728.91
5	5/1/99	733.76	664.86	68.91	99,660.01
6	6/1/99	733.76	664.40	69.36	99,590.64
7	7/1/99	733.76	663.94	69.83	99,520.82
8	8/1/99	733.76	663.47	70.29	99,450.52
9	9/1/99	733.76	663.00	70.76	99,379.76
10	10/1/99	733.76	662.53	71.23	99,308.53
11	11/1/99	733.76	662.06	71.71	99,236.82
12	12/1/99	733.76	661.58	72.19	99,164.64
Annual Totals		$8,805.17	$7,969.81	$835.36	
13	1/1/00	733.76	661.10	72.67	99,091.97
14	2/1/00	733.76	660.61	73.15	99,018.82
15	3/1/00	733.76	660.13	73.64	98,945.18
16	4/1/00	733.76	659.63	74.13	98,871.05
17	5/1/00	733.76	659.14	74.62	98,796.42
18	6/1/00	733.76	658.64	75.12	98,721.30
19	7/1/00	733.76	658.14	75.62	98,645.68
20	8/1/00	733.76	657.64	76.13	98,569.55
21	9/1/00	733.76	657.13	76.63	98,492.92
22	10/1/00	733.76	656.62	77.15	98,415.77
23	11/1/00	733.76	656.11	77.66	98,338.11
24	12/1/00	733.76	655.59	78.18	98,259.94
Annual Totals		$8,805.17	$7,900.48	$904.70	

of payment, payment amount, interest paid, principal payment, and loan balance. We used the sample $100,000 mortgage for 30 years at 8 percent compounded monthly to show an amortization schedule for the first two years of the loan.

INTERNAL RATE OF RETURN

The items discussed so far in this chapter provide us with a method of determining which formula or table to use, based on the type of financial terms and conditions that we face when obtaining a loan or making an investment. When we own a business or make an investment, however, we do not necessarily have neat little items that can be plugged into tables. For example, in January 1996, we bought 10,000 shares of stock in XYZ Company that were selling for $2 a share. We sold the shares in January 2000, for $3 a share, or $30,000. When we look at this initially, we believe that we made 50 percent on our investment, but we must take into consideration the time value of money, because purchasing power was lost during the four years that the money was invested in the stock. Therefore, we want to find the actual rate of return, or **internal rate of return,** that equates a dollar invested now with a dollar received in the future. From our previous discussion, we know that the present value equals future value times the present value factor. This, then, is our formula for the present value of a future lump sum. We know the present value, which is $20,000, and the future value received, which is $30,000. Once we find the factor, using simple algebra, we can then interpolate and find the actual rate of return. We enter the known values into our formula as follows:

$$PV = FV \times PVF$$
$$\$20,000 = \$30,000 \times PVF$$
$$PVF = \frac{\$20,000}{\$30,000} = 0.6667$$

To use the tables, we go to Appendix Table B-2, and go down to four periods. We then scan across the table and find that the PVF for 10 percent is 0.6830 and for 11 percent is 0.6587. So the actual rate of return is between 10 and 11 percent, because 0.6667 is between 0.6830 (10 percent) and 0.6587 (11 percent). If we want to come closer to the actual rate of return, we will have to interpolate. **Interpolation** is the process of using mathematics to find an unknown value between two known values.

The first step in performing interpolation is to subtract the 11 percent PVF (0.6587) from the 10 percent PVF (0.6830), to obtain 0.0243. We then subtract the actual PVF for the x rate, which is 0.6667, from the PVF for 10 percent (0.6830) and obtain 0.0163. We can express this graphically with the following diagram:

$$1\begin{bmatrix} ?\begin{bmatrix} 10\text{----}0.6830 \\ x\text{----}0.6667 \end{bmatrix}0.0163 \\ 11\text{----}0.6587 \end{bmatrix}0.0243$$

We actually solve for our unknown (?) algebraically. In the following formula, ? is our unknown distance from the lower interest rate i_1 to x, which is the internal rate of return that matches the factor 0.6667.

i_1 is the lower interest rate
i_2 is the higher interest rate

$$\frac{?}{i_2 - i_1} = \frac{\text{Partial distance}}{\text{Total distance}} \frac{(10\%PVF - X\%PVF)}{(10\%PVF - 11\%PVF)}$$

$$\frac{?}{11 - 10} = \frac{(0.6830 - 0.6667)}{(0.6830 - 0.6587)}$$

$$\frac{?}{1} = \frac{0.0163}{0.0243}$$

$$?(0.0243) = (1)(0.0163)$$

$$? = \frac{(1)(0.0163)}{0.0243} = 0.6708$$

$$IRR = X = i_1 + ? = 10\% + 0.6708\% = 10.67\%$$

Therefore, 10 percent plus the value of ? is equal to the actual rate of return, which is 10.67 percent.

Another formula for solving the internal rate of return problem when an amount invested culminates in a future lump sum is

$$IRR = \sqrt[n]{\frac{FV}{PV}} - 1$$

Using the previous problem with future value of $30,000 (amount received from our investment in four years) and present value of $20,000 (amount that we invested), we solve for IRR as follows:

$$IRR = \sqrt[n]{\frac{FV}{PV}} - 1$$

$$= \sqrt[4]{\frac{\$30,000}{\$20,000}} - 1$$

$$= \sqrt[4]{1.5} - 1 = 1.1067 - 1$$

$$= 0.1067 = 10.67\%$$

The preceding are examples of finding the IRR when we receive a lump-sum payment, have both present and future values, and the time element.

In other situations in business, we will receive an annuity. Say that you will have to spend $10,000 to develop a software program. The publisher estimates that you will receive royalties of $3,000 each year for four years, after which time the software will have to be updated, or the program will be obsolete. You want to know the actual rate of return over time that this payment of $3,000 gives you on your investment. To determine this we will have to use interpolation. From our previous discussion on annuities, we know that this problem involves determining the present value of an ordinary annuity. The formula is

$$PV = A(PVAF)$$
$$\$10,000 = \$3,000(PVAF)$$
$$PVAF = \frac{\$10,000}{\$3,000} = 3.3333$$

We then go to Appendix Table B-5, and go down to an n of 4. Moving across the table, we find for 6 percent a PVAF of 3.4651 and for 8 percent a PVAF of 3.3121. We are using 2 percent interest variation to show that the procedure can be used for any interest rate variation. Using the procedure shown in our previous example, the first step in the procedure for interpolation is to subtract the 8 percent PVAF (3.3121) from the 6 percent PVAF (3.4651), from which we obtain 0.1530. We then subtract the actual PVAF for the x rate, which is 3.3333, from the PVAF for 6 percent, which is 3.4651, and obtain 0.1318.

We can express this graphically with the following diagram:

$$2\begin{bmatrix} ?\begin{bmatrix} 6\text{----}3.4651 \\ x\text{----}3.3333 \end{bmatrix}0.1318 \\ 8\text{----}3.3121 \end{bmatrix}0.1530$$

We actually solve for our unknown ? algebraically (as follows) and find that ? = 1.7229. Six percent plus 1.7229 gives us an actual rate of return of 7.72 percent. The mathematical calculations for this are as follows:

$$\frac{?}{i_2 - i_1} = \frac{\text{Partial distance}}{\text{Total distance}} \frac{(6\%PVAF - x\%PVAF)}{(6\%PVAF - 8\%PVAF)}$$
$$\frac{?}{8 - 6} = \frac{(3.4651 - 3.3333)}{(3.4651 - 3.3121)}$$
$$\frac{?}{2} = \frac{0.1318}{0.1530}$$
$$?(0.1530) = (2)(0.1318)$$
$$? = \frac{(2)(0.1318)}{0.1530} = 1.7229$$
$$IRR = X = i_1 + ? = 6\% + 1.7229\% = 7.72\%$$

The results basically show that if you place the $10,000 in an account paying 7.72 percent interest, and you systematically withdraw $3,000 from the account each year, you will have exhausted the account in four years (i.e., the balance in the account at the end of four years will be zero).

If we did not have a table for reference, then we could solve the problem using a calculator. We first obtain the actual factor by dividing the present value by the annuity, since $PV = A \times PVAF$. We divide $10,000 by

$3,000 and obtain a value of 3.3333. We then use the formula for the present value of an ordinary annuity:

$$PV = A\left[\frac{(1 + i)^n - 1}{i(1 + i)^n}\right]$$

Because we know *PV* and *A,* we now use the formula in the brackets to do interpolation. We need to find a factor above 3.3333 and one below 3.3333. By trial and error, we choose an interest rate that we believe will have a present value annuity factor close to 3.3333. We initially used 6 percent and obtained a value of 3.4651 for the present value annuity factor; we also used 8 percent and obtained a PVAF of 3.3121.

We solved this problem on an Hewlett Packard (HP) 12c calculator by pressing the following keys, in the following sequence. To enter this formula in a calculator, we first must find the numerator and store it, then find the denominator and store it. We then divide the denominator into the numerator. Obviously, you must have a calculator with the functions discussed in the following procedure, or you cannot use a calculator to solve the problem.

Because the assumed IRR lies between an interest rate of 6 percent and 8 percent, we must find the present value annuity factors for each interest rate. We begin by finding the factor for 6 percent. Because the formula uses 1 + *i,* we press 1.06 ENTER. Then press 4, then press y^x, and see 1.2625. Now press 1, then press minus (−), and you will see 0.2625. Press the STO key, then press 1 to store this number as the numerator of the factor. Next press 0.06 ENTER, then press 1.06 ENTER, press 4 and press y^x, and you will see 1.2625. Then press the × key to multiply, and view 0.0757. This is the denominator that must be stored. Press STO and press 2. We then divide the denominator into the numerator as follows: Press RCL and 1, and see 0.2625; then press RCL and 2, and see 0.0757. Then press the divide key (÷), and see 3.4651. We then use the same procedure for 8 percent and find the factor of 3.3121. Interpolating between these two factors, as demonstrated previously, gives us an actual return of 7.72 percent.

Interpolation also can be used to find the actual interest rate used in the future value of an annuity problem. We will provide one more example. P. D. Attricks and his wife just had a baby girl. He believes that it will cost at least $100,000 to provide a college education for his daughter (future value) when she is 18 years old. P. D.'s father, Jerry Attricks, said he would put $2,000 (annuity) into an investment at the end of each year to ensure that his granddaughter would have enough funds to receive her education. This is a future value of an ordinary annuity problem where the future value is $100,000 and the annuity is $2,000. The time period is 18 years. Therefore,

$$Annuity(FVAF) = FV$$
$$\$2,000(FVAF) = \$100,000$$
$$FVAF = \frac{FV}{Annuity} = \frac{\$100,000}{\$2,000} = 50.0000$$

Using interpolation and Appendix Table B-3, we notice that for 18 years the FVAF for 10 percent is 45.5992 and for 11 percent is 50.3959. The 10 percent factor is lower and the 11 percent factor is higher than the actual factor of 50.0000, which matches with our required internal rate of return. Using the procedure for interpolation we obtain an IRR of 10.92 percent as shown:

$$\frac{?}{i_2 - i_1} = \frac{\text{Partial distance}}{\text{Total distance}} \frac{(x\%FVAF - 10\%FVAF)}{(11\%FVAF - 10\%FVAF)}$$
$$\frac{?}{11 - 10} = \frac{(50.0000 - 45.5992)}{(50.3959 - 45.5992)}$$
$$\frac{?}{1} = \frac{4.4008}{4.7967}$$
$$?(4.7967) = (1)(4.4008)$$
$$? = \frac{(1)(4.4008)}{4.7967} = 0.9175$$
$$\text{IRR} = X = i_1 + ? = 10\% + 0.9175\% =$$
$$10.9175\%, \text{rounded to } 10.92\%$$

Thus, Grandpa Jerry needs to seek out only those investments that will return a minimum of 10.92 percent per year, to reach his goal of $100,000 at the end of 18 years.

Solving for n or time

Another situation that we may encounter involves finding the amount of time that it takes a present sum of money to compound into a future value. If we invest $10,000 in a mutual fund that earns an interest rate of 12 percent annually, and we wish the investment to mature to $30,000, how long will we have to keep the $10,000 invested? This problem can be solved using a calculator that has a log function and using the following formula:

$$n = \frac{\log_{10} FV - \log_{10} PV}{\log_{10}(1 + i)}$$
$$= \frac{\log_{10} \$30,000 - \log_{10} \$10,000}{\log_{10}(1.12)}$$

$$= \frac{4.4771 - 4.000}{0.0492}$$

$$= \frac{0.4771}{0.0492} = 9.69 \text{ years}$$

Rule of 72

We can also find an approximation of the amount of time that it takes a present sum of money to double by dividing the number 72 by the interest rate earned on an investment. This procedure is known as the rule of seventy-two. If we invest $10,000 at 12 percent annually, it should take approximately 6 years for the invested amount to double to $20,000.

$$\text{Time for investment to double} = \frac{72}{\text{Annual interest rate}}$$

$$= \frac{72}{12} = 6 \text{ years}$$

Using the above formula, if we know the amount of time we want to wait for our money to double, we can find the annual interest rate that we must receive to reach our goal. Using the above we would be able to find the annual interest rate of 12 percent by dividing 72 by 6 years.

$$\text{Annual interest rate} = \frac{72}{\text{Time for investment to double}}$$

$$= \frac{72}{6} = 12 \text{ } percent$$

CONCLUSION

This chapter on the time value of money provides us with the tools that we require as financial managers and small business entrepreneurs to solve many of the actual problems faced in decision making. We covered the following areas:

- Simple and compound interest
- Bank discount
- Interest rate variances and stated and effective rates of interest
- Present and future values of lump sums
- Present and future values of both ordinary annuities and annuities due
- Finding rates of return through interpolation, by use of tables and by use of a calculator

Appendix A demonstrates how to place the formulas used in this chapter into spreadsheet programs.

We will use most of these formulas when making decisions on the purchase of equipment and the investment of money in personal or business ventures that will have a life of one year or more. The process for making these decisions is capital budgeting, which is the topic of our next chapter.

REVIEW AND DISCUSSION QUESTIONS

1. What is the relationship between the time value of money and inflation?
2. Compare simple interest to compound interest.
3. Distinguish between bank discount and simple interest.
4. Differentiate between a stated rate of interest and effective rate of interest.
5. What is the difference between the present value of an annuity and the future value of an annuity?
6. What is the difference between an ordinary annuity and an annuity due?
7. How do banks calculate the monthly payment on a loan?
8. Explain the rule of 72.

EXERCISES AND PROBLEMS

1. Jill Kramer borrowed $25,000 to pay for her child's education. Jill must repay the loan at the end of 5 months in one payment with an 11.5% simple interest rate.
   a. What is the total amount that Jill must repay in 5 months?
   b. How much interest does Jill repay?
2. Joe Jones went to his bank to find out how long it will take for $1,000 to amount to $1,350 at 9% simple interest. Please solve Joe's problem.
3. Hy Potenuse bought a $10,000 Treasury bill at a 5.15% discount for 13 weeks (91 days).
   a. How much does Hy pay for the bond?
   b. What is the effective rate of interest?
   c. Who is the borrower?
4. Alana Olsen borrowed $5,000 for 90 days from First Bank. The bank discounted the note at 10%.
   a. What proceeds did Olsen receive?
   b. What is the effective rate to the nearest basis point?
5. The face value of a simple interest note and simple discount note is $8,000. Assume both notes have 12% interest rates for 60 days. Calculate the following.
   a. The amount of interest charged for each?

    b. The maturity value of the simple interest note?

    c. The maturity value of the simple discount note?

    d. The amount the borrower receives for the simple interest note?

    e. The amount the borrower receives for the simple discount note?

  6. You deposit $760 in an account that compounds monthly at 6 percent. How much will you have in your account at the end of 10 years?

  7. A balloon payment on your house is due in 10 years, of $21,000. If you can earn an average of 5 percent per year for the 10-year period, how much will you have to place into an account today to have the $21,000 in 10 years?

  8. A financial institution quotes a rate of 6.45 percent compounded monthly. What is the effective rate for the year?

  9. If you want an effective rate of 10 percent, what is an acceptable quoted rate if money is compounded monthly?

10. If inflation averages 4 percent per year, how much purchasing power will $1.00 lose in 10 years?

11. How much will you pay for a $10,000 automobile in 20 years if the inflation rate averages 6 percent per year for 20 years?

12. You place $2,000 in a retirement account at the beginning of each year for 10 years. You believe the account will earn 12 percent per year, compounded quarterly. How much will you have in your retirement account in 10 years?

13. The city of South Podunk borrows $80,000 by issuing bonds. It plans to set up a sinking fund that will repay the loan at the end of 10 years. Assume a 10 percent interest rate per year. What should the city place into the fund at the end of each year to have $80,000 in the account to pay back their bondholders?

14. You deposit the following, at the beginning of each year, into a growth mutual fund that earns 18 percent per year:

Year	Deposit ($)
1	5,000
2	7,500
3	4,500
4	5,500
5	6,200

    How much should the fund be worth at the end of five years?

15. Congratulations! You have just won the lottery and have elected to receive $50,000 per year for 20 years. Assume that an 8 percent interest rate is used to evaluate the annuity and that you receive each payment at the beginning of the year.

    a. What is the present value of the lottery?

    b. How much interest is earned on the present value to make the $50,000-per-year payment?

16. Calculate the monthly mortgage payment made at the beginning of each month on a $100,000 mortgage. The mortgage is for 15 years and the interest rate is 7.5 percent.

17. You plan to retire at the age of 65 and believe you will live to be 90. You want to receive an annual retirement payment of $50,000. You have this money in an account that earns 10 percent annually.
    a. How much money will you need in the account when you reach 65 years old?
    b. You are currently 29 years of age. How much will you have to invest in this account for the next 36 years to have this amount in your account at age 65?

18. You just read an article that stated a college education costs approximately $35,000 at an average state university. If inflation is to average 5 percent per year, what would be the cost of a college education in 10 years?

19. Congratulations, it's a boy! Tom and Mary James just had a baby. They heard that the cost of providing a college education for this baby will be $100,000 in 18 years. Tom normally receives a Christmas bonus of $4,000 every year in the paycheck prior to Christmas. He read that a good stock mutual fund should pay him an average of 10 percent per year. Tom and Mary want to make sure their son has $100,000 for college. Consider each of the following questions.
    a. How much does Tom have to invest in this mutual fund at the end of each year to have $100,000 in 18 years?
    b. If the bonus is not paid until the first of the year, how much does Tom have to invest at the beginning of each year to have $100,000 in 18 years?
    c. Good news! Tom's father said he would provide for his grandson's education. He will put $10,000 in a government bond that pays 7 percent interest. His dad said this should be enough. Do you agree?
    d. If Mary has a savings account worth $50,000, how much would she have to set aside in this mutual fund to have the $100,000 for her son's education.

20. Sam is currently 30 years of age. He owns his own business and wants to retire at the age of 60. He has little confidence in the current social security system. He wants to retire with an annual income of $72,000 a year.
    a. If Sam believes he will live to age 90, how much does he have to accumulate by the time he reaches age 60 to receive $72,000 at the end of each year for the rest of his life? Sam believes he can earn 8 percent on his money.
    b. How much does he have to accumulate if he wants the payment of $72,000 at the beginning of each year?
    c. What dollar amount of interest will Sam have earned during retirement if he receives his $72,000 at the beginning of each year?

21. Regarding question 3, if Sam believes he will earn 10 percent on his investment for retirement, how much does he have to contribute to his retirement account at the beginning of each year to accumulate his retirement nest egg?

22. You have been shopping for a new home. You have a choice of financing. You can choose either a $200,000 mortgage at 8 percent for 30 years, or a $200,000 mortgage at 7 percent for 15 years.
    a. Calculate the monthly payment for both the 30-year and 15-year mortgages.
    b. Calculate the amount of interest paid over the life of the loan for both mortgages.
    c. Choose the best mortgage for you, and explain your answer.

23. On January 5, 1997, Mable bought 100 shares of ABC stock at $20 per share. On January 6, 2000, she sold her stock in ABC for $35 per share. What is the internal rate of return?

24. Icahn Tackel just signed an $11.5 million, four-year contract with an NFL team. He received a signing bonus of $2 million; $1.5 million at the end of the first year; $3 million at the end of the second year; $3.5 million at the end of the third year; and $1.5 million at the end of the fourth year. What is the present value of his contract if money can earn 8 percent per year?

25. You like to buy lottery tickets every week. The lottery pays an insurance company that will pay you an annuity. If you win a $1,000,000 lottery and elect to take an annuity, you get $50,000 per year at the beginning of each year for the next 20 years.
    a. How much will the state have to pay the insurance company if money can earn 6 percent?
    b. How much interest is earned on this lump-sum payment over the 20 years?
    c. If you take the cash rather than the annuity, the state will pay you $500,000 in one lump sum today. You will have to pay 40 percent of this in taxes. If you are currently working and invest this money at 10 percent, how much money will you have in a mutual fund at the end of 20 years?
    d. Are you better off with the annuity or should you take the cash? Explain.

26. Kay Serah buys 1,000 shares of stock at $3.00 per share in January of 1996. She sells the stock at $10 per share in January of 2000. What is Kay's IRR?

27. Kerry O'Key, an entrepreneur buys a piece of equipment for her lounge. The equipment costs $40,000 and will increase cash flow by $15,000 each year for 6 years. What is Ms. O'Key's Internal Rate of Return (Hint: use interpolation. IRR is between 25% and 30%).

28. Grandpa Eli Yale wants to send his grandchild to an Ivy League school. He heard that a college education would cost $200,000 in 18 years. If he invests $5,000 at the end of each year, what IRR must he obtain in order to reach his goal of $200,000?

29. Bylo Selhi wants to know how many years it will take for his mutual investment fund of $50,000 to reach $500,000 if his mutual fund pays an average of 12 percent per year.

30. Ira Schwabb wins the lottery and decides to take the one lump sum of $500,000 minus taxes. Ira receives a check for $300,000 after taxes using the rule of 72.

    a. How long will it take him to get $600,000 if he can earn 8 percent?

    b. How long will it take him to get $600,000 if he can earn 18 percent?

    c. How long will it take him to get $1,200,000 if he can earn 12 percent?

CAPITAL BUDGETING 9

Learning Objectives

When you have completed this chapter, you should be able to:

- Understand the purpose and need for capital budgeting.
- Explain the impact that government regulations may have on a company's capital budgeting decision.
- List and explain the steps required in making a capital budgeting decision.
- Distinguish between start-up costs, working capital commitment costs, and tax factor costs and the role each plays in the capital budgeting decision.
- Compare the relationship between increased efficiency benefits and tax factor benefits and understand their effect on a company's cash flow.
- Understand payback, net present value, profitability index, internal rate of return, and accounting rate of return as techniques of capital budgeting.

- Compute the payback of a capital budgeting project.
- Using time value of money, compute the net present value of a capital budgeting project.
- Given a company's investment costs, calculate the weighted average cost of capital.
- Calculate and compare a company's internal rate of return with its accounting rate of return.
- Determine how a company's capital budgeting decision makes a project mutually exclusive.
- Determine how a company's capital budgeting decision is influenced by capital rationing.
- Understand the importance of following up, controlling, and taking corrective action after a capital budgeting decision has been made.

As business owners, we constantly strive to ensure the profitability of our company by working hard to generate a high rate of return on both short-term and long-term investments. In Chapter 7 we discussed how we manage working capital to maintain liquidity and to meet our short-term obligations. We pointed out that excess cash could be invested temporarily in short-term marketable securities to generate a more positive return on investment without too much risk. We also mentioned that we invest in assets that are expected to result in cash returns for a period of one year or more. These investments in capital expenditures (assets having a useful life of one year or more) are expected to help generate increased revenues that will make our firm more profitable in the future. Our business has to constantly make decisions about whether to purchase new equipment and/or expand operations with the addition of new buildings. The method that we use to make these determinations is referred to as capital budgeting.

CAPITAL BUDGETING

Capital budgeting is the method we use to justify the acquisition of capital goods (those items that have a useful life in excess of one year). These long-term assets may be used by our business to generate increased cash flow by improving the efficiency and/or the effectiveness of our business. We purchase these assets only when we determine that the benefits we will receive over the life of the asset will exceed the costs of acquiring the asset and maintaining it over its useful life. Capital budgeting investments are based on the assumption that rates of return on investments, as well as the current inflation rate, will remain the same throughout the useful life of the investment.

A company should make the decision to enter into a specific project, acquire another company, or purchase a computer only if, after capital budgeting analysis, it is determined that the present value of the benefits received outweighs the present value of the costs incurred. It is important to note that future cash flow resulting from increased efficiency is a future benefit. These future benefits must be brought back, or translated, into the present and quantified for a profitable decision to be made. The value of future monies over time must be translated into a value now and matched with the costs incurred. These future monies or benefits should be measured in after-tax dollars or cash flows. The benefits received will vary from one investment to the next.

The risk involved in making an investment and the investment's ability to generate enough cash flow force companies to categorize capital budgeting decisions according to different standards. These standards are applied to determine whether specific projects or investments should be accepted or rejected. We find that some investments are a necessity for the well-being of a business. For example, a business will have to replace its worn-out equipment to continue operating. Hannah's Donut Shop delivery vans require replacement after several years, because of the amount of mileage put on the vehicles in distributing the product. Capital budgeting is used to make the most profitable decisions regarding the purchase of delivery vehicles.

FACTORS AFFECTING CAPITAL BUDGETING

CHANGES IN GOVERNMENT REGULATIONS

Government regulations placed on certain businesses often cost the company money in complying with the regulations. For example, the environment was found to be damaged by chlorofluorocarbon (CFC) emissions when automobile air conditioners are serviced. All automobile repair facilities that wished to continue to service air conditioners were forced to buy expensive recovery equipment. This mandatory requirement left a company that did not want to comply with only one choice—to quit servicing air-conditioning equipment. If we own an auto repair facility, we must use capital budgeting to determine if we want to comply with the new law or stop repairing and servicing air-conditioning equipment. First, we must determine how much revenue will be lost if we stop repairs. Second, we must determine the present value of the cost of compliance, which involves purchasing the CFC equipment and training our employees to use it. If the lost revenue (present value of the benefits we expect to receive) is greater than the cost of purchasing the equipment and training our employees to use the equipment, then we should buy the equipment. Conversely, if the lost revenue is less than the cost of the equipment and training, then we should cease to service air conditioners that use CFCs. Thus, the owners of a business need some method of determining if the current cost of purchasing the recovery equipment will be exceeded by the future revenues obtained by servicing air-conditioning equipment. The process of making the capital budgeting decision is the subject of this chapter.

We know from previous discussions that our goal in running a business is to make a profit, both now and in the future; hence, our business is always looking for ways to generate both additional revenue and cash flow. Cash flow is the actual cash in our pockets that can be used to pay bills. We often find that we incur additional expenses to increase revenue; but we also can generate additional cash by reducing costs. Numerous methods of cost reduction can be used to add to our cash flow. If we save $1 in expenses during the process of generating $2 in cash, then we have an additional $3. In other words, whatever amount we save through cost reduction can also be viewed as money earned. The benefits of increased cash flow and cost reduction are computed on an after-tax basis.

RESEARCH AND DEVELOPMENT

Another example of capital budgeting can be found in a company's new product development program. Companies must seek new products to remain competitive. The additional costs associated with new product development can be justified if the expected benefits to be received from the new product exceed the costs incurred. It is important to note the significant risk associated with new product development, because over half of all new products fail. When a product fails, it means that the expected benefits from the new product will not materialize, and therefore the benefits will not exceed the costs of developing the new product. Obviously, developing new products is a risky proposition. Risk may be overcome by acquiring companies that already have a proven product. Risk also can be minimized when companies make decisions that correspond to their existing company strategy.

CHANGES IN BUSINESS STRATEGY

In the 1980s, financial service businesses increased risk by changing strategies. With deregulation and changes in tax laws, many of them entered into businesses with little or no experience. When the economy changed, the risk associated with these changes in strategies increased. Financial managers did not change their strategies when the economy changed, and several businesses failed. Many of these failures could have been avoided if conservative strategies had been maintained or adopted through proper decision making. For example, the savings and loan institutions had traditionally financed home mortgages. In the 1970s, when market interest rates were low, these institutions loaned money (financed 30-year home mortgages) at rates ranging from 7 to 9 percent while paying their depositors rates of less than 5 percent. When interest rates soared in the late 1970s and early 1980s, to attract depositors, they had to offer interest rates of 12 percent or more. Hence the present value of the cost (interest rates given to depositors) exceeded the value of the benefits (interest rates collected on mortgages), and the result was a heavy loss for savings and loan institutions.

With changes in banking regulation, savings and loan institutions were allowed to enter new markets involving commercial real estate development. Financial managers saw the entry into these new markets as a way to reduce their losses from current interest rates and home mortgage collections. Thus, savings and loans changed their strategy and entered into markets (commercial real estate) where they had little or no experience. Many of them incurred risk that exceeded any benefits anticipated. The results were massive failure, bankruptcies, and corruption. Thousands of stockholders and bondholders lost most of their savings when these institutions failed. It is apparent that proper decision making was not used in the savings and loan industry.

To ensure proper decision making, a business should carefully take the necessary steps in making a capital budgeting decision. Five steps involved in capital budgeting are as follows:

1. *Formulate a proposal,* which serves the purpose of identifying the various costs incurred and benefits received in after-tax cash flows.
2. *Evaluate the data* generated with respect to the benefits and costs to see whether the investment will be profitable.
3. *Make a decision* about the data—choose the course of action that will provide the greatest future benefit while minimizing future costs.
4. *Follow up* on the capital budgeting decision through a post audit to see if the benefits received in reality exceed the additional costs incurred.
5. *Take corrective action* if the post audit indicates that the benefits received are not meeting our expectations.

 # FORMULATING A PROPOSAL

To formulate a proposal we must identify all costs and benefits associated with our project.

COSTS IN CAPITAL BUDGETING

Several costs must be determined when evaluating a capital budgeting decision. Those that are most often considered by business owners and managers are start-up costs, working capital commitment costs, and tax factor costs.

Start-up costs are the total dollars spent to get the project under way. These costs include acquisition costs for a new piece of equipment, training costs of employees, and any maintenance costs, as well as the costs of service agreements, hiring of new personnel, and/or changes in inventory, storage space, and so forth. We want to include all money that will have to be committed to the proposal. The acquisition cost of a new piece of equipment must include the cost of installing the equipment. The cost of hiring new personnel includes the cost associated with recruiting, interviewing, selecting, and training. Cash flow and revenue are not generated by a new project until after start-up costs are incurred.

We therefore must have sufficient financing to pay for all start-up costs without obtaining any additional cash flow. We strongly recommend using Gantt charts, as previously discussed, to chart all start-up costs over time. For a new business or a business expansion, start-up costs also would include utility deposits, security deposits on rented property, and possibly costs associated with construction of new facilities.

Working capital commitment costs involve maintaining specific levels of working capital that are required by lending institutions. Working capital, aside from cash, also consists of investments in inventory and accounts receivable. Banks and other lending institutions will not normally lend money to finance a capital budgeting investment unless the borrower shows possession of the working capital to make monthly payments. This money is legally tied up and is committed to the lender in such a manner that it cannot be used by the borrower for investment or other purposes. Funds tied up in inventory and accounts receivable cannot be used. Therefore, the working capital commitment is an opportunity cost that must be considered in formulating the proposal, because this money cannot be invested in any other area.

Tax factor costs will result from additional taxes that have to be paid. For example, your city, county, or state may have an annual property tax and personal property tax assessment. When you buy new equipment, or increase the value of your building, the assessor will include these additions when determining your tax liability.

BENEFITS IN CAPITAL BUDGETING

In identifying the benefits from a capital investment, we should note that most businesses derive their benefits from the increased amount of cash flow that the investment will bring, and the increased amount of efficiency that the investment will cause in day-to-day operations. Another factor is the ability of an organization to write off an investment, which in turn reduces its tax liability. We discussed the use of depreciation as a means of writing off an investment in Chapter 3; however, tax laws change so frequently that benefits from such information are unreliable. What must be stressed is the enhanced cash flow and increased efficiency that an asset investment—whether it be a piece of equipment, a new facility, or an acquisition—will bring. This ensures the success of a business by increasing its productivity via proper managerial decision making. It is important to note that decreasing the tax liability of a business is subject to modification as tax laws change. What appears to be a benefit today can very well change to a cost in the future as new legislation is enacted.

In dealing with increased efficiency, the benefit derived must have taxes paid on it before it can be deemed to be a true benefit. A company that will increase efficiency from the purchase of an asset to increase profit by $10,000 each year will pay taxes on $10,000. The tax rate may be as high as 39 percent, or $3,900, in which case the company can actually count on only $6,100 of benefit from $10,000 in profit; thus $6,100 is the increased future cash flow resulting from the purchase of the asset. In making the capital budgeting decision, we will see how the present value of this future cash flow benefit can be matched against the present value of the costs incurred in generating this benefit. After taxes are paid on increased profit, a cash flow benefit results. So $3,900 of taxes are paid on $10,000 worth of increased profit, resulting in $6,100 worth of benefit.

Conversely, a benefit resulting from reducing taxable income is equal to the amount saved in paying those taxes. Recall that we used $3,900 as the amount of tax paid on $10,000 worth of taxable income. If we can reduce the amount of taxable income by $10,000, then we save $3,900 in taxes, which is an increased cash flow benefit to the business. What we will attempt to show here is how to determine the present value of this future constant benefit of $3,900 saved in taxes per year. However, once again, uncertainty is present because tax laws change constantly. Thus cash flows from tax savings are merely estimates and have a large degree of uncertainty that further adds to the risk of the investment. This can be further exemplified by what transpired in the real estate industry. Tax savings decreased noticeably with the Tax Reform Act of 1986 which substantially changed the rules on depreciation.

Some companies use different depreciation methods for tax purposes and financial accounting purposes. The straight-line method takes a conservative approach to depreciation. Accelerated methods often are used for tax purposes and allow write-off of more income to save taxes and generate increased cash flow for a business, primarily because high depreciation in the early years of an asset's useful life results in a greater write-off and a further reduction in taxes paid on income. Thus, benefits will include all additional cash flows that accrue to our business as a result of making the capital budgeting decision. Those benefits that are most often considered are the tax factor benefits.

Tax factor benefits include those items that current tax laws will allow you to deduct or write off once the new investment is made. These items include annual depreciation, interest on loans, and/or investment tax credits. For example, you want to start a computer consulting business. You will need computers and peripheral equipment, office machinery (faxes, calculators, copy machines), and a good automobile to be used in visiting clients. The total cost of this equipment is $110,000, and this equipment is subject to a five-year straight-line depreciation method according to the Modified Accelerated Cost Recovery System (MACRS). You estimate that the equipment will be worth $10,000 (salvage value) at the end of the five years. Furthermore, you put $30,000 down and get a bank to finance the remainder at an annual rate of prime plus 4 percent. You estimate that you will be in a 28 percent tax bracket.

Calculating depreciation is accomplished by using the following procedure: (1) Subtract the salvage value of $10,000 from the cost of

$110,000, leaving $100,000 of wearing value to be depreciated over five years, straight line. (2) Determine annual depreciation. Divide the $100,000 by 5 (the number of years) to determine the annual depreciation of $20,000. (3) Calculate annual tax savings, which is a benefit and is derived by multiplying those items that can be deducted from income by the expected tax rate. Items that can be excluded from taxes, under current tax law, are annual depreciation and interest expenses. Therefore, annual depreciation of $20,000 can be deducted off of taxable income prior to calculating annual taxes. If you are in a 28 percent tax bracket, you will save 28 cents for every dollar of depreciation deducted, or 28 percent of $20,000, which is equal to $5,600 each year for five years.

Additional tax savings will be obtained because the annual interest that you will pay on the loan will be considered as a business expense. For example, say that the prime lending rate is 8.25 percent, as it was in October 1999. If the bank will finance the equipment loan at prime plus 4 percent, then your annual interest on this loan will be 12.25 percent compounded monthly. If you believe that interest rates will not change during the period of this loan, then each yearly payment of $24,160.666 can be calculated by finding the monthly loan payment of $2,013.3888 and multiplying by 12. We recommend that you obtain an amortization schedule from the bank or generate one from a spreadsheet program such as Microsoft Excel, Lotus 123, or some other program.

Table 9-1 is based on the following assumptions: We bought the $110,000 asset discussed here and financed $90,000 for five years at a stated rate of 12.25 percent. We also assumed that our tax bracket was 28 percent. Using these figures, we generated an amortization table and the following results: Annual interest for year 1 is $10,261.81; for year 2, $8,460.27; for year 3, $6,425.23; for year 4, $4,126.41; and for year 5, $1,529.62. Annual tax sav-

Table 9-1   Annual Interest Payments and Tax Savings for a Five-Year Loan

Amount Borrowed $ 90,000	Annual Interest Rate 12.25%	Number of Months 60	Monthly Payment $2,013.39	Income Tax Rate 28.00%
Year	Annual Loan Payment	Principal Payment	Interest Payment	Tax Savings
1	$ 24,160.67	$13,898.86	$ 10,261.81	$2,873.31
2	24,160.67	15,700.39	8,460.27	2,368.88
3	24,160.67	17,735.44	6,425.23	1,799.06
4	24,160.67	20,034.26	4,126.41	1,155.39
5	24,160.67	22,631.05	1,529.62	428.29
Totals	$ 120,803.33	$ 90,000.00	$30,803.33	$8,624.93

Note: Rounding may cause what appears to be an error of a penny in some columns.

ings are calculated in the same way as depreciation. Tax savings in year 1 equals 0.28 multiplied by $10,261.81, or $2,873.31. As shown in Table 9-1, the total tax savings expected over the life of the loan is $8,624.93. An interesting note with tax factor benefits is that the $120,803.33 which was repaid over five years, actually resulted in a cost to the business of $112,178.40 ($120,803.33 total loan payments − $8,624.93 total tax savings).

EVALUATING THE DATA— TECHNIQUES OF CAPITAL BUDGETING

Now that we understand the costs and benefits in a capital budgeting decision, it is time to discuss the methods of evaluating the data contained in our capital budgeting proposal.

There are several methods of evaluating the capital budgeting proposal. Businesses allocating capital properly use several techniques to make a profitable decision through a logical evaluation process. Six techniques used to ensure profitable capital budgeting decisions are those that employ the calculation of (1) payback, (2) net present value (NPV), (3) profitability index (PI), (4) internal rate of return (IRR), (5) accounting rate of return (ARR, also known as average rate of return), and (6) lowest total cost (LTC).

As discussed, capital budgeting determines whether the business should make an investment now that will eventually result in after-tax benefits. These techniques require us to forecast future cash flows resulting from increased revenue, increased operational efficiency or effectiveness, or tax benefits that allow our business to hold on to more of our income.

PAYBACK

Payback deals with the number of years that it will take a business to get back the money that it has invested in a project or asset. In determining payback, a business looks at how long an asset's cost will be tied up in the investment, as well as the project's profitability. To calculate payback we determine the investment cost and divide this by the annual after-tax benefits that the investment generates. The formula for calculating payback is

$$\text{Payback} = \frac{C}{\text{ATB}}$$

where

C = cost of the project
ATB = annual after-tax benefit of the project

If a company invests $25,000 in a project and generates $3,000 a year in after-tax benefits, then payback will occur in approximately 8.33 years (25,000/3,000 = 8.33). The advantages of payback are that it is easy to compute and simple to explain. It readily compares investments that have unequal initial costs. Its main disadvantages are that it does not consider the time value of money and it tends to concentrate on investments that satisfy immediate goals or those with a fast payback. How many businesspeople are willing to wait over eight years to recoup their investment, even though in the long run they can earn a substantial return on their investment?

NET PRESENT VALUE

The **net present value (NPV)** method of capital budgeting uses the time value of money by discounting future benefits and costs back to the present. It applies the present-value-of-a-stream-of-payments technique for even cash flows and the present-value-of-a-future-lump-sum technique for unequal yearly cash flows. The calculations are made using an interest rate that matches our cost of capital for the investment. This rate is used because the company must pay this cost on an annual basis to obtain the financial capital necessary to make the investment.

When making a capital budgeting decision, we must arrive at a forecast of future interest rates. The two interest rates that we must consider are: (1) the interest rate charged by the supplier of funds, or the lender, and (2) the interest rate that the borrower could receive by investing in some other enterprise. The latter is the borrower's opportunity cost.

The interest rate charged by the lender is a comfortable interest rate—one that the bank or lending institution finds acceptable and believes is realistic with regard to the future. Lenders use the following three components to determine this interest rate: (1) the real rate of return (the return that will be received after factoring out inflation), (2) the inflation premium (the expected average inflation rate for the term of the investment), and (3) the risk premium (the rate added to the interest rate to take into account the risk of the investment). For example, when a company goes into a new area of business, it will assume more risk (potential for failure) than if it had stayed in its original area. When the savings and loans went into commercial real estate, they did not include a sufficient risk premium and, therefore, entered into a market where they experienced losses that were much greater than anticipated. If the real rate of return is 3 percent and the inflation premium is 4 percent, then a risk-free investment will use an interest rate of 7 percent. For practical purposes this interest rate is the prime lending rate. It is the interest rate charged by lenders to companies that pose very little risk to the lender. Conversely, if the lender believes there is risk of default on the loan, then a risk premium will be added to this prime lending rate. If the risk premium is 4 percent, then 11 percent will be used as the loan rate charged by the lender.

The cost of capital to the borrower consists of the opportunity cost on the amount of equity invested in the business. It is the interest that is forgone because the business owner decided to invest in his or her own business rather than put the money in some other investment vehicle. For example, if you normally invest in government bonds that on an average have paid you 7.67 percent annual return over time, then 7.67 percent is your opportunity cost when you decide to invest your money in your own business. It is the amount you could have earned had you not invested in your own business. Therefore, we use both the lender's interest rate and the borrower's opportunity cost to determine the interest rate for the NPV method of capital budgeting. We combine these two rates into a weighted average cost of capital.

The **weighted average cost of capital (WACC)** is obtained by multiplying the cost of debt (rate that the lender charges) by its proportion of total funds raised, and multiplying the cost of equity (opportunity cost to the owner) by its proportion of total funds raised. For example, you are buying a piece of equipment for $100,000. You will put $30,000 down and finance the remaining $70,000. Using the interest rates discussed earlier, your opportunity cost is 7.67 percent for the $30,000 and 11 percent for the $70,000 loan. We obtain the proportions by dividing the total investment by the amount of the investment financed by each resource. Therefore, 30 percent of the investment is financed by the owner and 70 percent is financed by the lender:

$$\text{Owner's equity} + \text{Amount financed} = \text{Total amount paid}$$
$$\$30,000 \quad + \quad \$70,000 \quad = \quad \$100,000$$

$$\text{Equity proportion} = \frac{\text{Owner's equity}}{\text{Total amount paid}} = \frac{\$30,000}{\$100,000} = 0.30$$

$$\text{Debt proportion} = \frac{\text{Amount financed}}{\text{Total amount paid}} = \frac{\$70,000}{\$100,000} = 0.70$$

We then calculate the weighted average cost of capital as follows:

$$\text{WACC} = (\text{Equity cost})(\text{Equity proportion}) + (\text{Debt cost})(\text{Debt proportion})$$
$$= (0.0767)(0.30) + (0.11)(0.70)$$
$$= 0.0230 + 0.0770$$
$$= 0.1000, \text{ or } 10.00\%$$

This weighted average cost of capital is the interest rate used in calculating the NPV for capital budgeting. Most corporate financial textbooks would include common stock, preferred stock, bonds, and possibly loan financing in determining the WACC. For the small business owner, however, the two factors we use are sufficient, because bond financing is not available and there are not multiple classes of stock.

NPV considers all future cash flows over the asset's entire economic life, including benefits and costs. Once the present value of the benefits is determined, we then subtract the present value of the costs to determine if there is a positive NPV. The formula used in the NPV method of capital budgeting is

$$NPV = PVB - PVC$$

where

> NPV = net present value of the investment
> PVB = present value of the benefit as calculated in the following example
> PVC = present value of the cost of the investment as calculated in the following example

If NPV is positive using the WACC, the investment should be made. If NPV is negative using WACC, the investment should not be made, because it is matched against the present value of the costs of the investment. This can be illustrated in the following example. It will cost our company $100,000 to add a sales office to its current production facility. We estimate that we will increase our after-tax cash flow by $35,000 a year over seven years. Our weighted average cost of capital and our required rate of return or discount rate are 10 percent. Referring to Appendix Table B-5, we find that at 10 percent the present value of the annuity factor is 4.8684. Picture a money machine that earns interest on whatever amount of money is present in the machine at a specified time. If you started with $4.8684 (which is also the present value of an annuity factor), in a machine that was earning compound interest of 10 percent, then you could pull out $1 each year for seven years. At the end of seven years you would have pulled out your last dollar and nothing would be left in the machine. To get the present value associated with pulling out $35,000 per year for seven years, we would employ the following formula:

$$PVB = Annuity(PVAF)$$

where

> PVB = present value of the benefits
> Annuity = annual cash flow from the investment
> PVAF = present value annuity factor from Table B-5

From our example, PVB = \$35,000(4.8684) = \$170,394. Thus \$170,394 is the present value of \$35,000 a year for seven years at a required rate of return or discount rate of 10 percent. Although \$35,000 a year for seven years amounts to \$245,000 (7 years × \$35,000), the actual present value is \$170,394, because the \$35,000 received in the seventh year is worth less now than the \$35,000 received at the end of the first year. As explained in Chapter 8, money has a time value and an opportunity cost.

If we subtract the present value of the cost of \$100,000 from the present value of the benefit of \$170,394, we get \$70,394, which is the NPV. The addition of a sales office has a positive NPV, meaning that the office is expected to generate a return that will be higher than 10 percent. A business should accept an investment if the NPV is greater than zero. It should reject the investment if the NPV is less than zero. For example, if our estimated cash flow were \$19,000 per year for each of the next seven years, then we would receive \$133,000 in benefits over the next seven years. However, the present value of this cash flow is only \$92,500 (\$19,000 × 4.8684). Using the earlier procedure, we see that the NPV equals the \$92,500 PVB minus the \$100,000 PVC, which equals a negative \$7,500. Because NPV is negative at a weighted cost of capital of 10 percent, we should reject this investment.

NPV has two primary advantages: (1) Future cash flows that will be paid and received can be discounted back to the present so that a decision on the investment can be made now. (2) Interest rates are determined by and based on the weighted average cost of capital that takes risk into consideration. Note that a high-risk investment includes higher interest rates, which tend to lower the present value of the benefits. A low-risk investment includes lower interest rates, which tend to increase the present value of the benefits. The major disadvantage of NPV is that it requires estimates of future interest rates. These rates may change in the future. Additionally, it uses estimates of cash flow costs and benefits, which also may change in the future.

Because of the complexity of the NPV calculation, let us consider another example. You want to buy an automobile that is selling for \$20,000. You believe that you can use the car in your business to increase your cash flow by \$10,000 over the next five years. You also believe that you can sell the car at the end of five years for \$4,000. Table 9-2 shows the NPV calculations for this problem.

Recall that the salvage or residual value of an asset is what you might receive upon selling the asset when its useful life is completed. To help us with this decision, we must estimate the current value of selling an asset at a future date. In other words, we wish to determine the present amount of an estimated future residual value of an asset. You estimate that you can sell the automobile in five years for \$4,000. What is the present value of this \$4,000 lump-sum payment that you will receive in five years? To determine this value, you must use an interest rate that you believe is comparable to

Table 9-2   NPV of an Automobile Purchase

Item	Cash Flow per Time Period	PVAF at 10.00%	Present Value at 10%	PVAF at 14.00%	Present Value at 14%
Benefits					
Cash flow	$10,000.00 per year	3.7908	$37,908.00	3.4331	$34,331.00
Salvage value	$4,000.00 end of 5 years	0.6209	2,483.60	0.5194	2,077.60
PVB			$40,391.60		$36,408.60
Costs					
Purchase price	($20,000.00) present value		($20,000.00)		($20,000.00)
Insurance	($100.00) per month	47.4576	(4,745.76)	43.4784	(4,347.84)
Gas and maintenance	($300.00) per month	47.4576	(14,237.28)	43.4784	(13,043.52)
PVC			($38,983.04)		($37,391.36)
NPV = PVB – PVC			$ 1,408.56		($ 982.76)

your weighted average cost of capital or required rate of return. It is important to note that the interest rate chosen is based on an assumption that rates will not be changing over the next five years. If rates change, the present value of the future $4,000 lump sum will also change. Additionally, the $4,000 lump sum itself is only an estimate. The car could, and most probably will, be worth some amount other than $4,000 in five years.

Because we are using two estimated variables (cash flow and interest rate), we believe that you should take risk into consideration: Either underestimate the future residual value or add a risk premium to your required rate of return. For this problem, we added a risk premium of 4 percent to our required rate of return (WACC) of 10 percent that was used in the previous problem. Justification of the numbers in Table 9-2 is described as follows.

First you must calculate the present value of the benefits. The $10,000-per-year cash flow has a present value of $37,908 using 10 percent, and $34,331 using 14 percent, which takes risk into consideration. These figures were obtained by using the present value of an ordinary annuity factor, as the cash flow is not realized until the end of the year (ordinary annuity). You estimate that you can sell the car in five years for $4,000. This estimated figure can be obtained from any bank via the *Kelley Blue Book*.[1] The book provides the value of a five-year-old car of the same model and equipment that

---

[1] The *Kelley Blue Book* is used by most banks and lending institutions to provide book value on used automobiles. You can also find the book on the internet at *http://www.kellybluebook.com/*

you are buying. To avoid overestimating the future benefit, we recommend using the low book value. Using the present-value-of-a-future-lump-sum formula, or Appendix Table B-2, we arrive at a present value of $2,483.60 ($4,000 × 0.6209). Now let us add the risk premium of 4 percent, because you are unsure if you actually can get $4,000 for the car, or if interest rates in the future will stay at or below 10 percent. The present value of $4,000, using a 14 percent interest rate, is now only $2,077.60 ($4,000 × 0.5194). Therefore, the sum of the present value of the benefits (PVB) for a 10 percent assumption is $40,391.60, and for the approach using a 14 percent assumption is $36,408.60. Did you actually lose over $3,983? No, but the anticipated benefit as determined now in our capital budgeting decision is less than it was using the basic interest rate of 10 percent.

Your next step is to put in the present value of the car and the costs associated with using the vehicle over time. For an automobile, typical costs would include insurance, gas, and maintenance. Your records indicate that the insurance premium is $100 per month. Gas and maintenance for this car should be about $300 per month. We assume that these payments will be allocated (set aside) at the beginning of each month. Therefore, we will use the present value of an annuity due in our calculations. Calculating the present value of these costs and adding them to the present value of the automobile (we assume that $20,000 is paid for the automobile now) gives us a total present value of the costs of $38,983.04 at 10 percent and $37,391.36 at 14 percent. Using the formula NPV = PVB–PVC, we see that the car should be purchased at a risk level (WACC) of 10 percent because our NPV is positive at this rate ($1,408.56). If the risk level increases the rate to 14 percent, the car should not be purchased because the NPV is now negative ($982.76). In other words, at 10 percent the present value of the benefits exceeds the present value of the costs, as shown by the result of a positive NPV. When we increase the discount rate to 14 percent because of greater risk, the present value of the benefits is less than the present value of the costs, as shown by a negative net present value.

Most business loans are tied to the prime interest rate and are adjusted when the prime rate changes. It would be imprudent for a business owner to use a lower rate in decision making and not take into consideration that interest rates tend to fluctuate during the period of the loan. Because of the availability of personal computers, the small business owner now has the capability of analyzing the investment decision based on **sensitivity analysis**— the process of analyzing an investment using what-if situations. In this particular case, the interest rate variable can be modified and the resulting present value of benefits and costs can be analyzed to determine if specific situations meet the criteria of the investment decision. Therefore, we recommend that the small business owner or manager use the NPV technique in conjunction with sensitivity analysis to determine the value of an investment.

PROFITABILITY INDEX

The **profitability index (PI)** is the ratio of the present value of the benefits to the present value of the costs. The formula for PI is

$$PI = \frac{PVB}{PVC}$$

Using the previous sales office example, our investment has a present value of $170,394 and a cost of $100,000. The PI is 1.70, which means that at a discounted or required rate of return of 10 percent, a project will return approximately $1.70 in benefit for every dollar invested. This project is profitable because the PI is greater than one. We can see the relationship between NPV and profitability index as follows: A positive NPV will result in a PI greater than one, and a negative NPV will result in a PI that is less than one. For example, if our project had a PI of 0.85, this would indicate that for every dollar invested, the project was returning only 85 cents as benefit over time. The advantages of the profitability index are that it is easy to calculate once you have determined both PVB and PVC, that it is easy to explain, and that it provides a clear picture of cost-benefit analysis. The disadvantage is that it may give a false sense of security for a project if interest rate estimates are too low or cash flow estimates are too high.

INTERNAL RATE OF RETURN

The **internal rate of return (IRR)** is the actual rate of return of an investment and uses the time value of money in its calculation. The IRR is the interest rate that matches the present value of the cost of our investment directly against the present value of the future benefits received. The future benefits can be in the form of a stream of payments over a period of time or a lump sum (salvage value) received. The IRR is the interest rate that occurs when the NPV is zero. If the NPV is zero, then by definition, the present value of the costs must equal the present value of the benefits. The IRR is an interest rate that corresponds to a present value annuity factor that is found by dividing the present value of the cost by the period's cash flow. The formula for the IRR factor is

$$IRR\ factor = \frac{Present\ value\ of\ the\ cost\ of\ the\ investment}{Period's\ cash\ flow}$$

If an investment costs $25,000, then the present value of the $25,000 cost is also the present value of the $25,000 benefit, because the NPV equals zero. We estimate that the investment will provide a cash flow of $3,000 for 20 years. The internal rate of return (IRR) factor is identical to the present value annuity factor (PVAF) and is found by using the previous formula. Calculate *x* by dividing $25,000 by $3,000 and arrive at a value of 8.3333. We look in Appendix Table B-5, and go across the 20-year row to find the interest rate that corresponds to a factor of 8.3333. Note that 8.3333 falls between 8.5136 and 7.9633, which correspond to 10 percent and 11 percent, respectively. We now know that the IRR lies somewhere between 10 and 11 percent.

To find the actual IRR, we must interpolate. As discussed in Chapter 8, **interpolation** is the process of using mathematics to find an unknown value between two known values. We know that 7.9633 corresponds to an 11 percent interest rate and 8.5136 corresponds to a 10 percent interest rate. Because 8.3333 lies between these two known values, we interpolate by setting up the following proportion:

$$1\begin{bmatrix} ?\begin{bmatrix} 10 ---- 8.5136 \\ x ---- 8.3333 \end{bmatrix} 0.1803 \\ 11 ---- 7.9633 \end{bmatrix} 0.5503$$

In our proportion we take the difference between the lower-interest 10 percent PVAF of 8.5136 and the *x* IRR PVAF of 8.3333 and divide this difference of 0.1803 by the difference between the higher-interest-rate 11 percent PVAF of 7.9633 and the lower-interest-rate 10 percent PVAF of 8.5136 to get 0.5503. We now have the numerator of 0.1803 and the denominator of 0.5503, which is a proportion that we will set equal to ? divided by the difference in interest rates. Thus, ? divided by 1 equals 0.1803 divided by 0.5503. Solving for ?, we find that ? is 0.3276. We then add this number to the lower interest rate and get an internal rate of return of 10.33 percent. Mathematically, the proportion described here yields the following formula:

$$\frac{?}{i_2 - i_1} = \frac{\text{Partial distance } (10\%PVAF - x\%PVAF)}{\text{Total distance } (10\%PVAF - 11\%PVAF)}$$

$$\frac{?}{11 - 10} = \frac{(8.5136 - 8.3333)}{(8.5136 - 7.9633)}$$

$$\frac{?}{1} = \frac{0.1803}{0.5503}$$

$$?(0.5503) = (1)(0.1803)$$

$$? = \frac{(1)(0.1803)}{0.5503} = 0.3276$$

$$IRR = x = i_1 + ? = 10\% + 0.3276\% = 10.33\%$$

It is important to realize that not all investments produce consistently equal cash flows year after year—most investments produce unequal cash flows. Finding the IRR of an investment with unequal cash flows can be illustrated in the following example.

A company is considering the purchase of a new machine that would increase the speed of manufacturing electronic equipment. The annual cash flow projections are shown in Table 9-3. The cost of the machine is $66,000. To find the actual IRR we must interpolate. However, we will interpolate using present value dollars rather than factors, as in the equal cash flow example. First we have to find interest rates that provide us with projected present values of more than $66,000 and less than $66,000. Using trial and error or what-if analysis, we determine that rates of 20 percent and 25 percent, as shown in Table 9-4, meet the above mentioned criteria.

In our example, first we find the present value of the cash flows at 20 percent by using the present value of a future lump-sum formula for all individual cash flows. Next we find the present value in dollars of the cash flows at 25 percent.

We also wish to find the IRR, which is the interest rate that corresponds to a present value of $66,000. This is the present value of the investment cost. We know that $69,402.10 corresponds to a 20 percent interest rate and that $62,967.20 corresponds to a 25 percent interest rate. Because $66,000 lies between these two values we interpolate by setting up the following proportion:

$$5\left[?\begin{bmatrix} 20 ---- \$69,402.10 \\ x ---- \$66,000.00 \end{bmatrix} \$3,402.10 \atop 25 ---- \$62,967.20 \right] \$6,434.90$$

Table 9-3 Five-Year Projected Cash Flow Initial Investment: $66,000.00

Year	Projected Cash Flow
1	$21,000.00
2	29,000.00
3	36,000.00
4	16,000.00
5	8,000.00

Table 9-4 Present Value of an Unequal Stream of Projected Cash Benefits

Year	Projected Cash Flow	PVF for Interest of 20.00%	Present Value in Dollars	PVF for Interest of 25.00%	Present Value in Dollars
1	$21,000.00	0.8333	$17,499.30	0.8000	$16,800.00
2	29,000.00	0.6944	20,137.60	0.6400	18,560.00
3	36,000.00	0.5787	20,833.20	0.5120	18,432.00
4	16,000.00	0.4823	7,716.80	0.4096	6,553.60
5	8,000.00	0.4019	3,215.20	0.3277	2,621.60
Total PV			$69,402.10		$62,967.20

We set up a proportion in which we take the difference between the lower interest rate (20 percent) present value in dollars and the IRR present value in dollars which is $3,402.10. We divide by the difference between the lower interest rate's present value amount in dollars and the higher interest rate's present value amount in dollars which is $6,434.90. We now have the numerator of $3,402.10 and the denominator of $6,434.90, which is a proportion that we will set equal to ? divided by the difference in interest rates. Thus, ? divided by 5 equals $3,402.10 divided by $6,434.90. Solving for ?, we find that it equals 2.6435. We then add this number to the lower interest rate and get an internal rate of return of 22.64 percent. Mathematically, the proportion described here yields the following formula:

$$\frac{?}{i_2 - i_1} = \frac{\text{Partial distance } (20\%\text{PV\$} - x\%\text{PV\$})}{\text{Total distance } (20\%\text{PV\$} - 25\%\text{PV\$})}$$

$$\frac{?}{25 - 20} = \frac{(\$69,402.10 - \$66,000)}{(\$69,402.10 - \$62,967.20)}$$

$$\frac{?}{5} = \frac{\$3,402.10}{\$6,434.90}$$

$$?(\$6,434.90) = (5)(\$3,402.10)$$

$$? = \frac{(5)(\$3,402.10)}{\$6,434.90)} = \frac{\$17,010.50}{\$6,434.90} = 2.6435$$

$$\text{IRR} = x = i_1 + ? = 20\% + 2.6435\% = 22.64\%$$

As shown by the previous examples, the IRR follows the time value of money by discounting future benefits and costs back to the present. It is most appropriate for comparing investments with unequal initial cash outlays and unequal lives. A disadvantage of the IRR is that it requires complex interest calculations and may in some cases be difficult to explain. However, keep in mind that a business usually has a cutoff rate or hurdle rate (a minimum rate of return for investments) that is used with the NPV method. If the present value of the benefits exceeds the present value of the costs using this hurdle rate, then the internal rate of return is higher than the hurdle rate. Therefore, the IRR is only required by a business owner or manager who wants to know the actual return on investment. The method that we recommend for selecting an investment is the NPV method, because cash flows are assumed to be reinvested at the hurdle (WACC) rate. In using IRR, cash flows are assumed to be reinvested at the IRR. If a project shows an IRR of 38 percent, it is unrealistic to assume that cash flows could be reinvested at this rate. Because the NPV method uses an interest rate that is actually expected by both the investor and the lender, it is a more realistic approach.

ACCOUNTING RATE OF RETURN

The **accounting rate of return (ARR)** is the average annual income from a project divided by the average cost of the project. The accounting rate of return method bases its rate of return on income and does not incorporate the time value of money and the present value of future cash flows. In our preceding example, an individual spent $10,000 to develop a software program that generated $3,000 a year for four years. The accounting rate of return would be equal to the average amount of yearly income ($3,000) generated over the life of the project divided by the cost of the project ($10,000). The formula for ARR is

$$ARR = \left(\frac{\text{Average annual income}}{\text{Average cost of investment over its life}} \right)$$

Using this ARR example, $3,000 divided by $10,000 is a 30 percent accounting rate of return. This measure is not as accurate as the IRR, because the IRR tells us the actual rate of return, or how $10,000 will generate $3,000 over time. Our $10,000 investment is the discounted amount of a future stream of payments. From it we get our actual return. The accounting rate of return is an average return from income generated over an investment's life. The advantage of the ARR is that it is easy to calculate; however, there are several disadvantages. The ARR does not consider the time value of money. It also provides rates of return that are not realistic, because it is based on the average value of the investment over its life rather than the original cost. It uses average income without discounting each year's cash flow back to the present. We know that $3,000 received in the fourth year has less value presently than $3,000 received in the first year. The accounting rate of return assumes that each $3,000 cash flow provides the same benefit resulting in an ARR of 30 percent. Because the actual rate of return (IRR) is only 7.72 percent, we do not recommend using this method. We include it in this discussion so you understand that some advisors, to convince people to invest in a project, will use this method. According to our example, use of the ARR often shows returns that are far in excess of reality. For example, a $100,000 investment that gives off an annual return of $20,000 for 10 years provides an IRR between 15 and 16 percent. As a result, the accounting rate of return would be inflated to 20 percent.

LOWEST TOTAL COST

The **lowest total cost (LTC)** method of capital budgeting is similar to the net present value (NPV) method because it uses the time value of money by discounting future costs and benefits back to the present. It applies the present-value-of-a-stream-of-payments technique for even cash flows and the present-value-of-a-future-lump-sum technique for unequal yearly cash flows. The calculations are made using an interest rate that matches our weighted average cost of capital for the investment. This rate is used because the company must pay this cost on an annual basis to obtain the financial capital necessary to make the investment.

Businesses must replace equipment as it wears out. If a business is already in operation, then the capital budgeting decision often involves choosing the investment that provides the lowest total cost. Examples of these decisions would involve a delivery company that must replace its trucks, a bakery that replaces its ovens, or an office complex that replaces its air conditioning system.

The method used to determine the lowest present value of total cost is as follows: include all costs associated with two or more competing investments. Calculate the present value of these costs. Add the present value of any benefits (salvage value) that may be obtained on the investment. Select the investment with the lowest overall total cost.

Jonathan Lury is a contractor who must replace a long bed pick-up truck. Jonathan has the following constraints for his truck. He determines that the truck must have a towing capacity of 4,000 pounds and a cargo capacity of at least 3,000 pounds. He also needs an extended cab, as he often has to take three or four workers to the construction site. Jonathan developed Table 9-5 using information that he obtained for three models of different competing trucks.

Table 9-5 Lowest Total Cost (LTC) of a Truck Purchase

Category	Quantity
Fuel cost per gallon	$ 1.50
Annual Mileage	25,000
WACC	12.00%
Ownership in years	6
PVAF Table B-5 or Formula	4.1114
PVF Table B-2 or Formula	0.5066

	Truck Model A		Truck Model B		Truck Model C	
Category	(Costs) and Benefits	PV	(Costs) and Benefits	PV	(Costs) and Benefits	PV
Mileage Per Gallon	16		13		15	
Purchase Price	$ (26,955.00)	$ (26,955.00)	$ (25,695.00)	$ (25,695.00)	$ (30,556.00)	$ (30,556.00)
Annual Fuel Costs	(2,343.75)	(9,636.11)	(2,884.62)	(11,859.83)	(2,500.00)	(10,278.52)
Annual Insurance Cost	(1,347.40)	(5,539.71)	(1,532.44)	(6,300.49)	(1,358.52)	(5,585.43)
Salvage Value	10,800.00	5,471.62	10,800.00	5,471.62	12,250.00	6,206.23
Total Cost for 6 Years		$ (36,659.20)		$ (38,383.70)		$ (40,213.72)

Jonathan estimated that fuel costs $1.50 per gallon. He will drive his truck 25,000 miles per year for 6 years. His weighted average cost of capital (WACC) is 12 percent. The purchase price of each truck is its present value and is listed in Table 9-5. Jonathan obtained the EPA mileage estimates for city driving on each vehicle and computed the annual cost of fuel. He then calculated the present value of his fuel cost by using the formula, Present Value of an Ordinary Annuity. Maintenance costs on the 3 vehicles were the same. Therefore he did not include maintenance costs in the table. Jonathan called his insurance company and obtained an annual premium for each vehicle. He then calculated the present value of his insurance premiums. Using the Internet he obtained salvage values for six-year-old trucks. He determined the present value of the salvage value by using the formula, Present Value of a Future Lump Sum. Note the present value of the salvage value reduces the cost of each vehicle. Using this methodology, Jonathan then computes the total cost of each vehicle. Using the lowest total cost criteria he would purchase Truck Model A with a present value total cost of $36,659.20, as it has the lowest total cost of the three trucks. Note that it is not the least expensive truck to purchase. Truck Model A has a purchase price of $26,955 compared to Truck Model B that has a purchase price of $25,695. His decision however is based on the present value of the lowest total cost, not lowest initial cost.

The lowest total cost procedure will actually be used many times by the business owner because he or she must replace equipment on a regular basis. Net present value is not used to calculate this type of investment. Emphasis is placed on minimizing total expenses and their being somewhat offset by benefits. When this is the case, the lowest total cost method of capital budgeting should be used.

MAKING THE DECISION

If a firm has limited funds and a multitude of investments from which to choose, then it will find itself having to choose some alternatives and sacrifice others. Some investments are **mutually exclusive,** because one is chosen and the others are automatically sacrificed or excluded. For example, a business owner will evaluate several locations before opening a new business or expanding an existing one. If the owner decides to open in a single location, then the decision precludes all other sites and is a mutually exclusive decision even though most sites may have positive net present values. Referring to Table 9-6, if a business owner had less than $96,000 to invest, then location 1 would be the only choice— it is mutually exclusive. If he had $96,000 exactly, he could invest in two locations.

Investments that are not mutually exclusive are chosen because they have positive net present values. Using Table 9-6, if the firm had sufficient

Table 9-6 Capital Budgeting Choices

Business Location	Capital Investment Cost	Cumulative Investment Cost	Net Present Value
1	$ 50,000	$ 50,000	$ 125,000
2	46,000	96,000	121,000
3	52,000	148,000	119,000
4	47,500	195,500	116,000
5	67,300	262,800	115,000
6	48,000	310,800	113,000
7	63,000	373,800	112,500
8	48,700	422,500	111,000
9	54,200	476,700	110,250
10	62,500	539,200	(15,000)
11	48,500	587,700	(17,000)
12	65,000	652,700	(25,000)

capital, then the owner could open up to nine new sites because they all have a positive net present value, so the selection of one site does not preclude the selection of others. These investments are non–mutually exclusive. However, most businesses have limited access to capital, which often will require making capital rationing decisions.

Capital rationing is a constraint placed on the amount of funds that can be invested in a given time period. For a large corporation, this constraint is often artificial, because the corporation has a choice of issuing new bonds or stock. For most small businesses, this constraint results from limited funds. In our example linked to Table 9-6, if the owner could invest no more than $373,800, then he would choose to open seven new sites, even though nine have positive net present values (sites 10 through 12 would not be chosen by any business owner because they have a negative net present value).

 **FOLLOWING UP**

Following up consists of monitoring and controlling our cash flows. Monitoring is determining if the actual benefits received exceed the additional costs incurred on an ongoing basis. This is the equivalent of a post audit. A **post audit** requires the owner or manager to establish procedures that will determine how well the outcome of the decision correlates with the proposal. Cash inflows and outflows should be monitored by setting up a budget to determine if proposed costs and benefits are realized. Controlling, as we have said before, is a three-step process: (1) establish standards for measuring the project, (2) measure actual performance against the standards established, and (3) take corrective action if required. Establishing standards is the process of creating annual budgets based on our capital budgeting decision. This provides us with expected costs and benefits on an annual basis. Measuring actual performance is accomplished by comparing actual costs and benefits with our annual budget. Because of the seasonal nature of most businesses, the annual budget should be broken down into monthly budgets. Both cash inflow and cash outflow should operate within a range of acceptable variance. In reality, cash flows are based on a forecast, which we know will not be accurate. Taking corrective action is required only when actual cash flows are outside the parameters of the variances that we have established.

TAKING CORRECTIVE ACTION

Once we determine that our cash flows are outside of acceptable parameters, we must take corrective action. Taking corrective action from the viewpoint of the financial manager consists of cutting costs, increasing cash flows, or developing some method of doing both. For example, when Hannah's Donut Shop opened, it was the only donut shop within a five-mile radius. Sales and cash flow exceeded projections, and Hannah operated the donut shop using night bakers and finishers, while she worked the day shift. One year after the shop was opened, a national donut chain built a shop within one mile of Hannah's shop. Her sales declined by 30 percent. Specific fixed expenses such as rent and equipment payments to the bank could not be cut because she and her husband had signed long-term contracts. The shop had been staying open 24 hours a day. An audit of sales indicated that afternoon sales did not exceed the labor costs of the afternoon shift. So Hannah decided to cut operating hours and lay off the afternoon shift. This resulted in both reduced labor costs and lower utility bills, but the cuts were still not sufficient to offset the 30 percent reduction in sales due to the competition from the national chain.

Hannah and her husband, Phil, decided that they would have to work the night shift themselves and lay off the night baker and finisher. This procedure resulted in additional cost savings and a positive cash flow. The arrangement of Hannah and Phil working 12 to 14 hours a day, seven days a week, resulted in the business's turning a positive cash flow. They determined that the only way to increase sales consistently was to go after the industrial market. They realized that this market required consistency of product, competitive pricing, and prompt delivery. Phil developed baking and finishing procedures that resulted in meeting the required standards. Phoenix had several large factories with cafeterias for their employees. After developing the standards for product, Hannah hired a delivery driver who was paid based on his obtaining industrial accounts. Within one year, the cash flow from the industrial accounts was sufficient for Hannah to purchase an additional delivery vehicle, hire a night shift, and go back to working the day shift only.

From this scenario, it should be obvious that taking corrective action is not an instantaneous process. It requires carefully thought-out methods for cutting costs and increasing cash flows. It takes time, patience, and the commitment of the business owner.

CONCLUSION

Capital budgeting is the method we use to justify the acquisition of capital goods. It is a process of making a decision based on ensuring that the business owner or manager is entering into a project for which benefits exceed costs over time. Capital budgeting requires a five-step process:

1. Formulate a proposal, which serves the purpose of identifying the various costs incurred and benefits received in after-tax cash flows.
2. Evaluate the data generated with respect to the benefits and costs to see whether the investment will be profitable.
3. Make a decision by choosing the course of action that will provide the greatest future benefit while minimizing future costs.
4. Follow up on the capital budgeting decision through a post audit to see if the actual benefits received exceed the additional costs incurred.
5. Take corrective action if the post audit indicates that the benefits received are not meeting our expectations.

Evaluation of the data uses either payback, net present value, profitability index, internal rate of return, or accounting rate of return. We recommend using net present value and internal rate of return, although the actual choice is up to the owner or manager.

POSTSCRIPT

In the case of Hannah's Donut Shop, the perseverance of the owners paid off in the long run. The national chain closed its donut shop, and Hannah's again became the only donut shop within a five-mile radius. After 10 years, Hannah and Phil sold the shop. It is currently being operated by the new owners at a profit. Small businesses are the essence of the American enterprise system. We hope that this text will assist more people in successfully opening and operating small businesses.

Given the fact that we anticipate small business success, we must address one additional issue that impacts many small business owners and managers. Most business owners concentrate heavily on the day-to-day operational tactics to accomplish their immediate goal of making a profit. Many business owners fail to form an adequate strategy that revolves around their own personal finances. It is our intent to cover those areas of personal finance that are of utmost concern to the small business owner. Chapter 10 is devoted to personal finance and areas of concern to the small business entrepreneur.

REVIEW AND DISCUSSION QUESTIONS

1. What distinguishes a capital investment from other investments?
2. List and briefly explain the five-step capital budgeting process.
3. What are the various costs that must be evaluated in a capital budgeting decision?
4. What are some of the tax factor benefits of capital budgeting?
5. List the advantages and disadvantages of the payback method.
6. How does a company determine the interest rate it will use in making a net present value decision?
7. What are three components used by a lender in determining the interest rate charged for a loan?
8. What is the actual cost of capital to the borrower?
9. Describe the process of calculating net present value.
10. List two advantages of using net present value.
11. What is the relationship between net present value and profitability index?
12. What are the advantages of the profitability index method of capital budgeting?
13. How does the accounting rate of return differ from the internal rate of return?
14. Discuss the method of capital budgeting that you would use in your own business. Justify your decision.
15. What are the differences between mutually exclusive, non–mutually exclusive, and capital rationing decisions?
16. What is the three-step process of controlling?

EXERCISES AND PROBLEMS

1. What is the payback if the investment cost is $45,000 and the after tax benefit is $2000.
2. An interest payment of $650 in a 20% tax bracket would result in a tax savings of _____
3. Joe Morton buys a piece of equipment for $200,000. He puts down $40,000 and finances $160,000. Joe's opportunity cost is 12 percent, and the lender's interest rate is 11 percent. Find the weighted average cost of capital.

4. A $15,000 car is bought with a $3000 down payment. The balance is financed at 8% annual interest. If the opportunity cost is 10%, what is the weighted average cost of capital?

5. If the 10% annuity factor is 8.5136 and the 11% annuity factor is 7.9633, a present value annuity factor of 8.1234 correlates to an internal rate of return of_____ .

6. The Ohm Depot Co. is currently considering the purchase of a new machine that would increase the speed of manufacturing electronic equipment and save money. The net cost of the new machine is $66,000. The annual cash flows have the following projections:

year	amount
1	$21,000
2	29,000
3	36,000
4	16,000
5	8,000

If the cost of capital is 10 percent, find the following:

a. The present value of the benefits?

b. The net present value

c. The Internal rate of Return (Hint: use interpolation. IRR is between 20%–25%)

d. Payback

e. Profitability index

7. Georgia Boye is considering investing in a franchise which will require an initial outlay of $75,000. She has conducted market research and found that her after tax cash flows on the investment should be about $15,000 per year for the next seven years. The Franchiser stated that Georgia would generate a 20% return. Her cost of capital is 10%. Find the following:

a. The present value of the benefits

b. The present value of the costs

c. The net present value

d. The Internal rate of return (Hint: use interpolation. IRR is between 8% and 10%)

8. You want to buy a new computer for your business for net access on its own phone line. The computer system costs $5100. The new phone line costs $200 to install and has a $50 a month usage fee. You expect to buy the system with a $100 down payment financing the balance at 8% over the next four years and then sell the computer for $1000 when you upgrade. You expect a $500 a month increase in cash flow. You are in a 25% tax bracket.

a. The start up costs are_____

b. The present value of all the costs is_____

c. The present value of all the benefits is _____

d. The monthly payment for the computer will be_____

9. The LJB Company has to replace a freezer. The company is trying to decide between two alternatives. The two alternatives are as follows:

	Freezer A	Freezer B
Investment required	$29,000	$25,000
Annual electrical bill	3,000	4,000
Salvage value	6,000	5,000
Project life	11 years	11 years

The LJB Company cost of capital is 14%.

Which investment provides LJB with the lowest total cost?

10. You are considering the purchase of a beauty salon. The initial cost of this purchase would be $16,000. The after-tax cash flows from this investment should be $4,000 per year for the next 5 years. Your opportunity cost of capital is 10%. Please calculate the following:
   a. Payback—Would you buy the beauty salon based on payback if your required payback is less than three years?
   b. The Present Value of the Benefits (PVB)
   c. The Present Value of the Costs (PVC)
   d. The Net Present Value (NPV)—Would you buy the beauty salon based on NPV rules?
   e. Profitability Index (PI)—What does the profitability index mean in terms of buying the beauty salon?
   f. Internal Rate of Return (IRR) (hint: use interpolation)— Would you buy the beauty salon based on IRR rules?
   g. Accounting Rate of Return (ARR)—Would you buy the beauty salon based on the ARR?

11. Jim Coats has a sandwich shop in a downtown business district. Several of his customers have said that they would purchase from his shop more often if he offered a delivery service. Jim is considering establishing a delivery service to meet the needs of his market. He believes that he will have to purchase a fax machine, install a new phone line for the fax machine, purchase a delivery van, and hire at least one delivery person. Jim asks your advice in determining whether he should take on the delivery service venture.
   a. What steps would you recommend that Jim use in reaching a profitable decision?
   b. Explain to Jim what each step involves.

12. You decide to help Jim with his analysis. A good fax machine will cost $500 and function properly for five years. The phone company charges $300 for installing a new line and $60 a month for the line. A new delivery van costs $20,000 and can be financed for 60 months with a $4,000 down payment. Jim's bank will finance the van at 12 percent compounded monthly, which is also the rate that you calculated as his weighted average cost of capital. You found that a five-year-old van of this model sells for $5,000. After discussing the business venture with several retired restaurant owners at the local SCORE office, you believe that Jim, after paying his food costs, will increase his breakfast and lunch trade by $2,000 a month.

Jim can hire a part-time driver for $600 a month. The vehicle depreciates straight line for five years, or $3,000 per year. Jim is a sole proprietor and is in a 20 percent tax bracket. You estimate that it will cost Jim $300 a month to pay for maintenance, upkeep, and insurance on the van.

  a. If Jim decides to establish a delivery service and pays for the fax machine in cash, how much cash does he need now?

  b. What is the monthly payment for the delivery van?

  c. Using the time value of money and a five-year life for this project, what is the present value of all of Jim's costs?

  d. Using the time value of money and a five-year life for this project, what is the present value of all of Jim's benefits?

  e. What is the net present value of the delivery service?

  f. What is the profitability index of the delivery service?

  g. What is the payback?

  h. What recommendation would you give to Jim with regard to this project?

13. Kay Rite is considering investing in a franchise, which will require an initial outlay of $100,000. She has conducted market research and found that her after-tax cash flows on this investment should be about $20,000 a year for the next seven years. The franchiser stated that she will generate a 20 percent rate of return. She currently has her money in a mutual fund, which has grown at an average rate of 14 percent. Kay states to the franchiser that money has a time value and the actual rate of return according to her calculations is much less than 20 percent.

  a. Do you agree with the franchiser or with Kay?

  b. What rate of return is the franchiser using, and what method did he use to calculate it?

  c. What rate of return is Kay using, and what method did she use?

  d. Should Kay make the investment? Explain your answer.

14. Buster Block represents a video chain store that is expanding into a new, large metropolitan area. He currently has $2,000,000 to invest and wants to open several video stores. He found that each site will require a cash outlay of $230,000 for leasing, equipment, and initial inventory. Buster is currently looking at 20 sites. Fifteen sites have positive net present values; sites 16 through 20 have negative net present values.

  a. What is the maximum number of video stores in which Buster can invest for his company? Explain.

  b. How many stores can Buster open if his employer increases his budget to $5,000,000? Explain.

15. Buster's boss stated that after reviewing first-quarter earnings, the company decided to invest in only one store in the city. After evaluating the performance of the store, the company will determine if it wants to increase its presence in the area.

  a. If you were Buster, what method of evaluation would you use to recommend a site for a new video store?

  b. Explain how you would determine which site to invest in.

PERSONAL FINANCE 10

Learning Objectives

When you have completed this chapter, you should be able to:

♦ Understand the overall nature of risk as it pertains to both individuals and businesses.

♦ Distinguish between speculative and pure risk.

♦ Identify the programs employed by individuals and businesses in managing risk.

♦ Understand the role that insurance plays in the transfer of risk.

♦ Understand the role of capital accumulation in achieving financial success.

♦ Analyze and determine which investment vehicles to select in order to efficiently accumulate and preserve capital.

♦ Understand the importance of retirement planning.

♦ Distinguish between the various retirement programs and strategies available to the business owner and the individual.

♦ Understand the importance that estate planning plays for the individual and business owner in the transfer of wealth.

Personal finance is difficult to separate from business finance for the small business owner. First, the funds used to start and maintain the business are either your own or borrowed financial capital, which is used to acquire assets that will generate revenue for the business. In either case, as a small business owner, you are personally liable for all debts of the business. Conversely, all assets acquired by the business not only strengthen the business but also have a positive impact on your personal wealth. As your individual business assets increase your ability to borrow funds, your individual credit rating and the complexity of determining how to invest and protect these assets also increase. For example, excess cash should be invested in a manner that will guarantee your financial future and meet the liquidity needs of the business. Inventory, key personnel, and physical and real property must be safeguarded against loss. In financial terms, the methods of investing excess cash and guarding assets against loss are referred to as risk management.

RISK

Risk is a term that is based on the uncertainty of future outcomes. It involves both the probability that an expected outcome will occur, and the variability in that expected outcome. If there is no variability in future outcome, there is no risk. For example, when you buy a U.S. government bond that pays 5 percent annual interest, it is considered to be a risk-free investment, because the probability that the government will pay the interest is virtually 100 percent. If you buy a corporate bond, however, then the probability exists that the corporation may lose money and not be able to pay the interest on your bond. If the corporation goes into bankruptcy, then you may lose both the interest payment and the principal amount of your investment. Therefore, your risk in purchasing a corporate bond is higher than the risk of purchasing a U.S. government bond, and you would want to be compensated for the additional risk by having a risk premium added onto the investment. The risk premium for a bond is reflected in both the interest (coupon) rate that the corporation would have to pay to the bondholder and the discount from par that the bond would sell for. For the reader who is not familiar with the terms *coupon rate, discount rate,* and *par,* refer to "Bonds" later in this chapter. Both factors (coupon rate and discount amount) result in a higher rate of return, because of the variability and uncertainty of getting back your principal and interest.

For the businessperson, risk occurs when the possibility exists that a venture will fail or incur a loss versus the possibility that the business will succeed. In other words, risk is an uncertainty regarding the possibility that a loss may occur to a business and prevent it from generating a specific amount of revenue that will allow it to stay afloat.

The two types of risk are speculative risk and pure risk. **Speculative risk** involves a possible gain or loss, such as the risk of investing in the stock market or gambling in Las Vegas. This type of risk is uninsurable. **Pure risk** involves only a chance of loss or of experiencing a theft or fire. This type of risk is insurable. An example of speculative business risk involves new product introduction. If a business markets a new product and it fails, then the business has risked a great deal of time and capital only to find itself with excess unplanned inventory. This type of risk is uninsurable because just as the business experienced a loss, it also could have experienced a gain if the product had sold. This risk is speculative and is uninsurable.

An example of pure risk occurs if the business experiences a theft. If you have an insurance policy that includes theft, then your insurance will pay for the loss resulting from the theft, because a loss has actually occurred. If there had been no theft, there would have been no loss.

To have an insurable loss, the following criteria must apply:

1. Potential losses must be reasonably predictable for the insurance company to estimate the probability of a loss so that they can set the price of the insurance policy. If your business buys a liability policy and the number of your liability claims exceeds the probability predicted by the insurance company, then the price of liability premiums as charged by the insurance company will increase. If you have too many claims, your insurance premiums may increase to the point where your business can no longer support the payments and continue to make a profit. Additionally, the insurance company may cancel your coverage because it is no longer making a profit. We have seen this happen in the medical field, when some communities no longer have obstetricians because the cost of liability insurance has increased so much that they have chosen to exit the business of delivering babies.

2. The loss must be accidental. If the loss was incurred on purpose, then it is not covered by insurance.

3. The loss should be beyond the control of the insured. For example, the small business does not want to promote theft. When theft occurs, it is beyond the control of the business owners.

4. The loss should not be catastrophic to the insurance company. For example, it is difficult, if not impossible, to buy hurricane, earthquake, or flood insurance in certain areas.

IDENTIFICATION OF RISK EXPOSURE

As business owners, we have risk exposure when we place ourselves or our businesses in a situation in which there is uncertainty of outcomes. Marketing risk offers an example of a risk exposure. As indicated, a small business will suffer a loss if it brings the wrong product or products to market. A business, in its quest to increase sales, may extend credit to its customers. It may have a credit risk if these customers do not pay on time, and it definitely has a credit risk if they do not pay at all. The business is exposed to a loss because the owner thinks that revenue has been earned, but no money is ever received from the customers to increase cash on hand. These risks are not insurable. The loss of one's service to a business due to death or disability is insurable, however, as is the interruption of a business's activities due to fire or theft.

RISK MANAGEMENT

Risk management involves performing the management planning function in a manner that will reduce uncertainty. When uncertainty cannot be reduced, risk management should be used to control the risk at an acceptable level. Risk management applies to insurable business risks and involves a total approach to insuring against these risks. It includes programs to reduce risk, avoid risk, and transfer risk. One example of a program of **risk reduction** would be to have sprinkler systems installed in the business to curtail any damage that might be experienced during a fire.

A company that is financially unable to sustain or experience any risk can follow a program of **risk avoidance.** Here the company may avoid any physical hazard exposing it to risk. A method of risk avoidance in business would be a cash-only policy with no issuance of credit; thus, you would avoid the late payments and lack of payments associated with issuing credit. You may, however, face the risk of losing potential sales and becoming noncompetitive in your industry if the industry standard is to issue credit. Most firms recognize the fact that potential losses such as a fire might put them totally out of business because they do not have the capabilities to absorb large losses by themselves.

For the majority of firms, it is common and most feasible to engage in **risk transfer.** With this practice, risk is transferred to another party, usually a factor or an insurance company. A factor is some third party who, for a percentage of the accounts receivable, will provide you with immediate payment. The factor is responsible for collecting the payment, and the factor bears the risk of payment not being made. Therefore, when you use a factor, you can issue credit, but you do not have the risk associated with nonpayment as long as you comply with the requirements of the factor. The best example is companies that accept MasterCard, VISA, or American Express in payment for products or services. The company actually provides credit to its customers, but immediately transfers the risk to the factor (the credit card company). Of course, nothing is free. The factor will charge you a percentage of the accounts receivable as a collection fee. In other words, the risk associated with a particular event is transferred to someone else for a fee. Risk transfer to an insurance company will be explained in the next section of this chapter.

Risk assumption occurs when you believe that the loss you might incur is less than the cost of risk avoidance or risk transfer. Most of us are familiar with this concept in its relationship to carrying comprehensive insurance on an automobile. When the value of the car decreases to a certain point, we cancel our collision and comprehensive coverage, because the premiums exceed the value of the car. Another example occurs when firms grow. At some point a firm is large enough to become a self-insurer. If you own one pizza parlor and rely on it for your total income, then you had better use risk transfer and insure your building against fire, theft, and other potential losses in income. If you have 1,000 pizza parlors and one burns down, you have enough income generated by the others to rebuild, and you would not have to carry fire insurance. In addition, risk assumption may be the only alternative for a company, because it cannot find an insurance company to insure it against losses, for example, insuring a building against earthquake damage in certain areas of California.

LIFE, HEALTH, PROPERTY, AND LIABILITY INSURANCE

Life insurance will be discussed in terms of its basics. Permanent and term insurance are the basic types of life insurance. The business use of life insurance will be discussed in terms of key-man insurance, and group insurance, and health and retirement programs. Property and casualty insurance include fire, auto, theft, and liability insurance, and fidelity and surety bonds.

Life insurance is a method of transferring risk from the insured to the insurance company. This allows the insured to create an estate for his or her beneficiaries to receive upon the insured's death. The actual amount of life insurance should be based on the financial planning goals of the individual as discussed in this section. Normally, the amount of insurance that a person requires will depend on several factors including the number and ages of dependent children, the value of a business, the value of a home, and all other outstanding debts. The value also should include the earning potential of the insured and of a surviving spouse. Typically, the amount of insurance required will decrease as you get older, because you will have more equity in your home and business with time, and your children will reach an age at which they are no longer dependents and will not rely on you for their education and sustenance. Group insurance for life and health can be provided at a lower premium because of the reduced risk to the insurance company.

There are essentially two basic schools of thought with regard to life insurance, and several variations and combinations within these schools. The first school supports **term insurance,** which assumes that you pay the premium for pure life insurance. A term life insurance premium is based on the mortality rate of the insured's age group. Therefore, as your age increases, the premium (the payment you make to the insurance company) also will increase. Most term policies are issued with a level premium for a term of five years and then must be renewed at a higher rate. The second school supports **permanent** or **whole-life insurance,** which allocates part of the premium to building equity or cash value that can be used upon retirement or borrowed against in case of an emergency. If you die without a loan against the policy, however, the insurance company only pays the face value of the policy. Any cash value that you have accumulated will be retained by the insurance company. If you cancel a whole-life policy, you will receive a cash surrender value (CSV). If you cancel a term policy, there is no cash value returned.

In the late 1970s and early 1980s when interest rates skyrocketed, individuals took a hard look at their whole-life policy rates of return. They compared these returns with what they could be earning if their money was invested in stocks, bonds, or money market funds. In response, the insurance industry developed the universal life insurance policy to compete with investment products.

Under whole-life policies, premiums are set by the insurance companies based on long-term interest rates and actuarial tables. **Universal life insurance** is a policy in which purchasers set the premiums and the death benefits themselves. Premiums are set lower than whole-life policies, because at high interest rates a lower initial amount can generate the same investment return. However, if rates fall after the universal life policy is purchased, the premium may be inadequate to cover the death benefit. This creates a risk. The premium will need to be increased to maintain the policy in force.

Another variation of insurance is **variable life insurance.** This policy allows the individual to buy insurance and at the same time make choices among investment options; thus, all investment risk is placed on the policyholder. Investment choices may include a money market fund, bond fund, equity fund, or any combination.

Health insurance is purchased to transfer risk to an insurance company, to alleviate the cost of an illness or other health problem. Health insurance includes disability insurance, which lessens the cost of being disabled and losing the ability to earn an income. Health care costs have exceeded the inflation rate in the United States for several years, and these costs are a big concern of individuals, government, and business.

Many of today's business owners were born between 1946 and 1964. These individuals belong to the baby boomer generation. Baby boomers, because of their age, are concerned with retirement, risk, and death issues. In addition, these business owners should comprehend long-term care.

Long-term care insurance provides assistance for people who have chronic illnesses or are disabled for an extended period of time. Although most long-term care is needed by older individuals, young or middle-age individuals may require such care if they have been in an accident or experience a debilitating disease. In summation, a business owner will pay an affordable premium which will provide for benefits that lessen out-of-pocket expenses in the event that a mishap occurs. Today's policies cover care in a nursing home and home care. When considering long-term care insurance, we advise shopping several companies as they vary considerably with regard to waiting period, time and type of care, and premium.

Liability insurance is used to transfer the risk of property damage and personal injury that might result from your business operation or individual actions. In our litigious society, it is essential that individuals and businesses carry liability insurance. For example, if you are a plumber and are installing a water heater in a home, the possibility exists that the installation may be faulty and that damage to both the property and the occupants of the home may occur. Because you did the installation, you are personally liable for any damages that result from the installation. In the worst-case scenario, the home burns down because you or one of your employees failed to adequately tighten a natural gas fixture when the heater was installed. The house subsequently burned down and one of the occupants was seriously injured. Without liability insurance, you would probably lose your business and most of your personal assets. Liability insurance premiums vary with the degree of risk associated with your business and the amount of damages paid in a typical lawsuit. Therefore, the premiums for a plumber would be much lower than the premiums for a physician.

FINANCIAL PLANNING GOALS

The first step in the financial planning process, as in establishing a business, is to establish goals that are realistic and attainable. Every business owner desires to achieve financial success in life. We all have this general goal, but we have to become precise in terms of specific dollar amounts desired and the time frame for these financial goals. We must note that financial goals usually begin with the acquisition stage of capital accumulation involving savings and investments. Once acquired, our financial capital must be maintained and preserved. To actually preserve capital, we must invest in some vehicles that will provide us with a return that is greater than the inflation rate and that will take into consideration our individual tolerance for risk. Ultimately, our capital will be distributed through retirement income and/or estate transfer.

Tolerance for risk typically decreases with age due to the fact that we realize that we no longer have time to correct mistakes, and that we become more dependent on our financial capital to sustain us, because our ability to work decreases. For example, a young person who is just starting out can afford to take risks with regard to business and investments in order to accumulate wealth. If the young entrepreneur makes a mistake, he or she has the time to regroup and start again. An older person, however, normally will want a safer investment, because if a mistake is made, that person may not have the time to recover lost capital and may have to live in poverty. Therefore, once financial capital is accumulated, we must preserve and maintain it in an environment that is subject to both systematic and unsystematic risk as discussed in Chapter 1.

💲 INVESTMENTS

Investment vehicles are the specific financial instruments that we use to generate growth and income. Each investment vehicle will be described in this section.

CASH EQUIVALENTS

Cash equivalents are liquid assets that are invested in savings accounts or brokerage money market accounts. The money market consists of highly liquid current assets such as treasuries, bankers acceptances, certificates of deposits, and repurchase agreements. A **money market account** is a mutual fund that invests in the previous assets. These accounts earn interest and allow you to have liquidity for running your business. The interest earned on brokerage money market accounts is normally higher than the interest paid by banks on passbook savings accounts. However, most bank passbook savings accounts are federally insured through the Federal Deposit Insurance Corporation (FDIC), whereas brokerage accounts are insured by the brokerage house through the Securities Investment Protection Corporation (SIPC). There is a perception of increased risk in having funds held by a financial institution that is not federally insured. Therefore, having funds in a brokerage house rather than in a bank would be considered to have a higher risk; and as expected, we do find higher interest rates in brokerage accounts, because of the increased risk.

Although most bank savings accounts are of the passbook variety and normally require you to be present to withdraw funds, a money market brokerage account can normally be accessed with a check. However, these are not your usual bank checking accounts, because you are normally limited in some accounts to a minimum value for check writing ($500 to $1,000) and to the number of checks that can be written in a month. These accounts are useful for accumulating money for payment of items that are short term in nature, but not monthly—for example, payment of quarterly or semiannual taxes, insurance premiums, and in some cases retirement or profit sharing payments.

CERTIFICATES OF DEPOSIT

Certificates of deposit, or **CDs,** are promissory notes whereby a bank promises to pay the purchaser the principal amount plus interest after a stipulated period of time. Interest may be simple or compounded daily, monthly, or quarterly. CDs are issued for time periods as short as 30 days or as long as five years. As with most investments, the longer you tie up your money, the higher the interest rate, so you can expect to earn a higher return on a five-year CD than on a 30-day CD. It is important to note that if you purchase a five-year CD and need the money before it matures, you will pay a significant penalty that has the effect of decreasing the interest that you thought you would earn on the CD. Thus you would lose the liquidity available in savings and money market accounts for the additional interest that is earned on a CD. For this reason we do not recommend these investment vehicles unless you are extremely confident that the money will not have to be used during the maturity period.

You can time CD maturities in order to meet short- and long-term obligations. For example, six-month CD rates are normally 1/2 percent higher than passbook savings account rates. If you have a $10,000 property tax payment due in July and you have $10,000 of excess cash in December of the previous year, purchasing a six-month CD that is compounded daily will provide you with a little less than $25 of additional interest on the $10,000 during the six months.

BONDS

Bonds (government and corporate) are contractual agreements made between a borrower (government or corporation) and a lender of financial capital such as an individual, business, pension fund, mutual fund, or insurance company. There are several types of bonds, and several degrees of risk associated with them. We will discuss each type in ascending order of risk.

U.S. Treasury Bonds

U.S. treasury bonds are issued by the government of the United States to finance the government when its spending exceeds its tax revenue, which is referred to, on an annual basis, as the government having a deficit budget. The total amount of bonds issued by the government that are still outstanding at any given time is the national debt. Federal bonds are considered to be risk free or to have the least amount of risk, because they are backed by the full faith and credit of the federal government. Although short-term federal bills (T-bills) are risk free, long-term federal bonds are subject to interest rate swings and could be risky if you have to obtain the principal prior to maturity. In addition, the federal government is the only agency in the United States that can absolutely guarantee payment of interest, because it can print money. U.S. treasury bonds come in three varieties, which are based on the maturity dates of the bonds. **T-bills** (or treasury bills) are risk-free investments that mature in less than a year, typically in three or six months. **T-notes** are bonds that mature in 10 years or less, typically 10, 5, and 2 years. **Federal bonds** mature in periods that are greater than 10 years and range up to 30 years.

Municipal Bonds

Municipal bonds are issued by state and local governments, not the federal government, to finance projects. Municipal bonds are issued as either general revenue or general obligation bonds. **General revenue bonds** are issued to build specific projects for the municipality that will use the income from the project to pay the bondholder. For example, the city of Phoenix must expand its sewer system to provide sewer service for new homes. The city borrows the money, installs the sewer lines, and charges a sewer fee to homeowners. This money is then used to pay the bondholders. **General obligation bonds** are used to build projects that do not normally generate revenue such as public schools and roads, and these bonds are therefore based on the taxing ability of the municipality. For example, the city of Phoenix needs to widen the roads because of increased traffic flow. Because the city does not collect a road tax, it issues a general obligation bond and pays bondholders by collecting taxes in other areas (such as a sales tax). Interest payments on municipal bonds are free of federal income tax liability and are normally free of state and local taxes in the state in which they are issued. Therefore, they normally pay a lower interest rate than corporate bonds, but a higher rate than federal bonds; but this lower tax-free interest rate equates to a higher before-tax interest rate. For example, a tax-free municipal bond paying 7 percent issued to a taxpayer in the 40 percent bracket (federal and state combined) is equivalent to a taxable rate of 11.67 percent.

$$\text{Before-tax rate} = \frac{\text{Tax-free rate}}{1 - \text{tax rate}}$$

$$= \frac{0.07}{1 - 0.40} = 11.67\%$$

Corporate Bonds

Corporate bonds are issued by a public corporation that wants to borrow money to invest in assets that will help it earn revenue. These assets can be used as collateral and are pledged to the buyer of the bond in the event that the corporation cannot pay back the money due to the bondholder. When a corporation guarantees the bond in this manner, it is referred to as secured debt. The term **secured debt** refers to the fact that the corporation pledges specific assets to guarantee the bonds. For example, the Yantze Corporation wants to build a new office building that will cost $75 million. The corporation has only $25 million in cash for this project. It then issues $50 million in bonds and pledges the office building as collateral to the bondholders. When the bond is not backed by secured debt, it is referred to as a **debenture.** Debenture bondholders have a claim on the remaining assets of the company (those that are not secured).

Mechanics of Bond Financing

A brief explanation of several terms may help you to understand how bonds relate to your own personal goals. First, bonds are issued in denominations of $1,000. This is the **par value** of the bond—also referred to as the **face value** or **principal value** of the bond. This value never changes and is the amount of money that is paid to the bondholder at maturity (the due date of the bond). The **coupon rate** is the rate of interest that the issuer agrees to pay to the lender on an annual basis. This value also is referred to as the **stated** or **quoted rate,** and it never changes. For example, the Yantze Corporation issued a 10-year bond in January 2000 that pays 8 percent interest. If you bought this bond, you would receive $80 in interest payments each year until the year 2010. The $80 interest payment is calculated by multiplying the contractual 8 percent coupon rate by the par value of $1,000. The payments are normally made semiannually, or every six months. Therefore, you would receive a check for $40 twice a year from June 2000 until January 2010. At that time you would return the bond to the Yantze Corporation and receive a check for $1,000 (the maturity value of the bond). Please note that even if you do not return the bond, the corporation will no longer pay you interest, because their contract with you or whoever holds the bond was only for the life of the bond.

Corporate bonds are purchased through intermediaries (brokerage firms) and not directly from the corporation. We can buy bonds either when they are first issued (as in purchasing the bond mentioned earlier in January 2000) or in the aftermarket. Let us say we bought 10 Yantze bonds for $10,000 (at par $1,000 each) in January 2000, when the bonds were first issued at 8 percent. We now decide that we have another investment to make and no longer want to be a creditor of the Yantze Corporation. We can contact a broker and offer the bonds for sale. The price received for these bonds will depend on two primary factors—current market interest rates and risk.

The **current market interest rate** is the prevailing interest rate in the market on the day we decide to sell the bond. For example, if the current bond market rate is 12 percent, then a currently issued bond at par ($1,000) would have a coupon rate of 12 percent or pay $120 interest per annum. Therefore, any purchaser of a bond would want to earn 12 percent as the minimum rate on his or her investment. Consequently, when we sell our Yantze bonds in the current market, we cannot get the $1,000 par value for the bonds because Yantze will pay the new bondholder $80 or an 8 percent coupon rate on the face value. We must reduce the price (sell the bond at a discount) until the price of our bond will give the purchaser a market interest rate of 12 percent or more in annual interest on the amount that he pays for the bond. Bonds that are sold at a value above par are sold at a **premium;** bonds that are sold at a value below par are sold at a **discount.** The procedures for determining the current value of a bond were covered in Chapter 8 when we discussed the present value (PV) of an annuity and a lump sum. The method requires us to use the following factors:

1. Using current interest rates, find the present value of the bond's interest payments, paid over the remaining life of the bond. In the current example, our Yantze bond has five more years to maturity, with current market interest rates of 12 percent. Because the bond is paying 8 percent or $80 per year, you would want to determine how much money you would have to invest now at 12 percent to provide you with $80 per year for five years. Because Yantze will send you $40 checks semiannually, this is the same as receiving 10 payments of $40 at 6 percent interest (12 ÷ 6). We therefore want to find the present value of a $40 annuity for 10 periods at 6 percent interest. We use the formula PV = A (present value annuity factor) where **PV** is the present value of an annuity, A is the value of the annuity, and the annuity factor is obtained from Appendix Table B-5. Using Appendix Table B-5, we find a factor of 7.3601 for 10 periods at 6 percent. We then multiply this factor by the $40 annuity payment and determine that the PV is $294.40.

2. Using current interest rates, find the PV of the $1,000 maturity value of the bond, after 10 periods at 6 percent interest per period. First, we go to Appendix Table B-2 and find a factor of 0.5584. Using the formula PV = FV (Present value factor) we multiply the $1,000 future value payment by the 0.5584 from the table to obtain $558.40. Thus, if $558.40 were deposited in a bank today at 12 percent interest, it would grow to $1,000 in five years.

3. Therefore, as a bond purchaser, the maximum price that you would be willing to pay for this bond is $558.40 plus $294.40, or $852.80.

Additionally, we may have to sell our bond at a further discount that would give the purchaser an interest rate above 12 percent because of increased risk. For example, let us say that during the period of time from our initial purchase of the Yantze bond, in January 2000, until now, the Yantze Corporation has fallen on financial difficulties and its bond rating has gone from Aa (double a) to B. Note that, by definition, a B bond in Table 10-1 is considerably less attractive than an Aa bond. Because the investor perceives the purchase of this bond as being more risky, he or she will want an interest rate higher than 12 percent. These bonds are **junk bonds** (recently termed *high-income-yielding bonds* by the brokerage industry), because they have a rating of B or less. Therefore, the price that we have computed, $852.80, is the maximum price that a buyer would be willing to pay for this bond. Notice that 12 percent is the market rate which is based on systematic

Table 10-1 Corporate Bond Ratings

Key to Moody's Corporate Bond Ratings

Aaa

Bonds which are rated **Aaa** are judged to be of the best quality. They carry the smallest degree of investment risk and are generally referred to as "gilt edge." Interest payments are protected by a large or by an exceptionally stable margin and principal is secure. While the various, protective elements are likely to change, such changes as can be visualized are most unlikely to impair the fundamentally strong position of such issues.

Aa

Bonds which are rated **Aa** are judged to be of high quality by all standards. Together with the **Aaa** group they comprise what are generally known as high grade bonds. They are rated lower than the best bonds because margins of protection may not be as large as in **Aaa** securities or fluctuation of protective elements may be of greater amplitude or there may be other elements present which make the long term risks appear somewhat larger than in **Aaa** securities.

A

Bonds which are rated **A** possess many favorable investment attributes and are to be considered as upper medium grade obligations. Factors giving security to principal and interest are considered adequate but elements may be present which suggest a susceptibility to impairment sometime in the future.

Baa

Bonds which are rated **Baa** are considered as medium grade obligations, i.e., they are neither highly protected nor poorly secured. Interest payment and principal security appear adequate for the present but certain protective elements may be lacking or may be characteristically unreliable over any great length of time. Such bonds lack outstanding investment characteristics and in fact have speculative characteristics as well.

Ba

Bonds which are rated **Ba** are judged to have speculative elements; their future cannot be considered as well assured. Often the protection of interest and principal payments may be very moderate and thereby not well safeguarded during both good and bad times over the future. Uncertainty of position characterizes bonds in this class.

B

Bonds which are rated B generally lack characteristics of the desirable investment. Assurance of interest and principal payments or of maintenance of other terms of the contract over any long period of time may be small.

Caa

Bonds which are rated **Caa** are of poor standing. Such issues may be in default or there may be present elements of danger with respect to principal or interest.

Ca

Bonds which are rated **Ca** represent obligations which are speculative in a high degree. Such issues are often in default or have other marked shortcomings.

C

Bonds which are rated **C** are the lowest rated class of bonds and issues so rated can be regarded as having extremely poor prospects of ever attaining any real investment standing.

risk. However, Yantze has increased risk because of its B bond rating, so we would have to increase the discount and lower the price below $852.80 to give the bondholder an interest rate above 12 percent. Some bonds sell at very deep discounts when firms have poor bond ratings. When the Circle K Corporation was in chapter 11 bankruptcy in 1992, you could have purchased a $1,000 bond for $70. This is somewhat akin to playing the lottery. The market perceived that this company would not recover from bankruptcy, and therefore valued the bonds at 7 cents on the dollar. While in bankruptcy, a corporation normally ceases all payments to bondholders.

The only hope is that if the company is sold or emerges from bankruptcy, some payment will be made to the company's creditors—and bondholders are creditors.

STOCK

Common Stock

Common stock is issued by public or private corporations to raise financial capital. The stockholders (owners of shares of common stock) are the owners of the corporation. A share of stock represents ownership in the corporation, and each share of stock is normally worth one vote. Every public corporation must hold an annual meeting. The normal agenda for these meetings includes election of the members of the board of directors, selection of an independent auditor to perform the annual audit of the corporate books, and any other business deemed necessary by the owners. The board of directors is responsible for selecting the professional management of the corporation: the chief executive officer, the chairman of the board, and the president of the corporation. The stockholders determine who will sit on the board of directors; and the number of shares of common stock to be issued by the corporation is determined by the board of directors. They will assign a par value to the stock. The **par value** is an arbitrary dollar amount that is used for accounting purposes to determine the number of shares of stock that have been sold by the corporation.

The par value has no relationship to the actual market price of the stock. For example, the Yantze Corporation decides to issue 1 million shares of common stock at a par value of $1 per share, and the market is willing to buy this stock at an average price of $10 per share. We say that the market has paid in $9 per share of additional capital. Recall from our previous discussion on the accounting equation, Assets = Liabilities + Stockholder's equity. Because the common stock is the stockholder's (owner's) equity, the sale of these shares of stock will be listed on the balance sheet as follows: stock at par, $1 million ($1 × 1 million shares = $1 million); and additional paid-in capital, $9 million ($9 × 1 million shares = $9 million). Notice that the stockholder's equity is $10 million—the total amount raised by the Yantze

Corporation for the sale of this stock. In reality, the stock will have sold at a price slightly above $10 per share, because there will be charges to the corporation by the investment banking firms and brokerage firms who act as intermediaries between the corporation and potential investors. The initial sale of stock by a corporation to the public is the **primary securities market.**

Once the stock is initially sold by the corporation, all future sales of this stock are normally carried out by the owners of individual shares of stock in the **secondary securities market,** and not by the corporation. Common stocks normally have two values, book value and market value. The **book value** of the stock is the total stockholder's equity that is carried on the corporate balance sheet. It includes three factors: stock at par, additional paid-in capital, and retained earnings. Only one of these figures, retained earnings, will change, unless the corporation buys back stock or issues additional shares of stock. The total value of the owner's equity (Stock at par + Additional paid-in capital + Retained earnings) divided by the number of shares outstanding is the book value of a share of common stock. The formula is

$$\text{Book value per share of common stock} = \frac{\text{Total common stockholder's equity}}{\text{Number of shares of common stock outstanding}}$$

The **market value** of a share of stock is the price at which the owners of current shares are buying and selling the stock at the time that a share is actually traded. Several factors affect the market value of a share of stock:

1. **Supply and demand for shares** of the company stock. As discussed in Chapter 1, if there are more people who want to buy available shares in a specific corporation than there are people who are willing to offer shares for sale, then the share price will be bid up by competition. Conversely, when there are more shares available for sale than there are purchasers of the stock, then the price will fall. For example, when America West Airlines filed for chapter 11 bankruptcy, shareholders panicked and offered thousands of shares of stock for sale. Because of the company's financial position, there were very few takers, and the price of the stock fell from a high of $7.62 in 1991 to a low of $2.50 by June 28, 1991.

2. **Actual earnings and anticipation of changes in earnings** by the corporation. For example, if the Yantze Corporation announces that it has just received a patent for a new product that the market perceives as a best-seller, then the stock price will probably rise. However, if owners read an article that states that the Yantze Corporation has lost money, or has had a plant burn down, or has been involved in a product liability lawsuit, then the price of the

stock will probably fall. An additional factor is analysts' earnings expectations and the company's abilities to meet these expectations with actual earnings. For example, Cisco Systems on November 9, 1999, reported earnings of 24 cents a share, which was 1 cent better than analysts' estimates. The next day, Cisco stock increased $4.50 per share from $74.25 to $78.75 per share with over 40 million shares traded in the secondary market.

3. **The book value of the stock and the number of shares of stock outstanding.** For example, if the Yantze corporation currently has 1 million shares of stock outstanding, and the board of directors decides to issue an additional 1 million shares, then the book value of each share will be reduced by 50 percent and any earnings per share of the corporation also will be diluted because of the additional number of shares. This reduction will be reflected in a reduced market value of the stock.

4. **General economic conditions.** Economic conditions in general also will affect the price of a stock, even if the corporation does everything correctly. If the economy is in a recession, with a high unemployment rate, then corporate sales in general will be lower. Low sales will decrease corporate earnings. Therefore, the stock investor will not be willing to pay as high a price for the stock, because as a corporation's earnings decline, the price of the stock in the market will normally follow. Other factors in the economy can affect specific industries. For example, if oil prices increase because of an accord reached by the Organization of Petroleum Exporting Countries (OPEC) to cut supply, then the price of stocks of companies that are dependent on petroleum products, such as the airlines, will probably drop. Another economic factor is market interest rates. If interest rates in the market are rising, then money becomes more expensive to borrow, and thus it becomes more expensive for corporations to raise money through bond sales or bank borrowing. If corporations have to pay more interest on their debt, then they will not be able to make as much profit and stock prices in general will fall as a result of decreased earnings. The reverse of the preceding situations will normally lead to increasing stock prices.

Preferred Stock

Preferred stock (cumulative preferred, convertible preferred, and callable preferred) is also issued by a corporation to raise financial capital; however, it occupies an intermediate position between common stock and bonds.

Preferred stock is a hybrid vehicle because it has features of both bonds and common stock. Preferred stockholders are quasi owners of the corporation. They do not have voting rights, but are guaranteed a specific percentage return on their investments if the corporation pays a dividend. The original selling price and par value of preferred stock are the same, and preferred stock is normally sold at values of $25, $50, or $100 per share with a stated dividend that is a percentage of the sales price. For example, if the Yantze Corporation issues $1 million worth (10,000 shares) of preferred stock at $100 par value, paying $7 or 7 percent per share, then the purchaser knows in advance that he or she should receive a $7 dividend in each year that the corporation declares a dividend. Preferred stock has an important feature of the long-term bond (fixed annual payments), and owners relinquish their voting rights for this feature. However, like the common stockholders, they still have a residual claim on income; and in fact, their claim is senior to that of the common stockholders.

Continuing with our example of the Yantze Corporation, it has issued 1 million shares of common stock and 10,000 shares of preferred stock (10,000 shares × $100 per share = $1 million in preferred stock). The corporation makes an annual profit of $4 million and the board of directors determines that it will pay a dividend of $1 million and have retained earnings of $3 million. When a dividend is declared, the preferred stockholders receive their payment first (in this case, $7 × 10,000 shares). Dividend distributions are calculated as follows:

$$\text{Total dividend} = \text{Total preferred dividend} + \text{Total common stock dividend}$$

$$
\begin{aligned}
\text{Total common stock dividend} &= \text{Total dividend} - \text{Total preferred dividend} \\
&= \$1,000,000 - (\$7)(10,000 \text{ preferred shares}) \\
&= \$1,000,000 - \$70,000 \\
&= \$930,000
\end{aligned}
$$

$$
\begin{aligned}
\text{Common stock dividend per share} &= \frac{\text{Total common stock dividend}}{\text{Total number of shares of common stock outstanding}} \\
&= \frac{\$930,000}{1,000,000 \text{ shares}} = \$0.93 \text{ per share of common stock}
\end{aligned}
$$

Because each of the 10,000 shares of preferred stock will receive a dividend payment of $7, Yantze preferred stockholders receive $70,000 in total dividends. This leaves $930,000 to be paid to common stockholders. Because there are 1 million shares of common stock outstanding, each share of common stock will receive a dividend of 93 cents. Therefore, if you owned 1,000 shares of preferred stock, you would receive a dividend check for $7,000. If you owned 1,000 shares of common stock, you would receive a dividend check for $930.

Cumulative preferred stock.   This type of preferred stock has the following important feature. There may be a year or two, due to financial circumstances of a corporation, in which a dividend is not paid (the corporation may have lost money, or retained the earnings to finance some project). When the corporation decides to pay a dividend, the preferred stockholder will receive back dividends, or dividends in arrears. This feature is not available to common stockholders. Using our previous example, let us say that the Yantze Corporation had not paid any dividends during the past two years, and then decided to pay the $1 million dividend in the current year. The payout of dividends would be calculated as follows: There would be $70,000 for year 1, $70,000 for year 2, and $70,000 for the current year, or $210,000, in preferred dividends; therefore, the preferred stockholder would receive $21 per share in preferred dividends. The common stock dividend would then be calculated as $1,000,000– $210,000 = $790,000, or 79 cents a share. Most preferred stock is cumulative.

Convertible preferred stock.   This type of preferred stock may be exchanged for shares of common stock. If the preferred stock is convertible, this feature is stated when the stock is issued, with minimal time frames within which the option may be exercised. This feature is used to add value to a preferred stock issue, because the stock has the advantage of fixed earnings in the near term, but appreciates in value in the long term if the corporation's common stock does well in the market. Additionally, the preferred stockholders have the senior position on whatever funds are available to stockholders should the corporation be liquidated.

Callable preferred stock.   This type of preferred stock can be called back by the company at some specified price. It is not attractive to investors, so the company normally has to provide the investor with a call premium (an amount of money above the stock's current selling price). Companies normally call back preferred stock when interest rates are low, because they believe they can raise capital and pay less interest to the lender than they would pay in dividends to the preferred stockholder. For example, if the prime lending rate falls to 5 percent when the company has 7 percent preferred stock, then Yantze can borrow the $1 million to buy back the preferred stock and make interest payments of $50,000 per year, when it would have had to pay the preferred stockholder a dividend of $70,000. Another method that the company can use to raise capital when market interest rates are low is to issue common stock. Because stock prices are normally high when interest rates are low, the company could issue common stock and use the capital to call back the preferred stock. This would have the advantage of eliminating the entire $70,000 preferred dividend.

Strategies of Stock Investment

Strategies of stock investment are varied. Stocks are considered to be high-risk investments, because when you supply equity capital to a company you position yourself as a claimant on any income that the company may generate. As a small investor, however, you have such a small share of the company that you, in reality, have no voice in how your investment is used. Owning 100 shares of a corporation that has 30 million shares of common stock provides you with no real authority in regard to the corporation. Additionally, any corporation, regardless of size, may lose vast amounts of money (IBM lost over $5 billion, General Motors over $23 billion, and Ford over $7 billion in 1992), or may declare bankruptcy (TWA in 1991). When companies lose money, the market value of their stock goes down (IBM stock lost over half of its value during 1992). If the company goes into bankruptcy, you may very well lose all of your money, because the value of the stock can go to zero. On average, however, stockholders earn 9 percent on their investment each year. The problem is that, to earn this average, you must have stock in all publicly traded companies. Some will go bankrupt, and you will lose your investment; others will generate income far in excess of 9 percent. Thus, you will have to diversify your portfolio by owning stock in several corporations at the same time. To equal or beat this 9 percent average return, you must either spend inordinate amounts of time studying individual corporations, hire a broker in whom you have absolute confidence, or set up a pool of funds with other investors who have the same goals and risk tolerance level as you have. We believe that the best method of pooling your investment, based on goals and risk tolerance level, is to invest in mutual funds.

MUTUAL FUNDS

Mutual funds are companies that are involved in collecting the funds of investors and using these funds to purchase large blocks of stocks, bonds, or other investment vehicles. Each fund is established with a specific goal and risk objective. When you invest in a mutual fund, you are essentially hiring a professional manager to spend full time researching and purchasing those investment vehicles that will match your own individual goals. Basically, the investment objectives of most mutual funds fall into one or more of the following general categories.

Growth Funds

Growth funds are the most popular of mutual funds. They invest primarily in common stock of publicly held corporations and have as their objective capital appreciation. Growth funds vary from aggressive growth (investing in small high-tech companies that also provide high risk) to long-term growth (investing primarily in stable, well-established blue-chip companies with low risk) to sector funds that specialize in the stocks of specific industries (pharmaceuticals, chemicals, metals, etc.).

Income Funds

Income funds are attractive to people who are retired. These funds specialize in corporate and government bonds. Their objective is to provide the investor with a relatively high level of stable income. As with growth funds, the level of risk varies based on the specialized area of fund investment. Some funds will invest only in U.S. government bonds; others may invest only in high-quality corporate bonds or home mortgages (Ginnie Mae bond funds); and others may invest only in low-quality corporate bonds (junk bonds). These latter funds are normally listed as high-income or high-income-yielding bond funds.

Growth and Income Funds, or Balanced Funds

Growth and income funds, or **balanced funds,** invest in both stocks and bonds. These funds provide both capital growth, through stock and bond acquisition, and fixed income, through bond coupon payments. The balance is achieved because if there is a shift by investors out of the stock market, bond prices will normally increase because of increased demand for bonds. There is also an inverse relationship: If investors shift from bonds to stock, then stock prices are bid up by increased demand. These funds normally appeal to the investor who has moderate tolerance for risk.

Global and International Funds

Global and international funds have the same basic objectives as the balanced funds, but invest in stocks and bonds of companies primarily outside of the United States. These funds may be truly global (investing in opportunities in any area of the world), regional (European, Asian), or specialized (Japan, Israel, France).

Money Market Funds

Money market funds primarily invest in short-term, highly liquid investments such as CDs, short-term government treasuries, commercial paper, repurchase agreements, and banker's acceptances. These funds are the mutual fund equivalent of a checking account. If you hold money in a money market fund, you may request check-writing privileges; however, these are not normal checkbooks in that the number of checks you can write per month is limited and the minimum amount of the check may be set by the fund. These funds normally generate income above that which is being paid by commercial banks because they have a portfolio of investments. When you purchase a CD or treasury instrument through a commercial bank, you get only the interest rate of the specific vehicle. We (the authors) both have money market accounts so that we have some liquidity, but we use the accounts to shift assets to and from mutual funds, purchase stock, and make other investments.

Other Funds

Other funds include a whole category of specialized funds that are very high risk and operate in such areas as options, futures contracts, commodity markets, and currency exchanges. Because this book is primarily written for the nonfinancial entrepreneur and small businesses, we will not discuss these high-risk operations.

Mutual Fund Families

A **mutual fund family** is an investment group that may have mutual fund portfolios in all of the preceding categories. Fidelity, Janus, and Vanguard are examples of fund families. Each has several categories of mutual funds. A mutual fund family may sell no-load funds or load funds.

- ◆ **No-load funds** do not charge commissions on the amount invested. If you invest $100 and the fund share price is $10, you will purchase 10 shares. However, these funds may involve assessed charges when you sell the mutual fund shares.
- ◆ **Load funds** charge a commission on the initial investment, but have no sales charges when you sell the shares. If you invest $100 in a front-loaded fund that charges a commission of 5 percent, then you will purchase $95 worth of shares and pay $5 in commission.

There are advantages to both of these funds. No-load funds are primarily used by people who do their own research and determine which fund and which fund family to invest in. Load funds, because they involve a commission, are preferred by most brokers. However, it is in their best financial interest to provide you with advice that will make you a long-term client. One should choose funds and families that will meet individual investment needs. The choice of which type of fund to invest in is based on your own perceptions. The authors of this text invest primarily in no-load funds.

When you are in a family of funds, you can switch your investments from one fund to another without having to pay a transaction fee based on the amount transferred. This normally saves you time and paperwork.

Mutual fund families are based on the assumption that individuals will consider certain investment vehicles more appropriate than others over time, due to both individual and economic changes over time. For example, if you start investing when you are young and single, what type of investing will you do? Because you have no family and no responsibility to others, you probably will have a high tolerance for risk and will consider placing most of your investments in growth funds. Later, you then marry and have children who will need a college education. Your goals become more focused as you take on the additional responsibility of providing for your offspring's education. You might invest in growth mutual funds when your children are young, but as college age approaches, you will want to lock in the principal amount and be in a position to write checks for tuition, books, and other incidental expenses. At this point, you will want to switch some of your investments into money market funds, which guarantee principal, and still provide some growth in the form of interest. As you approach retirement, you will want to start to accumulate wealth for retirement; but after you retire, you will probably want to have a specified level of income, which may be accomplished by investing in low-risk income funds, rather than aggressive growth funds. As discussed earlier, if all of your investments are in a single family of funds (no-load, load), then you can switch from one investment vehicle to another without paying a transaction fee based on a percentage of the reallocated investment.

In addition to changes that occur because of your family circumstances, other factors in the economy may impact your investments. If you have invested in a growth fund that has been paying you 15 percent per year on average, and market interest rates go to 18 percent, as they did during the 1980s, then you may want to shift some of your investment from stock to bonds. As mentioned, bond prices decrease as interest rates increase, so you can buy more bonds with a given amount of investment principal. You can increase your wealth by this shift in investments. You were getting 15 percent in your growth fund, but now can get 18 percent interest on bonds. Now, when interest rates drop, the income generated from the bond fund will decrease, but the value of the bond fund shares will increase. With declining interest rates, there is a point at which you may decide to sell the bond fund and reinvest in stock funds. For the small investor, mutual fund families are probably the best investment vehicle.

REAL ESTATE

Real estate is an investment in land and buildings. In general, these investments fall into three separate categories: owner-occupied residential, nonowner-occupied residential, and commercial. Each category is treated differently for tax purposes and will be discussed separately.

Owner-Occupied Residential Real Estate

Owner-occupied residential real estate is any kind of building in which people live. It is limited by law to your primary residence and one additional vacation home. This property may or may not appreciate, (increase in market value) in the future. The factors that affect market value are based on the laws of supply and demand, as discussed in Chapter 1. However, real estate can be used as a form of savings that historically has kept pace with inflation. The house in which you live and have a right to own, because you are paying off a mortgage, is your investment in real estate. As you pay down your mortgage, you are building equity in the home, and this equity is a form of investment that you actually own. The equity comes in two forms, the paying down of the mortgage and the appreciation of home values in the market. Historically, housing has increased in value by about 10 percent a year, although in any given area, and for any time period, this may not be true. Therefore, an investment in a home is considered to be one that beats inflation over time. The tax advantage of home ownership is that you may subtract the interest paid on your mortgage from your personal income before determining your tax liability. Because of this, it normally pays the homeowner to itemize deductions for income tax purposes.

Nonowner-Occupied Residential Real Estate

Nonowner-occupied residential real estate is property that can be leased by the owner to the tenant for the purpose of generating income. This property may be in the form of houses, apartments, motels, or hotels. You can convert a residential property to nonowner-occupied residential property by renting out your house. Variations on this include living in one part of the house and renting out the other part (the portion of the house that you rent out is depreciable) and buying a rental house for investment. The property is subject to depreciation because it is an asset that generates income. Under tax law, the depreciation rate is not the same as that for commercial real estate. The advantages of owning nonowner-occupied residential real estate are primarily in tax benefits. The owner of the property may deduct mortgage interest, depreciation, and all other normal business expenses. These expenses would include employee salaries and expenses needed to help generate income (e.g., maintenance and repair of the property).

Commercial Real Estate

Commercial real estate is both land and improved property that is used by the owner to generate income. Examples are commercial office buildings, shopping centers, factories, and warehouses. Commercial property is subject to different depreciation rates than is nonowner-occupied residential property. Commercial property and nonowner-occupied residential property differ from owner-occupied residential property for tax purposes, because they can be depreciated and the interest payments on commercial mortgages are considered business expenses. There may be a large shift in commercial real estate value due to the impact of technology and on-line shopping via the internet. If this mode of shopping has a severe adverse effect on retail stores, then there may be a large shift from retail stores and malls to centralized warehouses which store and ship products purchased on the internet.

Real Estate Investment Trusts

A **real estate investment trust (REIT)** provides the investor with the opportunity to participate in the commercial and nonresidential real estate market. A REIT is a pooling of individual investor funds, much like a mutual fund. You buy shares in the trust; then the trust invests in real estate. If the investment value goes up, the shares appreciate; and when you sell the shares, you realize a gain as with any other investment. The shares will normally pay dividends, which can be taken as income or can be reinvested. Like all real estate investments, however , the property held by the trust may actually go down in value. When this happens, you lose money on your investment if you sell your shares. These investments are considered to be highly speculative and risky, and we do not recommend them.

PRECIOUS METALS

Precious metals fall into the area of commodity trading. They are primarily gold, silver, and platinum. Precious metals, especially gold, are considered to be hedges against inflation. With an increase in the inflation rate, the value of currency (in terms of its purchasing power) decreases. In some countries, this happens at such a fast rate that the currency of the country becomes worthless. Gold, on the other hand, is in universal demand and can maintain its value when transported across international boundaries. Investments in precious metals can be in the commodity itself (bars, coins, or bullion) or in mining stocks. Mutual funds that deal in precious metals actually deal in mining stocks rather than the commodity itself. Over time, however, precious metals are not as good an investment as equity, bonds, and real estate. These investments do not earn interest and depend primarily on their marketability at the time of sale. Most investment advisors recommend that no more than 5 percent of the average portfolio be invested in precious metals. If you do not want to invest in bullion, but would rather collect coins, then you are no longer investing in the commodity, but are investing in collectables.

COLLECTABLES

Collectables are items that become valuable or appreciate with time because of their scarcity. Some examples are coins, paintings, sculptures, antiques, stamps, and even baseball cards and comic books. The reason these items increase in value is there are more people who want the specific item than there are items available for sale. The primary reason is the particular item is no longer being produced. An artist such as Picasso can produce only a specific number of paintings during his lifetime. Because Picasso has died, there can never be another original Picasso. Therefore, the original Picasso becomes a collectable and will continue to increase in value because there are not enough paintings to allow everyone who wants one to have one.

Investing in collectables is highly speculative because much of its success depends on the marketability of the item when the owner wants to sell. There are also problems associated with insurance and security of collectables. If you place the item somewhere where you do not have high protection costs and insurance premiums (such as a bank vault or safety deposit box), then your access to the item is limited because you have to go to the storage facility to view the collectable. If you place it where you have constant access to it (such as on the wall in your home), then the insurance premiums and security issues become quite expensive because every one has access. Therefore, collectables have a tendency to lead to additional risk that is not associated with the purchasing price of the item, and this risk cuts into the profitability of the collectable. Hence many collectables look much more attractive on paper than they are in reality.

INVESTMENT STRATEGIES

SHORT-TERM INVESTMENT STRATEGIES

Short-term investment strategies are specifically developed to get a return on an investment in time periods that are normally less than one year. These investments include buying stock on margin, selling short, and option trading. These strategies are very speculative and incorporate very high risk. We do not recommend short-term strategies for small businesses or novice investors. We will provide a margin requirement example to demonstrate the risk. If you have a brokerage account, you may be able to buy on margin. Current margin requirements are 50 percent. Let us say that you have $5,000 in a brokerage account. You can purchase $10,000 in stock from the broker. He will use your $5,000 and loan you $5,000. You do this because you have read an article that says that the ABC Pharmaceutical Company has developed a cure for acquired immunodeficiency syndrome (AIDS). The article states that Food and Drug Administration (FDA) approval should be received next month. You therefore believe that the stock's price should increase. You purchase 1,000 shares of stock in the ABC Company for $10 a share on Monday. You use your $5,000 plus the broker's $5,000. You notice that the stock increases to $15 a share on Tuesday, and you sell the stock at $15. The shares are now worth $15,000. You pay your broker the $5,000 that was used on margin, and you now have a profit of $5,000 or a total of $10,000 in cash.

This is the ideal short-term investment. However, let us say that on Monday afternoon, the FDA finds that the potential AIDS cure causes prostate cancer and requires additional long-term studies. On Tuesday, the stock price falls to $5 a share. The broker calls the margin account and wants repayment of the $5,000 loan. You sell the stock at $5 a share and pay the broker. Now you have lost $5,000 and have no cash. This is an example of the speculative nature of short-term investing, and is why we recommend long-term strategies only.

LONG-TERM INVESTMENT STRATEGIES

Long-term investment strategies are developed to provide future income and growth. Long-term strategies include selecting investments based on individual goals that are established for some time in the future. These strategies include basic stock and bond investment strategies, retirement planning, and tax planning. Two basic techniques in stock investment are buy and hold and dollar cost averaging.

Buy and hold can be realized by purchasing common and preferred stock and holding on to it for a number of years. Because the basic objective of corporations is growth and profit over time, purchasing stock in these corporations also should provide you with growth and profit over time.

Dollar cost averaging involves regular systematic investments. Markets fluctuate over time. Prices of stocks increase and decrease. Most of us cannot predict the future and have limited funds for investment. Dollar cost averaging allows us to purchase an equal dollar amount of the same stock at equal time intervals (every month). For example, you buy or purchase $500 worth of XYZ mutual fund every month. In January you pay $50 per share and buy 10 shares. In February the price drops to $25 and you buy 20 shares. In March the price increases to $50 per share and you buy 10 shares. You now own 40 shares of this fund and paid an average price of $37.50 per share ($1,500 ÷ 40 shares = $37.50/share). The average price per share purchased is based on the total number of dollars invested divided by the number of shares purchased. This technique eliminates the problem of trying to guess what the market will do. Your dollar cost averaging will provide you with normal growth and income over time.

PENSION PLANNING

Pension planning consists of making plans to guarantee a system of conserving future income for the time when you choose to retire or are forced into retirement due to circumstances beyond your control. The three main sources of retirement income will be social security, employer-sponsored retirement plans, and personal savings. We currently have no control over social security, but have significant control over employer-sponsored retirement plans, and total control over personal savings. Our contention that we have significant control over employer-sponsored retirement plans is explained in detail as we define the different types of retirement plans in the following section.

RETIREMENT PLANS

Retirement plans are broken down into contribution-oriented plans, benefit-oriented plans, and combined plans that allow a portion of the investment to be classified as a contribution and the other portion to become a benefit. **Contribution-oriented plans** provide benefits to the retiree based on the account balance that has been accumulated during the working life of the pensioner. **Benefit-oriented plans** provide a defined benefit to the retiree at retirement, which is generally a percentage of the compensation paid to the employee during the last several years of employment and the total term of employment. An example would be military retirement pay. **Combined retirement plans** are designed by individuals or employers. They are based on factors that allow one to take maximum advantage of current tax law. Examples are plans that provide for both tax deferment of salaries and employer contributions into the retirement plan.

Tax consequences of all retirement accounts are as follows. If the money that is contributed is pretax dollars, then the tax on these dollars is deferred until they are withdrawn. If the money contributed is after-tax dollars, then only the return on the money invested is taxed when it is withdrawn, except in the case of the **Roth Individual Retirement Account (IRA).** For example, if your adjusted gross income is $20,000 and you contribute $2,000 in pretax dollars, then you will pay income tax on a recomputed adjusted gross income of $18,000 this year. If you retire in 20 years and use funds from your retirement account, all the money you withdraw is considered to be income and will be taxed at the rate that exists at the time of withdrawal. If, on the other hand, you contribute after-tax dollars, your adjusted gross income will remain $20,000 and you will pay current taxes on the entire $20,000. When you retire, if 20 percent of your retirement account consists of after-tax contributions that were made during your working years, and 80 percent consists of the return on your investment, then you will pay taxes on 80 percent of your retirement income, except in the case of the Roth IRA.

Note: The retirement plans discussed in this section were current in accordance with IRS Publication 560, and other IRS publications at the time the textbook was written. Because Congress continually updates tax laws and the IRS responds, it is our belief that the reader must check current tax laws pertaining to small business. Particular attention should be given to IRS Publication 560, Retirement Plans for Small Business.

Specific types of retirement plans are as follows:

◆ Individual retirement accounts, or IRAs, are plans that allow us to contribute current annual income into retirement accounts. The specific investment vehicle can be chosen by us, but the investments must be maintained by a trustee. There are several types of individual IRAs.

   1. Deductible IRAs are those in which you can contribute pretax dollars up to an amount specified by current law. In 1999 you could contribute earned income up to $2,000 ($4,000 for married couples filing jointly) of pretax income, provided you or your spouse was not covered by an employer-sponsored pension plan and your adjusted gross income did not exceed certain limitations.

   2. Nondeductible IRAs allow you to contribute the same amounts as deductible IRAs, but the contribution is after-tax dollars. For both of these plans, the returns on investment accumulate tax free until they are withdrawn. You can begin taking funds from these accounts at age 59 1/2, and must begin withdrawing at age 70 1/2.

   3. **Roth IRAs** allow you to contribute up to $2,000 of after-tax dollars. If the funds are held in the account for at least five years, then there are no taxes due. Your original contributions can be withdrawn tax free at any time. You may roll a current IRA into a Roth IRA, provided that you pay all taxes due on the distribution at your current tax rate. In a Roth IRA you can withdraw $10,000 penalty free and income tax free, provided the money is used to purchase a first home and the IRA is more than five years old. To qualify for a Roth IRA first home contribution, you must not have owned a home for the previous two years. Additionally, you can use the money to buy or build a first home for yourself, your children, or your grandchildren. As with other IRAs you can begin to take withdrawals at age 59 1/2, but the Roth IRA does not have an age limit with regard to mandatory withdrawals. Additionally, the Roth IRA can be established even if you contribute to an employee-sponsored retirement plan. The Roth IRA is also tax free to your heirs.

4. Educational IRAs allow for a nondeductible contribution of up to $500 for any child under the age of 18 years. These contributions are subject to certain phaseout and other limitations. The income from an educational IRA accumulates tax free and remains tax free as long as it is used for the child's higher educational expenses. Funds must be used before the student is 30. The account can be transferred between family members. Current law must be consulted prior to any distribution due to the complexity of the requirements.

♦ **Simplified employee pension (SEP) plans** are IRAs that are funded by employers. The employer contributes to a retirement account that covers the employee. For an employer to establish a SEP, all employees must agree to the account. If any employee does not choose to have an IRA, then the company cannot establish a SEP. These plans are common for the self-employed. The participating employee makes no contribution. Contributions can be up to 13.04 percent of self-employment income (15 percent of salary if you are an employee of your own corporation). The maximum annual contribution was limited to $24,000 in 1999. The advantages of the SEP are it can be opened as late as the extended due date of your income tax return, it is as easy to open as a deductible IRA but it allows much larger contributions, it is not subject to annual government reports, and the administrative expenses are quite low.

♦ In 1997, many firms considered switching over from a SEP IRA to a SIMPLE plan. SIMPLE (savings incentive match plan for employees) IRA plans may be established after 1996 by an employer who has fewer than 100 employees and each employee received at least $5,000 in employee compensation in each of the past two years. Each employee's contribution limit is $6,000 and is indexed for inflation in $500 increments. The company must match dollar for dollar of employee contributions up to 3 percent of salary or put in 2 percent of salary for all eligible employees regardless if they contribute. Participants are completely vested immediately.

♦ **Tax-sheltered annuities (TSAs)** are plans that allow employees of not-for-profit organizations (churches, public schools, charitable organizations, etc.) to establish a retirement fund that is purchased and approved by the employer. You can contribute up to 20 percent of annual salary on a pretax basis. Maximum contributions will be imposed by current tax law. Each pay period, the employer deducts the contribution from the paycheck and sends it to the contract administrator. The deduction is not subject to income taxes. The employees can begin drawing retirement pay when they retire, and they will then pay taxes on both the contributions and the earnings.

◆ **Keogh plans** are for self-employed individuals in sole proprietor-ships and partnerships. If you are self-employed, you can set up a self-directed retirement plan and contribute up to 20 percent of earned income with a limit of $30,000 per year. With a Keogh plan, you can define both the contribution amounts and the bene-fits derived from the account. If you choose to have a defined con-tribution plan based on a percentage of earned income, contribu-tions can vary from year to year since they are based on profit. They may be skipped if there were no profits one year. If you choose to have a defined benefit plan, annual contributions must be calculated by an actuary and you must make this contribution yearly. For example, you can determine that you want to retire with an annual income as high as a $130,000 limit and the amount that you must contribute each year will be determined by an actu-ary based on your income, target benefit, and years until retire-ment. Additionally, the actuary will look at the expected invest-ment returns.

◆ **Profit sharing plans** are established by employers who have de-termined that a portion of each dollar in profit will be allocated to the employees of the company. The method of allocation can vary, but is normally based on employee compensation and length of service. Annual contributions to these plans vary drastically be-cause profits fluctuate due to economic, industry, and specific company health. These plans almost never stand alone, but are in-corporated into other types of retirement plans, such as 401k re-tirement plans.

◆ **401k retirement plans** are established to accept employee con-tributions. The primary 401k plan is based on salary reduction. Employees may contribute a specified percentage of their pretax salary, which is collected by the employer as a payroll deduction. The employer may match a portion of the contribution on some basis such as 25 cents of employer contribution for every dollar of employee contribution. The employer also may choose the 401k as the vehicle for distributing profit sharing contributions. 401k plans allow for contributions of up to 15 percent of an employee's salary. The maximum allowed for 1999 was $10,000. The IRS states that 401k plans cannot favor highly compensated employees over lower paid workers. It is for this reason that $66,000 in earn-ings is the cutoff point for contributions made on salary. A modifi-cation of the 401k plan currently used today is the SIMPLE 401k. This plan allows employees to shelter up to $10,000 per year. It is for businesses with fewer than 100 employees.

Employers can contribute 3 percent of worker's compensa-tion. This plan has to be the only plan that the business offers and employers are spared the discrimination testing for highly compensated employees that a regular 401k plan is subject to.

♦ **Money purchase plans** are defined contribution plans established by the employer to contribute a fixed percentage of payroll into a retirement fund for the employees. The maximum contribution is 25 percent of payroll. The employee does not contribute to this plan, but all contributions are considered to be pretax income. The employer must contribute each year even if the company makes no profit.

♦ **Stock bonus plans** are similar to profit sharing plans, except that the employer contributes shares of stock, rather than money, into the retirement account. The employee is therefore investing primarily in the common stock of the employing firm. The employer gets a deduction for the value of the stock contributed to the plan, so the contribution is pretax dollars.

RETIREMENT STRATEGIES

Retirement strategies are the plans that individuals make to take care of themselves and their families when they can no longer work or no longer wish to work. As small business owners each of us has to determine which of the preceding plans, or combination of plans, should be used to establish future income for us and our employees. Certain basics, however, would benefit all individuals.

♦ Establish a goal or minimum income level that you desire when you retire. This should be at least 70 percent of your annual income at the time of retirement.

♦ Do not wait until you believe you can afford to start a retirement account, because if you wait, there will always be emergencies that require current income, and you will probably never start the account.

♦ Plan for capital preservation and continued growth. The principal amount of your retirement account should provide a return that gives you the desired income, and should continue to grow by at least the inflation rate that exists at the time of retirement. Because none of us know how long we will live after retirement, it is absolutely essential that the principal amount of our retirement account remain intact during our retirement years.

♦ Invest in instruments that provide you with a degree of risk that is comfortable to you (i.e., based on your tolerance for risk).

♦ If you work for an employer who provides you with a 401k or similar plan in which the money in the account is maintained by a trustee who is not the employer, then try to invest the maximum amount, but never less than the amount that the employer uses to calculate profit sharing or matching contributions. If your 401k plan accepts a 15 percent maximum contribution and the employer matches the first 3 percent, then you should invest at least 3 percent. Where else can you invest and earn 100 percent on your investment?

♦ Consider opening a Roth IRA even if you have an employer-sponsored plan.

RETIREMENT STRATEGY EXAMPLES

Table 10-2 provides a visual representation of two example retirement strategies, using a worst-case scenario and a best-case scenario from the retirement programs described previously. We assume that you begin investing in a retirement account at age 25. Your income at age 25 is $20,000, and you never receive a promotion, but you do get annual pay raises equal to the rate of inflation. We assume that the rate of inflation will average 5 percent until you retire. Therefore, your salary at retirement at age 65 will be $140,800. We know that this sounds unreasonable, but ask your father or grandfather how much they were making 40 years ago. We believe you will find that the figures match your parents' experiences.

The worst retirement program, from the viewpoint of annual contributions, is the IRA, which is limited to $2,000. If you invest $2,000 a year, and invest at the end of each year (worst case because the money does not earn anything during the year) in safe securities (U.S. government bonds or government bond mutual funds), you will earn an average yield of 7 percent. Your retirement nest egg will have a value of $399,270 when you retire. If you decide to retire on an income equal to 6 percent of your retirement account, your income will be $23,956 per year—hardly a comfortable retirement when your income before retirement was $140,800. This obviously will not meet the goal of 70 percent of income.

If you have a high tolerance for risk and place the $2,000 in a stock mutual fund that averages 15 percent annual return, your retirement account will have $3,558,181. If you take 6 percent as income, and let the remainder grow, your annual income will be $213,491, and will grow by an average of 9 percent each year. These are the two extremes. Most financial advisors would recommend a combined strategy in which all of your retirement dollars are diversified in various instrument vehicles. There are other factors that you should consider. In our example here, we assume that all contributions are pretax dollars, so the entire amount of your retirement income is subject to taxation at the rate that exists in the year you withdraw the income. If you made the contribution in after-tax dollars, then only the amount earned on the contribution would be subject to taxes. Several advisors recommend that a portion of contributions to retirement accounts be made in after-tax dollars, because none of us know what the

Table 10-2 Retirement Strategies

| | | $2,000 annual IRA Contribution | |
| | | | |
Age	Annual Income	Low-Risk Strategy (7%)	High-Risk Strategy (15%)
25	$20,000		
26	21,000	$ 2,000	$ 2,000
27	22,050	4,140	4,300
28	23,153	6,430	6,945
29	24,310	8,880	9,987
30	25,526	11,501	13,485
31	26,802	14,307	17,507
32	28,142	17,308	22,134
33	29,549	20,520	27,454
34	31,027	23,956	33,572
35	32,578	27,633	40,607
36	34,207	31,567	48,699
37	35,917	35,777	58,003
38	37,713	40,281	68,704
39	39,599	45,101	81,009
40	41,579	50,258	95,161
41	43,657	55,776	111,435
42	45,840	61,680	130,150
43	48,132	67,998	151,673
44	50,539	74,758	176,424
45	53,066	81,991	204,887
46	55,719	89,730	237,620
47	58,505	98,011	275,263
48	61,430	106,872	318,553
49	64,502	116,353	368,336
50	67,727	126,498	425,586
51	71,113	137,353	491,424
52	74,669	148,968	567,138
53	78,403	161,395	654,208
54	82,323	174,693	754,339
55	86,439	188,922	869,490
56	90,761	204,146	1,001,914
57	95,299	220,436	1,154,201
58	100,064	237,867	1,329,331
59	105,067	256,518	1,530,731
60	110,320	276,474	1,762,340
61	115,836	297,827	2,028,691
62	121,628	320,675	2,334,995
63	127,710	345,122	2,687,244
64	134,095	371,281	3,092,331
65	140,800	399,270	3,558,181
Retirement Income at 66		$ 23,956	$ 213,491

tax rates will be at the time of retirement, whereas we do know what current tax rates are.

A third example is based on making everyday life choices. An 18-year-old male decides to give up smoking for the next four years while he starts his college career. He estimates that he spends $3.50 per day on cigarettes or $1,277.50 per year (365 days × $3.50 per day). On a one-month basis he spends $106.46 ($1,277.50 ÷ 12 months per year). If he invests the $106.46 each month that he would have spent on cigarettes in a stock mutual fund earning 12 percent (12 percent per year is a monthly rate of 0.949 percent), he will have $6,434.82 at the end of four years. He now has several options: (1) Spend the money on a vacation; (2) put a down payment on a new car; (3) leave the money in the stock mutual fund until age 65 in a Roth IRA; or (4) leave the money in the stock mutual fund until age 70 in a Roth IRA. If he spends the money on a vacation he has nothing of lasting value except a few pictures and a suntan. If he spends the money on a car he will have a depreciating asset worth a small percentage of the original down payment. If he chooses the Roth IRA route and does not touch the money but keeps it in the stock mutual fund earning 12 percent, then he will have $841,223.46 at age 65. If he keeps it another five years to age 70, he will have $1,482,523.18. Since it is in a Roth IRA all of the above values are tax free.

ESTATE PLANNING

As a business owner you should plan for the use, conservation, and, in estate planning, the transfer of your wealth as efficiently as possible. Basically, you are doing financial planning with the anticipation of eventual death. It is in your best interest to create documents with proper professional advice to accomplish the goals we have just stated.

Property transfer at death is an inevitable fact. As a business owner, it is imperative that you plan for this transfer to be made in a manner that will allow the business to remain intact, rather than being dissolved. If you are a sole proprietor, your business will be transferred to your spouse or whomever you designate in your will. If you are in a partnership, the business will be transferred to the surviving partners, and possibly your spouse, in accordance with the partnership agreement.

In each of these instances, there will be large financial costs incurred by the business. For example, if you have very specific skills that are required by the business, your spouse or surviving partners will have to hire others who have these skills to take your place. The best method of handling this circumstance is through the use of a life insurance policy on each of the key personnel in the firm. The policy is purchased by the business so that adequate financial capital will be available to continue the business when one of the key people dies.

In other words, proper estate planning allows for the creation of capital (via life insurance) upon the death of one of the owners. In some partnership agreements, it is specified that the policy will be of sufficient value to allow the surviving partners to purchase the other's share of the business from the surviving spouse or family members.

Wills are written documents that provide direction to others as to how you want your wishes carried out after death. Everyone should have a will, but it is absolutely essential that married couples with children have wills, to ensure that their children are raised by people who will carry out their wishes. If you and your spouse both die, whom do you want to take care of your children? Do you want separate funds set aside for your children? Are there certain keepsakes and mementos that you want to go to a particular friend or relative? In other words, you are actually giving directions to others on how you want your assets distributed upon your death. Without a will, the government makes those decisions for you. Dying without a will is known as dying intestate. If you die intestate, the court will appoint an administrator to distribute your estate in accordance with the probate laws in your state.

Wills also describe how you want your probate property disposed of at death. **Probate** is a legal court process that addresses and focuses on the will and the probate estate. The probate property value is the value of the gross assets owned by the deceased, other than life insurance. For example, if you own a house that is valued at $300,000, and you owe $100,000, then the net estate is $200,000, but the gross estate for probate is $300,000. Because probate costs are a percentage of the gross estate, then good estate planning should remove as much of the gross assets as possible from the portion of the estate that is subject to probate. There are essentially two methods of accomplishing this, joint ownership with right of survivorship (temporary removal) and trusts (permanent removal).

In the first method, you purchase as many assets as possible with joint property ownership with right of survivorship. In other words, if the house were purchased only in your name and you died, then the entire value would be subject to probate. If you had purchased it in joint tenancy with your spouse, then there would be no probate on the property upon your death. However, when your spouse died, then all property would be subject to probate. There is one caveat to this process. If your spouse later wants to sell the house, your spouse must get the property into his or her name prior to sale. At that point, the deceased spouse's half of the property will be subject to probate. To totally remove the home from probate, you could place the home in a trust.

Trusts are legal arrangements that actually divide legal and beneficial interests among two or more people. The trust is created by a trustor or grantor, and beneficiaries or trustees are named by the trustor. The trustor also can be the trustee. The trust is a separate entity, similar to a corporation, that has a legal persona of its own. Property placed in a trust is separate from that of its owner, but it can be managed by the owner, because the owner can be the trustee. When a trust is set up during the life of the trustor, it is referred to as a **living trust.** When a trust is established at death, it is referred to as a **testamentary trust.** Trusts may also be revocable or irrevocable. A **revocable trust** is one in which the trustor has the right to cancel the trust during his or her lifetime. An **irrevocable trust** is unalterable during a person's lifetime. There are several legal and tax issues with relationship to revocable and irrevocable trusts that are too complex to handle in this text. Additionally, laws pertaining to trusts and taxes are constantly changing. Therefore, if you want to set up a will or a trust or some combination, we recommend that you seek professional legal advice.

CONCLUSION

Risk management for a small business owner is a must. We identify risk exposure and employ those methods that will guarantee both the continuation of the business and personal financial security. This requires that we establish financial goals that are viable and obtainable. Each owner has to base individual goals on a combination of factors that include personal tolerance for risk. The plan should include a mix of several financial vehicles, including insurance for pure risk and financial investment vehicles for speculative risk. We should select the investment vehicles based on where we wish to be at some future date, such as at retirement. The planning should include both business and individual pension planning to provide us with a lifestyle in retirement that we desire. Additionally, we want to include estate planning to ensure that our business continues after our death, and that our family will be provided for. Only through advanced planning and the proper implementation of these plans can we guarantee the future viability of our business and the ability to provide for our individual and our family's well-being.

REVIEW AND DISCUSSION QUESTIONS

1. Compare the risk of buying a U.S. government bond to that of buying a corporate bond.
2. Compare speculative risk and pure risk.
3. How can a business owner identify risk exposure?
4. What are some programs that an entrepreneur can use to reduce risk?
5. Compare whole-life and term insurance.
6. List and describe some investment vehicles that a small business owner might select.
7. What is the difference between the coupon rate of a bond and current market interest rate?
8. If the coupon rate on a bond is 8 percent and current market interest rates are 6 percent, should this bond be selling at a premium or a discount?

9. How do we determine the book value of a stock?
10. Compare cumulative, convertible, and callable preferred stock.
11. What is the difference between a mutual fund and a mutual fund family?
12. List and briefly describe three different types of mutual funds.
13. Compare a no-load mutual fund with a load mutual fund.
14. Compare short-term and long-term investment strategies.
15. What is the difference between a contribution- and benefit-oriented retirement plan?
16. What are the basic factors that should be considered when establishing an individual retirement plan?
17. How may a small business owner plan for the use, conservation, and transfer of wealth as efficiently as possible?
18. What is the role of trusts in estate planning?

EXERCISES AND PROBLEMS

1. You have a friend, Icahn Betitall, who just started a small business. He is paying a hefty premium for insurance. Icahn's insurance agent told him that he is insuring against the risk of loss on fire, theft, liability, and business interruption. Icahn also has policies for life, health, and automobiles.

   Icahn is planning a trip to Las Vegas. He plans to contact his agent and obtain a policy on the risk of losing his money at the blackjack table.
   a. What will you tell Icahn about being able to purchase such a policy?
   b. What are several methods that Icahn can choose to manage his risk exposure in Las Vegas?

2. Your city is expanding. There have been several problems with street flooding, which is affecting your business. You decide to attend a city council meeting during which there is a discussion on building storm and waste sewer lines in advance of construction. At the meeting, Tom Frank, the city manager, states that the city is prohibited by law from financing these projects through a sales or property tax. He states that after the new homes are built, the city will be able to charge a monthly sewer fee to each homeowner and business. He asks for suggestions on financing the new sewer system.
   a. What would you propose the city do to raise this money?
   b. Why is this investment vehicle attractive to investors?

3. Grandpa Russ thinks he needs a fixed income for the next 10 years. He currently has $10,000 in CDs, which are maturing at the end of this month. The CDs can be renewed for one year at 4 1/2 percent. Russ calls his broker, Ben Seller, and learns that his $10,000 can be put to better use by purchasing debentures issued by Grab-n-Run Incorporated. These bonds are 10-year bonds with a coupon rate of 8 percent, which is paid semiannually. The current market interest rate is 6 percent for bonds of a similar nature. The broker tells Grandpa Russ that he may buy the

bond for $1,400. Grandpa knows that he will have to pay a premium, but he believes that a $1,400 premium is too high.

   a. What is the maximum price you would tell Grandpa to pay for this bond?

   b. Compare the risk of the CD with the risk of the bond.

   c. What else would you advise Grandpa with regard to this type of investment?

4. Sarah Mix is a single, 30-year-old business owner who has $500 a month to invest. This money is in excess of the contribution to her company pension plan. Sarah hears that many of her friends are investing in mutual funds. Her grandfather, Grandpa Russ, invested in the stock market and lost everything. He advises her to invest only in bonds. Her uncle, Sam, thinks that she should invest in stock mutual funds, but only in conservatively managed funds that invest in U.S. blue-chip stocks. Sarah notes that her Grandpa is 70 years old and that her uncle is 55 years old. Her friend Jane, who is also 30 years old, said she only invests in small capital growth funds.

   a. What would you advise Sarah to invest in?

   b. Why do you think these people have different investment strategies?

5. Sarah Mix decides to invest in three funds, with $200 going into a small capital growth fund, $150 going into a large capital growth fund, and $150 into an international fund. She tracked the price she paid for stock in these funds over a six-month period as shown in Table 10-3.

   a. What was the average price paid per share in each mutual fund?

   b. How much has Sarah invested in mutual funds?

   c. What is the current value of her investment?

   d. Which fund is currently performing best for Sarah?

6. Larry Kraft owns a restaurant that is open seven days a week. He has 25 full-time employees, but has fairly high employee turnover. He believes that he can stabilize his workforce if he has a pension plan for his employees. Larry hears about a new plan called the SIMPLE. What are the qualifications and limitations for him to establish this plan?

Table 10-3 Price Per Share in Dollars

Month	Large Cap	Small Cap	International
1	35.45	27.00	29.00
2	32.35	27.25	28.50
3	28.36	26.55	28.00
4	32.15	28.00	28.25
5	33.12	28.50	28.75
6	35.00	27.60	29.00

7. Larry Kraft plans to open six more restaurants during the next five years. He believes that he will then have 125 employees.
   a. What recommendations would you make for Larry at this time?
   b. Could Larry set up a tax-sheltered annuity pension plan for his company?

8. Larry has expanded his business. When he met with his accountant at the end of the year, he learned that his total assets are in excess of $850,000. His accountant asked Larry if he had a will, and Larry said he had been too busy to develop one. His accountant strongly recommended that Larry contact an estate planning attorney.
   a. What advice do you think the estate planner will give Larry with respect to establishing a will?
   b. What would you advise?

9. You purchase a tax-free municipal bond paying an annual rate of 6 percent. Find the before tax rate if you are in the;
   a. 15% tax bracket?
   b. 28% tax bracket?
   c. 36% tax bracket?

10. A ten-year bond with a $1,000 face value has a coupon rate of 8 percent that it pays semi-annually. If current interest rates are 7 percent for bonds of a similar nature, calculate the price of the bond.

11. If a corporation has total assets of $85 million and total liabilities of $5 million. If the corporation has 4 million shares of common stock outstanding what is the book value per share of common stock.

12. If the book value of a company is $15 per share and the total common stockholder's equity is $45 million. How many shares of common stock has this corporation issued?

13. ABC corporation issues 10 million shares of common stock and 20 thousand shares of 8 percent preferred stock at $50 par. The corporation makes an annual profit of $10 million and the board of directors declares a $5 million dollar stock dividend.
    a. What is the preferred stock dividend per share?
    b. What is the commons stock dividend per share?

14. Best-Cost corporation issues 5 million shares of common stock and 100 thousand shares of 6 percent cumulative preferred stock at $100 par. The corporation has not paid any dividend during the past three years. The board of directors decides to pay $5 million in dividends for the current year.
    a. How much in dividends is paid for each share of preferred stock?
    b. What is the total amount of dividends paid to preferred stockholders?
    c. How much is the dividend payment for each share of common stock?
    d. What is the total amount of dividends paid to common stockholders?

15. David Nash has $100,000 to invest in a mutual fund.
    a. How many shares will he purchase in a no load mutual fund whose NAV is $50 per share?
    b. How many shares will he purchase in a loaded mutual fund whose NAV is $50 per share and has a front-loaded sales charge of 5 percent.

16. Jane Jones wants to purchase 1,000 shares of an Internet technology stock for $15 a share. She figures out that she needs $15 thousand dollars plus commission in order to purchase the stock. She currently has $8,000 of liquidity in her money market account.

   a. What can Jane borrow on margin in order to affect the transaction?

   b. Within a week the stock jumps to $50 per share, how much will she actually realize in profit after paying her broker?

   c. If the stock dropped to $5 per share, rather than increasing to $50 and the broker put in the margin call, how much would she have to pay the broker?

   d. Based on beginning account balance of $8 thousand, what is her loss?

17. You deposit the following at the end of each year into a growth mutual fund that earns 16% per year?

Year	Deposit
1	$4,000
2	3,500
3	2,500
4	2,000
5	1,700

   a. How much should the fund be worth at the end of 5 years?

   b. How much interest will you have earned in total?

18. Starting in the year 2000, Ira Roth places $2,000 in a Roth IRA in the beginning of each year for the next 40 years. Ira believes the account will earn 12 percent a year compounded yearly. How much will he have in his account in 40 years?

19. N. Ebriate, a college student at a party university, decides to forego beer drinking and invest the $100 he saves at the end of each month in a mutual fund that is currently earning 18 percent annually.

   a. How much will he have in his fund in four years upon graduation?

   b. If he graduates at the age of 22 and leaves this investment in the mutual fund without adding any additional funds, how much will he have at age 60?

   c. If he really enjoys his work and decides to leave the money in the fund until age 75, how much will he have?

   d. If he never touches this fund and dies at the age of 90, how much will he leave in his estate from only this investment?

Working with Spreadsheets

Many businesses and individuals will have a personal computer that can be used to automate the functions shown in this appendix. The following are formulas shown in the format of Microsoft Excel. Each of the formulas used in this appendix is presented with a problem. We then show how the problem is entered into Excel, so that we have the basic procedures and uses of these formulas.

Spreadsheet Basics

The following is an example of a spreadsheet:

	A	B	C	D	E	F	G
1							
2							
3							
4							
5					cell E5		

Most spreadsheet programs will accept the following standards:

1. *Cells.* All data are entered in cells. Cells are identified by column and row.
   - Columns are lettered across the top and are alphabetical, beginning with the letter *A*. The first column is A; second column, B; third column, C; and so forth. When the alphabet is exhausted, we then begin over with AA, AB, AC, and so forth; then BA, BB, BC, and so forth.
   - Rows are numbered, beginning with the number 1.
   - Cells are referred to by their column and row designation. For example, the cell for the fifth column and fifth row would be cell E5.
2. *Functions.* All functions must begin with an = (equal sign), a + (plus), or a − (minus). Spreadsheet programs may accept other characters,

but if you begin with any other keyboard symbol, the program assumes you are entering a title, rather than a mathematical function. Basic numbers can be entered as numbers (5, 5000, or 50). Note that numbers can contain commas. The number 5,000 is entered as 5000.

3. *Formatting.* Cells are formatted to display the entry or the result of calculation as you desire. Cells can be formatted in the following manner:

   a. **Text.** The entry is not used in calculations, even if it is a number. This is important when you enter items that you do not want to change accidentally. For example, if you had customer addresses and zip codes in a spreadsheet and if you were to enter a zip code, you would not want to accidentally add 5 to every zip code. You would format this column as text, rather than as a number.

   b. **Numerical formats.** There are several numerical formats that you can use. For business, we normally are concerned with using the following formats:

   ◆ **Number.** Number formats allow us to assign decimal places and basic styles. For example, we could enter a number as 5000.0124. If the specified cell is formatted as #,##0.00, then when we hit the ENTER key, it would show us 5,000.01. If we entered 5000.0156, we would see 5,000.02 when we hit the return key because the program would automatically round our entry to the number of decimal places we selected when we formatted the cell.

   ◆ **Accounting.** Accounting formats will normally display numbers as previously described, but include the $. Therefore, 5000.0124 would display as $5,000.01. We can also choose to have negative numbers display with parentheses or with the minus sign; $(-50$ would display as (50) or -50, depending on the format we choose.

   ◆ **Date.** When we choose date formatting, we will obtain a list of displays from which we can choose—for example, d/m/y or d-mmm-yy. When we enter a date in the cell, it will appear in the format we have chosen. Therefore, if we entered 3/29/96 having chosen the first format, it would display as 3/29/96; but if we had chosen the second format, it would display as 29 Mar 96.

   ◆ **Percentage.** When we choose a percentage format, the number we enter will display as a percentage and have the percent sign displayed. For example, if we choose 0% and enter .08, we will see 8%. However, if we choose 0.00% and enter .08, we will see 8.00%. A word of warning: If you enter 8, you will see 800%.

   ◆ **Fraction.** If we choose fraction formatting, we can enter fractions and have them display as such. For example, if we choose fraction formatting and enter 3/4, our display will be 3/4.

Note: The display you receive is based on how the cell is formatted. If we enter 3/4 and have percentage cell formatting, we will see 75%. On the other hand, if we have fraction formatting, we will see 3/4. And if we did not choose any formatting, we will see 4 Mar, because Excel assumes that a 3/4 entry should display as a date.

4. *Entering formulas and numbers.* Spreadsheet programs use the following keyboard characters for entering formulas:

   ♦ + for addition, − for subtraction, ⋆ for multiplication, / for division. Note: Make sure you use the normal slash and not the backslash (\) for division.

   ♦ = for equal to, >= for greater than or equal to, <= for less than or equal to.

   ♦ ^ to raise a number to a power. For example, 2^3 would be entered as 2^3.

   ♦ \$, preceding cell identifiers, to lock the position of the cell so that other cells can refer to this location for a formula or number. \$B\$5 would lock cell B5 so that it could be used in further calculations in other cells. Normally, when a cell is copied, the value of the subsequent cell increases; but if the cell is locked, it will not. For example: Cell A2 has the number 1, and cell A3 has the formula =A2+1; when we hit the return key, we will see the number 2. When we copy the formula in cell A3 to cell A4, we will see the formula as A3+1 and we will see the number 3. If, however, cell B5 had the number 10, and we entered the formula in cell A3 as =A2+\$B\$5, we would see the number 11. If we then copied this to cell A4, we would obtain the number 21, and would see the formula as =A3+\$B\$5. Notice that the A2 increases to A3, but the locked cell value does not change. Note: This capability of spreadsheets allows us to ask "what if" questions. With the present or future value factor formula located in cell B5, we could change the interest rates in cells A3 through some range of cells and obtain factors for several interest rates. This is the method that we used to construct the tables in this chapter.

   ♦ ( ) for calculations that are to be accomplished prior to the remainder of the formula.

   ♦ : to indicate a range of cells. For example, all cells from A2 through A15 would be entered as (A2:A15).

   ♦ *Functions.* Most spreadsheets have formulas that are already built in. These spreadsheets will have either a function key $\boxed{f\cdot}$ that can be clicked on with the mouse to see various functions that can be used or a help key that will allow you to type in the function you want to use and obtain the formula that the spreadsheet program uses. These will also provide you with the formula for the function. For example, in Excel, if you click on the function SUM, you will see SUM(number 1, number 2, ---), and below this you will see a brief explanation of what the SUM function does—in this case, "adds its arguments."

The following is an example of a spreadsheet and the use of the preceding formatting and mathematical standards. Row 1 is a title row, row 2 displays the entry that we type on the keyboard, row 3 shows the result of the entry with no formatting, and rows 4 and 5 show the results of the entry with formatting.

	A	B	C	D	E	F	G
1	Date	Principal	Interest	Formula	Formula	Formula	Formula
2	1/4/96	1000.00	.0725	=2*(3/4)	=2^3	=2*(3+5)	=B2*C2
3	1/4/96	1000	0.0725	1.5	8	16	72.5
4	4-Jan-96	1,000.00	7.25%	1.50	8.00	16.00	72.50
5	4-Jan	$1,000.00	$0.07	$1.50	$8.00	$16.00	$72.50

In row 1, we typed in the title of each column. In row 2, we show what number or formula was typed on the keyboard. In row 3, we see the result of pressing the enter key after our entry with no formatting. For row 4, we formatted cell A4 as date d-mmm-yy, cell B4 and cells D4 through G4 as number with two decimal places, and cell C4 as percentage with two decimal places. For row 5, we formatted cell A5 as date d-mmm, and cells B5 through G5 as accounting with two decimal places. As we discussed previously, formatting provides us with the result of our calculation in the form in which we want to view it.

Formula Entry

Simple Interest   The simple interest formula is $I = Prt,$ where $I =$ Interest, $P =$ Principal amount stated, $r =$ Rate, and $t =$ Time. What is the annual interest paid on a loan of $5,000, at 8 percent? To enter this formula into Excel, we would type the following:

$$= 5000*(.08)*(1)$$

The standard used in Excel for formula entry is to begin with the $=$ (equal sign); you can also begin entering a formula with the $+$ or $-$.

When we press the enter key, we will receive an answer of 400. How this result of our calculation appears on the screen will be based on formatting.

Compound Interest or Future Value of a Lump Sum

The formula for future value of a lump sum amount is

$$FV = PV(1+i)^n$$

What is the future value of $5,000 that earns interest of 12 percent, compounded monthly, for three years? We would enter this formula as $=5000\star(1+(.12/12))^\wedge(3\star12)$ and would obtain an answer of $7,153.84. We could also enter the amount in one cell, the formula for the factor in another cell, and the formula for the future value in a third cell. This would allow us to use any of the values to conduct a what-if analysis. A what-if analysis is known as sensitivity analysis. It allows you to create hypothetical situations that change the variables of the formula. This then allows you to compare several proposals at varying interest rates, or with varying terms. For example, you could compare a three-year note that compounds monthly at 8 percent to a three-year note compounding annually at 9 percent to determine which of two offers from two different banks is the best.

	A	B	C	D	E
1	FV	PV	annual i	n in years	Factor
2	=B2*E2	5000	.12	3	=(1+(C2/12))^(D2*12)
3	$7,153.84	$5,000.00	12%	3	1.430769
4					
5					

Again, we have used the same convention, with row 1 containing titles, row 2 containing the formula we would enter into a cell, and row 3 showing the formatted result of the formula after we hit the return key. If we check Appendix Table B-1 to this chapter, we note that the future value factor for 1 percent interest for 36 months is 1.4308. Please note that this is not the same factor we would get if the loan were not compounded monthly. We would then go to the 12 percent column for three time periods and obtain a factor of 1.4049.

Present Value of a Future Lump Sum

The formula for the present value of a future lump-sum amount is given as

$$PV = FV\left[\frac{1}{(1 + i)^n}\right]$$

If we have a trust that will pay us $50,000 in 10 years, and we assume that the inflation rate will be 5 percent for this 10-year period, what purchasing power will this $50,000 payment have? To obtain the present value factor for this problem directly, we would enter =(1/(1+.05)^10) and would obtain an answer of 0.613913. Using Appendix Table B-2 to verify our answer, we obtain a value of 0.6139. The difference is due to rounding. To obtain the present value, we multiply this factor by our lump-sum amount of $50,000 and obtain $30,695.66. The spreadsheet entries would look like the following:

	A	B	C	D	E
1	PV	FV	annual i	n in years	Factor
2	=B2*E2	50000	.05	10	=(1/(1+C2)^D2)
3	$30,695.66	$50,000.00	5%	10	0.613913
4					
5					

Future Value of an Ordinary Annuity

The formula for the future value of an ordinary annuity is given as

$$FV = A\left[\frac{(1 + i)^n - 1}{i}\right]$$

If you deposit $2,000 a year, at the end of each year, in an individual retirement account (IRA) for 20 years and assume you will get an average return of 8 percent compounded annually, how much will your account contain at the end of 20 years? The spreadsheet entries would look like the following:

	A	B	C	D	E
1	FV	A	annual i	n in years	Factor
2	=B2*E2	2000	.08	20	=((1+C2)^(D2) −1)/C2
3	$91,523.93	$2,000.00	8%	20	45.76196
4					
5					

We can again cross-check our calculations with Appendix Table B-2 and notice a factor of 45.7620, with the difference being in rounding. Our conclusion is that you will have approximately $91,524 in your retirement account in 20 years. This problem is realistic for many of us, because we have to wait until the last minute to fund our IRA. However, what if you knew that you would definitely be funding the IRA every year, and decided to invest at the beginning of the year, rather than at the end of the year? Then, we would be dealing with an annuity due.

Future Value of an Annuity Due

The formula for the future value of an annuity due is given as

$$FV = A\left\{\left[\frac{(1 + i)^{n+1} - 1}{i}\right] - 1\right\}$$

We use the same problem as in our previous example, with the only difference being that you place the $2,000 in your account at the beginning, rather than the end, of each year. The spreadsheet entries would look like the following:

	A	B	C	D	E
1	FV	A	annual i	n in years	Factor
2	=B2*E2	2000	.08	20	=(((((1+C2)^(D2+1)) −1)/(C2)) −1
3	$98,845.84	$2,000.00	8%	20	49.42292
4					
5					

Therefore, if we know that we would definitely be investing each year in an IRA, we would absolutely want to invest at the beginning of the year, rather than the end, because we would have an extra $7,321.91 in our account as a result of early investing.

Present Value of an Ordinary Annuity

The formula for the present value of an ordinary annuity is given as

$$PV = A\left[\frac{(1 + i)^n - 1}{i(1 + i)^n}\right]$$

You want to retire at the age of 60 and plan to live to 90. You want a retirement income of no less than $60,000 per year. How much do you need in your account when you are 60, if you plan to receive the money at the end of each year for the next 30 years, and assume the account will continue to earn an annual rate of 8 percent? The spreadsheet entries would look like the following:

	A	B	C	D	E
1	PV	A	annual i	n in years	Factor
2	=B2*E2	60000	.08	30	=(((1+C2)^(D2)) −1)/((C2*(1+C2)^(D2)))
3	$675,467.00	$60,000.00	8%	30	11.25778
4					
5					

So if you had $675,467 in this account, you would be able to have a 30-year income of $60,000. At the end of 30 years, you would have nothing left in the account. What if you wanted the income at the beginning, rather than at the end, of the year? Again, this would take us into the realm of an annuity due.

Present Value of an Annuity Due

We will use the same problem as before, except that you get your retirement check at the beginning of the year (January 1), rather than the end of the year (December 31). The formula for this (the present value of an annuity due) is given as

$$PV = A \left\{ \left[\frac{(1 + i)^{n-1} - 1}{i(1 + i)^{n-1}} \right] + 1 \right\}$$

The spreadsheet entries would look like the following:

	A	B	C	D	E
	A	*B*	*C*	*D*	*E*
1	PV	A	annual i	n in years	Factor
2	=B2*E2	60000	.08	30	=((((1+C2)^(D2−1))−1)/((C2)*(1+C2)^(D2−1)))+1
3	$729,504.36	$60,000.00	8%	30	12.15841
4					
5					

Notice that if you take the payment out at the beginning of each year, you have to have significantly more money in your account. With the ordinary annuity, you will only have to have $675,467; but with the annuity due, you will have to have $729,504. This means that you will have to generate an additional $54,037 in your account before you reach 60.

Time–Value–of–Money Tables

The following time-value-of-money tables will assist the reader:

♦ To provide a cross-reference for confirming values returned with calculators.

♦ To provide a cross-reference for confirming values returned with spreadsheets and other computer programs.

♦ To provide reference tables for solving time-value-of-money problems when calculators or computers are not readily available.

Table B-1 Future Value of a Lump Sum

Formula: $FV = PV(1 + i)^n$

Interest Rate (i)

Periods (n)	1%	2%	3%	4%	5%	6%	7%	8%	9%	10%	11%	12%	13%	14%	15%	16%	17%	18%	19%	20%
1	1.0100	1.0200	1.0300	1.0400	1.0500	1.0600	1.0700	1.0800	1.0900	1.1000	1.1100	1.1200	1.1300	1.1400	1.1500	1.1600	1.1700	1.1800	1.1900	1.2000
2	1.0201	1.0404	1.0609	1.0816	1.1025	1.1236	1.1449	1.1664	1.1881	1.2100	1.2321	1.2544	1.2769	1.2996	1.3225	1.3456	1.3689	1.3924	1.4161	1.4400
3	1.0303	1.0612	1.0927	1.1249	1.1576	1.1910	1.2250	1.2597	1.2950	1.3310	1.3676	1.4049	1.4429	1.4815	1.5209	1.5609	1.6016	1.6430	1.6852	1.7280
4	1.0406	1.0824	1.1255	1.1699	1.2155	1.2625	1.3108	1.3605	1.4116	1.4641	1.5181	1.5735	1.6305	1.6890	1.7490	1.8106	1.8739	1.9388	2.0053	2.0736
5	1.0510	1.1041	1.1593	1.2167	1.2763	1.3382	1.4026	1.4693	1.5386	1.6105	1.6851	1.7623	1.8424	1.9254	2.0114	2.1003	2.1924	2.2878	2.3864	2.4883
6	1.0615	1.1262	1.1941	1.2653	1.3401	1.4185	1.5007	1.5869	1.6771	1.7716	1.8704	1.9738	2.0820	2.1950	2.3131	2.4364	2.5652	2.6996	2.8398	2.9860
7	1.0721	1.1487	1.2299	1.3159	1.4071	1.5036	1.6058	1.7138	1.8280	1.9487	2.0762	2.2107	2.3526	2.5023	2.6600	2.8262	3.0012	3.1855	3.3793	3.5832
8	1.0829	1.1717	1.2668	1.3686	1.4775	1.5938	1.7182	1.8509	1.9926	2.1436	2.3045	2.4760	2.6584	2.8526	3.0590	3.2784	3.5115	3.7589	4.0214	4.2998
9	1.0937	1.1951	1.3048	1.4233	1.5513	1.6895	1.8385	1.9990	2.1719	2.3579	2.5580	2.7731	3.0040	3.2519	3.5179	3.8030	4.1084	4.4355	4.7854	5.1598
10	1.1046	1.2190	1.3439	1.4802	1.6289	1.7908	1.9672	2.1589	2.3674	2.5937	2.8394	3.1058	3.3946	3.7072	4.0456	4.4114	4.8068	5.2338	5.6947	6.1917
11	1.1157	1.2434	1.3842	1.5395	1.7103	1.8983	2.1049	2.3316	2.5804	2.8531	3.1518	3.4785	3.8359	4.2262	4.6524	5.1173	5.6240	6.1759	6.7767	7.4301
12	1.1268	1.2682	1.4258	1.6010	1.7959	2.0122	2.2522	2.5182	2.8127	3.1384	3.4985	3.8960	4.3345	4.8179	5.3503	5.9360	6.5801	7.2876	8.0642	8.9161
13	1.1381	1.2936	1.4685	1.6651	1.8856	2.1329	2.4098	2.7196	3.0658	3.4523	3.8833	4.3635	4.8980	5.4924	6.1528	6.8858	7.6987	8.5994	9.5964	10.6993
14	1.1495	1.3195	1.5126	1.7317	1.9799	2.2609	2.5785	2.9372	3.3417	3.7975	4.3104	4.8871	5.5348	6.2613	7.0757	7.9875	9.0075	10.1472	11.4198	12.8392
15	1.1610	1.3459	1.5580	1.8009	2.0789	2.3966	2.7590	3.1722	3.6425	4.1772	4.7846	5.4736	6.2543	7.1379	8.1371	9.2655	10.5387	11.9737	13.5895	15.4070
16	1.1726	1.3728	1.6047	1.8730	2.1829	2.5404	2.9522	3.4259	3.9703	4.5950	5.3109	6.1304	7.0673	8.1372	9.3576	10.7480	12.3303	14.1290	16.1715	18.4884
17	1.1843	1.4002	1.6528	1.9479	2.2920	2.6928	3.1588	3.7000	4.3276	5.0545	5.8951	6.8660	7.9861	9.2765	10.7613	12.4677	14.4265	16.6722	19.2441	22.1861
18	1.1961	1.4282	1.7024	2.0258	2.4066	2.8543	3.3799	3.9960	4.7171	5.5599	6.5436	7.6900	9.0243	10.5752	12.3755	14.4625	16.8790	19.6733	22.9005	26.6233
19	1.2081	1.4568	1.7535	2.1068	2.5270	3.0256	3.6165	4.3157	5.1417	6.1159	7.2633	8.6128	10.1974	12.0557	14.2318	16.7765	19.7484	23.2144	27.2516	31.9480
20	1.2202	1.4859	1.8061	2.1911	2.6533	3.2071	3.8697	4.6610	5.6044	6.7275	8.0623	9.6463	11.5231	13.7435	16.3665	19.4608	23.1056	27.3930	32.4294	38.3376
21	1.2324	1.5157	1.8603	2.2788	2.7860	3.3996	4.1406	5.0338	6.1088	7.4002	8.9492	10.8038	13.0211	15.6676	18.8215	22.5745	27.0336	32.3238	38.5910	46.0051
22	1.2447	1.5460	1.9161	2.3699	2.9253	3.6035	4.4304	5.4365	6.6586	8.1403	9.9336	12.1003	14.7138	17.8610	21.6447	26.1864	31.6293	38.1421	45.9233	55.2061
23	1.2572	1.5769	1.9736	2.4647	3.0715	3.8197	4.7405	5.8715	7.2579	8.9543	11.0263	13.5523	16.6266	20.3616	24.8915	30.3762	37.0062	45.0076	54.6487	66.2474
24	1.2697	1.6084	2.0328	2.5633	3.2251	4.0489	5.0724	6.3412	7.9111	9.8497	12.2392	15.1786	18.7881	23.2122	28.6252	35.2364	43.2973	53.1090	65.0320	79.4968
25	1.2824	1.6406	2.0938	2.6658	3.3864	4.2919	5.4274	6.8485	8.6231	10.8347	13.5855	17.0001	21.2305	26.4619	32.9190	40.8742	50.6578	62.6686	77.3881	95.3962
26	1.2953	1.6734	2.1566	2.7725	3.5557	4.5494	5.8074	7.3964	9.3992	11.9182	15.0799	19.0401	23.9905	30.1666	37.8568	47.4141	59.2697	73.9490	92.0918	114.4755
27	1.3082	1.7069	2.2213	2.8834	3.7335	4.8223	6.2139	7.9881	10.2451	13.1100	16.7386	21.3249	27.1093	34.3899	43.5353	55.0004	69.3455	87.2598	109.5893	137.3706
28	1.3213	1.7410	2.2879	2.9987	3.9201	5.1117	6.6488	8.6271	11.1671	14.4210	18.5799	23.8839	30.6335	39.2045	50.0656	63.8004	81.1342	102.9666	130.4112	164.8447
29	1.3345	1.7758	2.3566	3.1187	4.1161	5.4184	7.1143	9.3173	12.1722	15.8631	20.6237	26.7499	34.6158	44.6931	57.5755	74.0085	94.9271	121.5005	155.1893	197.8136
30	1.3478	1.8114	2.4273	3.2434	4.3219	5.7435	7.6123	10.0627	13.2677	17.4494	22.8923	29.9599	39.1159	50.9502	66.2118	85.8499	111.0647	143.3706	184.6753	237.3763
31	1.3613	1.8476	2.5001	3.3731	4.5380	6.0881	8.1451	10.8677	14.4618	19.1943	25.4104	33.5551	44.2010	58.0832	76.1435	99.5859	129.9456	169.1774	219.7636	284.8516
32	1.3749	1.8845	2.5751	3.5081	4.7649	6.4534	8.7153	11.7371	15.7633	21.1138	28.2056	37.5817	49.9471	66.2148	87.5651	115.5196	152.0364	199.6293	261.5187	341.8219
33	1.3887	1.9222	2.6523	3.6484	5.0032	6.8406	9.3253	12.6760	17.1820	23.2252	31.3082	42.0915	56.4402	75.4849	100.6998	134.0027	177.8826	235.5625	311.2073	410.1863
34	1.4026	1.9607	2.7319	3.7943	5.2533	7.2510	9.9781	13.6901	18.7284	25.5477	34.7521	47.1425	63.7774	86.0528	115.8048	155.4432	208.1226	277.9638	370.3366	492.2235
35	1.4166	1.9999	2.8139	3.9461	5.5160	7.6861	10.6766	14.7853	20.4140	28.1024	38.5749	52.7996	72.0685	98.1002	133.1755	180.3141	243.5035	327.9973	440.7006	590.6682
36	1.4308	2.0399	2.8983	4.1039	5.7918	8.1473	11.4239	15.9682	22.2512	30.9127	42.8181	59.1356	81.4374	111.8342	153.1519	209.1643	284.8991	387.0368	524.4337	708.8019

Table B-2 Present Value of a Future Lump Sum

Formula: $PV = FV\left[\dfrac{1}{(1+i)^n}\right]$

Interest Rate (i)

Periods (n)	1%	2%	3%	4%	5%	6%	7%	8%	9%	10%	11%	12%	13%	14%	15%	16%	17%	18%	19%	20%
1	0.9901	0.9804	0.9709	0.9615	0.9524	0.9434	0.9346	0.9259	0.9174	0.9091	0.9009	0.8929	0.8850	0.8772	0.8696	0.8621	0.8547	0.8475	0.8403	0.8333
2	0.9803	0.9612	0.9426	0.9246	0.9070	0.8900	0.8734	0.8573	0.8417	0.8264	0.8116	0.7972	0.7831	0.7695	0.7561	0.7432	0.7305	0.7182	0.7062	0.6944
3	0.9706	0.9423	0.9151	0.8890	0.8638	0.8396	0.8163	0.7938	0.7722	0.7513	0.7312	0.7118	0.6931	0.6750	0.6575	0.6407	0.6244	0.6086	0.5934	0.5787
4	0.9610	0.9238	0.8885	0.8548	0.8227	0.7921	0.7629	0.7350	0.7084	0.6830	0.6587	0.6355	0.6133	0.5921	0.5718	0.5523	0.5337	0.5158	0.4987	0.4823
5	0.9515	0.9057	0.8626	0.8219	0.7835	0.7473	0.7130	0.6806	0.6499	0.6209	0.5935	0.5674	0.5428	0.5194	0.4972	0.4761	0.4561	0.4371	0.4190	0.4019
6	0.9420	0.8880	0.8375	0.7903	0.7462	0.7050	0.6663	0.6302	0.5963	0.5645	0.5346	0.5066	0.4803	0.4556	0.4323	0.4104	0.3898	0.3704	0.3521	0.3349
7	0.9327	0.8706	0.8131	0.7599	0.7107	0.6651	0.6227	0.5835	0.5470	0.5132	0.4817	0.4523	0.4251	0.3996	0.3759	0.3538	0.3332	0.3139	0.2959	0.2791
8	0.9235	0.8535	0.7894	0.7307	0.6768	0.6274	0.5820	0.5403	0.5019	0.4665	0.4339	0.4039	0.3762	0.3506	0.3269	0.3050	0.2848	0.2660	0.2487	0.2326
9	0.9143	0.8368	0.7664	0.7026	0.6446	0.5919	0.5439	0.5002	0.4604	0.4241	0.3909	0.3606	0.3329	0.3075	0.2843	0.2630	0.2434	0.2255	0.2090	0.1938
10	0.9053	0.8203	0.7441	0.6756	0.6139	0.5584	0.5083	0.4632	0.4224	0.3855	0.3522	0.3220	0.2946	0.2697	0.2472	0.2267	0.2080	0.1911	0.1756	0.1615
11	0.8963	0.8043	0.7224	0.6496	0.5847	0.5268	0.4751	0.4289	0.3875	0.3505	0.3173	0.2875	0.2607	0.2366	0.2149	0.1954	0.1778	0.1619	0.1476	0.1346
12	0.8874	0.7885	0.7014	0.6246	0.5568	0.4970	0.4440	0.3971	0.3555	0.3186	0.2858	0.2567	0.2307	0.2076	0.1869	0.1685	0.1520	0.1372	0.1240	0.1122
13	0.8787	0.7730	0.6810	0.6006	0.5303	0.4688	0.4150	0.3677	0.3262	0.2897	0.2575	0.2292	0.2042	0.1821	0.1625	0.1452	0.1299	0.1163	0.1042	0.0935
14	0.8700	0.7579	0.6611	0.5775	0.5051	0.4423	0.3878	0.3405	0.2992	0.2633	0.2320	0.2046	0.1807	0.1597	0.1413	0.1252	0.1110	0.0985	0.0876	0.0779
15	0.8613	0.7430	0.6419	0.5553	0.4810	0.4173	0.3624	0.3152	0.2745	0.2394	0.2090	0.1827	0.1599	0.1401	0.1229	0.1079	0.0949	0.0835	0.0736	0.0649
16	0.8528	0.7284	0.6232	0.5339	0.4581	0.3936	0.3387	0.2919	0.2519	0.2176	0.1883	0.1631	0.1415	0.1229	0.1069	0.0930	0.0811	0.0708	0.0618	0.0541
17	0.8444	0.7142	0.6050	0.5134	0.4363	0.3714	0.3166	0.2703	0.2311	0.1978	0.1696	0.1456	0.1252	0.1078	0.0929	0.0802	0.0693	0.0600	0.0520	0.0451
18	0.8360	0.7002	0.5874	0.4936	0.4155	0.3503	0.2959	0.2502	0.2120	0.1799	0.1528	0.1300	0.1108	0.0946	0.0808	0.0691	0.0592	0.0508	0.0437	0.0376
19	0.8277	0.6864	0.5703	0.4746	0.3957	0.3305	0.2765	0.2317	0.1945	0.1635	0.1377	0.1161	0.0981	0.0829	0.0703	0.0596	0.0506	0.0431	0.0367	0.0313
20	0.8195	0.6730	0.5537	0.4564	0.3769	0.3118	0.2584	0.2145	0.1784	0.1486	0.1240	0.1037	0.0868	0.0728	0.0611	0.0514	0.0433	0.0365	0.0308	0.0261
21	0.8114	0.6598	0.5375	0.4388	0.3589	0.2942	0.2415	0.1987	0.1637	0.1351	0.1117	0.0926	0.0768	0.0638	0.0531	0.0443	0.0370	0.0309	0.0259	0.0217
22	0.8034	0.6468	0.5219	0.4220	0.3418	0.2775	0.2257	0.1839	0.1502	0.1228	0.1007	0.0826	0.0680	0.0560	0.0462	0.0382	0.0316	0.0262	0.0218	0.0181
23	0.7954	0.6342	0.5067	0.4057	0.3256	0.2618	0.2109	0.1703	0.1378	0.1117	0.0907	0.0738	0.0601	0.0491	0.0402	0.0329	0.0270	0.0222	0.0183	0.0151
24	0.7876	0.6217	0.4919	0.3901	0.3101	0.2470	0.1971	0.1577	0.1264	0.1015	0.0817	0.0659	0.0532	0.0431	0.0349	0.0284	0.0231	0.0188	0.0154	0.0126
25	0.7798	0.6095	0.4776	0.3751	0.2953	0.2330	0.1842	0.1460	0.1160	0.0923	0.0736	0.0588	0.0471	0.0378	0.0304	0.0245	0.0197	0.0160	0.0129	0.0105
26	0.7720	0.5976	0.4637	0.3607	0.2812	0.2198	0.1722	0.1352	0.1064	0.0839	0.0663	0.0525	0.0417	0.0331	0.0264	0.0211	0.0169	0.0135	0.0109	0.0087
27	0.7644	0.5859	0.4502	0.3468	0.2678	0.2074	0.1609	0.1252	0.0976	0.0763	0.0597	0.0469	0.0369	0.0291	0.0230	0.0182	0.0144	0.0115	0.0091	0.0073
28	0.7568	0.5744	0.4371	0.3335	0.2551	0.1956	0.1504	0.1159	0.0895	0.0693	0.0538	0.0419	0.0326	0.0255	0.0200	0.0157	0.0123	0.0097	0.0077	0.0061
29	0.7493	0.5631	0.4243	0.3207	0.2429	0.1846	0.1406	0.1073	0.0822	0.0630	0.0485	0.0374	0.0289	0.0224	0.0174	0.0135	0.0105	0.0082	0.0064	0.0051
30	0.7419	0.5521	0.4120	0.3083	0.2314	0.1741	0.1314	0.0994	0.0754	0.0573	0.0437	0.0334	0.0256	0.0196	0.0151	0.0116	0.0090	0.0070	0.0054	0.0042
31	0.7346	0.5412	0.4000	0.2965	0.2204	0.1643	0.1228	0.0920	0.0691	0.0521	0.0394	0.0298	0.0226	0.0172	0.0131	0.0100	0.0077	0.0059	0.0046	0.0035
32	0.7273	0.5306	0.3883	0.2851	0.2099	0.1550	0.1147	0.0852	0.0634	0.0474	0.0355	0.0266	0.0200	0.0151	0.0114	0.0087	0.0066	0.0050	0.0038	0.0029
33	0.7201	0.5202	0.3770	0.2741	0.1999	0.1462	0.1072	0.0789	0.0582	0.0431	0.0319	0.0238	0.0177	0.0132	0.0099	0.0075	0.0056	0.0042	0.0032	0.0024
34	0.7130	0.5100	0.3660	0.2636	0.1904	0.1379	0.1002	0.0730	0.0534	0.0391	0.0288	0.0212	0.0157	0.0116	0.0086	0.0064	0.0048	0.0036	0.0027	0.0020
35	0.7059	0.5000	0.3554	0.2534	0.1813	0.1301	0.0937	0.0676	0.0490	0.0356	0.0259	0.0189	0.0139	0.0102	0.0075	0.0055	0.0041	0.0030	0.0023	0.0017
36	0.6989	0.4902	0.3450	0.2437	0.1727	0.1227	0.0875	0.0626	0.0449	0.0323	0.0234	0.0169	0.0123	0.0089	0.0065	0.0048	0.0035	0.0026	0.0019	0.0014

Table B-3 Future Value of an Ordinary Annuity

Formula: $FV = A\left[\dfrac{(1+i)^n - 1}{i}\right]$

Interest Rate (i)

Periods (n)	1%	2%	3%	4%	5%	6%	7%	8%	9%	10%	11%	12%	13%	14%	15%	16%	17%	18%	19%	20%
1	1.000	1.000	1.000	1.000	1.000	1.000	1.000	1.000	1.000	1.000	1.000	1.000	1.000	1.000	1.000	1.000	1.000	1.000	1.000	1.000
2	2.0100	2.0200	2.0300	2.0400	2.0500	2.0600	2.0700	2.0800	2.0900	2.1000	2.1100	2.1200	2.1300	2.1400	2.1500	2.1600	2.1700	2.1800	2.1900	2.2000
3	3.0301	3.0604	3.0909	3.1216	3.1525	3.1836	3.2149	3.2464	3.2781	3.3100	3.3421	3.3744	3.4069	3.4396	3.4725	3.5056	3.5389	3.5724	3.6061	3.6400
4	4.0604	4.1216	4.1836	4.2465	4.3101	4.3746	4.4399	4.5061	4.5731	4.6410	4.7097	4.7793	4.8498	4.9211	4.9934	5.0665	5.1405	5.2154	5.2913	5.3680
5	5.1010	5.2040	5.3091	5.4163	5.5256	5.6371	5.7507	5.8666	5.9847	6.1051	6.2278	6.3528	6.4803	6.6101	6.7424	6.8771	7.0144	7.1542	7.2966	7.4416
6	6.1520	6.3081	6.4684	6.6330	6.8019	6.9753	7.1533	7.3359	7.5233	7.7156	7.9129	8.1152	8.3227	8.5355	8.7537	8.9775	9.2068	9.4420	9.6830	9.9299
7	7.2135	7.4343	7.6625	7.8983	8.1420	8.3938	8.6540	8.9228	9.2004	9.4872	9.7833	10.0890	10.4047	10.7305	11.0668	11.4139	11.7720	12.1415	12.5227	12.9159
8	8.2857	8.5830	8.8923	9.2142	9.5491	9.8975	10.2598	10.6366	11.0285	11.4359	11.8594	12.2997	12.7573	13.2328	13.7268	14.2401	14.7733	15.3270	15.9020	16.4991
9	9.3685	9.7546	10.1591	10.5828	11.0266	11.4913	11.9780	12.4876	13.0210	13.5795	14.1640	14.7757	15.4157	16.0853	16.7858	17.5185	18.2847	19.0859	19.9234	20.7989
10	10.4622	10.9497	11.4639	12.0061	12.5779	13.1808	13.8164	14.4866	15.1929	15.9374	16.7220	17.5487	18.4197	19.3373	20.3037	21.3215	22.3931	23.5213	24.7089	25.9587
11	11.5668	12.1687	12.8078	13.4864	14.2068	14.9716	15.7836	16.6455	17.5603	18.5312	19.5614	20.6546	21.8143	23.0445	24.3493	25.7329	27.1999	28.7551	30.4035	32.1504
12	12.6825	13.4121	14.1920	15.0258	15.9171	16.8699	17.8885	18.9771	20.1407	21.3843	22.7132	24.1331	25.6502	27.2707	29.0017	30.8502	32.8239	34.9311	37.1802	39.5805
13	13.8093	14.6803	15.6178	16.6268	17.7130	18.8821	20.1406	21.4953	22.9534	24.5227	26.2116	28.0291	29.9847	32.0887	34.3519	36.7862	39.4040	42.2187	45.2445	48.4966
14	14.9474	15.9739	17.0863	18.2919	19.5986	21.0151	22.5505	24.2149	26.0192	27.9750	30.0949	32.3926	34.8827	37.5811	40.5047	43.6720	47.1027	50.8180	54.8409	59.1959
15	16.0969	17.2934	18.5989	20.0236	21.5786	23.2760	25.1290	27.1521	29.3609	31.7725	34.4054	37.2797	40.4175	43.8424	47.5804	51.6595	56.1101	60.9653	66.2607	72.0351
16	17.2579	18.6393	20.1569	21.8245	23.6575	25.6725	27.8881	30.3243	33.0034	35.9497	39.1899	42.7533	46.6717	50.9804	55.7175	60.9250	66.6488	72.9390	79.8502	87.4421
17	18.4304	20.0121	21.7616	23.6975	25.8404	28.2129	30.8402	33.7502	36.9737	40.5447	44.5008	48.8837	53.7391	59.1176	65.0751	71.6730	78.9792	87.0680	96.0218	105.9306
18	19.6147	21.4123	23.4144	25.6454	28.1324	30.9057	33.9990	37.4502	41.3013	45.5992	50.3959	55.7497	61.7251	68.3941	75.8364	84.1407	93.4056	103.7403	115.2659	128.1167
19	20.8109	22.8406	25.1169	27.6712	30.5390	33.7600	37.3790	41.4463	46.0185	51.1591	56.9395	63.4397	70.7494	78.9692	88.2118	98.6032	110.2846	123.4135	138.1664	154.7400
20	22.0190	24.2974	26.8704	29.7781	33.0660	36.7856	40.9955	45.7620	51.1601	57.2750	64.2028	72.0524	80.9468	91.0249	102.4436	115.3797	130.0329	146.6280	165.4180	186.6880
21	23.2392	25.7833	28.6765	31.9692	35.7193	39.9927	44.8652	50.4229	56.7645	64.0025	72.2651	81.6987	92.4699	104.7684	118.8101	134.8405	153.1385	174.0210	197.8474	225.0256
22	24.4716	27.2990	30.5368	34.2480	38.5052	43.3923	49.0057	55.4568	62.8733	71.4027	81.2143	92.5026	105.4910	120.4360	137.6316	157.4150	180.1721	206.3448	236.4385	271.0307
23	25.7163	28.8450	32.4529	36.6179	41.4305	46.9958	53.4361	60.8933	69.5319	79.5430	91.1479	104.6029	120.2048	138.2970	159.2764	183.6014	211.8013	244.4868	282.3618	326.2369
24	26.9735	30.4219	34.4265	39.0826	44.5020	50.8156	58.1767	66.7648	76.7898	88.4973	102.1742	118.1552	136.8315	158.6586	184.1678	213.9776	248.8076	289.4945	337.0105	392.4842
25	28.2432	32.0303	36.4593	41.6459	47.7271	54.8645	63.2490	73.1059	84.7009	98.3471	114.4133	133.3339	155.6196	181.8708	212.7930	249.2140	292.1049	342.6035	402.0425	471.9811
26	29.5256	33.6709	38.5530	44.3117	51.1135	59.1564	68.6765	79.9544	93.3240	109.1818	127.9988	150.3339	176.8501	208.3327	245.7120	290.0883	342.7627	405.2721	479.4306	567.3773
27	30.8209	35.3443	40.7096	47.0842	54.6691	63.7058	74.4838	87.3508	102.7231	121.0999	143.0786	169.3740	200.8406	238.4993	283.5688	337.5024	402.0323	479.2211	571.5224	681.8528
28	32.1291	37.0512	42.9309	49.9676	58.4026	68.5281	80.6977	95.3388	112.9682	134.2099	159.8173	190.6989	227.9499	272.8892	327.1041	392.5028	471.3778	566.4809	681.1116	819.2233
29	33.4504	38.7922	45.2189	52.9663	62.3227	73.6398	87.3465	103.9659	124.1354	148.6309	178.3972	214.5828	258.5834	312.0937	377.1697	456.3032	552.5121	669.4475	811.5228	984.0680
30	34.7849	40.5681	47.5754	56.0849	66.4388	79.0582	94.4608	113.2832	136.3075	164.4940	199.0209	241.3327	293.1992	356.7868	434.7451	530.3117	647.4391	790.9480	966.7122	1,181.8816
31	36.1327	42.3794	50.0027	59.3283	70.7608	84.8017	102.0730	123.3459	149.5752	181.9434	221.9132	271.2926	332.3151	407.7370	500.9569	616.1616	758.5038	934.3186	1,151.3875	1,419.2579
32	37.4941	44.2270	52.5028	62.7015	75.2988	90.8898	110.2182	134.2135	164.0370	201.1378	247.3236	304.8477	376.5161	465.8202	577.1005	715.7475	888.4494	1,103.4960	1,371.1511	1,704.1095
33	38.8690	46.1116	55.0778	66.2095	80.0638	97.3432	118.9334	145.9506	179.8003	222.2515	275.5292	342.4294	426.4632	532.0350	664.6655	831.2671	1,040.4858	1,303.1253	1,632.6698	2,045.9314
34	40.2577	48.0338	57.7302	69.8579	85.0670	104.1838	128.2588	158.6267	196.9823	245.4767	306.8374	384.5210	482.9034	607.5199	765.3654	965.2698	1,218.3684	1,538.6878	1,943.8771	2,456.1176
35	41.6603	49.9945	60.4621	73.6522	90.3203	111.4348	138.2369	172.3168	215.7108	271.0244	341.5896	431.6635	546.6808	693.5727	881.1702	1,120.7130	1,426.4910	1,816.6516	2,314.2137	2,948.3411
36	43.0769	51.9944	63.2759	77.5983	95.8363	119.1209	148.9135	187.1021	236.1247	299.1268	380.1644	484.4631	618.7493	791.6729	1,014.3457	1,301.0270	1,669.9945	2,144.6489	2,754.9143	3,539.0094

Table B-4 Future Value of an Annuity Due

Formula: $FV = A\left[\left[\dfrac{(1+i)^{(n+1)} - 1}{i}\right] - 1\right]$

Interest Rate (i)

Periods (n)	1%	2%	3%	4%	5%	6%	7%	8%	9%	10%	11%	12%	13%	14%	15%	16%	17%	18%	19%	20%
1	1.0100	1.0200	1.0300	1.0400	1.0500	1.0600	1.0700	1.0800	1.0900	1.1000	1.1100	1.1200	1.1300	1.1400	1.1500	1.1600	1.1700	1.1800	1.1900	1.2000
2	2.0301	2.0604	2.0909	2.1216	2.1525	2.1836	2.2149	2.2464	2.2781	2.3100	2.3421	2.3744	2.4069	2.4396	2.4725	2.5056	2.5389	2.5724	2.6061	2.6400
3	3.0604	3.1216	3.1836	3.2465	3.3101	3.3746	3.4399	3.5061	3.5731	3.6410	3.7097	3.7793	3.8498	3.9211	3.9934	4.0665	4.1405	4.2154	4.2913	4.3680
4	4.1010	4.2040	4.3091	4.4163	4.5256	4.6371	4.7507	4.8666	4.9847	5.1051	5.2278	5.3528	5.4803	5.6101	5.7424	5.8771	6.0144	6.1542	6.2966	6.4416
5	5.1520	5.3081	5.4684	5.6330	5.8019	5.9753	6.1533	6.3359	6.5233	6.7156	6.9129	7.1152	7.3227	7.5355	7.7537	7.9775	8.2068	8.4420	8.6830	8.9299
6	6.2135	6.4343	6.6625	6.8983	7.1420	7.3938	7.6540	7.9228	8.2004	8.4872	8.7833	9.0890	9.4047	9.7305	10.0668	10.4139	10.7720	11.1415	11.5227	11.9159
7	7.2857	7.5830	7.8923	8.2142	8.5491	8.8975	9.2598	9.6366	10.0285	10.4359	10.8594	11.2997	11.7573	12.2328	12.7268	13.2401	13.7733	14.3270	14.9020	15.4991
8	8.3685	8.7546	9.1591	9.5828	10.0266	10.4913	10.9780	11.4876	12.0210	12.5795	13.1640	13.7757	14.4157	15.0853	15.7858	16.5185	17.2847	18.0859	18.9234	19.7989
9	9.4622	9.9497	10.4639	11.0061	11.5779	12.1808	12.8164	13.4866	14.1929	14.9374	15.7220	16.5487	17.4197	18.3373	19.3037	20.3215	21.3931	22.5213	23.7089	24.9587
10	10.5668	11.1687	11.8078	12.4864	13.2068	13.9716	14.7836	15.6455	16.5603	17.5312	18.5614	19.6546	20.8143	22.0445	23.3493	24.7329	26.1999	27.7551	29.4035	31.1504
11	11.6825	12.4121	13.1920	14.0258	14.9171	15.8699	16.8885	17.9771	19.1407	20.3843	21.7132	23.1331	24.6502	26.2707	28.0017	29.8502	31.8239	33.9311	36.1802	38.5805
12	12.8093	13.6803	14.6178	15.6268	16.7130	17.8821	19.1406	20.4953	21.9534	23.5227	25.2116	27.0291	28.9847	31.0887	33.3519	35.7862	38.4040	41.2187	44.2445	47.4966
13	13.9474	14.9739	16.0863	17.2919	18.5986	20.0151	21.5505	23.2149	25.0192	26.9750	29.0949	31.3926	33.8827	36.5811	39.5047	42.6720	46.1027	49.8180	53.8409	58.1959
14	15.0969	16.2934	17.5989	19.0236	20.5786	22.2760	24.1290	26.1521	28.3609	30.7725	33.4054	36.2797	39.4175	42.8424	46.5804	50.6595	55.1101	59.9653	65.2607	71.0351
15	16.2579	17.6393	19.1569	20.8245	22.6575	24.6725	26.8881	29.3243	32.0034	34.9497	38.1899	41.7533	45.6717	49.9804	54.7175	59.9250	65.6488	71.9390	78.8502	86.4421
16	17.4304	19.0121	20.7616	22.6975	24.8404	27.2129	29.8402	32.7502	35.9737	39.5447	43.5008	47.8837	52.7391	58.1176	64.0751	70.6730	77.9792	86.0680	95.0218	104.9306
17	18.6147	20.4123	22.4144	24.6454	27.1324	29.9057	32.9990	36.4502	40.3013	44.5992	49.3959	54.7497	60.7251	67.3941	74.8364	83.1407	92.4056	102.7403	114.2659	127.1167
18	19.8109	21.8406	24.1169	26.6712	29.5390	32.7600	36.3790	40.4463	45.0185	50.1591	55.9395	62.4397	69.7494	77.9692	87.2118	97.6032	109.2846	122.4135	137.1664	153.7400
19	21.0190	23.2974	25.8704	28.7781	32.0660	35.7856	39.9955	44.7620	50.1601	56.2750	63.2028	71.0524	79.9468	90.0249	101.4436	114.3797	129.0329	145.6280	164.4180	185.6880
20	22.2392	24.7833	27.6765	30.9692	34.7193	38.9927	43.8652	49.4229	55.7645	63.0025	71.2651	80.6987	91.4699	103.7684	117.8101	133.8405	152.1385	173.0210	196.8474	224.0256
21	23.4716	26.2990	29.5368	33.2480	37.5052	42.3923	48.0057	54.4568	61.8733	70.4027	80.2143	91.5026	104.4910	119.4360	136.6316	156.4150	179.1721	205.3448	235.4385	270.0307
22	24.7163	27.8450	31.4529	35.6179	40.4305	45.9958	52.4361	59.8933	68.5319	78.5430	90.1479	103.6029	119.2048	137.2970	158.2764	182.6014	210.8013	243.4868	281.3618	325.2369
23	25.9735	29.4219	33.4265	38.0826	43.5020	49.8156	57.1767	65.7648	75.7898	87.4973	101.1742	117.1552	135.8315	157.6586	183.1678	212.9776	247.8076	288.4945	336.0105	391.4842
24	27.2432	31.0303	35.4593	40.6459	46.7271	53.8645	62.2490	72.1059	83.7009	97.3471	113.4133	132.3339	154.6196	180.8708	211.7930	248.2140	291.1049	341.6035	401.0425	470.9811
25	28.5256	32.6709	37.5530	43.3117	50.1135	58.1564	67.6765	78.9544	92.3240	108.1818	126.9988	149.3339	175.8501	207.3327	244.7120	289.0883	341.7627	404.2721	478.4306	566.3773
26	29.8209	34.3443	39.7096	46.0842	53.6691	62.7058	73.4838	86.3508	101.7231	120.0999	142.0786	168.3740	199.8406	237.4993	282.5688	336.5024	401.0323	478.2211	570.5224	680.8528
27	31.1291	36.0512	41.9309	48.9676	57.4026	67.5281	79.6977	94.3388	111.9682	133.2099	158.8173	189.6989	226.9499	271.8892	326.1041	391.5028	470.3778	565.4809	680.1116	818.2233
28	32.4504	37.7922	44.2189	51.9663	61.3227	72.6398	86.3465	102.9659	123.1354	147.6309	177.3972	213.5828	257.5834	311.0937	376.1697	455.3032	551.5121	668.4475	810.5228	983.0680
29	33.7849	39.5681	46.5754	55.0849	65.4388	78.0582	93.4608	112.2832	135.3075	163.4940	198.0209	240.3327	292.1992	355.7868	433.7451	529.3117	646.4391	789.9480	965.7122	1,180.8816
30	35.1327	41.3794	49.0027	58.3283	69.7608	83.8017	101.0730	122.3459	148.5752	180.9434	220.9132	270.2926	331.3151	406.7370	499.9569	615.1616	757.5038	933.3186	1,150.3875	1,418.2579
31	36.4941	43.2270	51.5028	61.7015	74.2988	89.8898	109.2182	133.2135	163.0370	200.1378	246.3236	303.8477	375.5161	464.8202	576.1005	714.7475	887.4494	1,102.4960	1,370.1511	1,703.1095
32	37.8690	45.1116	54.0778	65.2095	79.0638	96.3432	117.9334	144.9506	178.8003	221.2515	274.5292	341.4294	425.4632	531.0350	663.6655	830.2671	1,039.4858	1,302.1253	1,631.6698	2,044.9314
33	39.2577	47.0338	56.7302	68.8579	84.0670	103.1838	127.2588	157.6267	195.9823	244.4767	305.8374	383.5210	481.9034	606.5199	764.3654	964.2698	1,217.3684	1,537.6878	1,942.8771	2,445.1176
34	40.6603	48.9945	59.4621	72.6522	89.3203	110.4348	137.2369	171.3168	214.7108	270.0244	340.5896	430.6635	545.6808	692.5727	880.1702	1,119.7130	1,425.4910	1,815.6516	2,313.2137	2,947.3411
35	42.0769	50.9944	62.2759	76.5983	94.8363	118.1209	147.9135	186.1021	235.1247	298.1268	379.1644	483.4631	617.7493	790.6729	1,013.3457	1,300.0270	1,668.9945	2,143.6489	2,753.9143	3,538.0094
36	43.5076	53.0343	65.1742	80.7022	100.6281	126.2681	159.3374	202.0703	257.3759	329.0395	421.9825	542.5987	699.1867	902.5071	1,166.4975	1,509.1914	1,953.8936	2,530.6857	3,278.3481	4,246.8112

Table B-5 Present Value of an Ordinary Annuity

Formula: $PV = A\left[\dfrac{(1+i)^n - 1}{i(1+i)^n}\right]$

Interest Rate (i)

Periods (n)	1%	2%	3%	4%	5%	6%	7%	8%	9%	10%	11%	12%	13%	14%	15%	16%	17%	18%	19%	20%
1	0.9901	0.9804	0.9709	0.9615	0.9524	0.9434	0.9346	0.9259	0.9174	0.9091	0.9009	0.8929	0.8850	0.8772	0.8696	0.8621	0.8547	0.8475	0.8403	0.8333
2	1.9704	1.9416	1.9135	1.8861	1.8594	1.8334	1.8080	1.7833	1.7591	1.7355	1.7125	1.6901	1.6681	1.6467	1.6257	1.6052	1.5852	1.5656	1.5465	1.5278
3	2.9410	2.8839	2.8286	2.7751	2.7232	2.6730	2.6243	2.5771	2.5313	2.4869	2.4437	2.4018	2.3612	2.3216	2.2832	2.2459	2.2096	2.1743	2.1399	2.1065
4	3.9020	3.8077	3.7171	3.6299	3.5460	3.4651	3.3872	3.3121	3.2397	3.1699	3.1024	3.0373	2.9745	2.9137	2.8550	2.7982	2.7432	2.6901	2.6386	2.5887
5	4.8534	4.7135	4.5797	4.4518	4.3295	4.2124	4.1002	3.9927	3.8897	3.7908	3.6959	3.6048	3.5172	3.4331	3.3522	3.2743	3.1993	3.1272	3.0576	2.9906
6	5.7955	5.6014	5.4172	5.2421	5.0757	4.9173	4.7665	4.6229	4.4859	4.3553	4.2305	4.1114	3.9975	3.8887	3.7845	3.6847	3.5892	3.4976	3.4098	3.3255
7	6.7282	6.4720	6.2303	6.0021	5.7864	5.5824	5.3893	5.2064	5.0330	4.8684	4.7122	4.5638	4.4226	4.2883	4.1604	4.0386	3.9224	3.8115	3.7057	3.6046
8	7.6517	7.3255	7.0197	6.7327	6.4632	6.2098	5.9713	5.7466	5.5348	5.3349	5.1461	4.9676	4.7988	4.6389	4.4873	4.3436	4.2072	4.0776	3.9544	3.8372
9	8.5660	8.1622	7.7861	7.4353	7.1078	6.8017	6.5152	6.2469	5.9952	5.7590	5.5370	5.3282	5.1317	5.9464	4.7716	4.6065	4.4506	4.3030	4.1633	4.0310
10	9.4713	8.9826	8.5302	8.1109	7.7217	7.3601	7.0236	6.7101	6.4177	6.1446	5.8892	5.6502	5.4262	5.2161	5.0188	4.8332	4.6586	4.4941	4.3389	4.1925
11	10.3676	9.7868	9.2526	8.7605	8.3064	7.8869	7.4987	7.1390	6.8052	6.4951	6.2065	5.9377	5.6869	5.4527	5.2337	5.0286	4.8364	4.6560	4.4865	4.3271
12	11.2551	10.5753	9.9540	9.3851	8.8633	8.3838	7.9427	7.5361	7.1607	6.8137	6.4924	6.1944	5.9176	5.6603	5.4206	5.1971	4.9884	4.7932	4.6105	4.4392
13	12.1337	11.3484	10.6350	9.9856	9.3936	8.8527	8.3577	7.9038	7.4869	7.1034	6.7499	6.4235	6.1218	5.8424	5.5831	5.3423	5.1183	4.9095	4.7147	4.5327
14	13.0037	12.1062	11.2961	10.5631	9.8986	9.2950	8.7455	8.2442	7.7862	7.3667	6.9819	6.6282	6.3025	6.0021	5.7245	5.4675	5.2293	5.0081	4.8023	4.6106
15	13.8651	12.8493	11.9379	11.1184	10.3797	9.7122	9.1079	8.5595	8.0607	7.6061	7.1909	6.8109	6.4624	6.1422	5.8474	5.5755	5.3242	5.0916	4.8759	4.6755
16	14.7179	13.5777	12.5611	11.6523	10.8378	10.1059	9.4466	8.8514	8.3126	7.8237	7.3792	6.9740	6.6039	6.2651	5.9542	5.6685	5.4053	5.1624	4.9377	4.7296
17	15.5623	14.2919	13.1661	12.1657	11.2741	10.4773	9.7632	9.1216	8.5436	8.0216	7.5488	7.1196	6.7291	6.3729	6.0472	5.7487	5.4746	5.2223	4.9897	4.7746
18	16.3983	14.9920	13.7535	12.6593	11.6896	10.8276	10.0591	9.3719	8.7556	8.2014	7.7016	7.2497	6.8399	6.4674	6.1280	5.8178	5.5339	5.2732	5.0333	4.8122
19	17.2260	15.6785	14.3238	13.1339	12.0853	11.1581	10.3356	9.6036	8.9501	8.3649	7.8393	7.3658	6.9380	6.5504	6.1982	5.8775	5.5845	5.3162	5.0700	4.8435
20	18.0456	16.3514	14.8775	13.5903	12.4622	11.4699	10.5940	9.8181	9.1285	8.5136	7.9633	7.4694	7.0248	6.6231	6.2593	5.9288	5.6278	5.3527	5.1009	4.8696
21	18.8570	17.0112	15.4150	14.0292	12.8212	11.7641	10.8355	10.0168	9.2922	8.6487	8.0751	7.5620	7.1016	6.6870	6.3125	5.9731	5.6648	5.3837	5.1268	4.8913
22	19.6604	17.6580	15.9369	14.4511	13.1630	12.0416	11.0612	10.2007	9.4424	8.7715	8.1757	7.6446	7.1695	6.7429	6.3587	6.0113	5.6964	5.4099	5.1486	4.9094
23	20.4558	18.2922	16.4436	14.8568	13.4886	12.3034	11.2722	10.3711	9.5802	8.8832	8.2664	7.7184	7.2297	6.7921	6.3968	6.0442	5.7234	5.4321	5.1668	4.9245
24	21.2434	18.9139	16.9355	15.2470	13.7986	12.5504	11.4693	10.5288	9.7066	8.9847	8.3481	7.7843	7.2829	6.8351	6.4338	6.0726	5.7465	5.4509	5.1822	4.9371
25	22.0232	19.5235	17.4131	15.6221	14.0939	12.7834	11.6536	10.6748	9.8226	9.0770	8.4217	7.8431	7.3300	6.8729	6.4641	6.0971	5.7662	5.4669	5.1951	4.9476
26	22.7952	20.1210	17.8768	15.9828	14.3752	13.0032	11.8258	10.8100	9.9290	9.1609	8.4881	7.8957	7.3717	6.9061	6.4906	6.1182	5.7831	5.4804	5.2060	4.9563
27	23.5596	20.7069	18.3270	16.3296	14.6430	13.2105	11.9867	10.9352	10.0266	9.2372	8.5478	7.9426	7.4086	6.9352	6.5135	6.1364	5.7975	5.4919	5.2151	4.9636
28	24.3164	21.2813	18.7641	16.6631	14.8981	13.4062	12.1371	11.0511	10.1161	9.3066	8.6016	7.9844	7.4412	6.9607	6.5335	6.1520	5.8099	5.5016	5.2228	4.9697
29	25.0658	21.8444	19.1885	16.9637	15.1411	13.5907	12.2777	11.1584	10.1983	9.3696	8.6501	8.0218	7.4701	6.9830	6.5509	6.1656	5.8204	5.5098	5.2292	4.9747
30	25.8077	22.3965	19.6004	17.2920	15.3725	13.7648	12.4090	11.2578	10.2737	9.4269	8.6938	8.0552	7.4957	7.0027	6.5660	6.1772	5.8294	5.5168	5.2347	4.9789
31	26.5423	22.9377	20.0004	17.5885	15.5928	13.9291	12.5318	11.3498	10.3426	9.4790	8.7331	8.0850	7.5183	7.0199	6.5791	6.1872	5.8371	5.5227	5.2392	4.9824
32	27.2696	23.4683	20.3888	17.8736	15.8027	14.0840	12.6466	11.4350	10.4062	9.5264	8.7686	8.1116	7.5383	7.0350	6.5905	6.1959	5.8437	5.5277	5.2430	4.9854
33	27.9897	23.9886	20.7658	18.1476	16.0025	14.2302	12.7538	11.5139	10.4644	9.5694	8.8005	8.1354	7.5560	7.0482	6.6005	6.2034	5.8493	5.5320	5.2462	4.9878
34	28.7027	24.4986	21.1318	18.4112	16.1929	14.3681	12.8540	11.5869	10.5178	9.6086	8.8293	8.1566	7.5717	7.0599	6.6091	6.2098	5.8541	5.5356	5.2489	4.9898
35	29.4086	24.9986	21.4872	18.6646	16.3742	14.4982	12.9477	11.6546	10.5668	9.6442	8.8552	8.1755	7.5856	7.0700	6.6166	6.2153	5.8582	5.5386	5.2512	4.9915
36	30.1075	25.4888	21.8323	18.9083	16.5469	14.6210	13.0352	11.7172	10.6118	9.6765	8.8786	8.1924	7.5979	7.0790	6.6231	6.2201	5.8617	5.5412	5.2531	4.9929

Table B-6 Present Value of an Annuity Due

Formula: $PV = A\left\{\left[\dfrac{(1+i)^{(n-1)} - 1}{i(1+i)^{(n-1)}}\right] + 1\right\}$

Interest Rate (i)

Periods (n)	1%	2%	3%	4%	5%	6%	7%	8%	9%	10%	11%	12%	13%	14%	15%	16%	17%	18%	19%	20%
1	1.0000	1.0000	1.0000	1.0000	1.0000	1.0000	1.0000	1.0000	1.0000	1.0000	1.0000	1.0000	1.0000	1.0000	1.0000	1.0000	1.0000	1.0000	1.0000	1.0000
2	1.9901	1.9804	1.9709	1.9615	1.9524	1.9434	1.9346	1.9259	1.9174	1.9091	1.9009	1.8929	1.8850	1.8772	1.8696	1.8621	1.8547	1.8475	1.8403	1.8333
3	2.9704	2.9416	2.9135	2.8861	2.8594	2.8334	2.8080	2.7833	2.7591	2.7355	2.7125	2.6901	2.6681	2.6467	2.6257	2.6052	2.5852	2.5656	2.5465	2.5278
4	3.9410	3.8839	3.8286	3.7751	3.7232	3.6730	3.6243	3.5771	3.5313	3.4869	3.4437	3.4018	3.3612	3.3216	3.2832	3.2459	3.2096	3.1743	3.1399	3.1065
5	4.9020	4.8077	4.7171	4.6299	4.5460	4.4651	4.3872	4.3121	4.2397	4.1699	4.1024	4.0373	3.9745	3.9137	3.8550	3.7982	3.7432	3.6901	3.6386	3.5887
6	5.8534	5.7135	5.5797	5.4518	5.3295	5.2124	5.1002	4.9927	4.8897	4.7908	4.6959	4.6048	4.5172	4.4331	4.3522	4.2743	4.1993	4.1272	4.0576	3.9906
7	6.7955	6.6014	6.4172	6.2421	6.0757	5.9173	5.7665	5.6229	5.4859	5.3553	5.2305	5.1114	4.9975	4.8887	4.7845	4.6847	4.5892	4.4976	4.4098	4.3255
8	7.7282	7.4720	7.2303	7.0021	6.7864	6.5824	6.3893	6.2064	6.0330	5.8684	5.7122	5.5638	5.4226	5.2883	5.1604	5.0386	4.9224	4.8115	4.7057	4.6046
9	8.6517	8.3255	8.0197	7.7327	7.4632	7.2098	6.9713	6.7466	6.5348	6.3349	6.1461	5.9676	5.7988	5.6389	5.4873	5.3436	5.2072	5.0776	4.9544	4.8372
10	9.5660	9.1622	8.7861	8.4353	8.1078	7.8017	7.5152	7.2469	6.9952	6.7590	6.5370	6.3282	6.1317	5.9464	5.7716	5.6065	5.4506	5.3030	5.1633	5.0310
11	10.4713	9.9826	9.5302	9.1109	8.7217	8.3601	8.0236	7.7101	7.4177	7.1446	6.8892	6.6502	6.4262	6.2161	6.0188	5.8332	5.6586	5.4941	5.3389	5.1925
12	11.3676	10.7868	10.2526	9.7605	9.3064	8.8869	8.4987	8.1390	7.8052	7.4951	7.2065	6.9377	6.6869	6.4527	6.2337	6.0286	5.8364	5.6560	5.4865	5.3271
13	12.2551	11.5753	10.9540	10.3851	9.8633	9.3838	8.9427	8.5361	8.1607	7.8137	7.4924	7.1944	6.9176	6.6603	6.4206	6.1971	5.9884	5.7932	5.6105	5.4392
14	13.1337	12.3484	11.6350	10.9856	10.3936	9.8527	9.3577	8.9038	8.4869	8.1034	7.7499	7.4235	7.1218	6.8424	6.5831	6.3423	6.1183	5.9095	5.7147	5.5327
15	14.0037	13.1062	12.2961	11.5631	10.8986	10.2950	9.7455	9.2442	8.7862	8.3667	7.9819	7.6282	7.3025	7.0021	6.7245	6.4675	6.2293	6.0081	5.8023	5.6106
16	14.8651	13.8493	12.9379	12.1184	11.3797	10.7122	10.1079	9.5595	9.0607	8.6061	8.1909	7.8109	7.4624	7.1422	6.8474	6.5755	6.3242	6.0916	5.8759	5.6755
17	15.7179	14.5777	13.5611	12.6523	11.8378	11.1059	10.4466	9.8514	9.3126	8.8237	8.3792	7.9740	7.6039	7.2651	6.9542	6.6685	6.4053	6.1624	5.9377	5.7296
18	16.5623	15.2919	14.1661	13.1657	12.2741	11.4773	10.7632	10.1216	9.5436	9.0216	8.5488	8.1196	7.7291	7.3729	7.0472	6.7487	6.4746	6.2223	5.9897	5.7746
19	17.3983	15.9920	14.7535	13.6593	12.6896	11.8276	11.0591	10.3719	9.7556	9.2014	8.7016	8.2497	7.8399	7.4674	7.1280	6.8178	6.5339	6.2732	6.0333	5.8122
20	18.2260	16.6785	15.3238	14.1339	13.0853	12.1581	11.3356	10.6036	9.9501	9.3649	8.8393	8.3658	7.9380	7.5504	7.1982	6.8775	6.5845	6.3162	6.0700	5.8435
21	19.0456	17.3514	15.8775	14.5903	13.4622	12.4699	11.5940	10.8181	10.1285	9.5136	8.9633	8.4694	8.0248	7.6231	7.2593	6.9288	6.6278	6.3527	6.1009	5.8696
22	19.8570	18.0112	16.4150	15.0292	13.8212	12.7641	11.8355	11.0168	10.2922	9.6487	9.0751	8.5620	8.1016	7.6870	7.3125	6.9731	6.6648	6.3837	6.1268	5.8913
23	20.6604	18.6580	16.9369	15.4511	14.1630	13.0416	12.0612	11.2007	10.4424	9.7715	9.1757	8.6446	8.1695	7.7429	7.3587	7.0113	6.6964	6.4099	6.1486	5.9094
24	21.4558	19.2922	17.4436	15.8568	14.4886	13.3034	12.2722	11.3711	10.5802	9.8832	9.2664	8.7184	8.2297	7.7921	7.3988	7.0442	6.7234	6.4321	6.1668	5.9245
25	22.2434	19.9139	17.9355	16.2470	14.7986	13.5504	12.4693	11.5288	10.7066	9.9847	9.3481	8.7843	8.2829	7.8351	7.4338	7.0726	6.7465	6.4509	6.1822	5.9371
26	23.0232	20.5235	18.4131	16.6221	15.0939	13.7834	12.6536	11.6748	10.8226	10.0770	9.4217	8.8431	8.3300	7.8729	7.4641	7.0971	6.7662	6.4669	6.1951	5.9476
27	23.7952	21.1210	18.8768	16.9828	15.3752	14.0032	12.8258	11.8100	10.9290	10.1609	9.4881	8.8957	8.3717	7.9061	7.4906	7.1182	6.7831	6.4804	6.2060	5.9563
28	24.4596	21.7069	19.3270	17.3296	15.6430	14.2105	12.9867	11.9352	11.0266	10.2372	9.5478	8.9426	8.4086	7.9352	7.5135	7.1364	6.7975	6.4919	6.2151	5.9636
29	25.3164	22.2813	19.7641	17.6631	15.8981	14.4062	13.1371	12.0511	11.1161	10.3066	9.6016	8.9844	8.4412	7.9607	7.5335	7.1520	6.8099	6.5016	6.2228	5.9697
30	26.0658	22.8444	20.1885	17.9837	16.1411	14.5907	13.2777	12.1584	11.1983	10.3696	9.6501	9.0218	8.4701	7.9830	7.5509	7.1656	6.8204	6.5098	6.2292	5.9747
31	26.8077	23.3965	20.6004	18.2920	16.3725	14.7648	13.4090	12.2578	11.2737	10.4269	9.6938	9.0552	8.4957	8.0027	7.5660	7.1772	6.8294	6.5168	6.2347	5.9789
32	27.5423	23.9377	21.0004	18.5885	16.5928	14.9291	13.5318	12.3498	11.3426	10.4790	9.7331	9.0850	8.5183	8.0199	7.5791	7.1872	6.8371	6.5227	6.2392	5.9824
33	28.2696	24.4683	21.3888	18.8736	16.8027	15.0840	13.6466	12.4350	11.4062	10.5264	9.7686	9.1116	8.5383	8.0350	7.5905	7.1959	6.8437	6.5277	6.2430	5.9854
34	28.9897	24.9886	21.7658	19.1476	17.0025	15.2302	13.7538	12.5139	11.4644	10.5694	9.8005	9.1354	8.5560	8.0482	7.6005	7.2034	6.8493	6.5320	6.2462	5.9878
35	29.7027	25.4986	22.1318	19.4112	17.1929	15.3681	13.8540	12.5869	11.5178	10.6086	9.8293	9.1566	8.5717	8.0599	7.6091	7.2098	6.8541	6.5356	6.2489	5.9898
36	30.4086	25.9986	22.4872	19.6646	17.3742	15.4982	13.9477	12.6546	11.5668	10.6442	9.8552	9.1755	8.5856	8.0700	7.6166	7.2153	6.8582	6.5386	6.2512	5.9915

Answers to Even Numbered Exercises and Problems

Chapter 1

2. 3 appliance repairs per hour times $30 = $90 marginal revenue product. Maximum hourly wage equals marginal revenue product or $90.

4. Sara Lee's opportunity cost was Bean Counters CPA at $35,000.

6. They would most likely raise either the discount rate, the federal funds rate, or both. They could also sell more government securities to decrease the money supply.

Chapter 2

2. The memo that Jerry received relates to the strategic overall plan for his company. When Jerry develops a personnel plan he will be working on a functional plan (personnel) designed to support the strategic plan.

4. $6,000 which is your cost. Common stockholders cannot lose more than their initial investment when a company is sued or goes bankrupt.

6. **Strengths** include the fact that Barry has five years of experience, dry cleaning business is already established, assumable lease, fixed rent for next five years, commercial accounts for 20% of business. **Weakness,** none listed. **Opportunities** include fact that business is located in a busy shopping center, population is growing at 6% a year, residential area with residents being professional and wearing suits to work, no new competition because of favorable zoning. **Threats** include competition from price cutting business across the street.

Chapter 3

2. Answer is individualized. No single correct answer.

4. Income statement Davey Jones Family.

Income:		
Salaries	$42,000	
Interest Income	150	
Dividend Income	190	
Total Income		$42,340
Fixed Expenses:		
Mortgage Payment	7,980	
Automobile Payment	3,060	
Student Loan Payment	1,700	
Property Taxes	1,100	
Insurance	2,100	
Income Taxes	9,700	
Total Fixed Expenses		25,640
Variable Expenses:		
Food	2,400	
Transportation	1,200	
Utilities	3,000	
Clothes and personal	2,000	
Recreation and vacation	2,000	
Total Variable Expenses		10,600
Total Expenses		36,240
Disposable Income		$6,100
(Cash balance at end of the year)		

6.

Net Sales	$500,000	
Cost of Goods Sold	250,000	
Gross Profit		250,000
Operating Expenses		
Salaries	100,000	
Rent	24,000	
Utilities	25,000	
Payroll Taxes	25,000	
Insurance	12,000	
Total Operating Expenses		186,000
Operating Income		64,000
Interest Expenses	5,450	
Net Income		$58,550

8. $1,500,000 + $3,675,000 = $5,175,000$ Total Retained Earnings.
$1,000,000 + $12,500,000 + $5,175,000 = $18,675,000$.

Chapter 4

2. **Table 4-3   Balance Sheet, Sample Company**

	1996	Vertical Analysis 1996	1997	Vertical Analysis 1997
Current Assets	7,000,000	46.67%	9,000,000	60.00%
Total Fixed Assets	8,000,000	53.33%	6,000,000	40.00%
Total Assets	15,000,000	100.00%	15,000,000	100.00%
Current Liabilities	$ 3,000,000	20.00%	1,000,000	6.67%
Long Term Debt	4,000,000	26.67%	4,000,000	26.67%
Owner's Equity	8,000,000	53.33%	10,000,000	66.67%
Total Liabilities & Owner's Equity	15,000,000	100.00%	15,000,000	100.00%

4. Public library sources would include Dun's Review, Value Line Investment Survey, Moody's, Standard & Poors, New York Times archives, Wall Street Journal archives, Investor's Business Daily, Barrons, Zack's Financial, and several others that the instructor of the course may have access to. Internet resources include EDGAR, http://finance.yahoo.com gives immediate news stories on companies, stocksmart, the websites of business sections of large national newspapers, and many search engines such as **GOOGLE, CNET, YAHOO, EXCITE, HOT-BOT, ALTA-VISTA,** and several others that the instructor may suggest. We would also include businesswire, prwire, Dow Jones news retrieval, Associated Press, and **EDGAR** online. The most important source is often the company's own home page http://www.starbucks.com/

6. **Table 4-5, Starbucks Corporation Consolidated Balance Sheet**

Values in Thousands except share data

	09/27/98	09/28/97	HORIZONTAL
Cash and cash equivalents	$101,663	$70,126	44.97%
Short-term investments	21,874	83,504	−73.80%
Accounts receivable	50,972	31,231	63.21%
Inventories	143,118	119,767	19.50%
Prepaid expenses and other current assets	11,205	8,763	27.87%
Deferred income taxes, net	8,448	4,164	102.88%
Total current assets	337,280	317,555	6.21%
Joint ventures and other investments	38,917	34,464	12.92%
Property, plant, and equipment, net	600,794	488,791	22.91%
Deposits and other assets	15,764	16,342	−3.54%
Total Assets	$992,755	$857,152	15.82%
Liabilities and Shareholders' Equity			
Current Liabilities:			
Accounts payable	$54,446	$47,987	13.46%
Checks drawn in excess of bank balances	33,634	28,582	17.68%
Accrued compensation and related costs	35,941	25,894	38.80%
Accrued occupancy costs	17,526	12,184	43.84%
Other accrued expenses	37,928	30,829	23.03%
Total current liabilities	179,475	145,476	23.37%
Deferred income taxes, net	18,983	12,946	46.63%
Convertible subordinated debentures	—	165,020	
Commitments and contingencies (notes 5, 9, and 13)			
Shareholders' Equity:			
Common stock—Authorized, 150,000,000 shares; issued and outstanding, 89,633,478 (includes 424,275 common stock units) and 80,559,023 shares, respectively	589,214	391,284	50.58%
Retained earnings, including cumulative translation adjustment of $(6,631) and $(1,511) respectively, and net unrealized holding (loss)/gain on investments of $(532) and $63, respectively	205,083	142,426	43.99%
Total shareholders' equity	794,297	533,710	48.83%
Total	$992,755	$857,152	15.82%

*SECURITIES AND EXCHANGE COMMISSION, Washington DC 20549, FORM 10-K/A, located on the Internet at http://www.edgar-online.com

a. Assets increased by 15.82 percent, total current liabilities increased by 23.37 percent, total liabilities decreased by 38.64 percent and owner's equity increased by 48.83 percent.

b. Yes.

8. a.

Ratio	1998	1997
Operating profit margin	109,216/1,308,702=0.0835	86,199/975,389=0.0884
Net profit margin	68,372/1,308,702=0.0522	55,211/975,389=0.0566
Operating return on assets	109,216/992,755=0.11	86,199/857,152=0.1006
Net return on assets	68,372/992,755=0.0689	55,211/857,152=0.0644
Return on equity	68,372/794,297=0.0861	55,211/533,710=0.1034

b. Operating profit margin means that for every dollar in net sales the company earns a percentage of net sales as a result of operations. Net profit margin means that for every dollar in net sales the company earns a percentage of net sales as a result of operations, paying interest, and taxes. Operating return on assets is the percentage of operating income that each dollar of assets generates. Net return on assets is the percentage of net income that each dollar of assets generates. Return on equity is the percentage of net income generated by each dollar of owner's equity.

c. Starbucks was stable from 1997 to 1998, with respect to profitability. Operating return on assets, net return on assets were stable. However, the return on equity decreased due to a large increase in retained earnings and a lowering of the debt to asset ratio.

10. a.

Ratio	1998	1997
Inventory turnover	578,483/(143,118+119,767)/2=4.4010	Cannot be determined.
Times interest earned	109,216/1,381=79.08	86,199/7,282=11.8373
Total asset turnover	1,308,702/992,755=1.3183	975,389/857,152=1.1379
Fixed asset turnover	1,308,702/655,475=1.9966	975,389/539,637=1.8075

b. The 4.4010 inventory turnover ratio means that inventory is used up on the average of 4.4010 times per year in 1998. The times interest earned ratio means that Starbucks operating income exceeds the interest it has to pay by a multiple of 79.08 in 1998 and 11.8373 in 1997. Total asset turnover indicates that for each dollar of assets committed they generated $1.32 in sales in 1998 and $1.14 in 1997. Fixed asset turnover indicates that for each dollar of fixed assets, Starbucks generated $1.997 in sales in 1998 and $1.81 in sales in 1997. This indicates that of the assets committed, both total and fixed, a sufficient amount of sales is being generated.

c. The student paragraph should incorporate the data from both a and b above. They should discuss the fact that Starbucks operating income could decline 79 times and it could still meet its interest payments.

12. Library assignment, no definitive answer.

14. $EPS = \dfrac{\$1,375,486 - \$1,000,000 \text{ preferred stock dividend}}{3,000,000 \text{ shares of common stock}} = \dfrac{\$375,486}{3,000,000 \text{ shares}}$

$EPS = \$0.1252 \text{ per share}$

Chapter 5

2. a. Jim is more efficient because he gets a higher return on his money.
   b. They are both effective because each one got the desired return.

4. a. Revenues $150,000
       Expenses   <u>110,000</u>
       Profit $ 40,000
   b. Was earning $40,000 with accounting firm so entrepreneurial profit is zero.

6. They can try to declare Chapter 11 bankruptcy, but chances are that they will be denied as they have nothing of value to sell. In this instance they will probably be forced into Chapter 7 bankruptcy and will have to sell any assets of the corporation in order to satisfy their debt. The good news is that they incorporated, so they do not face personal bankruptcy as only the assets of the corporation will be sold to pay off creditors' claims. NOTE: With a small corporation, often the owners must personally guarantee notes and loans. If this is the case, then the two engineers are personally liable for the $150,000 loan.

8. a. CM $= 1 - 0.65 = 0.35$ or 35%
   b. Total fixed costs are $3,350 which is $1,500 + 500 + 100 + 1,250$. BE $=$ FC $\div$ contribution margin $= \$3,350 \div 0.35 = \$9,571.43$.
   c. BE $+$ Profit $= (\$3,350 + \$2,000) \div 0.35 = \$15,285.71$.

   d.

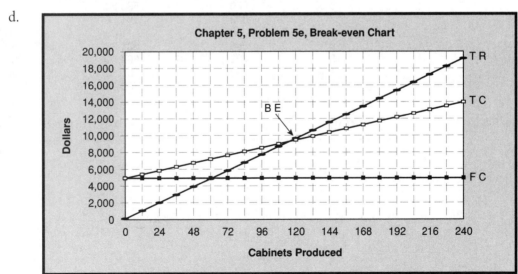

10. a. CM = $70
    b. BEQ = 286 skateboards
    c. BE$ = $45,760
    d. BEQ = 429 skateboards
    e. Monthly revenue = $64,000

Chapter 6

2. a. He should use demographic information on the new community and compare it to the information for his existing health club members. He needs information on traffic patterns, rent, utilities, and other factors that affect general operating expenses and; then compare those to his current successful clubs. He wants sites that compare favorably to his current sites.
   b. Judgmental models, but specifically he would use the historical analogy to determine the specific site. Market research would also be used to determine if the new community's residents have the same general demographic characteristics as his current customers.

4. a. $y = a + bx = 22.2 + 1.6x$
   b. 35
   c. year
   d. demand

6.

Time Period	Actual Sales $(000)	Weighted Moving Average Forecast	Absolute Deviation
1	445		
2	478		
3	525		
4	660	497.06	162.94
5	570	588.18	18.18
6	600	588.53	11.47
7	632	601.76	30.24
8	648	611.65	36.35
9	690	634.82	55.18
10	725	667.41	57.59
11	750	701.12	48.88
12		732.06	
Sum			420.82
n			8.00
MAD			52.60

   a. 732.06
   b. 52.60

8. a. Income Statement

Income statement for current and next year.

Actual this year pro forma next year

Sales	$200,000	$240,000
COG	140,000	168,000
Gross Profit	$ 60,000	$ 2,000
Operating Expenses		
Rent	18,000	18,540
Utilities	8,400	9,240
Insurance	2,000	2,400
Equipment	3,500	3,500
Total Operating Expenses	31,900	33,680
Operating Profit	$ 28,100	$ 38,320
Interest Expense	10,000	9,000
Net Profit (income)	$ 18,100	$ 29,320

b. Percentage change is $[(\text{new} - \text{old}) \div \text{old}] \times 100 = [(29,320 - 18,100)18,100] \times 100 = 61.99\%$.

c. Profit margin = net income/sales. For our current year, profit margin = $18,100/200,000 = 0.0905$, or 9.05%. For our pro forma year, profit margin = $29,320 \div 240,000 = 0.1222$, or 12.22%.

d. In your business, assets and liabilities have historically varied with sales. Assets are normally 80 percent of sales, and liabilities are normally 55 percent of sales. Percentage of sales method equation is:

Δsales$\star$(asset/sales) $- \Delta$sales$\star$(liabilities/sales) $- $ (S2)$\star$(P)$\star$(1-owner payout) = required financing

$40,000 \star 0.80 - \$40,000 \star 0.55 - (240,000) \star (0.1222) \star (1) = $ required financing

$32,000 - \$22,000 - 29,328 = - \$19,328 = $ required financing. Since this figure is negative, the business does not require any external financing, because it has internally financed any buildup in assets. NOTE: If the owner drew $20,000; he would have to have some external financing because there would not be enough money from internal financing to cover the shortfall.

10. a.

Pro Forma Cash Budget to solve Problem 5.a), preceding page

Monthly Cash Receipts

	November	December	January	February	March
Sales	15,000	17,000	15,000	20,000	25,000
Current Month Collection at 20% of Sales	3,000	3,400	3,000	4,000	5,000
Outstanding Current Month Accounts Receivable	12,000	13,600	12,000	16,000	20,000
60% of AR Collected Month Following Sale		7,200	8,160	7,200	9,600
40% of AR Collected 2nd Month Following Sale			4,800	5,440	4,800
Total Receipts			15,960	16,640	19,400

Monthly Cash Payments

Estimated Cash Payments			4,500	5,500	5,200
Total Payments			4,500	5,500	5,200

Monthly Cash Budget

Total Receipts			15,960	16,640	19,400
Total Payments			4,500	5,500	5,200
Net Cash Flow			11,460	11,140	14,200

b. We have 40 percent of February accounts receivable of 16,000, or $6,400, plus 100 percent of March accounts receivable of $20,000, for a total accounts receivable of $26,400.

c. No because all of the cash budgets have a positive balance.

12. $6,037.50 in new financing.

Chapter 7

2. $205.48

4. a. The total annual cost to Jane is $50 per month times 12 months for equipment and bank charges, or $600.

b. She would save $590 in bad check losses. She would also earn $(3 \div 365) = 0.001$ daily interest times 362 days, worth of interest times $400 average checking balance, and she makes an additional $11.90. Therefore, the benefits are $600.90 and the costs are $600.

c. With this problem, it is a toss-up. Would she lose some customers by not accepting checks and only accepting debit cards? If she lost just one customer whose checks were good due to this new policy, her costs of $600 would definitely outweigh her benefits.

6. Accounts receivable turn over = 4, Collection days = 91.25 or 92. With net 30, he is collecting in 92 days. He should age accounts receivable and determine if some accounts are uncollectable or have to be turned over to a collection agency.

8. a. 290.3069 or rounded up to 291.

b. Since the EOQ is greater than 200 hammers we would order the EOQ and take advantage of the quantity discount.

10. a. Roses and Carnations make up approximately 75 percent of our total cost of inventory, they are the A items.
   b. C items that make up approximately 10 percent of our total cost are bud vases, glass bowls, wrapping paper, ribbons, and pins.
12. a. 2 percent discount if paid within ten days, otherwise the entire amount is due within 30 days.
   b. 3 percent discount if paid within 15 days, otherwise the entire amount is due within 60 days.
   c. the entire amount is due by day 40.
   d. a. 36.73 percent, b. 24.74 percent, and no effective rate for c.
14. a. $20,566.66.
   b. $21,423.60
   c. 101.39 percent

Chapter 8

2. 3.89 years
4. a. $4,876.71
   b. 10.25%
6. $fv = 760 \left(1 + \dfrac{.06}{12}\right)^{120} = 760(1.8194) = 1,382.74$
8.
$(1 + i)^n - 1 = \left(1 + \dfrac{0.0645}{12}\right)^{12} - 1 = (1.0054)^{12} - 1 = 1.0664 - 1 = 0.0664 = 6.64\%$

10. The dollar lost 32 cents in purchasing power.
12. $FV = A\left\{\left(\dfrac{(1 + i)^{n+1} - 1}{i}\right) - 1\right\} = \$2,000(20.2840) = \$40,567.91$

14. $48,347.46
16. $927.01
18. $57,011.31
20. a. $810,560.40   b. $875,405.23 c. $1,284,594.77
22. a. 30 year, $1,467.53, 15 year $1,911. 30 or savings of $443.77 per month.
   b. 30 year interest $328,310, 15 year $184,276.80 savings $104,398.20
   c. no correct answer depends on student circumstance.
24. $9,841,862.97
26. 35.12%
28. 8.66%
30. a. 9 years   b. 6 years   c. 12 years

Chapter 9

2. $130.00

3.
$$WACC = \left(\frac{12,000}{15,000}\right)(0.08) + \left(\frac{3,000}{15,000}\right)(0.10) = 0.084 \text{ or } 8.4\%$$

6. year   Amount   PVF   PV

Year	Amount	PVF	PV
1	$21,000	0.9091	$19,090.91
2	29,000	0.8264	23,966.94
3	36,000	0.7513	27,047.33
4	16,000	0.6830	10,928.22
5	8,000	0.6209	4,967.37
			$86,000.77

    a. $86,000.77

    b. $20,000.77

    c. 22.54%

    d. 2.44 years

    e. 1.3030

8.   a. $300

    b. $7,348.10

    c. $16,095.75

    d. $122.06

10. a. 4 years.

    b. $15,163.15

    c. $16,000

    d. ($836.85)

    e. 0.9477

    f. 7.93%

    g. 25%

12. a. $4,800   b. $355.91   c. $63,956   d. $94,910.08

    e. $30,953.24   f. 1.4840

    h. 0.54 years h. Recommend because it is profitable.

14. a. 8 stores b. 21 stores, but only 15 have positive NPVs.

Chapter 10

2. a. The proposal would be for the city to issue general revenue municipal bonds.

    b. Interest payments made on municipal bonds are exempt from federal income tax. Additionally, since the bonds are being issued by the city, the interest is also free from state and local income taxes.

4. a. Because Sarah is young, she should definitely invest in mutual funds. We would ask her to evaluate her own tolerance for risk because, at her age, she may have a relatively high tolerance for risk. We would probably advise a diversified mutual fund portfolio, with a percentage of her money going into an aggressive growth (small cap stock) fund, some in a long-term growth (blue chip stock) fund, and some in a global fund. She may also consider a balanced fund as well as sector funds.

   b. Grandpa Russ is seventy years old and typically would have a very low risk tolerance. He would primarily be interested in protecting his principal and minimizing his risk. This would best be served by government bonds, government bond mutual funds, and CDs.

6. In order for him to invest in the Savings Incentive Match Plan for Employees (SIMPLE) he has to have fewer than one-hundred employees and each employee has to have received at least $5,000 in employee compensation in each of the past two years. The company must match, dollar for dollar, the employee's contribution up to 3 percent of salary or put in 2 percent of salary for all eligible employees even if they do not contribute. Each employee's contribution limit is $6,000 per annum.

8. a. He will tell Larry to establish the will because he doesn't want him to die intestate. The estate planner would want Larry to have a written document to indicate Larry's wishes with regard to the disposition of his assets upon death.

   b. We would recommend that Larry put his assets into a revocable living trust. Since assets in a trust do not have to go through probate, money will be saved for his heirs as probate costs are a percentage of the gross estate.

10. $568.50 + $502.57 = $1,071.07

12. 3,000,000 shares

14. a. $24 b. $2,400,000 c. 52 cents d. $2,600,000

16. a. She can borrow $8,000 but only would borrow $7,000 plus commission.

   b. $35 per share profit.

   c. She has to pay the broker back the $7,000 plus commission.

   d. She lost her $8,000 investment + $2,000 for the broker's commission.

18. $1,718,284.78

Case Study

Hannah's Donut Shop: A Case Study of Performance, Measurement, and Manufacturing Design in a Service Environment

Reprinted by permission, Journal of Systems Improvement, a journal of the International Society for Systems Improvement. WINTER/SPRING 1995, Vol. 1, No. 1.

Abstract

This article represents a one-year case study of Hannah's Donut Shop, an independent retail and wholesale donut shop, located in Phoenix, Arizona. The shop had shown marginal returns or losses during its first five years of operation. The manufacturing operation most closely resembles a job shop, in which small batches are produced to satisfy customer demand. The case study involves a one-year application of the Five Focusing Steps of the Theory of Constraints (TOC). Results of this application resulted in sales increases of 62 percent, operating profit increases of 485 percent, and net profit increases of 531 percent.

Introduction

We are including the case study on Hannah's Donut Shop because it provides you with a factual account of some of the problems that small companies must overcome to survive and be successful. We used theory of constraints (TOC) to analyze the problems that the shop experienced. This book, however, is not about TOC; it is about small business finance. The case study should be read as the true life story of a small business and what the owners did to make it successful. One of the things that you will learn from this account is that a business has no memory. Because of changes in customer preferences and employees, items and procedures that are not written down and described well tend to be forgotten. When quality deteriorates, customers are lost. We therefore provide some of the measures that the shop undertook to ensure consistency of product. Readers who have no interest in processes may omit reading the section, "Description of the Manufacturing Process." Readers who are interested in learning more about TOC should check out the references at the end of this case study.

Background

When developing a case study of a small business, it is important to determine the background of the owner, and her reasons for beginning the business enterprise. An interview with Hannah follows:

I am an educator by trade, and I enjoyed the field very much. Everywhere we went I was always able to find a job within religious school education as I am not a public school educator. In 1969, during our twelfth year as an Air Force family, Phil went to Vietnam which brought about tremendous changes in my life and the lives of my family. In the days that followed there were many lonely hours of the day, but it seemed that one in particular was morning coffee. We really enjoyed that time together to discuss the coming day, work schedule, children's programs, et cetera. When Phil left for Vietnam, mornings were intolerable. I would drop my daughter off at preschool, but I couldn't stand the concept of coming home to an empty house. So I would stop in at this donut shop as they are wonderful places to go for breakfast. Donut people are very special people because there is a warmth, kindness and acceptance that you find in donut shop patrons. When you break bread together and eat together, you have made a friend. First of all you are sitting at a counter rather than a lonely table and you're with the lady at the right, or the gentleman on your left. You are sharing something that you can say, "Wow, doesn't this taste great, or isn't this good, or did you read this in the paper?" Somehow, it's fast and it's quick but there is a very comfortable feeling. It's one of the very few places that a woman can walk in and sit down, talk to another adult, and not appear to be looking for anything else. You're just going to a donut shop for a nice cup of coffee and a donut, and then you are off and you feel that you can face the day.

So every day for the rest of the year that my husband was in Vietnam, I would go to the donut shop. And after a while you get to know the names of the people. You know that it's just "Hi Jim, hi Mary." If you miss one day, they want to know who's sick or what's wrong. It's a very interesting extended family, but keep in mind that you don't know anyone's last name. There is no great depth to this friendship, but there is a certain amount of caring that goes on. Everyone knew my husband was in Vietnam, and they knew how many days were left until he was coming home. When he finally returned home, after a certain amount of time had passed, it was off to the donut shop to meet all my new donut shop friends, so they could personally welcome him home as well.

Then we were off, back to our Air Force tours and on to the next city and the next donut shop. I was still in education but I was hooked on donuts. Now however, every time I would go into a donut shop, the only difference was I began to say, "If it was my shop I would do it this way, or that way. Or if I were the owner of this donut shop I would do it a different way" and my husband patiently listened. As Phil approached retirement, I was offered a wonderful job in Phoenix. He felt that since I had travelled with him for twenty-three moves in twenty-three years, maybe it was his turn to follow me.

So we came to Phoenix and within the first several years of our Phoenix stay I was happy with my job. As the aggravation and frustration with the job grew, the donuts started to look better and happier. And, my coming home day after day, saying, "You know, if I only had a donut shop." So finally he said one day, "Look, you know, either we're going to look into it and do it, or forget it as we're getting too old to keep talking about it." So we looked into it and found this franchise that I loved. I mean, they had this fabulous product, this wonderful donut.

Historical Background

This is a case study of Hannah's Donut Shop (HDS), a small retail and wholesale donut shop located in Phoenix, Arizona. HDS began operation in December 1985 as a member of a regional franchise. Hannah had considered purchasing a donut shop and decided to obtain experience in the industry prior to making a purchase decision. She worked for six months in a regional franchise donut shop. When she became convinced that this was what she wanted to do, she and her husband signed the franchise agreement and she opened her own shop. By December 1986, HDS was in trouble. The franchiser had a new chief executive officer (CEO) who attempted to expand the franchise from a regional chain to a national chain. Franchiser management concentrated on expansion, and franchiser service to HDS became nonexistent. At this point, HDS began to keep detailed records of conversations with the franchiser, and cost differentials between franchiser product and independent purchase of similar products with comparable quality. HDS determined that operating with the franchiser's raw materials plus franchise fees resulted in a 13 percent increase in raw material cost as compared to purchasing the product as an independent shop. Also, the franchiser changed vendors three times during the first eighteen months of operation. This resulted in changes in quality of product and eliminated standardization of product among shops, one of the primary advantages of franchising.

On February 20, 1987, the franchiser filed for Chapter 11 bankruptcy. HDS entered into suit, claiming breach of contract on the part of the franchiser, and ceased paying franchise and advertising fees to the franchiser. The court determined that the franchiser had in fact breached the contract and released HDS from all obligations to the franchiser in May 1988. Hannah changed the name of her shop and became an independent. The financial position of HDS at that time indicated that accumulated losses for the first two years of operation were $97,000.

Now HDS had to select its own vendors for product. The owners believed that quality and service were the two primary factors relating to success. They therefore tested products from the five primary vendors in the metropolitan area and selected two vendors who they believed provided the best quality. One vendor was selected for all donut products and another for muffin and paper products.

Up to this point, the HDS owners could be described as following an "analyzer" strategy for their business [5]. They attempted to conform to industry standards and kept their books in accordance with traditional cost accounting methodology. HDS had previously determined that the retail marketing area for their product was within three miles of the store on weekends, and extended to ten miles north of the shop on weekdays, when they sold primarily to commuters. The shop was located on the commuting side of the road for morning traffic, and 90 percent of all product was sold on a daily basis prior to 10 A.M.

Environmental Changes

The environment had changed significantly between the time the shop opened in 1985 and 1991. In 1985 a retail, freestanding donut shop could make a profit because these locales were virtually the only place that donuts could be purchased. By 1991 four new supermarkets that had in-store bakeries had been built within Hannah's retail marketing area. These stores offered a convenience factor with which the freestanding shop could not compete. The shopper could purchase donut products at the supermarket and did not have to make another stop. However, shoppers were willing to make the extra stop if the donut shop had what was perceived by the customer to be a superior product.

In January 1991 the owners read *The Goal* and became interested in its applicability to the shop [3]. In June 1991 Hannah's husband attended a Jonah conference on the theory of constraints (TOC) held at the University of Georgia. Upon his return, he and Hannah decided that TOC, if it was as powerful as indicated in the course, should be applicable to Hannah's Donut Shop.

Changes in Measurement Systems

From the time that the shop became an independent enterprise until June 1991, the owners were using traditional cost accounting procedures. Cost of goods was determined by adding raw material costs and direct labor costs (salaries of production workers). The results of these bookkeeping procedures indicated that cost of sales was approximately 68 percent of sales as seen in Table 1. The generation of selling prices for finished product using these procedures resulted in noncompetitive prices.

One of the first actions taken by the owners was to direct the bookkeeper to change the accounting system to one that conformed to the throughput principles of the theory of constraints [2, 4]. All production wages were moved to the operating expense category, and the cost-of-goods section of the income statement now contained only raw material costs and the cost of paper goods that were sold as part of the product (packaging, etc.) moving wages to operating expenses did not, of course, alter the bottom line (net profit) on the income statement, but it did allow the owners to determine a true and relevant cost of goods and to develop pricing strategies based on this actual variable cost (Table 1).

An analysis of the two break-even charts, using the first six months of 1991 data, indicates how powerful this concept is when using break-even analysis and the standard break-even formula (Table 1 and Figure 1).

$$\text{Break–even dollars} = \frac{\text{Fixed costs}}{1 - \text{Variable costs as a percentage of sales}}$$

Table 1 Income Statement, January 1 through June 30, 1991

Hannah's Donut Shop
Income Statement, January 1, 1991, through June 30, 1991

Cost Accounting Method			Theory of Constraints Method		
	$000	*Percentage of Sales*		*$000*	*Percentage of Sales*
Sales			Sales		
Retail sales	46.2	49.1	Retail sales	46.2	49.1
Wholesale sales	47.9	50.9	Wholesale sales	47.9	50.9
Total sales	94.1	100.0	Total sales	94.1	100.0
Cost of sales			Cost of sales		
Raw materials	32.1	34.1	Raw materials	32.1	34.1
Production labor	31.8	33.8			
Total cost of sales	63.9	67.9	Total cost of sales	32.1	34.1
Gross profit	30.2	32.1	Gross profit = Sales −Raw materials =Throughput	62.0	65.9
Operating expenses	27.9	29.6	Operating expenses	59.7	63.4
Net profit	2.3	2.4	Net profit	2.3	2.4

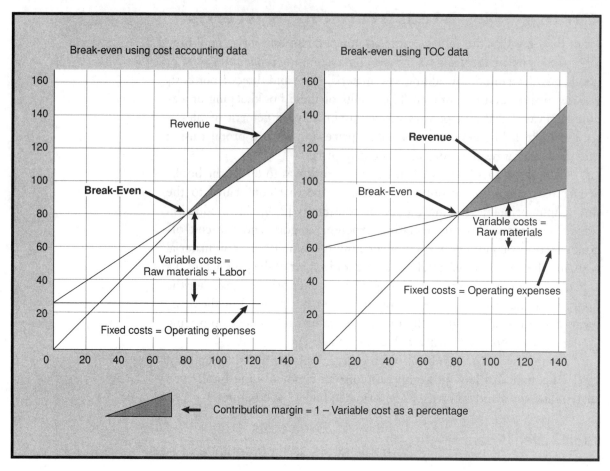

FIGURE 1
Break-Even Analysis using data from Table 1

There exists a true break-even point, of no profit and no loss, for any business. Under a given set of conditions, this point will be the same regardless of the categorization of expenses, labor, and so forth. But, as Figure 1 graphically shows, the a priori *perception* as to where that point will occur when the business is up and running depends on the categorizations. A firm using traditional break-even point analysis could easily delude itself into thinking it could profitably compete at lower volumes than are actually possible. Such delusion could lead to losses that would only be found when after-the-fact variance reports brought reality to bear on the projected (fictitious) profits. In the same manner, a firm could easily misinterpret the true marginal cost of a product, which could lead to noncompetitive pricing of its product.

As Figure 1, which uses the 1991 data from Table 1, shows, the break-even point for standard cost accounting is $86,900; with TOC, it is $90,590. It would appear that use of TOC yields break-even points that are unreasonable. We would contend that TOC presents a true picture because it considers production labor as a fixed cost, rather than as a variable cost that increases at a linear rate with production. Additionally, when one considers the difference in contribution margin (cost accounting, 32.1 percent; TOC, 65.9 percent), one realizes that if operating expenses can be held in check, then the firm can make a much higher profit with significantly fewer sales. For example, if the firm wanted to make $10,000 in profit, it would have to sell $118,000 + using cost accounting, but only $105,000 + using TOC. Realizing this, we see that the TOC firm is in a much better position to land contracts by using competitive bids that reflect actual costs rather than inflated accounting costs. Using the new figures, HDS was able to adjust prices to become more competitive in the wholesale arena. This resulted in large increases in throughput dollars and net profits, as indicated in the comparison of 1991 and 1992 data for the first year of operation under the throughput model (Table 2).

Changes in Strategy

HDS had been selling some product at the wholesale level, as do most competitors in this industry. Baked goods are sold to retailing customers (e.g., convenience stores) who resell the product. The traditional practices of the industry require the bakery to repurchase all unsold merchandise. For example, when $10 of product is delivered on a given day, and $4 of product remains unsold, the vendor will credit the reseller with $4 and only bill $6. This has a significant effect on throughput (defined as sales minus raw material costs) [2]. Because raw material costs are now correctly seen to represent approximately 30 percent of sales price, the gross profit on such a "sale with returns" would net $3 throughput ($10 revenue–$3 COGS–$4 returns = $3), not the original $7 (10 − 3 = 7). Interesting to note is the fact that, prior to looking at the situation from a throughput viewpoint, the tradi-

Table 2 Income Statement, First Six Months 1991 and 1992

	Hannah's Donut Shop Income Statements for Periods Indicated			
Category	Jan 1 through Jun 30, 1992	Percentage of Sales	Jan 1 through Jun 30, 1991	Percentage of Sales
Revenues				
Retail sales	72,335	45.5	46,197	49.1
Wholesale sales	86,516	54.5	47,878	50.9
Total revenues	158,851	100.0	94,075	100.0
Cost of sales				
Raw materials	50,164	31.6	32,091	34.1
Total cost of sales	50,164	31.6	32,091	34.1
Gross profit (loss)	108,687	68.4	61,984	65.9
Operating expenses	90,056	56.7	59,337	63.1
Operating profit	18,631	11.7	2,647	2.8
Interest expense	(897)	−0.6	(388)	−0.4
Net profit (loss)	17,734	11.2	2,259	2.4

tional analysis would have shown zero dollars as the result, because the cost of goods was previously considered to be about 60 percent of sales ($10 revenue − $6 COGS − $4 returns = $0). In any case, the throughput decreases because of the returns. Another significant factor relates to the fact that donut products (finished goods) have a very short shelf life (twelve hours for raised products to fifteen hours for cake products). Therefore all returned products are scrapped, because they have no residual value.

This "scrap factor," per industry standards, does not apply in cases of wholesale sales to end users (e.g., hospitals, industrial cafeterias, and restaurants). Purchases by these institutions are final, with no allowances for returns. HDS determined that throughput increases could best be achieved by concentrating on this second category of sales and by stopping all sales to convenience stores, unless the convenience store agreed to a no-buy-back policy.

The shop had actually shown a pattern of declining wholesale sales between 1988 and 1990, during which time sales declined from $108,853 to $92,728, a decrease of 14.8 percent. This was because several wholesale accounts had canceled because of product inconsistency, even though new accounts were being solicited. HDS realized there was a significant problem. Before the new market segmentation strategy of selling only to customers who would not require buy-back could be implemented, significant improvements in quality had to be realized.

In addition, if significant production increases could not be accomplished by the night shift, no additional accounts could be established. The night shift, with current production methods, could only produce $500 to $550 worth of finished goods per shift. Because donuts are primarily served in the morning, wholesale accounts had to be delivered by 6 A.M. each day or customers would refuse the product. An additional shift would not be added at an earlier time because the product would exceed the shelf life of finished goods. The night shift worked from 8 P.M. to 4 A.M.

As previously indicated, the owners had complete confidence in the quality of their raw materials and realized that the inconsistency in product must be in the internal production procedures. They set out to solve this problem through use of the five-step focusing process contained within TOC [4]. Up to this point, HDS had been using the production methods established by the franchiser, including personal assignments and batch sizes. Most of the procedures given by the franchiser appeared to be standard for the industry, as evidenced by the comments of HDS's bakers who had previously worked for other bakeries (Dunkin Donuts, Winchels, etc.). The standard procedure was to mix the minimum number of batches, based on the shelf life of the raised donut as it sat on the baker's table, or based on bowl capacity for cake donuts.

There are essentially two different processes used in the production of donuts, one for cake donuts and one for raised donuts (see Figure 2, and

Description of the Manufacturing Process, located at the end of this case study). There are three people who work the night shift at HDS. These people and their duties are described as follows:

- The **baker,** who traditionally is responsible for cutting raised product, serving as shift supervisor, and setting the pace for the night crew.
- The **fryer,** who is responsible for frying all donut products in a machine known as the fryer.
- The **finisher,** who applies frosting and toppings (nuts, coconut, candy sprinkles, etc.), and fills donuts after they are processed by the fryer. The finisher assists the fryer with glazing product, waits on retail customers, and may assist the baker by operating the mixer and performing any other duties as required by the baker. The finisher normally comes to work two hours after the fryer and baker begins the bake so that there is sufficient product to process.

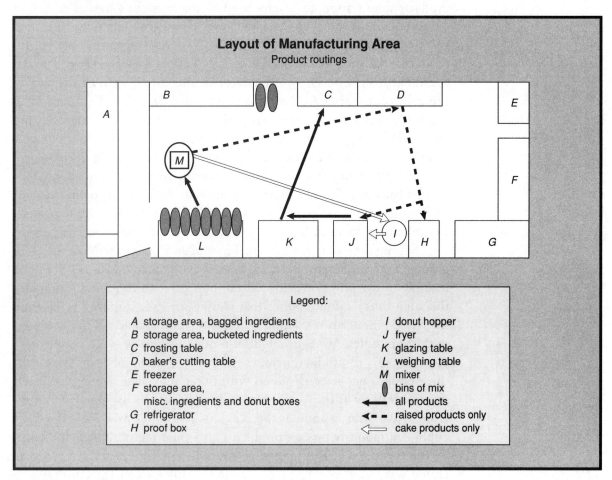

FIGURE 2
Layout of Manufacturing Area

Implementing the Five–Step Process and Drum Buffer Rope

Step One

Step one of the TOC focusing process [2, 4] is to **identify the system's constraint(s).** The owners determined that the fryer (the physical machine) was definitely the constraint. All processes prior to the fryer had excess capacity, and components to be processed by the fryer were continuously in queue. Therefore the **fryer became the drum** in this process.

Step Two

The owners then concentrated on the second step of the process, which is to **decide how to exploit the system's constraint(s).** Several of the products were waiting to be processed by the fryer for a period of well in excess of their shelf life. This resulted in the fryer's spending some time processing products of inferior quality. If the fryer was to process only quality products, and process them continuously, several adjustments had to be made. The first, however, involved **determining the length of the buffer** (optimum batch sizes for both cake and raised products). Optimum cake batch size was set at twenty-two pounds eight ounces via the following analysis: Because the fryer can process three pounds of cake in four minutes, and thirty minutes is the maximum time the product can sit in the queue prior to processing (without losing quality), the maximum number of process batches is 7.5 (30 minutes/4 minutes = 7.5 three-pound process batches). With a three-pound process batch, 22.5 pounds is the maximum cake batch size that can be processed by the fryer in thirty minutes.

Setting the batch size for raised product is a little more complex. The product rises in the proof box for twenty minutes, and can stay in queue (outside of the proof box) for ten minutes prior to frying. This provides the same thirty-minute buffer that is used for cake donuts. Frying time for raised product is two minutes. Thus fifteen batches can be processed in thirty minutes. Average weight of product in queue is 2.5 pounds, because the mix of product includes about the same number of items with three pounds per screen as items with two pounds per screen. The batch size was thus set at thirty-seven pounds eight ounces. If these batches arrived at the fryer as soon as the previous batch was processed, the fryer could continuously process product. This would require **tying the rope to the fryer** and redefining individual tasks to ensure that the fryer (machine) was never idle. These procedures would exploit the constraint in an optimum way.

Step Three

The next obvious step, according to TOC, is to **subordinate everything else to the decision made in the previous step.** This was accomplished by reviewing all duties performed by the fryer (in this case the person doing the frying). The normal process was for the fryer to mix a batch of cake, fry the product, and mix the next batch of cake. While the fryer was frying the first batch, the baker (bakers typically concentrate on producing only raised product) would put on the first batch of raised dough (normally a fifty-pound batch). Using this process, the fryer was spending approximately twenty minutes out of each hour measuring and mixing product. In addition, the baker often had fifty pounds of raised product waiting to be fried, while the fryer was still concentrating on cake products.

The Change Process

One of the first steps was to provide the baker with a copy of *The Goal* [3] and let her read it at her own pace. Changes in duties were often suggested by her; other changes were directed by the owners only after the owners had worked the night shift with the crew to determine how actual flow conformed to theoretical flow (this was essentially a pilot production run). The resulting process involved the following changes:

1. The baker mixes all products for the fryer, rather than the fryer mixing the product.
2. When the fryer is down to six pounds of cake product in the hopper (approximately eight minutes' worth of processing time), the baker mixes the next batch of cake product. This procedure ties the rope to the fryer.
3. To keep the fryer (machine) operating continuously, the baker or finisher continues to process product while the fryer (person) is on break.
4. The baker begins mixing raised dough when the fryer is halfway through processing the next-to-last batch of cake product.
5. Premixed raised products are placed in the proof box by the baker when the fryer starts processing the last batch of cake product.
6. The raised dough now mixes for fifteen minutes, rests in the bowl for twenty minutes, rests on the table for twenty minutes, and is ready to be cut into various raised products fifty-five minutes after the mixing process began.
7. As raised product is processed by the baker, it is placed in the proof box, and it is ready to fry twenty minutes later.
    Note: *Returning to step 3, the fryer has approximately one hour and fifteen minutes of processing time when the baker begins mixing the raised*

> *dough—fifteen minutes for the next-to-last batch of cake product, thirty minutes for the last batch of cake product, and thirty minutes for the fritters. It also takes one hour and fifteen minutes from the time the raised product begins mixing until the product is ready to fry.*

8. The baker, while waiting for the dough to rise on the table, measures out the next batch of raised product and places it in the bowl at the mixer. When the batch is ready to cut, the baker turns on the mixer. It takes approximately forty minutes for the baker to cut the batch of raised dough into product.

9. Before the cut is finished, the next batch of raised dough is placed on the table.

10. Steps 5 through 9 continue until all of the baking requirements are completed. These steps are required to tie the rope for the raised product.

Step Four

Step four (**elevate the system's constraint[s]**) of the five focusing steps was not used because the constraint was broken by the exploitation and subordination process.

Step Five

Step five of the TOC focusing process indicates the following: **if, in the previous steps, a constraint has been broken,** then one should **go back to step one, but do not allow inertia to** take effect and **cause a system's constraint,** because TOC is a process of continuous improvement.

Results

After we accomplished the first three steps of the TOC focusing process, the following results were noted. Potential production per shift increased from $500 to $1,000 with no additional operating expense. This allowed the owners to establish a goal of soliciting an additional $500 per day in wholesale accounts. If more than $500 per day in wholesale accounts was realized, and these accounts could be serviced prior to 6 A.M., then additional sales could be accomplished by shifting some of the night bake, which included retail product, to the day shift. The night shift could generate just enough retail product to open the store and stock the shelves, and the day shift would bake fresh product for retail sales during the day.

Training the night crew and establishing a change in measurement systems were critical for success of the process; these efforts took the owners approximately three months. Changes in measurement included paying the baker a salary rather than an hourly wage, notifying employees that they would share in a bonus every six months that was equal to 10 percent of total profit, and paying the baker overtime if she worked in excess of eight hours in a shift because of the volume of the bake. After implementation of these procedures, the night shift was actually finishing its work in six hours, rather than eight, and the product quality was consistently high.

Improvement in quality could be accurately measured by the amount of shortening consumed in the process. As indicated in Description of the Manufacturing Process (at the end of this case study), when a raised donut is overproofed, it absorbs more shortening. The same is true when cake donut batter stays in queue too long and the temperature rises (which is the normal situation, because the hopper for cake donuts is physically located between the proof box and the fryer, as you can see in Figure 2). Shortening consumption decreased by 30 percent after the new process was instituted, resulting in a 2.5 percent decrease in cost of goods while simultaneously increasing the product quality. Thus in this case, the cost of improving quality was actually negative.

Shifting Constraints

The TOC model is still being applied at the shop, and it has been used several times, because the constraint has been shifting between the shop and the market. In July 1991, one of Hannah's major accounts notified her that they were going to change vendors. Rather than accepting this, the situation that had existed prior to June 1991, Hannah asked what it would take to keep the account. The customer stated that the problem was with the muffins that were provided by the shop. They were too dry and did not have a long enough shelf life. Hannah's customer in this case was a major hotel that served breakfast to its patrons as part of the room cost. Hannah asked for one week, and stated that if she did not provide a superior product by that time, then she would understand being terminated as a vendor.

Hannah called per primary vendor and asked for the moistest muffin mix with the longest shelf life. The vendor introduced and demonstrated a superior product that had a three-day, rather than eighteen-hour, shelf life. Hannah baked several dozen muffins and provided them to the customer for taste testing. Not only did the customer stay, but muffin production and throughput increased between July 1991 and December 1992 by 1,000 percent at the retail level (from 4 dozen per week to 42 dozen per week) and by 675 percent at the wholesale level (from 28 dozen per week to 217 dozen per week). Due to this increase in muffin production, the oven became a constraint, and in August 1992, this constraint was elevated by the purchase of another oven.

Due to the three-day shelf life, and the fact that wholesale muffins are baked to order and retail muffins are maintained at a level where they are baked and sold daily, there is no waste in this product. All sales result in throughput because HDS carries no more than twenty-four hours' worth of finished goods inventory for an item with a seventy-two-hour shelf life.

The shop landed two large accounts in January 1992, the service and quality were such that these customers notified others, and by March 1992, Hannah had a waiting list of wholesale customers. The ability to deliver product to customers with current delivery vehicles became a constraint. The shop purchased another delivery vehicle and established two routes in the greater metropolitan area after determining that the increase in operating expense (monthly costs of operating the new vehicle) would be more than offset by the increase in throughput. During the last year, Hannah has more than doubled the number of wholesale customers (from fifteen to thirty-five) without losing any accounts. All deliveries are being made between 1:30 A.M. and 6 A.M.

Summary

The shop has been operating under theory of constraints principles for just over one year. The results, using data from 1991 (prior to TOC) and 1992 (after implementation), are shown in Table 3. These results indicate that the theory of constraints can be applied to the service industry (quasi-manufacturing sector) and result in significant improvements. The application of the focusing steps of the theory can be easily seen and understood in this simple environment. The theory is thus seen in its simplicity, and the steps taken by the shop owners are illustrated for the benefit of those who would apply this new theory to their own industry. The three measures of TOC, net profit, ROI, and cash (a necessary condition, not a goal), have increased significantly.

Table 3 Results of TOC Implementation, First Year

	Hannah's Donut Shop		
	Income Statements for Periods Indicated		
Category	**Jan 1 through Dec. 31, 1992**	**Jan 1 through Dec. 31, 1991**	**Percentage Change**
Sales			
Retail sales	149,618	96,183	55.55
Wholesale sales	177,878	106,441	67.11
Total sales	327,496	202,624	61.63
Cost of sales			
Raw materials	103,020	68,516	50.36
Total cost of sales	103,020	68,516	50.36
Gross profit (loss)	224,476	134,108	67.38
Operating expenses	187,549	127,264	47.37
Operating profit	40,038	6,844	485.01
Interest expense	3,111	993	213.29
Net profit (loss)	36,927	5,851	531.12
ROI	87.99%	30.94%	
Cash	15,670	3,112	403.53

Application of the theory resulted in the owner's shifting from being analyzers to being "prospectors" [5] and from a "cost world" to a "throughput world" thinking process [2].

Description of the Manufacturing Process

Cake Donut Process

Raw material for cake donuts comes premixed in bags; the only things that is added is water. Each type of cake donut has a different mix-water ratio, and each has a specified mixing time and resting time. For example: The recipe for a plain cake donut requires four pounds eight ounces of mix to two pounds of water (2.25/1 ratio), to be mixed for forty-five seconds in second gear and forty-five seconds in third gear, with no resting time. However, the recipe for a devil's food donut calls for three pounds of mix to one pound eight ounces of water (2/1 ratio), to be mixed for one minute in second gear and one minute in third gear, and to rest for five minutes. The approximate yield is one dozen donuts for each pound of mix. Bowl capacity is twenty-five pounds of mix.

The process used in Hannah's Donut Shop is as follows: Mix product (M), move to hopper (I), and place mix in hopper. The hopper holds the mix while it is hand cranked into the fryer (J). The variation in temperature between the mix and fryer is critical. The fryer is normally set to 375 degrees Fahrenheit; the mix should be 73 degrees Fahrenheit when it enters the fryer. This mix temperature is accomplished during the mixing process by measuring the temperature of the mix and adjusting the temperature of the water to provide an overall temperature of 73 degrees. The frying process takes approximately 3 1/2 minutes—one minute to crank three dozen donuts into the fryer, where they fry for one minute; thirty seconds to turn the donuts over; and another one minute for frying on the second side. The donuts are then removed from the fryer, at which point they are either glazed (K) or placed next to the frosting table (C) for finishing.

Cake Donut Quality Problems

The cake donut batter has a shelf life of approximately thirty minutes. If it sits for longer than this, there are two factors that affect quality. If the temperature of the batter rises, the donut flattens out in the fryer and resembles a pancake with a hole in the middle; also, this mix will take on additional shortening and the resulting donut will be greasy. If the temperature of the batter falls, the donut will ball up and become quite thick; frying time will have to be increased, because the center of the donut will be raw if the donut is fried only for the normal two minutes.

Raised Donut Process

HDS uses a raised donut product that uses the following ingredients: raised donut base (mix), unbleached bread flour, yeast, and water. The ingredients are added to the mixing bowl and mixed for fifteen minutes (*M*). The dough is left in the mixing bowl to rise for twenty minutes. The dough is then placed on the baker's table (*D*), cut into loaves, and covered. It then rises for another twenty minutes. The dough is then rolled out and cut into end product (donuts, filled donuts, long johns, etc.). After being cut, the product is placed in the proof box (*H*) for approximately twenty minutes. The proof box is a steam cabinet for donuts. With the increased heat and humidity, the donut rises in approximately twenty minutes. It also maintains its moisture content as a result of the humidity. After proofing, the product is fried (*J*) for forty-five seconds on each side, with approximately thirty seconds required to turn the product. The product is then either glazed (*K*) or frosted (*C*).

Raised Donut Quality Problems

Raised dough has a table shelf life of approximately one hour. However, an experienced baker can normally roll and cut fifty pounds of raised dough in thirty minutes. Two to three dozen raised items (depending on product) are placed on a frying screen and then placed in the proof box. When donuts stay in the proof box for an extended period, they develop small air pockets. These pockets will absorb shortening when the donut is fried, and the product will be greasy. The standard procedure is to remove the product from the proof box after twenty minutes and place it on a rack for frying. However, if the product sits out of the proof box for an extended period (this varies with temperature and humidity of the bakery), the product loses moisture and shrinks. The result is end product of varying sizes (quality).

References

1. Fearon, H. E., W. A. Ruch, and C. D. Wieters. *Fundamentals of Production: Operations Management.* St. Paul: West Publishing Company, 1989.

2. Goldraft, E. M. *Theory of Constraints.* Croton-on-Hudson, N.Y.: North River Press, 1990.

3. Goldratt, E. M., and J. Cox. *The Goal.* Rev. ed. Croton-on-Hudson, N.Y.: North River Press, 1992.

4. Goldratt, E. M., and R. E. Fox, *The Race.* Croton-on-Hudson, N.Y.: North River Press, 1990.

5. Miles, R. E., and C. C. Snow. *Organization Strategy: Structure and Process.* New York: McGraw-Hill, 1978.

Glossary

10-K   See Form 10-K.

401k plans   Retirement plans established to accept employee contributions via salary reductions. Employers may match a portion of the employee's contribution. The 401k is also a vehicle for distributing profit sharing contributions.

503b   See tax sheltered annuity.

Absolute deviation   The difference between the actual amount and the forecasted amount is always expressed as a positive number. Represented mathematically by a vertical line on either side of the numbers (e.g. $|8 - 10| = 2$).

Absolute value   The absolute value of any number is positive and is represented mathematically by two vertical lines drawn on either side of a number or equation. The absolute value of $|5 - 8|$ is 3.

Accelerated Cost Recover System (ACRS)   A U. S. depreciation schedule that covered items which were placed in use prior to January 1, 1987.

Accounting profit   Is what a business has left from its revenues after paying all of its expenses. Is typically shown on the bottom of a business income statement.

Accounting rate of return (ARR)   In capital budgeting, it is the rate of return on an investment that is found by dividing the average annual income by the average cost.

Accounts payable   Are debts of a business which are owed to vendors.

Accounts receivable turnover   A ratio that allows a business to determine how fast a company is turning its credit sales into cash. It states the number of times per year a company collects its accounts receivable. The formula is credit sales divided by accounts receivable.

Accounts receivable   A current asset carried on the balance sheet which indicates the amount owed to our firm due to credit sales. The value of credit sales for which the money has not been collected.

Accrual method of accounting   A method of accounting that recognizes revenue when earned and expenses when incurred.

Accrued liabilities   The obligations of firm that are accumulated during the normal course of business and are paid after the books are closed.

Accumulated depreciation   The total depreciation (wearing allowance) that an asset has on a balance sheet, from the asset's acquisition, until the asset is disposed of by the business.

Acid test ratio   *See* quick ratio.

Activity ratios   Those ratios that indicate how efficiently a business is using its assets.

Additional paid in capital   The equity contributions to a corporation in excess of the par value of common stock as shown on a corporate balance sheet.

Amortization   The reduction of the loan balance by applying each month principal payment is amortization.

Annuity   A stream of payments paid or received.

Annuity due   Payments which are made or received at the beginning of each time period.

Asset   An item that is used or owned by an individual or a business.

Average collection period   A ratio that divides the number of days in a year by accounts receivable turnover and determines how many days, on average, it takes a company to collect its accounts receivable.

Balance sheet   A financial statement that lists all assets, liabilities, and equity of a company or individual at a given point in time. The balance sheet uses the basic accounting equation which is *Assets = Liabilities + Owner's Equity.*

Balanced mutual funds   Mutual funds that invest in both stocks and bonds. They provide both capital growth and fixed income.

Bank discount   An amount of interest deducted from the amount you wish to borrow. It is calculated by multiplying what you wish to borrow by the bank discount rate and the amount of time that the loan is in effect.

Bankruptcy, Chapter 11   *See* Chapter 11 bankruptcy.

Bankruptcy, Chapter 7   *See* Chapter 7 bankruptcy.

Bankruptcy   Is a state of insolvency where the liabilities of a firm or individual exceed the assets and the firm or individual does not have sufficient cash flow to make payment to creditors.

Bond   A contractual agreement made between a borrower (government or corporation) and a lender (individual, pension fund, mutual fund, insurance company).

Book value   The value of a fixed asset on a company's books after depreciation has been accounted for. Also the value of a share of common stock based upon the amount of common stockholder's equity divided by the number of outstanding shares of common stock.

Break-even analysis   A process of determining how many units of production must be sold, or how much revenue must be obtained, before a business begins to earn a profit.

Break-even chart   A graph that is used to visually depict total revenue, total cost, break even, profit and loss in terms of sales volume.

Break-even dollars (BE$)   The dollar amount of revenue that equals the total cost. The formula is fixed costs divided by one minus variable costs expressed as a percentage of net sales.

Break-even quantity (BEQ)   The number of units that must be produced in order to cover the total costs of production. The formula is fixed costs divided by sales price minus variable costs.

Buy and hold   A method of investing where once purchased the investment is held for a number of years.

Callable preferred stock   The preferred stock of a corporation that may be redeemed by the corporation at a specified price plus a premium.

Capacity   A term used in credit evaluation to determine whether or not a customer has enough cash flow or disposable income to pay back a loan or pay off a bill.

Capital Asset   A plant, facility, equipment, machinery, or factory used in business to increase revenue or sales.

Capital Asset   A plant, facility, equipment, machinery, or factory used in business to increase revenue or sales.

Capital Budgeting   A method used by a business to justify the acquisition of those items that have a useful life of one year or more. Capital budgeting aids the decision maker by comparing the costs and benefits of a project.

Capital intensive   A business concern that has heavy investment in machinery and equipment and low labor costs as a percentage of its production costs.

Capital rationing   When a constraint is placed on the amount of funds that can be invested in a given time period then capital rationing is being used.

Capital resources   Capital resources consist of economic capital and financial capital.

Character   A term used in credit evaluation to determine if a customer has paid his or her bills on time in the past and has favorable credit references.

Cash discounts   A discount which is offered to credit customers as an incentive to get them to pay promptly. For example 2/10, net 30.

Cash equivalent   Are liquid assets that are invested in savings accounts or money market brokerage accounts.

Cash flow statement   *See* Statement of Cash Flow.

Cash flows from financing activities   The section of a statement of cash flow that includes cash received from stocks or bonds, the actual cash paid to owners in the form of dividends, and the repayment of long term debt.

Cash flows from investing activities   The section of a statement of cash flow which identifies all long term investments made by a firm. It includes cash paid for the acquisitions and cash received from sales of investments.

Cash flows from operating activities   The first section of a statement of cash flow which identifies all operating sources and uses of cash.

Causal models   Also known as exogenous or external models they take into account variables in the general economy that affect the sales of a firm or industry. For example housing starts would be the cause for increased sales of plumbing fixtures.

Certificate of deposit (CD)   Are promissory notes issued primarily by banks where the promissor (bank) agrees to pay the purchaser (promissee) the principal amount plus interest after a stipulated period of time.

Certified Public Accountant (CPA)   A public accountant who has passed a rigorous examination administered by the American Institute of Certified Public Accountants and has completed a work experience requirement (normally two years) prescribed by the state.

Ceteris paribus   A Latin phrase which means that all else remains the same.

Chapter 11 bankruptcy   A form of bankruptcy where a business seeks court protection while it develops a plan to pay off its creditors.

Chapter 7 bankruptcy   A form of bankruptcy that requires the company to liquidate all of its assets and make payment to its creditors.

Collateral   A term used in credit evaluation to determine the ability of a customer to satisfy a debt or pay a creditor by selling assets for cash. In finance and banking collateral is the asset which is actually used to secure a loan.

Collectables   Items that have a tendency to appreciate in value over time due to their scarcity. Examples include coins, paintings, and sculptures.

Collections float   The amount of time that elapses between your depositing a debtor's check in your account and the check's clearing the bank.

Commercial real estate   Land and improved property that is used by the owner to generate income.

Common stock   Stock which is issued by public or private corporations to raised financial capital. Stock is issued in shares and each share represents ownership of the corporation.

Compound interest   The interest that is earned or charged on both the principal amount and on the accrued interest that has been previously earned. The formula is $FV = PV (1 + I)^n$.

Consumer price index (CPI)   A measure of inflation which represents a market basket of goods that the average American purchase each month.

Contribution margin   The amount of profit that will be made by a company on each unit which is sold above the break even quantity.

Controlling   A three-step process that involves establishing standards, measuring performance against standards, and taking corrective action when necessary.

Convertible preferred stock   The preferred stock of a corporation that may be exchanged for shares of common stock.

Corporate bond   A bond issued by a public corporation that wants to borrow money to invest in assets that will help it earn revenue.

Corporation (C corporation)   A form of business that is incorporated in one of the fifty states. Ownership is based on shares of stock or percentage of ownership. A corporation is a legal entity that may accomplish all of the tasks that can be accomplished by an individual.

Cost of goods sold (COGS)   Normally includes the cost of materials, direct labor, and overhead allocated specifically to the product.

Coupon rate   The stated rate or nominal rate of interest that is contractual and attached to a bond. The coupon payment is calculated by multiplying the coupon rate by the face amount of the bond.

Credit evaluation   A method of determining which customers are allowed to use credit based on established credit standards such as character, capacity and collateral.

Creditor   An individual, business firm, institution, or government that has money which is due presently or in the future.

Credit terms   The requirements that a business establishes for the payment of a loan (the use of credit by a customer).

Cumulative discounts   A discount offered by a vendor to a customer which is based on the total quantity purchased during the vendor's fiscal year.

Cumulative preferred stock   Preferred stock where the owner's receive back dividends for those years when a dividend was not paid by a corporation.

Current assets   Assets that have a useful life of one year or less. Examples are cash, accounts receivable, and inventories.

Current liabilities   All of those obligations that a firm expects to pay off during the accounting year. Examples of current liabilities include accounts payable, notes payable, and taxes payable.

Current ratio   A liquidity ratio where total current assets are divided by total current liabilities.

Cyclical variation   The variation in company sales due to economic cycles such as recessions and growth.

Debenture   A corporate bond that is not backed by the collateral of the company.

Debt ratios   See leverage ratios.

Debt-to-equity ratio   A ratio that indicates what percentage of the owner's equity is debt. The formula is total liabilities divided by owner's equity.

Debt-to-total-assets ratio   A ratio that indicates what percentage of a business' assets is owned by creditors. The formula is total liabilities divided by total assets.

Delphi method   A qualitative forecasting method which uses a panel of experts to obtain a consensus of opinion.

Demand curve   A curve that is obtained by horizontally summing the quantity demanded at various prices in the marketplace.

Demand table   A table that is generated by determining how much of an item people are willing to purchase at various prices in the marketplace.

Dependent variable   A variable that relies on other variables for its value. In the formula $y = a + bx$, y is the dependent variable.

Depreciation   A dollar value assigned to the wearing out of a business asset during its useful life.

Directing (leading)   Leading and motivating employees to accomplish the goals of the business.

Disbursement float   The time that elapses between payment by check and the check's actually clearing the bank.

Discount rate   The rate of interest that the Federal Reserve charges banks to borrow money from the FED.

Discretionary income   The income that one has after paying taxes and fixed expenses such as rent and insurance.

Disposable income   The income that one has after paying federal, state, and city taxes. This income can either be spent (consumed) or saved.

Dividend   An after tax payment that may be made by a corporation to a stockholder. These are usually declared by the board of directors of the company.

Dollar cost averaging   A method of investing by making regular systematic payments over time in order to take advantage of market fluctuations. It allows us to purchase an equal dollar amount of an investment at equal time intervals.

Earnings before taxes   The amount of income that a corporation has before paying corporate taxes to the government. Shown on corporate income statements.

Earning power   Is the product of a company's ability to generate income on the amount of revenue it receives (net profit margin) and its ability to maximize sales revenue from proper asset employment (total asset turnover). The formula is net profit margin times total asset turnover.

Earnings per share   How much a corporation has earned for each share of common stock outstanding. The formula is net profit minus preferred dividends divided by the number of shares of common stock.

Economic Capital   Those items that man manufactures by combining natural and human resources. Includes buildings, machinery, and equipment used by business and government. Economic Capital, Physical Capital, or Fixed Assets are often used synonymously.

Economic order quantity (EOQ)   The quantity of items for a business to order which balances the ordering costs against the storage costs of inventory. The most economic quantity to order to minimize overall inventory costs.

EDGAR   See Electronic Data Gathering and Retrieval System.

Effective rate   The rate of interest that is actually earned or charged when compounding is taken into consideration.

Effectiveness   Effectiveness is accomplishing a specific task or reaching a goal.

Efficiency   Efficiency is obtaining the highest possible return with the minimum use of resources.

Electronic Data Gathering and Retrieval System (EDGAR)   A Securities and Exchange (SEC) computer filing system used by public corporations to file reports required by the SEC. The SEC provides the public with access to this computer filing system.

Electronic funds transfer   Electronic funds transfer is a process used to immediately transfer funds from one bank account to another via computer.

Entrepreneur (Entrepreneurial resources)   An individual who assumes risk and begins business enterprises. The entrepreneur combines land, labor, and capital resources to produce a good or service that society values more highly than the sum of the individual parts.

Entrepreneurial profit   An amount that is earned above and beyond what the entrepreneur would have earned if he or she had chosen to invest time and money in some other enterprise. It is most closely related to the economic concept of opportunity cost.

Equilibrium   The point where a supply curve and demand curve for a market intersect.

Estate planning   A method of planning for use, conservation, and transfer of wealth as efficiently as possible. It is financial planning with the anticipation of eventual death.

Exponential smoothing forecasting model   A forecasting model that uses a smoothing constant α_as an adjustment in determining the forecast. The assumption is that both the forecast of current period sales and actual sales can be used to predict future sales. The higher the value of alpha the more emphasis that is placed on current period sales.

Face value   *See* Par value.

Factoring   The process of a business selling its accounts receivable to another firm at a discount off of the original sales price.

Federal funds rate   The interest rate that banks charge each other for overnight loans. The minimum amount of these loans is $1 million.

Federal Insurance Contribution Act (FICA)   Taxes paid by a wage earner and a business to the Federal government for Social Security and Medicare. Social Security tax is 6.20 percent for wage earner and business for total of 12.4 percent on the first $65,800 of earned income in 1997. Medicare is 1.45 percent for the wage earner and 1.45 percent for the business or a total of 2.90 percent on all earned income. The total FICA contribution can be as high as 15.30 percent.

Federal Treasury Bills   U. S. Government bonds of 3 month, 6 month and one year duration that are issued at a discount.

Federal Reserve   The central bank of the United States, often called the FED. It is the banker's bank. The United States is divided into twelve districts with each district having a Federal Reserve Bank.

Finance   Any transaction in which money or a moneylike instrument is exchanged for money or a moneylike instrument.

Financial Accounting Standards Board (FASB)   An independent board responsible for establishing and interpreting Generally Accepted Accounting Principles (GAAP). Founded in 1973 it succeeded and continued the activities of the Accounting Principles Board (APB). Works in conjunction with the Securities and Exchange Commission (SEC).

Financial Asset   Assets such as stocks, bonds, or savings that may be used to increase revenue and acquire capital assets.

Financial Capital   A dollar value claim on economic capital. Financial capital may include cash, accounts receivable, stocks, or bonds.

Financial planning   Financial planning consists of establishing monetary goals and developing method and processes for achieving these goals.

Financial leverage   Financing a company with other peoples' money.

Financial Statement (personal form)   A form required by a bank when one applies for a loan. Consists of two segments, a statement of financial position and a personal cash flow statement.

Finished goods   The inventories that a company has which are actually sold by the business. Finished goods also include spare parts and repair parts.

Fixed asset turnover   A ratio that indicates how efficiently fixed assets are being used to generate revenue for the firm. The formula is net sales divided by fixed assets.

Fixed assets (use assets)   Assets that have a useful life of one year or more. Also see capital asset.

Fixed costs   See operating expenses.

Fixed expenses   Expenses over which we have little or no control, such as mortgage payments, automobile loan or lease payment, property taxes, insurance, and income taxes.

Forecast   A quantifiable estimate of the future.

Forecasting   The process and procedures used to develop a forecast. In business it is normally the process of estimating future demand for a business' products and services.

Form 10-K   An annual report that most public corporations must file with the Securities and Exchange Commission (SEC). The Form 10-K provides a comprehensive overview of the corporation's business. The report must be filed within 90 days after the end of the company's fiscal year and is filed electronically through EDGAR.

Franchise   A business in which the buyer, who is the franchisee, purchases the rights to sell the goods and services of the seller, who is the franchiser.

Functional planning   Planning for a business that is driven by strategic planning. Function planning is related to specific functional areas of our business such as personnel, finance, operations, and marketing.

Gantt chart   A chart that uses time on its horizontal axis and tasks to be performed on its vertical axis. Developed by Henry Gantt and used extensively in business planning. Gantt charts are often generated by project management software programs.

General obligation bond   A municipal bond that is used to build projects that do not normally generate revenue. The bond holder is paid on the taxing ability of the municipality.

General partner   Is in charge of day-to-day operations and is personally liable for the partnership.

General revenue bond   A municipal bond issued to build specific projects that use the income from the project to pay the bond holder.

Generally Accepted Accounting Principles (GAAP)   Rules, procedures and guidelines that accounting follows as acceptable accounting practices.

Goal   A measurable objective that can be reached in a specific time frame. All goals must be measurable, achievable, and have a time frame.

Gross income   All of the money received from all sources during a year. This would include wages, tips, interest earned on savings and bonds, income from rental property, and profits to entrepreneurs.

Gross profit margin   A ratio that is used to determine how much gross profit is generated by each dollar of net sales. The formula is gross profit divided by net sales.

Gross profit   Determined by subtracting cost of goods sold (COGS) from net sales.

Gross working capital   The current assets of a business which consist of cash, marketable securities, accounts receivable and inventory.

Growth mutual funds   Mutual funds that invest primarily in corporate common stock with an investment goal of capital appreciation.

Historical analogy   A qualitative forecast that uses historic similarities to project the possible success or failure of new products or services.

Horizontal analysis   A process of determining the percentage increase or decrease in an account on a financial statement from a base time period to successive time periods.

Human resources (labor)   The mental and physical talents of human beings.

Income mutual funds   Mutual funds that invest primarily in government and corporate bonds to provide the investor with stable income.

Income statement   A financial statement that shows what has happened to a business during a specific accounting period with regard to revenues and expenditures.

Independent variable   A variable that does not depend on other variables for its value. It is the actual observation of data which is made. In the formula $y = a + bx$, x is the independent variable.

Individual retirement accounts (IRA's)   Retirement plans that allow one to contribute current annual income that have favorable tax treatment. They allow accumulation of tax deferred benefits until withdrawal.

Inflation   An increase in the average price of goods. Most often measured by the Consumer Price Index (CPI).

Insurance   The transfer of risk to a third party for a premium.

Insurance, health   The transfer of risk to an insurance company to alleviate the cost of an illness or a disability.

Insurance, liability   The transfer of risk to an insurance company to alleviate the cost of property damage and personal injury to others as a result of your action.

Insurance, life (whole life, universal life, term, variable)   The transfer of risk to an insurance company for a premium by one who has an insurable interest in the life of an individual. Life insurance can be purchased by a company, spouse, child, etc.

Insurance, long term care   An insurance policy which provides assistance for people who have a chronic illness or are disabled for an extended period of time.

Insurance, property   The transfer of risk to an insurance company for a premium by one who has an insurable interest in the property.

Interest   The rent charged for money borrowed or loaned. The premium paid to the supplier of funds by the user (demander) of funds.

Interest expense   Interest accrued during an accounting period on money borrowed by a company. Found on an income statement.

Internal rate of return (IRR)   The actual rate of return on an investment that takes into consideration the time value of money. It is that specific interest rate where the present value of the benefits equals the present value of the cost. At the IRR net present value (NPV) is equal to zero and the profitability index (PI) is equal to one.

Interpolation   The process of using mathematics to find an unknown value that lies between two known values.

Inventory turnover   A ratio used to indicate how efficiently a firm is moving its inventory. It is stated as how many times per year a firm moves its average inventory.

Inventory   The items that a business has in stock which have not been sold.

Invested assets   Those assets found on a statement of financial position which are marketable securities such as stocks, bonds, and life insurance cash values. These items are normally listed on a business balance sheet under current assets.

Investment vehicle   Any item which allows one to attain an investment goal. Examples are stocks, bonds, savings, accounts, real estate, etc.

Irrevocable trusts   A trust that cannot be changed by the grantor or trustees once it is established.

Judgmental models   Forecasting models which are qualitative and essentially use estimates based on expert opinion.

Keogh plan   A retirement plan for self-employed individuals in sole proprietorships and partnerships. Under the laws governing Keogh a retirement plan can be established based on profit sharing, money purchase or paired. The percentage and total contribution may differ depending on the type of Keogh plan selected.

Junk bonds   A bond issued by a corporation or municipal government which is rated B or less and sold at a deep discount from the face amount ($1,000).

Labor intensive   A business concern that has relatively low investment in machinery and equipment and relatively high labor costs as a percentage of its production costs.

Land   *See* natural resources.

Law of demand   As the price of an item decreases people will demand a larger quantity of that item, *ceteris paribus.*

Law of supply   As the payment for or price of an item increases, the quantity of the item supplied to the market will increase, *ceteris paribus.*

Leverage (debt) ratios   Ratios which indicate what percentage of the assets of a business actually belong to the owners and what percentage is subject to creditors claims.

Liabilities   That part of assets that is owed to others.

Limited Liability Company (LLC)   A hybrid business entity having features of both partnerships and corporations. If formed properly it will be taxed as a partnership and its members will enjoy limited liability like corporate shareholders.

Limited partner   An investor in a partnership who is not involved in day to day operations and whose liability is limited to the amount of his or her investment in the partnership.

Limited partnership   A partnership having one or more general partners and several limited partners.

Linear regression model   A time series forecasting model that uses a statistical method known as least squared regression. Regression models are typically used for intermediate and long term forecasts.

Line of credit   A credit limit extended to a business which may be drawn upon when required by the business. There are no payments due on the line of credit unless the business actually borrows the money.

Liquidity ratios   A ratio which determines how much of a firms current assets are available to meet short term creditor's claims.

Liquidity   A measure of how fast an asset can be converted into cash.

Living trust   A trust that is set up during the life of the trustor.

Load mutual funds   Mutual funds that charge a commission on the initial investment.

Lockbox   A post office box that is opened by an agent of the bank and checks received there are immediately deposited in a company account.

Long-term debt   It is the debt that a company owes that it does not expect to pay during the current accounting year. Used synonymously with long-term liabilities. Found on the company's balance sheet.

Lowest total cost   A method of using time value of money by discounting future costs and benefits to determine the lowest total cost of a capital budgeting decision.

M1   *See* Money Supply (M1).

M2   *See* Money supply (M2).

Maintenance, repair, and operating (MRO) supplies   The inventories of a firm that are used in normal operations and are not manufactured or sold by the firm.

Management   The process of working with or through others to achieve an individual or business goal by efficiently and effectively using resources.

Marginal   The last additional unit that one measures. The addition of one more unit of measurement.

Marginal cost   The cost of hiring one more unit of labor or the cost of producing one more unit of output.

Marginal physical product   The additional product that results from hiring one more unit of labor.

Marginal revenue product   The additional revenue a business obtains when it adds one more unit of labor. Can also be the additional revenue a business obtains when it adds one more machine or other fixed asset.

Market   A market is any organized effort through which buyers and sellers freely exchange goods and services.

Market research   A qualitative method of forecasting which uses surveys, tests, and observations to project sales.

Market ratios   Ratios which are used by investors to determine if they should invest capital in a company in exchange for ownership.

Market value   The value of a share of common stock that the investor is willing to pay in the market place. Also the value of any asset that an investor is willing to pay in the marketplace.

Marketable securities   Those investment vehicles that include U.S. treasury bills, government, government and corporate bonds, and stock.

Maturity value   *See* Par value.

Mean absolute deviation (MAD)   A measure of how closely a forecasting model compares to actual data.

Medicare   See Federal Insurance Contribution Act (FICA).

Modified Accelerated Cost Recovery System (MACRS)   A U.S. depreciation schedule which became effective for assets placed in use on or after January 1, 1987.

Monetary policy   Governmental action to change the supply of money to expand or contract economic activity.

Money market mutual funds   Mutual funds that invest primarily in short term highly liquid investments such as CDs, short term government treasuries, commercial paper, repurchase agreements, and banker's acceptances. These funds are the mutual fund equivalent of a checking account.

Money purchase plans   A retirement plan which is a defined contribution plan established by an employer who contributes a fixed percentage of payroll into a retirement fund for employees. The employer must contribute each year even if the company does not make a profit.

Money supply (M1) Money in circulation plus the money in checking accounts.

Money supply (M2) M1 + money in passbook savings accounts + money market accounts + small time deposits (CDs).

Moving average forecasting model A forecasting model which assumes some recent time periods are the best predictor of future sales.

Municipal Bond A bond that is issued by a government agency other than the federal government. Usually state and local governments issue these bonds to finance projects.

Mutual fund family An investment group that has a portfolio of mutual funds with different goals and objectives.

Mutual fund A pool of money which is invested by a manager in specific investment vehicles with a defined goal and risk objective.

Mutually exclusive When several choices are available, but selection criteria obligates the decision maker to select only one and exclude all other choices.

Natural resources (land) Consist of natural products such as minerals, land, and wildlife.

Net cost rate factor The actual percentage of the list price paid after taking all successive trade discounts.

Net income The profit after provision for income taxes and interest expenses for the corporation, and the profit after interest expense for the sole proprietorship, partnership, LLC, or Subchapter S corporation. This is the bottom line of a business income statement.

Net present value (NPV) In capital budgeting, it is a technique which uses the time value of money by discounting future benefits and costs back to the present. The NPV is the difference between the present value of the benefits and the present value of the costs.

Net profit margin A ratio that is used to determine how much a firm earned on each dollar of net sales after paying its obligations of tax and interest. The formula is net profit divided by net sales.

Net return on assets (ROA) also known as return on investment (ROI) A ratio that determines how much a firm earns on each dollar in assets after paying both interest and taxes. The formula is net profit divided by total assets.

Net sales The revenue that a business has after accounting for returns and allowances. Net sales equals gross sales minus returns and allowances.

Net working capital The difference between a business' total current assets and its total current liabilities. It is a measure of a company in terms of liquidity.

Net worth The assets of an individual or firm minus its liabilities.

No load mutual funds Mutual funds that do not charge a commission on an initial investment.

Noise (random variation) The changes in company sales that cannot be explained by trend, cyclical, or seasonal variation.

Non-owner-occupied residential real estate Real estate which is rented by the owner to the tenant with the purpose of generating income.

Notes payable A businesses promise to pay a creditor or lender an amount owed plus interest for a specified period of time, normally one year or less.

Open market operations The purchase and sale of U.S. securities by the Federal Reserve.

Operating expenses (fixed costs) Those payments for expenses of a business that are not directly related to revenues or cost of goods sold.

Operating income   The result of subtracting operating expenses from gross profit on an income statement.

Operating profit margin   A ratio which is used to determine how much each dollar of sales generates in operating income. The formula is operating income divided by net sales.

Operating return on assets   A ratio which determines how much a company earns on each dollar of assets prior to paying interest and taxes. The formula is operating income divided by total assets.

Opportunity cost   The highest value that is surrendered when a decision is made. If you give up a $30,000 a year job to attend school full time, the decision was to attend school, the opportunity cost was $30,000.

Ordinary annuity   Payments which are made or received at the end of each time period.

Organizing   A structure developed by managers that will allow them to carry out a plan.

Owner's equity   The net worth of a company or individual. It is found by subtracting total liabilities from total assets.

Owner-occupied residential real estate   Real estate that is purchased as your primary residence or your one additional vacation home.

Par value (bonds)   The value of a bond which is printed on the bond and is the value at which the bond is redeemed for by the issuer at maturity. This is also referred to as the face value, maturity value, or principal value of a bond. For corporate bonds the face value is $1,000.

Par value (stock)   An arbitrary value placed on each share of stock when a corporation issues stock. This is the face value of one share of stock and does not normally change during the life of the corporation.

Partnership (general partnership)   An association of two or more persons who carry out a business as co-owners for a profit.

Payback   In capital budgeting, a technique of determining the number of years it will take a business to get back the money it has invested in a project or an asset.

Pension planning   *See* retirement plans.

Percentage of sales method for determining new financing   A method of determining how much new financing a company will need in the future based upon the fact that assets and liabilities historically vary with sales.

Percentage of sales method for calculating a pro forma balance sheet   A method of calculating a pro forma balance sheet based upon the fact that assets and liabilities historically vary with sales.

Personal cash flow statement   A personal income statement consisting of all annual income before taxes and outflows of fixed expenses and variable expenses.

Petty cash   A cash fund that is normally used to pay for small daily items such as postage or minor supplies.

Planning   A systematic process that takes us from some current state to some future desired state.

Post audit   Procedures that determine how well the outcome of a decision correlates with the proposal.

Preferred stock   A hybrid vehicle which has features of both bonds and common stock. Owner's of preferred stock are guaranteed a percentage return on their investment but are stockholders with no voting rights.

Price   The amount of money that a company charges for a product or service.

Price earnings ratio   A ratio that indicated what multiple of earnings per share investors are willing to pay for the stock. The formula is market price of stock divided by earnings per share.

Primary securities market   The initial sale of stock by a corporation to the public.

Prime rate   The rate of interest that a bank charges to its very best customers.

Principal value   *See* Par value.

Private corporation   A corporation that has been formed under state law, but does not sell its shares of stock to the public.

Pro forma financial statement   A financial statement that is developed to project the future condition of a business based upon a forecast.

Probate   A legal court process that addresses and focuses in on an individuals estate at the time of death.

Proceeds   The amount you receive after the bank discount (D) is deducted from the maturity value of the loan (S).

Profit   An absolute number (actual dollar value) that is earned on an investment.

Profit sharing plans   A retirement plan which is established by employers who have determined that a portion of each dollar in profit will be allocated to employees of the company. Allocation is normally based on employee compensation and length of service.

Profitability Index (PI)   In capital budgeting, a ratio that consists of the present value of the benefits divided by the present value of the costs. If the PI is greater than one the investment also has a positive net present value.

Profitability ratios   Ratios that determine how much of an investment will be returned from either earnings on revenues or appreciation of assets.

Profitability   The return on investment (ROI); it is measured by dividing net profit by total assets.

Progressive taxes   A tax that takes a larger percentage of your income as your income increases.

Proportional taxes   A tax where the percentage paid stays the same regardless of income.

Provision for income taxes   The total of corporate tax that is owed to federal, state, and possibly municipal governments.

Public corporation   A corporation whose stock is traded on the open market.

Pure risk   *See* Risk, pure.

Quantity discount   A discount offered by vendors to customers who order items in large quantities. The vendor specifies the minimum quantity that will qualify for the discount.

Quick ratio (Acid test ratio)   A liquidity ratio that divides current assets minus a company's inventory by current liabilities. It measures the liquidity of a company without liquidating its inventory in meeting current obligations.

Quoted Rate   The rate of interest that is listed, normally on an annual basis, and it disregards compounding. This also may be referred to as the stated rate.

Random variation   *See* Noise.

Ratio   A relationship between two variables expressed as a fraction.

Ratio analysis   A process used to determine the health of a business as it compares to other firms in the same industry or similar industries. The process makes use of mathematical ratios to express numbers.

Raw materials   The inventories that a production company uses in producing its final product.

Real estate investment trust (REIT)   A pool on investors that participate in buying shares in the trust. The trust buys real estate.

Regression   *See* Linear regression model.

Regressive taxes   A tax that takes a higher percentage of your income as your income decreases.

Reserve requirement   A percentage of deposits that are placed in banks to conduct daily operations which cannot be used for loans. Reserve requirements are established by the FED. These reserves must be kept in the banks vault or kept on deposit with the FED.

Retained earnings   The amount of a corporation's profit that is not distributed to the owner's but is retained by a corporation for future investment.

Retirement plans (Pension)   The establishment of an investment structure to accumulate wealth for use upon retirement. Under current law most plans require that money may be withdrawn after age 59 and one-half and money must be withdrawn after age 70 and one-half.

Retirement plans, benefit oriented   A defined benefit plan to the retiree based on employment longevity and compensation.

Retirement plans, combined   A plan designed by individuals and the employer which are based on tax deferred salary contributions and employer contributions.

Retirement plans, contribution oriented   A plan where benefits to the retiree are based upon an account balance that has been accumulated during the employees tenure.

Returns and allowances   A method of accounting for providing the customer with an avenue to return unwanted items as well as providing discounts to the customer for taking advantage of special promotions.

Return on equity (ROE)   A ratio that indicates to the stockholder or individual owner what each dollar of his or her investment is generating in net income. The formula is net profit divided by owner's equity.

Return on investment (ROI)   *See* Return on assets (ROA).

Revenues   The money generated due to sales of a product and services for a company.

Revocable trusts   A trust in which the trustor has the right to cancel the trust during his or her lifetime.

Risk   The probability that an expected outcome will occur, and the variability in that expected outcome. In financial terms the probability that the actual return on an investment will be different from the desired return.

Risk assumption   When you believe that the loss you might incur is less than the cost of risk avoidance or risk transfer.

Risk avoidance   A method of managing a business by distancing yourself from a hazard that may cause a loss. Example: Dealing in cash only to avoid credit risk.

Risk exposure   The placement of a business in a situation in which there is uncertainty of outcome. Smoking cigarettes for an individual is risk exposure, some but not all smokers will get cancer. Introducing a new product for a business is risk exposure, some but not all products will succeed.

Risk premium   An interest rate that is added onto the real rate of return that takes into consideration the risk of a project.

Risk reduction   A program used by a business or individual to lessen the severity of an outcome due to risk. Fastening your seat belt or having air bags in a car are methods of risk reduction.

Risk transfer   Having another party assume the risk and agree to pay you for your loss as long as you pay the fee (or premium) charged by the agency assuming the risk. Example: A fire insurance policy on your house.

Risk, pure   Pure risk involves only the chance of loss and it is therefore insurable. Example: Having your house catch on fire is pure risk.

Risk, speculative   Speculative risk is the risk in which there may be a possible gain or loss which is uninsurable. Example: Buying a lottery ticket is speculative risk. You can either gain a dollar or more or lose a dollar.

Roth IRA   An individual retirement account that allows you to contribute up to $2,000 of after tax dollars. The earnings on this account are tax free.

Rule of 72   An approximation of the amount of time that it takes for a present sum of money to double by dividing the number 72 by the annual interest rate.

Salvage (residual) value   The value of an asset after it has been depreciated over its useful life.

Savings incentive match plan for employees (SIMPLE)   An IRA that may be established (after 1996) by an employer that has fewer than 100 employees. The company must match dollar for dollar the employees contribution up to three percent of salary.

Scarcity   A condition that exists because human beings want more than they currently have.

Seasonal variation   The variation that exists in company sales based on predicable differences in climate, holidays, and buyer behavior.

Secondary securities market   A market where stock is bought and sold by the existing owners of individual shares.

Secured debt   Debt of a company or individual that is backed by specific assets which are pledged to guarantee the debt.

Securities and Exchange Commission (SEC)   An agency that regulates the sale and exchange of publicly traded securities. The SEC is an independent, nonpartisan, quasijudicial regulatory agency with responsibility for administering the federal securities laws.

Sensitivity analysis   Is also known as what-if analysis. It uses a mathematical spreadsheet program, or other computer program, that allows us to change some variable to determine what would happen with a decision when the variable was changed. For example: What would be the result of loan payments on a loan at various interest rates?

Service Corps of Retired Executives (SCORE)   A consulting service provided by the Small Business Administration which consists of a group of retired business owners and managers who have years of experience in various businesses.

Short-term debt   The obligations of a business that will be paid during the current accounting period, normally one year or less.

Simple interest   The amount of money earned on the principal amount stated.

Simplified employee pension plans (SEPS)   IRAs that are funded by employers. SEPS are common for the self-employed, the participating employee makes no contribution.

Single equivalent discount   A discount which is equal to one hundred percent of the list price minus the actual percentage of the list price paid (net cost rate factor).

Slope   Slope is the rise of a line (change in y) divided by the run of a line (change in x). In the formula $y = a + bx$, b is the slope of the line.

Smoothing constant   A value (alpha α) assigned by the forecaster to adjust the forecast based on the forecaster's assumption of the relationship of sales in one time period and sales in the next time period. Used in Exponential Smoothing forecasting model.

Social Security   *See* Federal Insurance Contribution Act.

Sole proprietorship   A business which is operated by an individual for his or her own profit.

Speculative risk   *See* Risk, speculative.

Staffing   Obtaining the most capable personnel in order to implement business plans.

Start-up costs   All of the dollars that a business spends to get a project under way. Start-up costs normally include acquisition costs, training costs, and maintenance costs.

Stated (quoted) rate   The rate of interest that is listed, normally on an annual basis, and it disregards compounding.

Statement of cash flows   A financial statement that determines what has happened to the working capital account (the amount of cash available) of a company between the beginning and end of an accounting period.

Statement of financial position   On a personal balance sheet, it indicates all of the items that are owned and all of the items that are owed by an individual or family at a specific point in time.

Stock bonus plans   A retirement plan where the employer contributes shares of stock rather than money into a retirement account.

Stock   Ownership in a corporation that is divided into shares. The individual shares are referred to as stock.

Strategic planning   Establishing an overall long range plan for a business.

Strategic plans   The long range overall plans for a business.

Subchapter S corporation   One that is privately held, has more than one owner but not more than seventy-five, and is granted Subchapter S status by the Internal Revenue Service. Subchapter S corporations have favorable tax status.

Supply curve   A curve that is generated from a supply table by horizontally summing the total product or service provided at various prices in the marketplace.

Supply table   A table that is generated by determining how much of a product or service people and business will be willing and able to provide to the market at various prices.

SWOT   An acronym that stands for strengths, weaknesses, opportunities, and threats. These pertain to both the internal workings (strengths, weaknesses) and external factors (opportunities, threats) external factors of a company.

Systematic risk   Risk that is associated with economic, political, and sociological changes that affect all participants on an equal basis.

Tax factor benefits   In capital budgeting, the benefits that current tax law will allow a business to deduct or write off once a new investment is made.

Tax factor costs   In capital budgeting, the calculation of the costs that will result in additional taxes that will have to be paid by a firm.

Tax sheltered annuities (TSA's)   Retirement plans that allow employees of not-for-profit organizations to establish a retirement fund that is purchased and approved by the employer.

Taxes   Payments to government for goods and services provided by government.

Taxes payable   The accrued taxes that are owed by a business, but not actually paid as of the date of the business balance sheet. An example would be sales taxes collected in December would not be paid to the state until January of the following year.

Taxes   Payments to government for goods and services provided by government.

T-bill   U. S. treasury bond that matures in less than one year, typically three and six months.

T-bond   U. S. treasury bond that has a maturity greater than ten years.

Testamentary trust   A trust that is established at the death of the trustor.

Theory of Constraints (TOC)   A theory developed by Eliyahu M. Goldratt that is used to find business' primary problem(s) (constraints), generate a simple solution to the problem, and provide an implementation strategy.

Time series forecasting models   Forecasting models that use historical records that are readily available within a firm or industry to predict future sales.

Times-interest-earned   A ratio that shows the relationship between operating income and the amount of interest in dollars the company has to pay to its creditors on an annual basis. The formula is operating income divided by interest.

Time value of money   The loss of purchasing power that occurs over time as a result of inflation.

T-note   U. S. treasury bonds that mature in ten years or less.

Total asset turnover   A ratio that indicates how efficiently total assets are being used to generate revenue for the firm. The formula is net sales divided by total assets.

Total assets   The sum of current and fixed assets.

Trade discount   These are amounts deducted from the list price of items when specific services are performed by the customer. Normally given by manufacturers to wholesalers or retailers.

Trend variation   The change in sales over time which is represented by a straight line that depicts changes in sales over time. The trend line uses least square regression to eliminate seasonal variation, cyclical variation, and noise.

Trusts   A trust is a legal entity similar to a corporation that has a legal persona of its own. Property placed in a trust is separate from that of its owner. A trust is created by a trustor or grantor and beneficiaries or trustees are named by the trustor.

Unsecured debt   A debt that is not backed by collateral.

Unsystematic risk   Risk that is unique to an individual, firm, or industry.

Use assets   *See* Fixed assets.

Treasury bonds   Bonds issued by the Government of the United States.

Variable costs   Are costs directly driven by the volume of product flow.

Variable expenses   Pertains to a personal cash flow statement. Expenses over which we have some control such as food, clothing and automobile expenses.

Variance   A deviation from the norm. If a company establishes a personnel budget at $250,000 and actual spending is $260,000 then the variance is a negative $10,000.

Vertical analysis   A process of using a single variable on a financial statement as a constant and determining how all of the other variables relate as a percentage of the single variable.

Warranty   The guarantee that a product or service will perform under certain terms and conditions. Normally lists the remedy the purchaser may pursue if the warranty is not carried out.

Weighted average cost of capital (WACC)   The method of determining a company's cost of capital when it takes into consideration the rate charged by the lender(s) and the opportunity cost foregone by the borrower(s). Using these rates and the proportion of total financing funded by the lender and borrower, the WACC is calculated.

Weighted moving average forecasting model   A model which assumed that some recent time periods are a more accurate predictor of sales than previous time periods, but that the predictive ability of the time periods used is not equal.

Will   A document directing how you want your wishes carried out after death with regard to disposition of property.

Work-in-process   The inventories that a firm uses while in the assembly or transformation process.

Working capital   The current assets and current liabilities of a business.

Working capital commitment costs   In capital budgeting, the costs of maintaining a specific level of working capital that are required by lending institutions. Examples would include inventory and accounts receivable costs committed to back up a loan.

Working capital management   The ability to effectively and efficiently control current assets and current liabilities in a manner that will provide our firm with maximum return on its assets and will minimize payments for its liabilities.

Index